THE

RENAISSANCE IN

HISTORICAL THOUGHT

Five Centuries of Interpretation

WALLACE K. FERGUSON
Professor of History, New York University

HOUGHTON MIFFLIN COMPANY

The Riverside Press Cambridge

CB
361
.F373

To the Memory of

PRESERVED SMITH

the teacher and friend
to whom I owe more
than I was ever able to repay

CONTENTS

PREFACE

FOR CENTURIES the idea of a Renaissance at the end of the Middle Ages has been an active agent in shaping conceptions of the development of Western European civilization. But, though the idea has enjoyed so long a life, conceptions of the nature of the Renaissance, of its sources, its extent, and its essential spirit have varied from generation to generation. Confined at first to a rebirth of art or of classical culture, the notion of the Renaissance was broadened as scholars of each successive generation added to it what they regarded as the essence of modern, as opposed to medieval, civilization. As the Renaissance receded into the past, it also acquired more finite chronological limits. It gradually ceased to be something still taking place and became an event which had occurred in a more or less definite period in the past. Finally the process of expanding the content of the rebirth, while at the same time limiting it to a past age, culminated in the conception of the Renaissance as a period in the history of European civilization, a period characterized by a spirit common to all aspects of its culture.

The completion of this process was the work of an historian of great genius. Jacob Burckhardt wove together selected threads from the varied strands of humanist, Protestant, rationalist, Romantic, liberal, and idealist traditions, but the resulting pattern was essentially a new creation. His interpretation of the Renaissance won universal acceptance in the decades following 1860, and remained almost unchallenged for half a century. It became, indeed, *the* traditional interpretation, an established orthodoxy. And, as tradition too long maintained excites innovation, and orthodoxy which has become conventional provokes heresy, so the Burckhardtian interpretation became in time a formula that cried aloud for revision. But, though revision followed revision, and Burckhardt's Renaissance was amended and its chronological and geographical scope expanded or contracted to suit the current thesis, though it was in the end rejected by many scholars in whole or in part, no other generally accepted interpretation arose to take its place. The fortunate period in which historians could agree on what they meant by the Renaissance had ended. Yet the idea of the Renaissance could not be ignored or allowed to slip quietly into obsolescence as a figment of nineteenth-century historical imagination. The interpretation of the age we know as the Renaissance is crucial to any conception of the nature and evolution of medieval and modern culture. Until the traditional interpretation is replaced by another on which there can be some general agreement, its opponents will probably be the least likely to let it rest in peace.

Under these circumstances, the Renaissance has become a controversial problem, over which learned men have argued with all the vigor of theologians debating the freedom of the will. The protagonists in this controversy have mostly been specialists in some aspect of Renaissance history, though the medievalists have also taken an active part, but echoes of the clamor have been clearly audible in adjacent fields. It has become a disturbing situation for historians whose specialty impinges upon the Renaissance — as whose does not? — and who were accustomed to refer to it with confidence as a known phenomenon. The conflict of the specialists has forced many such to uneasy and imprecise qualifications or to some face-saving phrase such as "the so-called Renaissance." Nor has this feeling of uncertainty been confined to historians of other fields who could not spare the time to investigate the problem. Many specialists have been equally confused and more deeply concerned. In the present situation, indeed, every thoughtful historian of the Renaissance seems faced by an inescapable dilemma. He must either work out for himself a tenable interpretation, selecting and combining such elements of the various conflicting interpretations as seem to him valid, or he must abandon altogether a useful and time-honored periodic concept, with no substitute to take its place.

Out of my own preoccupation with this dilemma two books have emerged. The first, an attempt, not altogether satisfactory, to sketch in brief form a coherent interpretation of the Renaissance, was published in 1940.[1] But I had meanwhile become increasingly aware that the problem of the Renaissance is a double problem. It concerns not only the objective facts, the undoctored incidents that actually occurred, but also the subjective conception of the nature of these facts, and these conceptions have a history of their own. It seemed to me, therefore, that some of the present confusion regarding the Renaissance might be resolved, or that, at least, the conflicting interpretations might be in some degree rationalized, by a study of the historical development of the idea of the Renaissance and of the interpretations presented during the past five hundred years. I began the present work with that idea in mind during the academic year 1939–40, during which time I was able to devote my whole attention to the problem, thanks to a fellowship from the John Simon Guggenheim Foundation and a sabbatical leave from New York University. To both of these institutions I wish to express my gratitude for the boon of a year free from academic duties. My thanks are also due to the officials of the Widener Library at Harvard for the ungrudging hospitality with which they placed their unrivaled resources at my disposal.

The work begun under such fortunate circumstances was interrupted and delayed in the following years by the minor irritations and extra duties that accompany academic life in wartime. The unforeseen delay in completing the book, however, was caused to a greater degree by a change in my own conception of its nature, a change which resulted in a considerably more extensive study than I had originally planned. As the work progressed, I found that to trace the history of the interpretation of the Renaissance in any meaningful way it was necessary to write a running commentary on the history of modern historiography, and that what I was contemplating was in fact a *Beitrag* to the intellectual history of modern times. To have followed the lure of this larger goal to its logical conclusion would have been disastrous. The book, if it had ever been finished, would have grown beyond all due proportion and the original purpose would have been lost in the process. What I have tried to achieve is, instead, a compromise and

[1] W. K. Ferguson, *The Renaissance* (New York, 1940).

like all compromises not wholly satisfactory. I have kept the history
of the interpretation of the Renaissance consistently in mind as the
central theme of the book, but have attempted at the same time, so far
as this was possible in a reasonable space, to trace the changing ideas
of history, the varying preconceptions of historians, and the fashions
in historical thought during the past five centuries, with the interpretation of the Renaissance used as the touchstone by which they
might be assayed.

Other problems arose which also tended to expand the scope of the
work and delay its completion. Conceptions of the Renaissance proved
to be so closely related to interpretations of the Middle Ages on the
one hand, and on the other to historians' attitudes toward the culture
of their own time, that both had to be awarded more than passing
attention. Further, the idea of the Renaissance has frequently developed along special lines in the history of particular aspects of culture,
such as art, literature, philosophy, or science, so that it became necessary
at times to trace the shifting currents of historiography or criticism in
each of these and other fields, in the full awareness, moreover, that
no specialist would be satisfied with the results. Finally, there was the
problem of space. I wanted the book to remain within readable size,
but that entailed the painful excision of a good deal of material. To
paraphrase a well-worn epigram, I could have written a book twice the
size in half the time.

In accordance with my determination to keep the book within
readable limits, I abandoned any attempt to include all the important
works on the Renaissance. It was not, in any case, the purpose of the
work to present a critical bibliography of histories of the Renaissance,
but rather to trace the variations in conception and interpretation. For
that reason I have included some very bad histories and omitted some
very good ones. And in reviewing them, I have concentrated attention on the ideas of the Renaissance they present rather than on their
factual content. The criterion of selection was twofold. I tried, first,
to select for treatment those works, including works of philosophy, art
criticism, and *belles lettres,* as well as histories, which influenced trends
of interpretation, and, second, to include a sufficient number of typical
examples, chosen more or less at random, to illustrate the changing

fashions. Any reader will no doubt find a number of favorites unaccountably missing.

In the interest of readability, I have translated all titles cited in the body of the text. Full citation to the original titles will be found in the footnotes, with added notes to English translations where I have been aware that they exist. Page numbers refer always to editions in the original language unless otherwise stated. Quotations are most commonly in my own translation. When I have quoted directly from a translation, though at times amending the wording to bring it closer to the original text, I have cited the corresponding pages of the original text, with a following citation to the translated edition contained in square brackets.

I completed the writing of the manuscript, save for a final revision, in September, 1946. Preoccupation with other tasks, however, prevented me from finishing the revision until September, 1947, at which time the manuscript was sent to the publishers. Some of the relevant historical works which appeared between those two dates I was able to work into the text. Those which were published, or which came to my attention after September, 1947, I have been forced to ignore or, at best, I have been able to accord them only inadequate mention in the footnotes.

To the many friends with whom I discussed the work during the long period of its gestation, I wish to express my thanks for their patience and for the encouragement they offered when my own faith in it had grown dim. My thanks are most especially due to Geoffrey Bruun, Jean Hecht, and Leo Gershoy, who read the manuscript, to Winifred Carroll Ferguson, who edited it with an unerring eye for irregularities, and to Margaret Wing, who read and reread the proof and assisted in compiling the index, and whose philological erudition saved the work from many errors, some of them of a rather shocking sort. To all of these, once more my thanks!

WALLACE K. FERGUSON

CHAPTER ONE

The Early Humanist Tradition in Italy[1]

It has become a commonplace to say that the traditional conception of the Renaissance as a new age in the history of Western civilization, a period of rebirth after centuries of medieval darkness, arose during the Renaissance itself; and it is more or less true. It might be more accurate, however, to say that the humanists furnished the materials for such an interpretation of the course of European history and for the scheme of periodization adopted by later generations trained in the classical school. Living in the midst of a rapidly changing society and culture, the men of the Renaissance could scarcely be expected to envisage their own age as an integrated whole, nor to perceive clearly its relation to the past. Their cultural interests and their conception of what constituted history, despite their growing historical sense, were too narrow for that. The Italian humanists were undoubtedly conscious of living in the midst of a great cultural revival, but their awareness of what was new in their age was limited to classical literature and learning and the fine arts. Within this narrow field they established the foundations for the threefold periodization of European history which was to be the conventional pattern for centuries to come; but they did so more by the implications inherent in their whole attitude toward past and present culture than by their more explicit passing comments or by the briefly outlined sketches of the history of culture which appear here and there in their works. When

---

[1] Much of the material in this chapter was originally published as an article: W. K. Ferguson, "Humanist Views of the Renaissance," *American Historical Review*, XLV (1939), 1–28.

they turned to what they regarded as history proper, their scheme of historical development was radically different.

Several important studies in recent years have demonstrated, with a wealth of examples, how frequently the humanists of both Italy and the northern countries employed the metaphors of rebirth, revival, or resuscitation, all of which imply a previous death, or the contrasting metaphors of darkness and light, to denote their conception of the history of literature, learning, and the fine arts from antiquity, through the Middle Ages, to their own time.[2] The use of these metaphors is undoubtedly significant and in the majority of instances indicates that the writer had in mind a fairly clear and coherent historical scheme of the course of cultural history. At the same time, they must be examined carefully in relation to context if we are to avoid the danger of reading into them a too clear conception of the distinctive character of the new age as a whole and of its historical relation to the past. The perils attendant upon unrestrained generalization from dubious symbolism and isolated instances of the metaphor of rebirth are particularly evident in the work of Konrad Burdach.[3] We will be on safer ground if we extend our research to include the most complete discussions of their own age in its relation to the past to be found in the works of the Renaissance writers, and if we restrict our interest

2 See especially, L. Varga, *Das Schlagwort vom "finsteren Mittelalter"* (Vienna, 1932); F. Simone, "La Coscienza della Rinascita negli humanisti," *La Rinascita,* II (1939), 838–71; III (1940), 163–86; H. Weisinger, "The Self-Awareness of the Renaissance as a Criterion of the Renaissance," *Papers of the Michigan Academy* XXIX (1944), 561–67; "Renaissance Theories of the Revival of the Fine Arts," *Italica,* XX (1943), 163–70; "The Renaissance Theory of the Reaction against the Middle Ages as a Cause of the Renaissance," *Speculum,* XX (1945), 461–67. I had seen none of the above when this chapter was first published as an article. The evidence they adduce has impressed upon me more strongly how widespread was the humanist schematization of cultural history, but has not otherwise altered my original opinions. For earlier research into the origins of the Renaissance idea, see K. Brandi, *Das Werden der Renaissance* (Göttingen, 1908); J. Huizinga, "Das Problem der Renaissance," in his *Wege der Kulturgeschichte* (Munich, 1930), 89–139; K. Borinski, "Die Weltwiedergeburtsidee in den neueren Zeiten," *Sitzungsberichte der Preussischen Akademie der Wissenschaften* (1910), I. Abh., pp. 1–130.

3 Cf. K. Burdach, "Sinn und Ursprung der Worte Renaissance und Reformation," *Sitzungsberichte der Preussischen Akademie der Wissenschaften* (1910), 594–646; *Rienzo und die geistige Wandlung seiner Zeit* (2 vols., Berlin, 1913–28); and *Deutsche Renaissance* (Berlin, 1916). For discussion of Burdach's thesis and method, see below, pp. 306 ff.

in the metaphors of rebirth or of light and darkness to those instances where the context clearly indicates an historical application. We may then be able to answer more definitely the question of what the Italian humanists thought regarding the historical development of European civilization and the periodization of history, and especially what they thought had been revived in their own or preceding generations, when they thought the revivals in specific fields took place, and through what agency.

THE POLITICAL HISTORIES OF THE ITALIAN HUMANISTS

The age of the Renaissance saw the birth of modern historiography.[4] Nearly all the leading Italian humanists wrote formal history with a literary and historical sophistication that set their work clearly apart from the chronicles of the preceding centuries. Here, then, would seem to be the most obvious source for the humanists' view of their own age in its relation to the past. Yet the student who turns hopefully to the historical works of the humanists for the history of medieval and Renaissance civilization will be quickly disillusioned. As a result, humanist histories have been almost entirely ignored in the search for early evidences of the Renaissance concept, and in general they have been treated very superficially by students of Renaissance culture. There is reason for this neglect. Taking the classical historians as models, the humanists restricted the scope of history to a literary narrative of political and military events. For them it was quite true that history was simply past politics. They scarcely mentioned the economic life of the people and, though many of them commented elsewhere on the development of literature and art, they excluded these subjects from their formal histories as pertaining to a different genre.

4 For general discussion of Italian Renaissance historiography, see E. Fueter, *Geschichte der neueren Historiographie* (Munich, 1936), pp. 9 ff; P. Joachimsen, *Geschichtsauffassung und Geschichtschreibung in Deutschland unter dem Einfluss des Humanismus* (Leipzig, 1910), pp. 18 ff; H. Baron, "Das Erwachen des historischen Denkens im Humanismus des Quattrocento," *Historische Zeitschrift,* CXLVII (1932), 5–20; M. Ritter, *Die Entwicklung der Geschichtswissenschaft an den führenden Werken betrachtet* (Munich, 1919), pp. 125–204; B. Croce, *History, its Theory and Practice* (Eng. trans., New York, 1921), pp. 224–42; J. W. Thompson, *A History of Historical Writing* (New York, 1942), I, 473–509.

Moreover, the classical Latin that was their greatest pride has failed to make a favorable impression on many modern critics. Since Burckhardt it has been the fashion to dismiss them as sterile imitators of Livy and Sallust and to deplore the lack of definite chronology, local color, and specific realism, which resulted from their use of a rhetorical style and of a vocabulary that was not adapted to postclassical institutions.[5]

Still, whatever may be the justice of this criticism, and it is at least open to question,[6] the best of the humanist histories were certainly far superior to the medieval chronicles in perspective, coherent organization, and critical sense. Above all, the Italian humanists took an essential step in the direction of sound historical thought when they abandoned the medieval habit of seeking supernatural causes for historical events. They no longer saw history merely as the working out of Divine Providence; they saw it rather as the record of human activity, inspired by human motives. A part of this advance, but only a part, must be ascribed to the advantages of a classical education. The humanist historians were not only classical scholars; they were also laymen who had had wide experience in business, law, government, or diplomacy. Even those whose connection with the papal curia or whose search for benefices had given them a nominal status as clergy had a thoroughly lay point of view. They represented at once the secular attitude of the educated urban laity and the practical politics and diplomacy of the newly developed Italian states. The humanists brought to the writing of history an appreciation of the part played by individuals, parties, and states that was far beyond the range of the monastic chroniclers, and also a knowledge of the past and a breadth of political experience greater than had been enjoyed by the chroniclers of the medieval communes. They wrote a different kind of history from that of the Middle Ages not only because they had a different kind of education but because they lived in a different economic,

---

[5] J. Burckhardt, *Die Cultur der Renaissance in Italien* (Basel, 1860), pp. 238 ff; cf. V. Rossi, *Il Quattrocento* (Milan, 1933), pp. 169 ff; F. Schevill, *History of Florence* (New York, 1936), p. xvii.

[6] Cf. E. Santini, *Leonardo Bruni Aretino e i suoi "Historiarum Florentini populi libri XII"* (Pisa, 1910), p. 88; W. Goetz, "Renaissance und Antike," *Historische Zeitschrift*, CXIII (1914), 254 f.

social, and political environment. And because they expressed the ideas and interests of the most influential classes of their day, their work is of real significance for the history of Renaissance culture, and their picture of their own and past ages, despite its unfortunate limitation to political history, is too important to be ignored.

The character of historiography in any age depends on the purpose as well as on the knowledge and training of the historian. And, if the aims of the humanist historians were not entirely modern, neither were they entirely medieval. An Italian humanist, asked to justify his writing of history, might have replied that it is a form of literature, highly regarded by the ancients and presenting attractive opportunities for the exercise of style; that it has great practical value since it teaches moral, ethical, and political lessons; and, finally, that his history celebrated the past and present glories of his native land or of the state to which it was dedicated.[7] On all three points the humanists' conception of history differed from that of the feudal, communal, and ecclesiastical chroniclers of the Middle Ages. The literary aim was more conscious and much more important. The pragmatic purpose, though less original, differed from that of the theological historians by its emphasis on practical ethical and moral problems rather than on examples of divine intervention in human affairs, by its evaluation of political necessity, and by its glorification of the quite untheological *virtù* of great men. The patriotic purpose was almost entirely new in its exclusive devotion to the history of the state or the nation, and was the most compelling motive of the three. Neither the universal view of the medieval churchmen nor the narrow particularism of feudal lords and communal burghers could produce the clear perception of the state or the nation as the unit of historical development that resulted from the evolution of the territorial states in Italy and, somewhat later, of the national states in the North.

The new political point of view and the patriotic purpose of the humanist historians led them to a new organization and periodization of history. It also reinforced their natural tendency toward a

---

[7] Cf. R. Sabbadini, *Il metodo degli umanisti* (Florence, 1920), pp. 78–85; for the practical and moral value of history, see L Bruni, *De studiis et litteris ad illustrem Dominam Baptistam de Malatesta tractatulus* (Zschopau, 1880), p. 10.

secular interpretation. Their task was to write the political history of the Italian states. And since these arose only after the collapse of the Roman Empire, those of the historians who did not limit their work to contemporary events naturally began their story with the decline of the empire and carried it through the period in which the communes arose and grew into powerful territorial states. In the early period they usually treated the whole Italian scene, later narrowing the story to one state, though still discussing the others in relation to it. The history of Italy was thus separated from world history, and history as a whole was divided in practice into two great periods, that of antiquity and that which followed the decline of the Roman Empire. It was a conception of history radically different from that common in the Middle Ages, its scope limited to national and secular interests.

The medieval churchmen had written history from a universal point of view, *sub specie aeternitatis*. Their world chronicles were constructed on a basis of theology and were shaped by concepts of a divinely ordained universal church with its secular counterpart in a universal empire. They divided human history either into Six Ages, corresponding to the six days of creation, or into the Four Monarchies mentioned in the prophecy of Daniel (2:40).[8] The fourth and last of these monarchies had been definitely identified by St. Jerome with the Roman Empire. Under the influence of Augustine and Orosius the idea of the Roman Empire as the last of the world monarchies, which should continue until the beginning of the reign of Antichrist, was transferred from the pagan to the Christian empire, and belief in the necessary continuity of the Roman Empire was maintained throughout the Middle Ages by the fiction of the *translatio imperii ad Francos* or *ad Teutonicos*.[9] As long as historical thought remained within this framework of supernatural teleology there could be no idea of a distinction between ancient Roman civilization and that of the age following the break up of the empire nor of a rising civilization after

---

[8] Cf. G. Falco, *La polemica sul medio evo* (Turin, 1933), pp. 1 ff; H. Spangenberg, "Die Perioden der Weltgeschichte," *Historische Zeitschrift*, CXXVII (1923), pp. 7 f. For discussion of the general character of medieval historiography, see Thompson, Vol. I; Croce, pp. 200–223; H. von Eicken, *Geschichte und System der mittelalterlichen Weltanschauung* (4th ed. Stuttgart, 1923), pp. 641–71.

[9] Cf. W. Rehm, *Der Untergang Roms im abendländischen Denken* (Leipzig, 1930), pp. 27 ff.

the darkest period was passed. Many of the medieval historians, as Otto of Freising, were aware of the decline of the Roman Empire, but only as a symptom of the general senescence of a world approaching its end. In any case it was regarded as the continuous decline of a universal empire still existing in their own day. This view of the empire was still accepted in Dante's time and formed the basis of his political theories in the *De monarchia*. Such an organization of world history was perfectly adapted to the needs of medieval theologians and fitted the conception of the unity and universal character of the *Respublica Christiana*. It could not satisfy the humanist historians, who were primarily interested in the secular history of Italy and the Italian states.

The transition from medieval to Renaissance modes of thought was in this as in all other respects a gradual one. The *Florentine Chronicle* [10] of Giovanni Villani, written during the first half of the fourteenth century, marks one of the early stages. Like the humanists who followed him as historians of Florence, Villani was a layman and a practical man of affairs. His discussion of contemporary economic and political life in Florence was based on astute and independent observation. But his general conceptions of the world conformed in the main to the conventional pattern of medieval religious thought.[11] He could not separate the history of Florence from the theological setting of universal history — the *Chronicle* begins with the Tower of Babel — and in every event he perceived the guiding hand of Divine Providence. Nevertheless, the body of his work deals specifically with the secular history of his native city, and toward the end of his book he made a valiant effort to construct a scheme of periodization that would meet the demands of Florentine rather than of world history.[12] Based on the periodic conjunction of certain planets, it was not a very happy historical device, but it served the purpose of marking the decline of the Roman Empire under the shock of the barbarian invasions as the beginning of a new era in the history of Italy.

[10] G. Villani, *Croniche fiorentine,* best found in L. A. Muratori, *Rerum Italicarum scriptores* (Milan, 1723–51), XIII.

[11] Cf. E. Mehl, *Die Weltanschauung des Giovanni Villani* (Leipzig, 1927), pp. 181 ff *et passim;* Schevill, p. 227.

[12] Villani, xii, 41; cf. Mehl, pp. 169 ff.

With Petrarch the division between ancient and later history took on a new meaning, founded on a romantic admiration for pagan Roman literature, the city of Rome, and the ideal of republican virtue. He drew a definite line between the period of purely Roman history and the Christian-barbarian era that followed. Defining his terms, he called the period prior to the adoption of Christianity by the Roman emperors "ancient" (antiqua), the period from that event down to his own age "modern" (nova).[13] And this modern age he qualified consistently as one of barbarism and "darkness" (tenebrae).[14] Petrarch, indeed, may well be regarded as the originator of the conception of the "dark ages," which was for centuries to dominate the interpretation of medieval history, and furnish the contrasting background for the Renaissance.[15] The idea of a dark age was itself not new. Christian writers had long thought of the period of pagan antiquity before the dawn of Christianity as an age of darkness.[16] By shifting the metaphor from the sphere of religion to that of culture and its application from pagan antiquity to the Christian Middle Ages, Petrarch set the tone for the humanists' secular interpretation of history. But though most of the later humanists followed Petrarch's inversion of the religious periodization of history and agreed with his conception of the cultural darkness of the Middle Ages, they did not share his lack of interest in what he called modern history. With his nostalgic feeling for the purely Roman past, Petrarch had nothing but contempt for the age of the barbarians. It was, he thought, unworthy of historical consideration and so better forgotten. For him, history was exclusively Roman; it could be nothing but "the praise of Rome."[17] He therefore limited his own major historical work to the lives of illustrious Romans.[18] He

---

[13] Petrarch, *Epistolae de rebus familiaribus,* VI, 2, ed. J. Fracassetti (Florence, 1859), I, 314; "et dicantur antiquae quaecumque ante celebratum Romae et veneratum Romanis principibus Christi nomen; novae autem ex illo usque ad hanc aetatem."

[14] *Ibid.,* XX, 8, ed. Fracassetti, III, 30 f.

[15] Cf. T. E. Mommsen, "Petrarch's Conception of the 'Dark Ages,'" *Speculum,* XVII (1942), 226–42, which seems to establish this point beyond doubt.

[16] Cf. Simone in *Rinascita,* III, 177 ff.

[17] Cf. Petrarch, *Apologia contra cuiusdam anonymi Galli calumnias,* in *Opera Omnia* (Basel, 1554), p. 1187: "Quid est enim aliud omnis historia quam Romana laus?"

[18] For discussion of the stages by which Petrarch restricted the *De viris illustribus* to purely Roman subjects, see Mommsen, pp. 228 ff.

also rejected the idea of the *translatio imperii*. The Roman *imperium* was inalienable, having sprung from the virtue of the Roman people. "If the Roman *imperium* is not in Rome, where," he asked, "is it?"[19] But if Petrarch did not share the medieval faith in the continuation of the Roman Empire, he had an equally unhistorical faith in the mystical continuation of the *virtus Romana* among the degenerate Roman populace of his own day and in the possibility of a political rebirth of the ancient republic, whence his enthusiastic approval of Cola di Rienzi's fantastic revolution.[20]

This identification of virtuous republican Rome with the papal city as it was in the fourteenth century bore so little relation to reality that it made no great impression on the later Italian humanists. They were profoundly influenced by Petrarch's admiration for Roman antiquity, but they shared neither his pessimistic view of the contemporary political scene nor his hopes for a rebirth of the Roman state. Their patriotism was of a different sort. It was focused primarily upon particular states or cities, though no Italian could be completely lacking in the national consciousness which sprang from a clear perception of his own superiority over the barbarians. Moreover, they no longer thought of the Roman Empire as having been translated across the Alps. Like Petrarch, then, the later Italian humanists looked upon the history of ancient Rome as the first stage in the history of the Italian people. Like him they closed one historical period and opened another with the decline of the Roman Empire. But whereas Petrarch confined his historical writing to the ancient period, their special local patriotism drew their attention chiefly to the second period in which the modern Italian states arose and flourished.

Florence, always the leader in the cultural movements of the Renaissance, produced the first true humanist historian in Leonardo Bruni, the chancellor and ranking scholar of the republic. In his *History of the Florentine People*,[21] which was cut short by his death

[19] Petrarch, *Liber sine nomine*, ep. IV, in P. Puir, *Petrarcas 'Buch ohne Namen' und die päpstliche Kurie* (Halle, 1925), p. 176.
[20] Cf. H. W. Eppelsheimer, *Petrarca* (Bonn, 1926), 78; 100 ff; Burdach, *Rienzo*.
[21] L. Bruni, *Historiarum Florentini populi libri xii* in Muratori, XIX, 3 (new ed. by E. Santini, Città di Castello, 1914). See discussion in B. L. Ullman, "Leonardo Bruni and Humanist Historiography," *Medievalia et Humanistica*, IV (1946), 45–61.

in 1444, all the characteristic traits of the literary school of humanist historiography appeared in full maturity. It was a semi-official work, encouraged by the state government, typical of the new history both in its patriotic purpose and in its purely secular attitude. It also set a high standard for style and coherence, for the critical use of sources and rejection of legend, and for the interpretation of political history in the light of human motives and natural causes. It was to serve as a model for generations of literary historians both in Italy and the North.

For all its universal appeal, however, Bruni's history was distinctively Florentine in tone. Historians elsewhere might adopt his formal technique, but his strongly republican interpretation of history could not be taken over by the humanists who wrote at the command of kings and princes. Bruni had all the theoretical republican enthusiasm of his fellow-citizens on the eve of the Medici domination, and he had absorbed the ethical and moral interests of Florentine burgher humanism from his early tutor, Coluccio Salutati. His own thought, too, had been profoundly influenced by Aristotle's *Politics* with its emphasis on the connection between civic virtue and the life of the city-state.[22] More than any other historian of his age he perceived the vitally important role of the free Italian communes in the evolution of modern Italy. Consequently he regarded the dissolution of the Roman Empire less as an unrelieved disaster than as a necessary prelude to the rise of the communes, thus providing, as Santini observes, the first historical justification of the Middle Ages.[23]

Bruni's feeling for political liberty with its attendant civic virtues colored his whole interpretation of the decline of the Roman Empire and the later revival of the Italian cities. Rome reached the apex of her power in the days of the republic; the decline began with the loss of political freedom under the despotism of the emperors. "The Roman *imperium* began to go to ruin when first the name of Caesar fell like a disaster upon the city." Freedom ended with the appearance of the imperial title, "and following liberty, virtue departed." [24] Bruni traced the sources of the empire's weakness directly to the moral effects

22 See H. Baron's introduction to his edition of L. Bruni, *Humanistisch-phil-osophische Schriften* (Leipzig, 1928), pp. xviii ff.
23 Santini, *Bruni e i suoi Hist.*, pp. 41 ff.
24 Bruni, *Historiarum*, p. 14.

of despotism, just as he ascribed the greatness of the republic to the moral qualities engendered by freedom. At first the strength of Rome enabled her to keep her enemies at bay despite the internal ills resulting from imperial rule. But after Constantine had moved the capital to the East, Italy and the western provinces were neglected and were repeatedly "inundated" by the floods of barbarian invasion.[25] It is clear that for Bruni the Roman Empire in the West ended with the barbarian invasions. Like Petrarch, he insisted on the exclusively Roman character of the *imperium* and refused to regard its revival by Charlemagne as other than a usurpation.[26]

Having broken with the theory of the continuity of the Roman Empire, Bruni was free to break also with the tradition of continuous decline. The whole tenor of his work indicates an awareness of the rising fortunes of Italy after the break-up of the Carolingian Empire. And in one significant passage, following his discussion of Charlemagne, he furnished an explicit statement of his theory of the revival of medieval Italy. Here he noted that after the empire departed into Germany and when few of the emperors kept a permanent residence in Italy, visiting the country only for brief campaigns, the cities of Italy gradually began to be mindful of their freedom and to think less of the imperial authority. Thereupon "such cities throughout Italy as had survived the various barbarian floods began to grow and flourish and return to their original power."[27] Here again political freedom was the decisive factor. As soon as they had recovered it, the Italian cities began to revive. The darkest period was then past, and from that point Bruni's history was the story of the growth of the communes and of their struggle for independence, until, with the collapse of the Hohenstaufen empire, he turned more specifically to the history of Florence.

The *History of the Florentine People* established a widely accepted norm for the organization and periodization of state history. The next step was to fix a definite chronological boundary between Roman and later history and to expand the history of the Italian states into a history of Italy since the fall of Rome. This was the contribution of the learned papal secretary, Flavio Biondo of Forlì. His *History from the*

---

[25] *Ibid.*, p. 15.   [26] *Ibid.*, pp. 22 f; 25.   [27] *Ibid.*, p. 23.

Decline of the Roman Empire (1439-1453),[28] though strongly influenced by Bruni, was original in both method and purpose. It was a careful, critical work, scholarly rather than literary, based on the best and oldest sources available, and covering the history of all Italy together with a running commentary on the Eastern Empire. There was little deep historical insight in Biondo's work, but it was more accurate and more comprehensive than the literary state histories. It had the virtues as well as the vices of the historical text book. Indeed, with its plenitude of definite dates, its factual treatment of events, and its incredibly heavy style, it is unhappily reminiscent of innumerable later texts similarly entitled. The humanists damned Biondo with faint praise because of his hopelessly unclassical style, yet they paid him the sincere compliment of plagiarizing his work more extensively than that of any other historian.[29]

Unlike the majority of the humanist historians, Biondo was not inspired by official patronage. He was led to undertake his history by a sincere, if somewhat antiquarian, love of all evidences of the Italian past. He had a profound admiration for ancient Roman civilization and a stronger feeling for the empire than had the republican Bruni, but he had also a genuine affection for the later centuries, as was amply demonstrated in his geographical and antiquarian study of Italy's past, the *Italy Illustrated* (1446).[30] Moreover, the Middle Ages presented the irresistible appeal of a virgin field. As he explained in the opening sentences of the *History,* the period of Rome's growth and power had been celebrated by many good historians, but the age that followed her decline was shrouded in darkness. It was his purpose, therefore, to restore to the light the history of the thousand and thirty years following the sack of Rome by the Goths in 412 (*recte* 410). When he wrote this introduction he had, as a matter of fact,

---

28 F. Biondo, *Historiarum ab inclinatione Romanorum imperii decades* (first ed. Venice, 1483; I use the Froben edition of Biondo's works, Basel, 1531). For Biondo and his work see B. Nogara, ed., *Scritti inediti e rari di Biondo Flavio* (Rome, 1927), Introd.

29 Fueter, pp. 16; 109. Aeneas Silvius wrote an epitome of the *Historiarum,* covering its naked learning with a decent raiment of Ciceronian prose. Aeneas Silvius, *Opera* (Basel, 1551), pp. 144–281. Elsewhere he described Biondo's work as "opus certe laboriosum et utile, verum expolitore emendatoreque dignum." Aeneas Silvius, *Commentarii* (Frankfurt, 1614), p. 310.

30 F. Biondo, *Italia illustrata* (Basel, 1531).

already completed the history of the final thirty years (1412–42) in twelve books, which in the finished work formed the third *Decade*, or group of ten books, and the beginning of a fourth. The first two *Decades*, then, were devoted to the even thousand years between the decline of Rome and what he regarded as contemporary history, that is, to the Middle Ages, though he did not, of course, use that term. The first *Decade* ended with the war of Pepin against the Lombards in 752, a well-chosen turning point in Italian history.

This definite chronological scheme was one of the most significant features of Biondo's history. His insistence on the date 412 for the beginning of Rome's decline drew a sharp line between the period of ancient history and that which followed. Throughout the first *Decade* he dated events from that year, and in the introduction he justified his position in a lengthy argument against the opinion of those who, like Bruni, thought that the decline of Rome began with the emperors and those who would date it from the removal of the capital to Constantinople. The empire, he argued, continued to grow in power or, at least, to hold its own till the time of Theodosius the Great. Whatever the underlying causes of weakness, the actual decline began with the sack of Rome.[31] This emphasis on an external, if dramatic, event may indicate a more superficial view of history than that of Bruni, but it made a lasting impression simply because it was definite and hence memorable.

The decline and desolation of Italy through the barbarian invasions is the theme of the first *Decade*. Like Bruni, however, Biondo realized that the decline was a temporary phase, ending at some vague chronological point after the Lombard wars with the rising vigor of the Italian cities.[32] The tone of the second *Decade* is noticeably more cheerful and he began to date events by the conventional *anno salutis* rather than the arbitrary *anno inclinationis Romanorum imperii* which he had used hitherto. He had already explained his conception of the significant factors in Italian history in a rare philosophical aside at the beginning of *Decade* I, Book 3. The preceding book had ended

[31] Biondo, *Historiarum*, p. 4.

[32] Cf. Brandi, p. 6; and Joachimsen, *Geschichtsauffassung*, p. 24, to the contrary. Borinski, p. 107, notes that in his *Roma instaurata* Biondo seems to end the decline with the conclusion of the Lombard wars.

with the abdication of Romulus Augustulus, the last emperor of Roman race. This abominable event, he wrote, recalled the memory of those indignities which had long restrained him from writing, for shame had almost deterred him when he contemplated commencing his history with the decline, or rather the destruction, of the Roman Empire. It galled him to recount the injuries done to his country and his ancestors. But the hope held before him of narrating the origin of new cities and most distinguished peoples, whose excellence has restored the Roman dignity of Italy, gave him heart so that he could write without any feeling of shame. He then proceeded to list the cities that had grown great through God's special kindness to Italy, by whose wealth and the vigor of their inhabitants the dignity and glory of Italy existed once more.[33] Again, as with Bruni, there is the implication that the fall of Rome was not an unrelieved disaster, and the proud consciousness of the rising power of Italy through her cities, once they were left free to work out their own salvation.

In Biondo's view, then, the revival of Italy began with the rise of the communes. There is no indication that he saw a Renaissance at the end of the Middle Ages. There is, however, in the neat chronological organization of his work and in the introduction to the third *Decade,* where he rejoiced at having completed the history of the thousand years from 412 to 1412, a faint suggestion that he regarded those thousand years as forming a historical epoch in some way distinct from contemporary history.[34] It is difficult to say how much of this was due to a preconceived historical pattern. The work on the thirty years from 1412 to 1442 was written first, so that the introductory remarks must have been an afterthought. And so far as the thousand year period is given any characterization, it is only as the period following the decline of Rome, during which no good history was written. In the contemporary period, the author did not have to depend in the same way on unsatisfactory sources, since the events fell within the memory of living men. This is an obvious distinction and one that could have no permanent value. Still his organization may have helped to set the idea of a thousand-year Middle Ages for later historians to whom the year 1412 no longer had the significance it held for Biondo.

[33] Biondo, *Historiarum,* p. 30.   [34] *Ibid.,* p. 393.

Bruni and Biondo were, each in his own way, the pioneers of humanist historiography. The other Italian humanists followed faithfully in their footsteps, imitating the style and method of Bruni and borrowing material, often without acknowledgment, from Biondo. Even Machiavelli adhered fairly closely to the pattern in his *Florentine History* (1525).[35] Beginning with the barbarian invasions, he devoted half of the work to the period "from the decline of the Roman Empire" to the accession of the Medici in 1434. The first book, in which he surveyed the history of the whole of Italy during that period, leaned heavily upon Biondo. Machiavelli departed from precedent, however, by adding to the common reasons given for the decline of Rome a cyclical theory, which made the alternate rise and decline of states a kind of natural law. "The reason is," he argued, "that valor produces peace; peace, repose; repose, disorder; disorder, ruin; so from disorder order springs; from order virtue; and from this glory and good fortune." It followed that the decline of the ancient empire must be succeeded by a new period of rising strength.

And [he concluded] although nothing has subsequently arisen from the ruins of Rome at all corresponding to her ancient greatness . . . . still there was so much bravery and intelligence in some of the new cities and governments that afterwards sprang up, that although none ever acquired dominion over the rest, they were, nevertheless, so balanced and regulated amongst themselves as to enable them to live in freedom and defend their country from the barbarians.[36]

For all his faith in the incomparable greatness of Rome, then, Machiavelli was far from thinking of the Middle Ages as an unfortunate period in the history of Italy. The misfortunes which most troubled his patriotic soul came in his own day. Hence he regarded the contemporary history of his native land with a pessimistic eye. It might be noted in passing that, while Machiavelli's historical work furnished little sustenance for the Renaissance idea, it did nevertheless exert a considerable influence upon later interpretations of the age, notably upon the Romantic conception of the "wicked Renaissance."

[35] N. Machiavelli, *Istorie fiorentine* (Florence, 1532). Eng. trans. (London, 1901).
[36] *Ibid.*, V, I [p. 203].

His cold-blooded analysis of contemporary political corruption and his vivid portraits of such ruthless egocentrics as Cesare Borgia made a lasting impression, an impression to which Guicciardini's disillusioned estimate of his fellow Italians also contributed in no small degree.[37]

The humanists are particularly interesting for our purpose because they introduced new trends in historical thought, which were to have a decided influence upon future interpretations. It would be an error, however, to regard their ideas as shared by all Renaissance historians. Medieval conceptions of all kinds were still widely held, and the medieval forms of world history still found expression and enjoyed a considerable popularity. Five years after the death of Bruni, the saintly Antonio Pierozzi, Archbishop of Florence, completed a *Universal Chronicle* (1459),[38] which showed not the slightest sign of the new historical ideas and methods. In neither his historical interpretation nor his attitude toward pagan antiquity, is there evidence that the good archbishop had ever heard of the humanists or their work. The *Chronicle* was divinely motivated history, a compilation based on the usual medieval sources, with the Six Ages and the Four Monarchies supplying its chronological structure and determining its historical philosophy. More modern was the *Supplement of Chronicles* (1483)[39] of Fra Jacopo Filippo Foresti of Bergamo, but it too remained well within the scholastic tradition, though with humanist overtones. These chronicles were especially popular in Germany, where they were most frequently published and where they exerted a strong influence on the early semi-scholastic school of humanist historiography.[40]

While most of the humanists avoided the world chronicle, there is one notable exception in the *History from the Creation of the World to the Year of Human Salvation 1504* (1498-1504)[41] of Marcantonio Coccio, called Sabellicus. Writing under the patronage of the Vene-

37 Cf. Fueter, p. 79.
38 A. Pierozzi, *Chronicon universale* (Nuremberg, 1484). Cf. Joachimsen, *Geschichtsauffassung*, pp. 80 ff.
39 J. F. Foresti, *Supplementum Chronicarum* (Venice, 1483).
40 Cf. Joachimsen, *Geschichtsauffassung*, p. 86.
41 Sabellicus, *Rapsodie historiarum enneadum ab orbe condito ad annum salutis humane 1504* (first ed. Venice, 1498-1504; I use the ed. of Paris, 1509).

tian government,[42] Sabellicus undertook the ambitious task of adapting the methods and periodization of Bruni and Biondo to universal history, a field hitherto monopolized by theologians. Though distinctly pious, he broke completely with the tradition of ecclesiastical world chronicle. His treatment of ancient history, whether sacred or profane, was free from theological interpretation. He followed a strictly chronological scheme throughout, rejecting the doctrine of the Four Monarchies,[43] and breaking his work into two major parts at the sack of Rome in 412 (Biondo's date). The first seven *Enneades,* which ended at that point, were first published separately; the remaining four, beginning with the founding of Venice, were added later.[44]

We have lingered over the formal historical writing of the Italian humanists longer, perhaps, than may seem justified by the slight contribution it made to the growth of the modern conception of the Renaissance. If, however, the histories written during that period showed few signs of the idea of the Renaissance, that fact is of more than negative importance. On the other hand, it should not be regarded as too significant. The formal historical work of the humanists was restricted arbitrarily to the political sphere, and the Renaissance has always belonged primarily to *Kulturgeschichte.* The political historians have never taken much cognizance of it, at least until recent years when even political history has been so impregnated with ideas drawn from cultural history as to have lost its exclusive character. At the same time, the humanist historians did make certain definite contributions to the modern organization and periodization of history, which were not without significance for the problem of the Renaissance. They broke with the theological world history of the medieval chroniclers, abandoned the idea of perpetual decline, and established

[42] Sabellicus had already published a history of Venice, *Rerum Venetarum ab urbe condita libri xxxiii* (Venice, 1487), in which he borrowed heavily from Biondo. Cf. R. Bersi, "Le fonti della prima decade delle 'Historiarum rerum Venetarum' di Marcantonio Sabellico," *Nuovo archivio Veneto,* N. S., XIX (1910), 422–60; XX (1910), 115–62.

[43] Sabellicus, *Rapsodie,* I, f. civo ff. Falco (p. 30) believes he sees traces of the six ages in the first six *Enneades.*

[44] That the division at 412 was not due to chance but represented a conscious historical scheme seems clear from Sabellicus' discussion in the Preface, and in the *Epistola apologetica,* appended to the first part. *Rapsodie,* II, f. ccxxvvo.

a new periodization on secular grounds, thereby setting up one of the two boundaries of the Middle Ages. And the Middle Ages are an essential prerequisite to the Renaissance in the conceptual as well as the chronological sense. Their conception of the Middle Ages, however, remained incomplete. The nearer side was left open and, in political history at least, they were far from regarding it as merely a period of regrettable time between antiquity and their own age. For their more positive influence on later ideas of both the Middle Ages and the Renaissance, we must leave their formal histories and turn to their comments on the evolution of literature and the arts.

HUMANIST VIEWS OF THE HISTORY OF LITERATURE AND ART

The exclusion of literature, learning, and art from their formal historical work was part of the price paid by the humanists for the invaluable guidance of their classical models. For the history of culture they were forced to utilize other media less well adapted to the purpose. One of the most common was the biography or series of biographies of writers and artists. Unfortunately these forms offered little opportunity for the coherent treatment of cultural evolution over a long period. They were designed primarily to celebrate the achievements of great men, thus strengthening a tendency which among the humanists needed no encouragement. Yet their historical studies, together with their conscious efforts to restore the literature and learning of antiquity, gave the humanists a sense of the passage of time and of changes in civilization that led them to consider the problems of cultural decline and revival. Lacking a literary form that would permit full development of this theme, they produced no complete cultural history, but they did frequently insert into biographies, prefaces, and other works brief summaries of the history of the particular branch of culture suggested by the subject under discussion.

The general picture of European history presented in these parenthetical essays into the history of culture was in certain respects similar to that found in the humanist political histories; but there were also differences of great significance for the growth of the Renaissance concept. In both political and cultural history the humanists emphasized the ages and events which held the greatest current interest for themselves and their patrons. In both fields the fall of Rome and the barbarian invasions were events of epoch-making importance. But it was only in political history that the humanists were drawn to the study of the Middle Ages in which the present Italian cities and states were founded. Urban laymen as most of them were and trained in the reverent study of the ancient classics, the Italian humanists found the feudal literature, the scholastic learning, and the symbolic religious art of the Middle Ages alien to them: alien to them as humanists and doubly alien to them as Italians, for the most vigorous forms of medieval culture were indigenous to France rather than to Italy. Thus, although their scheme of cultural history coincided with the political in marking a definite periodic break at the end of Roman civilization, in separating Italian from world history, and in concentrating on secular activity, it departed from the political scheme by blandly ignoring the greater part of the Middle Ages. From the decline of antique culture they usually leaped directly to the recent revival of Italian art and letters, that is, to the Renaissance.

The keynote of the new conception of cultural history was struck by one of the earliest of the humanists, Giovanni Boccaccio. In his *Life of Dante*,[45] he proclaimed the great Florentine poet the first to open the way for the Muses who had been banished from Italy. Through him dead poetry was reawakened to life. And in the *Decameron*,[46] recounting an anecdote about Giotto, he praised the life-like character of his painting and hailed the painter as one of the chief glories of Florence because he had restored the art of painting to the light. Thereafter the idea of a recent restoration of letters and art, after a long period in which both had disappeared, formed the basis of all humanist cultural history. Boccaccio was apparently the first to assert it, but he did so only in passing. It was first developed at length by Filippo Villani.

Villani's pioneer work on the history of literature and art was the *Book concerning the Famous Citizens of the City of Florence*,[47]

---

[45] G. Boccaccio, *La vita di Dante,* in A. Solerti, ed., *Le vite di Dante, Petrarca e Boccaccio scritti fino al secolo* XVII (Milan, s. a., c. 1904).

[46] G. Boccaccio, *Decamerone,* VI, 5.

[47] F. Villani, *Liber de civitatis Florentiae famosis civibus* (ed. G. C. Galletti, Florence, 1847). Fueter (p. 94) dates it 1382; but A. Philippi, *Der Begriff der*

written toward the end of the fourteenth century. It opened with the lives of the poets, first Claudian, then Dante, Petrarch, Boccaccio, and others. Villani apparently felt that the absence of representatives from the nine centuries between Claudian and Dante called for some explanation. He therefore began the life of Dante with a brief sketch of literary history from the decline of Rome. Since he was writing only about famous Florentine citizens, it was natural that he should exclude those medieval writers who had not the good fortune to be born in Florence. However, that was not the reason he gave. Rather, Villani's argument implied that there were simply no poets of note between the fifth century and the fourteenth.

> After Claudian, who was well nigh the last of the poets whom ancient times brought forth [he asserted], almost all poetry decayed, because of the weakness and avarice of the emperors, and also perhaps because art was no longer prized, since the Catholic faith began to abhor the figments of poetic imagination as a pernicious and a vain thing. Poetry, therefore, lying prostrate without honor or dignity, that great man Dante Allagherii [sic] recalled it as from an abyss of shadows into the light, and giving it his hand, set the fallen art upon its feet. [48]

This vivid, if somewhat redundant, metaphor suggests a sudden and recent revival of letters, but offers no clue to the cause. A rationalization of the new interest in poetry, however, and on quite unusual grounds, followed immediately. Dante, he said, had reconciled the fictions of the poets with moral and natural philosophy and with Christian literature, and had shown that the ancient poets were divinely inspired to prophesy the Christian mysteries, thus making poetry pleasing not only to the learned, but also to the common and uneducated (plebeis et idiotis), of whom the number is infinite.

In a later chapter Villani turned to the Florentine painters, "who raised up the bloodless and almost extinct arts." [49] He gave credit for the first step in the revival of painting to Cimabue, and it is noteworthy that he made Cimabue's service consist not of closer imitation of the ancients, but rather of the skill and genius with which he recalled art to natural similitude. Before Cimabue, Villani asserted, Greek and Latin painting had lain dead for many centuries, and he pointed to the pictures adorning the churches as evidence of the crude technique of the earlier artists. "After him," he continued, "the road to a new art having been opened, Giotto, who not only can be compared with the illustrious painters of antiquity but surpassed them in skill and genius, restored painting to its ancient dignity and greatest fame." [50] Here again he emphasized the close resemblance to nature of Giotto's pictures, which seemed "to live and breathe."

That Cimabue and Giotto were the originating geniuses in the revival of Italian painting was destined to become a permanent axiom in the history of art. Dante, on the other hand, was soon replaced by Petrarch in the role of the restorer of good literature.[51] This shift followed naturally upon the growing enthusiasm of the humanists for the ancient tongues to the prejudice of the *volgare*. So much is made clear by the comparison of the two poets in Leonardo Bruni's *Lives of Dante and Petrarch* (1436).[52] Bruni admired Dante and took patriotic satisfaction in the fame he had brought to Florence.[53] But his admiration was tempered by the fact that Dante was "more accomplished in the vulgar style and in rhyme than in the Latin and literary style." [54] The reason for this, Bruni added, was that "none of the men of his century understood how to write gracefully in prose or in Latin verse, but were raw and coarse and without skill in letters." [55] The true literary revival began with Petrarch. To explain this situation Bruni inserted a sketch of the history of Latin letters since the age of Cicero.[56]

This little essay on the decline and revival of literature is one of the most interesting of its kind, for Bruni was more concerned with the causes of historical change than were most of the humanists, and he had already worked out a theory of the causes of political decline and

[50] *Ibid.*
[51] Cf. H. Weisinger, "Who Began the Revival of Learning? The Renaissance Point of View," *Papers of the Michigan Academy of Science, Art and Letters,* XXX (1944), 625–38.
[52] L. Bruni, *Vite di Dante e del Petrarca,* in A. Solerti, ed., *Autobiografie e vite de' maggiori scrittori italiani* (Milan, 1903), pp. 93–123.
[53] *Ibid.,* p. 94.   [54] *Ibid.,* p. 109; cf. p. 123.
[55] *Ibid.,* p. 110.   [56] *Ibid.,* pp. 115 ff.

revival in his *History of the Florentine People.* He now applied a similar theory to the history of Latin and Italian letters. Latin literature reached its highest peak of perfection in the time of Cicero, that is, at the end of the Republic. Thereafter both Rome and her literature began to decline, and for the same reason, because the Roman people had lost their freedom under the tyrannous emperors. Finally, after centuries of decline, the Goths and Lombards, "barbarous and foreign nations," came and completed the destruction of Latin style. But, as in his political history, Bruni saw the dark period of barbarian conquest followed by an upward movement as soon as the Italian people began to recover their freedom. Then, he said, "the cities of Tuscany and others began to regain their strength and to pay attention to learning and to the refinement of their coarse style, and thus gradually recovered literary vigor." [57] Bruni evidently regarded the literary revival as later and slower than the political, however, for he insisted that it was a feeble movement and that the men of that age were without true taste, being given more to writing in Italian verse than in Latin, so that even in Dante's time there were few who understood the "literary" style, and they but poorly. Petrarch was the first "who possessed such grace and genius that he could recognize and recall to the light the ancient elegance of style, which had been lost and extinguished." And even Petrarch did not attain perfection, though he pointed the way for others to follow. Later Bruni added an appendix, as it were, to this sketch of the literary revival; in his *Commentary on Things Done in his own Time (ca.* 1440) [58] he tells with vast enthusiasm how Chrysoloras brought Greek back to Italy after it had been forgotten there for seven hundred years.

A more complete account of the restoration of the classics appeared a few years after this in Biondo's *Italy Illustrated,*[59] written between the years 1448 and 1458. The subject was suggested in the midst of his description of Ravenna by the fame of John of Ravenna (Giovanni

---

[57] *Ibid.,* p. 117.

[58] L. Bruni, *Rerum suo tempore gestarum commentarius,* Muratori, XIX, Part III (ed. C. di Pierro, 1926), p. 431; cf. Bruni's preface to his translation of Plato's *Phaedrus* in Baron, *Brunis humanistisch-philosophische Schriften,* p. 125.

[59] F. Biondo, *Italia illustrata* (first ed. 1474; I use Froben ed., Basel, 1531), pp. 346 f.

Malpaghini), whom he cited as the first to restore the present flourishing study of eloquence to Italy. True to his conception of historical periodization, Biondo dated the decline of letters from the decline of the Roman Empire, that is, from the early fifth century. There were few or almost none who wrote Latin with any elegance after the Doctors of the Church, Ambrose, Jerome, and Augustine, unless one might include St. Gregory and the Venerable Bede, who were near the same time, and, much later, St. Bernard. Ignoring the *volgare* altogether, Biondo leaped straight from St. Bernard to Petrarch, who "first began to awaken poetry and eloquence." Like Bruni, however, he refused to credit Petrarch with attaining the full flower of Ciceronian eloquence, adding the shrewd comment that for this we must blame Petrarch's lack of books rather than of intelligence. After discussing the limited number and poor quality of the Ciceronian works at Petrarch's disposal, Biondo continued the story of the revival of ancient literature with the teaching of John of Ravenna and Emmanuel Chrysoloras and an imposing list of the men who gained from these two a love of Ciceronian style and of Greek letters. Then followed an account, too long to be summarized here, of the search for old manuscripts at the Council of Constance and elsewhere, of the founding of new classical schools like those of Vittorino and Guarino, and of the work of the most distinguished humanists of the first half of the fifteenth century. It is a remarkable survey of the contemporary humanist movement, filled with enthusiastic appreciation of the advances made since the generation of Petrarch.

This critical awareness of the progressive improvement in classical style became more pronounced as the century advanced. It formed the *leitmotif* of Paolo Cortese's *Dialogue of Learned Men*,[60] dedicated to Lorenzo de' Medici in 1490, the most comprehensive discussion written during the *Quattrocento* of the humanists who revived classical letters. Cortese was a Ciceronian purist.[61] He had nothing but contempt for the vernacular and judged his predecessors by the single standard of correct classical style. Beyond that, nothing seemed impor-

[60] P. Cortese, *Dialogus de hominibus doctis*, in Villani, *De civitatis* (ed. Galletti), pp. 221–48.

[61] Cf. Erasmus, *Ciceronianus, Opera Omnia*, ed. J. Clericus (Leyden, 1703–06), I, 1023 f.

tant, except a knowledge of Greek, which he evidently regarded as the original source of *humanitas*. His account of the learned men of Italy opened with Chrysoloras, through whom the Italians, "altogether ignorant of literary practise or art, were first vehemently excited to the study of eloquence by the knowledge of Greek letters." [62] Cortese's theory that it was the Greek revival which caused the awakening of a new taste for Ciceronian Latin was unusual but not unique. [63] It was probably a heritage from Cicero himself, who had firmly believed that Greek literature was the source and inspiration of Latin taste and style. The recognition of Chrysoloras as the founder of Greek studies in Italy was, of course, a commonplace among the humanists. It was only at a much later time that the Greek revival was dated from the fall of Constantinople.

At this point in Cortese's *Dialogue* one of the interlocutors mentioned Dante and Petrarch, who had flourished before Chrysoloras. But the chief speaker replied, quite untroubled by the objection, that he had begun with Chrysoloras because eloquence was generally regarded as having arisen at that time and he would limit his discussion to those writers who came out of Chrysoloras's brilliant workshop. As for Dante, he had great genius, but the colors of his work, like those of the old pictures, have faded. It was indeed marvelous that he could explain things so difficult and abstruse in the vulgar tongue, "but would that he had been able to express his thoughts as well in Latin." Petrarch, he continued, "possessed such magnitude of intellect and memory that he was the first who dared to recall the study of eloquence to the light, for it was by the influence of his genius that Italy was first stimulated and impelled to study." His speech, however, "was not Latin." His sentences were too concise, his wording abject, and his composition diligent rather than elegant. His Italian poems demonstrate what he might have accomplished "had he possessed the light and splendor of Latin speech, but to the man born in the dregs of all the centuries those ornaments of writing were lacking." Thus Cortese on the unfortunate Petrarch. Boccaccio, John of Ravenna, and Coluccio Salutati were in no better case. The first Italian humanist accorded high, though still qualified, praise was

[62] Cortese, pp. 223 f.   [63] See reference to Aeneas Silvius, below p. 26.

Leonardo Bruni. Thereafter Cortese commented on the whole list of Italian classical scholars until he came to his own generation. Those still living he omitted in accordance with a recognized convention, but the dialogue ended with the suggestion that it was fairer to those great men of the earlier period, who freed eloquence from the bondage of the barbarians, not to compare them with the men of the present, for though the former were versed in all forms of learning, they had not attained the flower of Latin oratory.[64]

In contrast to the increasing elegance of the century since Chryso-loras, the preceding period seemed to Cortese one of complete degrada-tion for letters. And he had reasons. At one point in the *Dialogue,* the mentor undertook to explain why the study of eloquence had been entirely withdrawn from Italy.[65] In the first place, the translation of the imperial residence from Rome to Thrace did great damage to literature, for by that emigration Italy was thrown open to the vio-lence of the barbarians, and the power of the Roman people was de-stroyed. The barbarians poured into Italy and, after overturning every-thing, intermingled with the Roman race. Nor were they content with a single plundering raid, but for nearly a thousand years held Italy in bitter distress. The result of this was a close interrelation with the barbarian peoples, a Latin speech befouled with innumerable accretions, and the destruction of an infinite number of books, so that the intelligence of men born in that time was deprived of energy and languished immersed in barbarism. The medieval ignorance of good letters, therefore, was all the fault of the barbarians, and he had al-ready suggested in the preface that the restoration of learning came when Italy was freed from vexation at their hands, though the four-teenth century seems a little late for that.

The *Quattrocento* witnessed many variations upon the theme of medieval darkness and the recent restoration of literature and the arts. We have noted the most coherent and comprehensive of these. Some briefer comments from the other humanists may be worth noting, however, in illustration of both the general uniformity of the concep-tion and the variety of opinion concerning the dates and authors of the new cultural movements.[66]

---

[64] Cortese, p. 236.   [65] *Ibid.,* p. 223.
[66] For further illustrations see the articles by Simone and Weisinger cited above.

Thus Matteo Palmieri, writing in 1436 or thereabouts, proclaimed
Giotto the restorer of painting, but ascribed the revival of Latin letters
after eight hundred years of neglect to his friend and contemporary,
Leonardo Bruni.[67] This flattering tribute to a famous fellow-citizen
was endorsed by the Florentine bookseller, Vespasiano da Bisticci, although he included Fra Ambrogio Traversari and Poggio Bracciolini
with Bruni as responsible for the renewal of the Latin tongue which
had been dead and buried a thousand years or more.[68] Vespasiano also
recognized Dante as the first Florentine writer for more than a thousand years and admitted that Petrarch had done much to revive Latin
though never approaching Traversari and Bruni.[69] Poggio, on the
other hand, attributed the flowering of the almost extinct liberal disciplines in that golden age to the patronage of Pope Nicholas V.[70] But
Poggio was a papal secretary as well as a Florentine citizen and he had
good reason to appreciate the generosity of the humanist pope. Aeneas
Silvius, too, observed the phenomenon of the literary revival but was
less definite about its original authors. Bruni he thought the greatest
of the early humanists, while noting that he had been taught by
Coluccio Salutati and, later, by Chrysoloras who had introduced the
ancient style of writing and the Ciceronion manner into Italy.[71] He
insisted, however, that Bruni far surpassed Salutati, for the latter retained certain of the ineptitudes of his age.

So ran the complacent chorus of the humanists, carrying conviction
beyond the strictly humanist circle. Even the good friar, Jacopo Filippo
Foresti, after having found learned men to praise all through the
Middle Ages and having hailed Dante as not only the first Florentine
poet but also a distinguished theologian,[72] accepted the contradictory
humanist thesis when he came to Petrarch, Chrysoloras, John of
Ravenna, and the other champions of classical letters.[73] While follow-

67 M. Palmieri, *Della vita civile* (Milan, 1825), pp. 46 f.
68 Vespasiano da Bisticci, *Vite di uomini illustri del secolo XV* (Florence, 1938),
pp. 261; 450. Eng. trans. (New York, 1926).
69 *Ibid.*, pp. 10; 261.
70 Poggio Bracciolini, "Oratio V ad summum Pontificem Nycholaum V," *Opera*
(Strassburg, 1513), fo. 109vo f.
71 Aeneas Silvius, *De viris illustribus* (Stuttgart, 1842), No. xvi, p. 23.
72 Foresti, *Supplementum Chronicarum*, fo. 246 vo.
73 *Ibid.*, ffo. 251vo; 262 f; 269vo.

ing Biondo closely on most points, Fra Jacopo made one addition that was entirely his own idea, proudly asserting that it was his fellow citizen, Gasparino da Barzizza of Bergamo, who first resuscitated the moribund Latin literature, raising it "as though from the depths." [74]

The artists of the *Quattrocento,* too, accepted the general pattern of cultural history outlined by their humanist friends, though adding to it from their more specialized knowledge of the arts.[75] Knowing little and caring less about the work of their medieval predecessors beyond the Alps, the Italian artists concentrated their attention on the Italian scene. Ghiberti's account in his second *Commentary (ca.* 1455) [76] is characteristic. Ancient art declined in the age of Constantine; then followed six hundred years devoid of all art until the Byzantines introduced the awkward *maniera Greca;* finally, natural painting was revived by Cimabue and Giotto, but especially by the latter. Thereafter, Ghiberti traced the progress of the Giottesque school in Florence to his own time, though he also noted the contributions of the Sienese painters and the Pisan sculptors. Leo Battista Alberti, on the other hand, ascribed the founding of the new arts entirely to his contemporaries, Brunelleschi, Donatello, Ghiberti, Luca della Robbia, and others. These he thought equal to the ancients, if not greater in genius, since they had produced so much beauty without teachers or models.[77] Brunelleschi continued to be regarded as the originator of the new style of architecture in contrast to the Gothic, but for most of the artists Cimabue and Giotto remained the conventional founders of the new painting.

Glancing back over the comments on cultural history that we have cited, one can find ample inspiration for the later conceptions of both the Middle Ages and the Renaissance. Both humanists and artists were agreed that, for a long period between antiquity and their own time, literature and the arts were dead or hidden in darkness, and

---

[74] *Ibid.,* fo. 269vo.

[75] For discussion and examples see A. Philippi, *Der Begriff der Renaissance* (Leipzig, 1912), pp. 15 ff.

[76] See summary in Philippi, pp. 15 ff. For discussion of contemporary histories of fifteenth century art, see J. Schlosser, *Die Kunstliteratur* (Vienna, 1924), pp. 87–105.

[77] L. B. Alberti, *Trattato della pittura* (1436), in H. Janitschek, ed., *Kleinere kunsttheoretische Schriften* (Vienna, 1877), p. 49.

that they had since been revived or restored to the light of day. The actual metaphor of rebirth does not occur, but there is nearly always some equivalent expression. Nevertheless, it would be dangerous to read into these fragmentary essays on the history of art and letters a too clear perception of the general differentiation between the Middle Ages and the Renaissance as periods in the history of civilization. Almost always the idea of revival is limited to one specific branch of Italian culture. Occasional expressions of consciousness of a more general revival and of the dawn of a new era may indeed be found among the humanist writings. Thus Marsilio Ficino: "It is undoubtedly a golden age which has restored to the light the liberal arts that had almost been destroyed: grammar, eloquence, painting, architecture, sculpture, music. And that all in Florence." [78] The last phrase is not without significance. Lorenzo Valla, too, remarked upon the fact that not only letters but also the kindred arts of painting, sculpture, and architecture were long dead but "in this age were raised up and lived again." [79] But even when thus extended, the humanist idea of the Renaissance was limited strictly to the intellectual and aesthetic forms of culture.

[78] Cited in J. Nordström, *Moyen Age et Renaissance* (Paris, 1933), p. 18. For similar comments on the revival of culture in Florence, see Vespasiano, p. 10; and N. Machiavelli, *Dell' arte della guerra* (Milan, 1878), p. 228.

[79] L. Valla, *De linguae Latinae elegantia* (Lyons, 1538), p. 8.

CHAPTER TWO

The Humanist Tradition as Altered by
Northern Humanism and the Reformation

THE ITALIAN HUMANISTS of the fifteenth and early sixteenth centuries set the tone of secular state histories for the following two hundred years. They also established the fundamental basis for the conception of the decline and revival of learning and the arts that was to prevail until the Romantic movement. But as humanist historiography spread beyond the Alps its content and character were diluted and altered by the infusion of alien elements. French, English, and German humanists viewed history through the astigmatic lenses of national consciousness. So, indeed, had the Italians. But if the northern humanists were but following the example of their Italian masters in this, the resulting picture was warped in different places. And when national bias was less discernible, as in Erasmus and his circle, an active campaign for the reform of religion as well as education lent a new emphasis to the conception of the medieval *lacuna* and the revival of culture. If the Erasmians were faithful to the tradition of Italian humanism, it was decidedly in their fashion. Thus, even before the Reformation, the humanist view of cultural history had undergone some changes, losing something of its earlier integration. The Protestant reformers revolutionized it still further, giving it a new orientation and a new teleological significance.

THE PATRIOTIC HISTORIANS IN THE NORTH

Modern historiography was the child of the Renaissance in the northern lands as in Italy, a direct descendant of the humanism which

29

spread from Italy across the continent in the late fifteenth century.[1] Jealous of the priority of the Italians in the patriotic presentation of their political history, the governments of the northern states commissioned humanist historians to perform a similar service for them. The new historiography came at an opportune moment for France and England. It coincided with the spread of printing and a notable increase in lay education and also with the growing national consciousness that accompanied the political centralization of the national states. The historians who learned their trade in Italy or from Italian models were thus able to count on both a wider and more interested public than had existed earlier and the direct patronage of royal governments. The task of the national state historians was sufficiently similar to that of their Italian prototypes so that they had little need for originality. They had merely to adapt to the requirements of the national states the form and method of state history worked out by the school of Bruni, together with the antiquarian research founded by Biondo. After the Italian importations, Paolo Emilio and Polydor Vergil, who introduced humanist historiography into France and England respectively, the majority of the northern historians — Du Haillan, Belleforest, De Thou, Mézeray, Camden, Bacon, and the rest — were natives and wrote for the most part in the national language, without, however, departing far from the humanist precedent in style or method. Like the Italian historians, they were concerned with the history of states that had originated during the early Middle Ages. Their work, therefore, began where ancient history ended, and they carried the national story without a break down through the Middle Ages to their own time.

In comments on the history of literature and learning, however, the French humanists also took over from the Italians the idea that there had been a break in historical development since the Middle Ages and a recent restoration or rebirth. The latter term, indeed, seems to have occurred more commonly in the North than in Italy. Jean Plattard[2]

---

[1] Cf. E. Fueter, *Geschichte der neueren Historiographie* (Munich, 1936), pp. 137 ff.

[2] J. Plattard, " 'Restitution des bonnes lettres' et 'Renaissance'," in *Mélanges offerts par ses amis et ses élèves à M. Gustave Lanson* (Paris, 1922), pp. 128–31.

and Franco Simone [3] have both demonstrated, with a wealth of examples which makes repetition here unnecessary, that the early French humanists, like Jean de Montreuil, Nicole de Clémanges, Guillaume Tardif, and Robert Gaguin, as well as their sixteenth century successors, Guillaume Budé, Clément Marot, Rabelais, Louis le Roy, and others, all echoed the familiar humanist refrain of the contrast between present light and past darkness or of the rebirth or restoration of good letters after they had been neglected, dead, and buried during the centuries since the great age of antiquity. Most of the French writers generously acknowledged the priority of the Italians as the original agents of the literary revival. Jean Despautère, in particular, declared most specifically that it was Petrarch "who not without divine inspiration about the year 1340 opened war on the barbarians; and, recalling the Muses who had fled, vehemently excited the study of eloquence." [4]

At the same time, national pride was frequently evident in the emphasis placed by the French humanists upon their own national revival, and it served to alter, if but slightly, the historical scheme as established in Italy. Jacques Amyot, dedicating his translation of Plutarch to Henry II in 1559, may indeed be said to have enunciated what was long to remain the peculiarly French conception of the *renaissance des lettres* when he reminded the king "that the great King Francis, your father, happily founded good letters and made them to be reborn (renaistre) and to flourish in this noble kingdom." [5] In common with other northern scholars the French humanists were prone to overlook upon occasion the priority of the Italian revival. They would admit it, no doubt, if pressed, but they might also pass over it in discreet silence. They were the more likely to do so when connecting the restoration of classical letters with the purification of sacred learning, a field in which Erasmus and his fellows had a more justifiable claim to priority. Thus Budé noted that it was his friend Erasmus who had cleansed sacred literature and, what was more im-

[3] F. Simone, "La Coscienza della Rinascita negli humanisti," *La Rinascita*, II (1939), 838–71; III (1940), 163–86.

[4] J. Despautère, *Ars versificatoria* (Paris, 1516), Preface.

[5] J. Amyot, *Les vies des hommes illustres . . . . par Plutarque de Chaeronée* *translate de Grec en François* (Paris, 1582), I, a iii.

portant, had caused "sacred truth itself to emerge from the Cimmerian darkness" of scholastic discipline. And he added that if theology was ever "to shine forth from the filth of the sophist school" it would be "because of the commencement made during our time." [6] But even when classical learning alone was being considered, Erasmus was frequently cited as the author of the literary revival, as when Jacques Charron asserted that he was "the first to raise up good letters at the time when they were being reborn (renascentes tum jam bonas litteras) and were emerging from their barbaric squalor." [7] More commonly, however, the suggestion of a revival more recent than the Italian was merely implied in such phrases as "in our time." [8] This, it is true, is but a minor variation upon the humanist theme. In general the French humanists were in accord with the scheme of historical development already outlined by the Italians.

German humanist historians, on the other hand, did not find the Italian schemes of political and cultural history entirely to their liking. It was, therefore, in Germany that the new historiography diverged most widely from the humanist norm.[9] The Holy Roman Empire, which had progressed from decentralized feudalism under the medieval emperors to a disintegrated particularism under the House of Austria, provided no effective focus for a national state history. The movement toward the centralization of state government, which was characteristic of the age, operated in the rising territorial states rather than in the empire as a whole. German national consciousness thus lacked the substantial substratum of political reality to be found in England and France. In this respect Germany resembled Italy rather than the national states, but with the important difference that the

6 G. Budé to C. Tunstall, May 19, 1517, in P. S. Allen, ed., *Opus epistolarum Des. Erasmi Roterodami* (Oxford, 1906–41), II, 567.
7 Erasmus, *Adagia,* ed. J. Charron (Paris, 1571), fo. a iii.
8 Cf. G. Budé, *De Philologia,* in Budé, *Lucubrationes variae* (Basel, 1557), fo. 87 A: "Cum igitur litteras vitae restitutas postliminio aetates nostrae vidiamus." Cf. fo. 88.
9 The best special study is P. Joachimsen, *Geschichtsauffassung und Geschichtschreibung in Deutschland unter dem Einfluss des Humanismus* (Leipzig, 1910); see also, F. Schnabel, *Deutschlands geschichtliche Quellen und Darstellungen in der Neuzeit* (Leipzig, 1931), I, 63 ff; F. X. Wegele, *Geschichte der deutschen Historiographie seit dem Auftreten des Humanismus* (Munich, 1885), pp. 30 ff; Fueter, pp. 181 ff.

German territorial states were not so highly developed as the Italians, while the empire, despite its real weakness, still held a strong emotional appeal to Germanic pride. The German historians could apply the Italian technique of secular state history to neither the separate principalities nor the empire with any degree of satisfaction. Nevertheless, a powerful strain of patriotic sentiment ran through German humanism from Konrad Celtis to Ulrich von Hutten and aroused a vital interest in German history.

Though much preoccupied with the task of providing the various princely houses with distinguished if fanciful genealogies, the humanist historians were motivated most strongly by a patriotic sentiment that was Germanic in the broadest sense. They searched the archives for evidences of the German past, unearthing and publishing such sources as the *Nibelungenlied*, Ligurinus, Otto of Freising, Einhard, and the poems of Hroswitha, not to mention the very doubtful history of Hunibald (1514),[10] which was apparently invented by the Abbot Trithemius to supply much-needed information about the early Franks. They also made good use of the newly discovered *Germania* of Tacitus [11] and of the even more stimulating Berosus forgery (1498) of Annius of Viterbo,[12] which traced the genealogy of the German *Stämme* back to Noah. These enabled the humanists to furnish the German people with an ancient history comparable in antiquity to that of the Romans. But, for much the same reason, they were also very much interested in medieval history, where their enthusiasm was aroused by the Holy Roman Empire. The *translatio imperii ad Teutonicos* was the outward and visible sign of an inward and spiritual equality with the Roman race. The patriotism of the German humanists, indeed, was Pan-Germanic, less political than

---

[10] J. Trithemius, *De origine gentis Francorum compendium, ex duodecim ultimis Hunibaldi libris* (1514), in Trithemius, *Opera historica omnia,* ed. M. Freher (Frankfurt, 1601), I, 63–99. Cf. J. J. Hermes, *Über das Leben und die Schriften des Johannes von Trittenheim, genannt Trithemius* (Brüm, 1901), p. 26.

[11] Cf. P. Joachimsen, "Tacitus im deutschen Humanismus," *Neue Jahrbücher für das klassische Altertum, Geschichte und deutsche Literatur,* XXVII (1911), 687–717; Schnabel, p. 76 f.

[12] Annius of Viterbo (Giovanni Nanni), *Antiquitatum variarum volumina xvii cum commentariis* (Rome, 1498). Cf. F. Gotthelf, *Das deutsche Altertum in den Anschauungen des 16. und 17. Jahrhunderts* (Berlin, 1900), pp. 5 ff.

cultural, less national than racial.[13] It drew its emotional force in large part from resentment against the arrogant claims to cultural superiority voiced by the Italian scholars, who habitually referred to the Germans as barbarians.[14] This, it is true, did not keep them from a zealous absorption of the new learning imported from Italy, nor from a reverence for Latin antiquity almost equal to that of the Italians, but it did give a different motive to their historical research, which resulted in the paradox of nationalist world history.

The German humanists were drawn to the theme of universal history, with all its traditional theological connotations, for a variety of reasons. Only on the stage of world history could they find an adequate setting for the heroic antiquity they were building for the German people about the Berosus legend and the *Germania*. Moreover, they had no rising national state to write about, and the empire needed all the support that could be found in the doctrine of the Four Monarchies to make it a respectable subject for patriotic pride. Finally, they could not forget that the theory of universal monarchy, which was inseparably bound up with the ecclesiastical tradition of universal history, gave to the German emperors a claim to sovereignty over all Christian peoples. Thus, though heavily indebted to the Italian historians, they were prevented by the nature of their historical interest from adopting to the full either the secular attitude or the critical method of the southern humanists. On the whole, they found more aid and comfort in the unhumanistic world chronicles of Foresti and Antonio Pierozzi than in Sabellicus[15] or the humanist state histories. There was, indeed, a closer kinship between certain strains of early German humanism and scholasticism than has often been supposed,[16] and nowhere was this more evident than in their historiography.

13 "Zum ersten Male wurde jetzt das Deutschtum in rassenhaftem Gegensatze zum römischen und romanischen Wesen empfunden." Schnabel, p. 75. See also H. Reiss, *Motive des patriotischen Stolzes bei ben deutschen Humanisten* (Freiberg, 1934).

14 See, for example, the resentment of Italian arrogance expressed in Konrad Celtis, *Fünf Bücher Epigramme,* ed. K. Hartfelder (Berlin, 1881), pp. 20; 26; 35; 49; 122; and Erasmus, *Stultitiae Laus, Opera Omnia,* ed. J. Clericus (Leyden, 1703–06), IV, 448; cf. Allen, IV, 280, n. 67.

15 See above p. 16 f.

16 Cf. H. Hermelink, *Die religiösen Reformbestrebungen des deutschen Humanismus* (Tübingen, 1907); G. Ritter, *Studien zur Spätscholastik,* 2 vols. (Heidelberg, 1921–22).

The first of the humanist world histories, the *Book of Chronicles* (1493) [17] of the Nuremberg physician, Hartmann Schedel, was scarcely more than "a scholastic work in humanist clothing," [18] a rewriting of Foresti, with excerpts, all too few, from Aeneas Silvius and Biondo. It was soon surpassed, however, by Johannes Nauclerus's more critical and independent work, the *Chronicles of All Ages and of All Memorable Peoples* (1516).[19] Nauclerus belonged to the older generation of northern humanists, having been born between 1425 and 1430. He had had some experience of public life as *Hofmeister* to Eberhard of Württemberg and was later Professor of Canon Law at Tübingen. It was with this combination of political and legal background that in his old age he began the writing of a world chronicle. From the humanists he had learned to use ancient and medieval sources with fair discrimination, but he made no attempt to break with the major lines of the traditional scholastic organization. He retained the time-honored six ages, and added an equally unhumanistic periodization by the generations of Christ. Moreover, his critical sense was not strong enough to withstand the temptation of the Pseudo-Berosus. That charming fable, indeed, must have seemed to a German patriot too good to be untrue. And, for all its universal scope, Nauclerus's *Chronicle* was essentially a vehicle for the expression of German patriotism.

Here the German race appeared as the aboriginal people, the *Urvolk* of Europe, and later as the conquerors whose blood and vigor were injected into the British, French, and Italian nations during the victorious era of the *Völkerwanderung*. The coronation of Charlemagne provided Nauclerus with a further opportunity to celebrate the divinely ordained superiority of the German people. He had no doubt that the Roman Empire was in reality transferred to the Germans in the person of Charles,[20] and the event moved him to a digressive

---

[17] H. Schedel, *Liber chronicarum* (Nuremberg, 1493).

[18] Joachimsen, *Geschichtsauffassung*, p. 91.

[19] J. Nauclerus, *Memorabilium omnis aetatis et omnium gentium chronici commentarii* (Tübingen, 1516; I use ed. Cologne, 1544).

[20] "Eo die imperium Romanum a Graecis in persona Caroli Magni translatum est in Germanos . . . ." *Ibid.*, p. 619.

Laus Germaniae[21] that would warm the heart of the most immoderate believer in the innate superiority of the German race. A little later he drew the lesson still more clearly in an address to the German princes of his own day, urging them to follow in the footsteps of their great progenitors. He reminded them that God had chosen them before all others to dominate all nations and had given them the sovereignty of the world.[22] He admitted that there were other people who for fortitude and Christian faith were not to be neglected, but to the Germans God had given empire, glory, and most excellent renown. And again he repeated that to the Germans alone of Christian peoples the *imperium mundi* had been entrusted by Divine Providence, so that whatever happened in the world was their business, since no limits had been prescribed to their power, and "wherever people exist they should be subjected to their rule." One is reminded of the particularism of sixteenth century Germany only in the special praise that Nauclerus reserved for the Hohenstaufen emperors who were of his own Swabian *Stamm*.

The *Chronicle* of Nauclerus was much used by historians of the following generation, but it was his successor Aventinus who first presented the historical thesis of the "national humanists" in a popular form that at once secured for it a wide reading public. Johannes Turmair, called Aventinus, was a restless, far-wandering scholar, who had carried on his researches in all parts of Germany and the neighboring lands. As a student under Konrad Celtis at Ingolstadt and Vienna he had imbibed the old master's enthusiasm for German history and its sources, and when at last in 1517 he settled down in the congenial post of court historian to the Duke of Bavaria, he was prepared to devote the rest of his life to the task of celebrating the historic past of the German people. His great work, the *Annals of the Dukes of Bavaria* (1519–21), which he himself later revised and translated into the national tongue as *The Bavarian Chronicle* (1526–33),[23] was os-

---

21 "Quae enim est natio alia sub coelo, ubi tanta et tam syncera nobilitas, ubi tot generosi proceres, ubi tot fortissimi milites, quibus ex innata animi fortitudine contra hostes videtur . . . ." *Ibid.,* p. 620.

22 "Vos prae omnibus eligit Deus, ut dominaremini omni nationi, vobis data est monarchia mundi." *Ibid.,* p. 630.

23 Aventinus, *Annales ducum Boiariae* (Basel, 1580); *Bayerische Chronik* (Frankfurt, 1566); both eds. in Aventinus, *Sämtliche Werke* (Munich, 1881–1906), II–IV.

tensibly a history of the Bavarian *Stamm*, but in reality it was a history of the German race placed against the background of world history. Using with equal freedom Tacitus, Berosus, and his own imagination, Aventinus constructed a magnificently vivid and detailed picture of the early Germans from the foundation of the race by Tuitschen, the son of Noah.[24] Strongly moral as well as patriotic, his conception of German antiquity survived the historical revisionism of the Protestant reformers and remained the accepted standard for more than two centuries.[25] Aventinus himself had definitely Protestant leanings, which appeared in the anticlerical and antipapal tone of his presentation of medieval history. Here the empire was the central theme. For him Charles the Great was both pure German and the true successor of the Roman Emperors, having been elected by the Romans themselves. And he took no little satisfaction from the thought of the Roman people being forced to appeal for aid to their ancient enemies, the Germans.[26] The decline of the empire in later centuries depressed him, but he clung to the prophetic hope embodied in the doctrine of the Four Monarchies.

Meanwhile, some attempts had been made to separate German history from universal history,[27] but the patriotic use of world history remained the dominant trend among the German historians and shaped their conception of the past. As a result they lacked the motive for a clear periodization along the lines drawn by their Italian predecessors. They had no reason to draw a line of demarcation between ancient history and what we know as the Middle Ages. In fact, both the extension of German history into the misty past of the early tribes and the belief in the continuity of the Roman Empire through the Middle Ages militated against such a distinction. Like the political historians in Italy, they were greatly interested in medieval history, but because it represented a second heroic period for the German race rather than because it showed the rise of new, independent

---

[24] *Ibid.*, IV, 52 ff.
[25] Gotthelf, pp. 8 ff; cf. Schnabel, pp. 100 ff.
[26] Aventinus, *Werke*, V, 127; cf. IV, 618.
[27] See, for example, J. Wimpfeling, *Epitoma rerum Germanicarum usque ad nostra tempora* (Strassburg, 1505); and Beatus Rhenanus, *Rerum Germanicarum libri iii* (Basel, 1531).

states whose history belonged to a new age. Finally, having retained the ecclesiastical pattern of universal history, the German humanists were unable to discard the supernatural, teleological interpretation inherent in it, and so failed to create a purely secular national history.

Carried over into the field of cultural history, this view of the past also hindered the development of a clear pattern of the decline and revival of literature, learning, and the arts. Not that the German humanists could be unaware of the decline of Roman civilization nor of the recent restoration of culture. The Italian tradition, their own reverence for antiquity, and their pride in the achievements of their age were all too strong for that. Despite his enthusiasm for medieval German literature, Konrad Celtis rejoiced over the revival of Greek and Latin as the great good fortune of his generation.[28] Nauclerus praised the liberality of Nicholas V, who had used his power of patronage to such good effect that Greek and Latin letters, "which had lain in darkness and oblivion for six hundred years," had now recovered their splendor.[29] Aventinus, too, hailed the papal Maecenas, but gave credit for the original revival to Dante, whom he noted with patriotic pride as among the learned men who had supported the imperial theory.[30] Johann Reuchlin recalled with pleasure the impression made upon him by the city of Florence, "in which all the best arts were reborn (renascebantur)."[31] And among the German artists, Albrecht Dürer noted that the art of painting, which was honored by the Greeks and Romans, was lost and lay hidden for a thousand years, until it was brought to the light of day again by the Italians within the last two hundred years.[32] But the theme of decline and revival was not their story as it was that of the Italians. The German humanists could take little patriotic satisfaction from contemplating the destruction of Roman culture by the barbarians or the recent restoration of literature and the arts by the Italians. Nor were they as willing as the Italian humanists to ignore the culture of the medieval period, Germany's age of heroic dominance. On the contrary, only by turning to

[28] Celtis, *Epigramme,* p. 84.   [29] Nauclerus, p. 950.
[30] Aventinus, *Werke,* V, 460.
[31] J. Reuchlin, *Briefwechsel,* ed. L. Geiger (Tübingen, 1875), p. 104.
[32] E. Heidrick, ed., *Albrecht Dürers schriftlicher Nachlass* (Berlin, 1920), p. 223; cf. p. 250.

the Middle Ages could they provide Germany with a respectable literary history.

The German humanists produced very few of the biographical summaries of cultural history that were so dear to the Italians. The only two of any significance, both by the indefatigable Abbot Trithemius, demonstrate very clearly the profound difference between the patriotic humanism of the two nations. Trithemius was both monk and humanist, combining ecclesiastical tradition with the new learning. His *On Ecclesiastical Writers* (1494) [33] contains notices of some 962 clerical authors from the beginning of the Christian Church to his own time. Among the later writers a number of the Italian humanists appear, and there is a definite suggestion of the Italian conception of the revival of learning in his notices on Petrarch and Gasparino da Barzizza, but as these were almost certainly taken straight from Foresti that fact loses most of its significance. [34] In any case, the major weight falls upon the Middle Ages. This is even more true of his *Catalogue* of German writers (1495). [35] Here his purpose was to show that since its conversion to Christianity Germany had at all times shone with learning, and to combat those who, "walking blindly through the history of the ages, despised Germany as sterile and empty of the good arts." [36]

THE ERASMIAN HUMANISTS

The strain of national patriotism was but one element in northern humanism, and that not the most vital. Humanism was an international as well as a national phenomenon, its devotees held together by strong bonds of mutual interest until the Protestant Reformation broke the unity of Western Christendom beyond all hope of repair. Above all it was an intellectual revolution with religious overtones. A large number of the northern humanists were more keenly interested

[33] J. Trithemius, *De scriptoribus ecclesiasticis* (Basel, 1494), *Opera historica omnia,* I.

[34] Cf. *ibid.,* I, 322; 345 and J. F. Foresti, *Supplementum chronicarum* (Venice, 1483), ffo. 251[vo]; 269[vo].

[35] J. Trithemius, *Catalogus illustrium virorum Germaniam suis ingeniis et lucubrationibus exornantium* (1925), *Opera historica omnia,* I.

[36] *Ibid.,* I, 122.

in the problem of reforming the Church, religion, and education than
in asserting the past glories of their native land. This was particularly
true of those scholars in England, France, the Netherlands, and Germany who followed the leadership of Erasmus of Rotterdam, uniting
to combat abuses in the worldly church and to fight against the out-
worn forms of both religion and learning represented by the conservative monks and theologians who still dominated the northern schools.
And from this rather self-conscious alignment of the children of light
against the powers of medieval darkness there emerged a new conception of cultural history, different from that of the Italians in motivation and emphasis, and radically different from that inherent in the
scheme of the patriotic German historians. Divergent as their interests
were, however, the "Christian humanist" and "national humanist"
movements were not altogether mutually exclusive. They operated
on different levels and many of the German scholars were drawn
toward both. Nevertheless, the historians who, like Beatus Rhenanus
and Vadianus,[37] were most strongly influenced by Erasmus were the
most objectively critical and the furthest removed from the combination of Pan-Germanic patriotism and scholastic interpretation of
world history that marked the greater part of German historiography.

Erasmus himself had too little national consciousness to be interested
in the history of any country for its own sake, nor would political
history, with its inevitable theme of warfare and civil tumult, have
attracted him in any case. Yet he was by no means indifferent to
history. He valued it, as did most of the humanists, for the instructive examples it furnished of good and bad conduct, of political wisdom and folly. He also made excellent use of the technique of historical criticism in his *Life of St. Jerome* (1516),[38] and in his editions
of the ancient pagan and Christian authors. His most influential historical thought, however, was that implicit in his whole program for
the reform of religion and good letters. The central conception of that

[37] See work of Rhenanus cited above, p. 37, and Vadianus (Joachim von
Watt), *Chronik der Äbte von St. Gallen*, in J. von Watt, *Deutsche historische
Schriften*, ed. E. Götzinger (St. Gallen, 1875), I.
[38] Erasmus, *Hieronymi Stridonensis Vita*, pub. as introduction to Erasmus's ed.
of St. Jerome, *Omnia Opera* (Basel, 1516); new ed. in W. K. Ferguson, ed., *Erasmi
Opuscula, A Supplement to the Opera Omnia* (The Hague, 1933), pp. 134 ff.

program was the necessity of returning to the original sources of pure Christianity and classical culture. Erasmus believed that the necessary reformation could be brought about only by restoring both religion and learning to their ancient purity and by clearing away the mass of barbaric accretions that had grown up around both during the past thousand years. Hence his insistence on the study of the three ancient tongues as a prerequisite to theology; [39] hence his own scholarly editions not only of the classics but of the Fathers and the Greek New Testament; hence, too, his constant comparisons of contemporary ecclesiastical institutions and practices, of churchmen and theologians, with the simple, ideal Christianity, the *Philosophia Christi,* presented in the early Christian writings.

Erasmus was convinced that both religion and good letters had declined sadly after the age of the last classical writers and the great Church Fathers. In the intervening period both had been barbarized, nor were they yet wholly delivered from the hands of the barbarians. For that he blamed the medieval system of education, which still survived in most of the schools. The enemy therefore was scholasticism. The *Praise of Folly,* the *Colloquies* and, indeed, all his popular works abound in satirical attacks upon the bad Latin, the crabbed learning, the barren subtlety, and the needlessly elaborate theology of the schoolmen. It was, of course, grossly unfair to confuse the contemporary exponents of a decadent scholasticism with the great medieval doctors. But Erasmus was too deeply involved in conflict with the former to make troublesome distinctions. For him all were barbarians, and the culture of the medieval centuries which the schoolmen had dominated was therefore barbarous.

The prince of the humanists began his life-long struggle against the barbarians at an early age. He was still a restless young monk in the monastery at Steyn when he wrote the first draft of the *Book against the Barbarians,* though he did not publish it until some thirty years later (1520) and then with a few very significant additions. [40]

---

[39] Cf. Erasmus, *Ratio sive methodus compendio perveniendi ad veram theologiam, Opera Omnia,* V, 75 ff.

[40] Erasmus, *Antibarbarorum liber* (Basel, 1520), *Opera Omnia,* X, 1691, ff; new ed. in A. Hyma, *The Youth of Erasmus* (Ann Arbor, 1930), pp. 242–331, with variations between the MS and later ed. of 1520. See discussion, *ibid.,* pp. 182 ff.

It is an enthusiastic defense of ancient literature and an equally enthusiastic denunciation of all who were opposed thereto. Among these, though only in the later edition, the monks and friars are singled out for special attention. The book is in the dialogue form so popular with the humanists. The discussion soon turns to the causes of that "vast calamity," the decline of ancient letters, whereupon one of the speakers presents an interpretation which was considerably strengthened in the published edition. He suggests that perhaps the fault lay with those Christians of the post-Patristic period who felt that, since the need for learning as a weapon against the pagans had ended, pure religion and learning did not go well together. Lest learning should be entirely lost, however, the task of caring for it was relegated to the monks. These for a time cultivated it well enough, but afterwards turned to luxury. The result was that, with languages and antiquity neglected, a new kind of confused doctrine was born, "a truly unlearned learning," through which not only the humane disciplines but theology itself was vitiated.[41] In the later discussion the point is made repeatedly that Jerome, Augustine, and the other Fathers, and even Bede, were well versed in the classic authors.[42] The damage was done after their time. The burden of the argument is that good theology and good learning degenerated together, and that the barbarians — the "Goths"[43] — who destroyed them were the medieval monks and doctors.

But, while railing against the medieval schoolmen whose commentaries obscured rather than illuminated the best authors and who made bad Latin out of good Greek,[44] Erasmus reserved his choicest invective for their living disciples. "O contemtores servum pecus, quos vel ipsi derideant asini!"[45] They hated good letters simply because they themselves were ignorant. They preached to fools and the unlearned multitude that to know Greek is heresy, that to speak as Cicero spoke is heresy.[46] They cried "Beware! He is a poet, not a Christian."[47] This indeed was a common theme with Erasmus, born

[41] Erasmus, *Opera Omnia*, 1696 A–C (added in 1520).
[42] *Ibid.*, 1710 A–B; 1717 F–1718 A; 1737 D ff.
[43] *Ibid.*, 1706 C.   [44] *Ibid.*, 1705 F.
[45] *Ibid.*, 1707 B (added in 1520).   [46] *Ibid.*, 1699 E (added in 1520).
[47] *Ibid.*, 1700 C (added in 1520).

of his experience with the uproar that greeted the *Praise of Folly,* his edition of the New Testament, and the founding of the Collegium Trilingue at Louvain.[48] The Reuchlin controversy provided further evidence. What aroused Erasmus to a kind of exasperated fury was his belief that the rebirth of good Latin and Greek letters and of pure Christianity had already begun, but was being wilfully obstructed by the selfish ignorance of "aged parrots who could not hope to change their tongue." [49] The opposition, he felt, arose from those who had a vested interest in the old forms of education. They conspired zealously against good letters, so he wrote to Martin van Dorp in 1515, fearing lest, "si renascantur bonae litterae et si resipiscat mundus," they would be found to know nothing who before were commonly thought to be ignorant of nothing.[50]

The phrase "renascantur bonae literae" is characteristic of Erasmus's thought.[51] He believed as firmly as any of the Italians that there had been a rebirth of good literature, but his view was broader than theirs and included all the countries of Europe. His first essay on the subject dates from his monastic youth. At about the time when he was writing the first draft of the *Book against the Barbarians,* he wrote to his friend Cornelius Gerard a long account of the men who had revived ancient eloquence in Germany and the Netherlands as well as in Italy.[52] And not only had good letters been raised from the grave, but also the neighboring arts of painting, sculpture, and architecture. In ancient times, he continued, all the arts and especially the study of eloquence had flourished. Then came the barbarians and destroyed them so that not a vestige was left. Thereafter illiterate teachers taught what they did not understand, producing verbose commentaries, ridiculous grammatical rules, "deliramentaque innumera." Had this barbaric breed of men continued, there is no telling into what new kind of speech poetry would have been turned. But from this fate it was rescued by Lorenzo Valla and Filelfo. The reference to the fine arts is almost unique in Erasmus's writings and was probably inspired by

[48] Cf. Allen, *Opus epistolarum Erasmi,* Epp. 1007, 47–53; 1033, 234–40; On the Collegium Trilingue, see Ferguson, pp. 191 ff.

[49] Allen, Ep. 761, 64.   [50] *Ibid.,* Ep. 337, 326–329.

[51] Cf. *ibid.,* Epp. 117, 27; 862, 2 ff; 967, 128.

[52] *Ibid.,* Ep. 23 (June, 1489 [?]).

Valla's preface to *On the Elegance of the Latin Language.*[53] Erasmus seemed almost unaware of the artistic achievements of his age, but he never lost interest in the restoration of classical style throughout Europe. Nearly forty years later (1528), he presented in the *Dialogue entitled the Ciceronian* [54] a remarkably complete and critical survey of the modern writers in Italy, France, England, the Netherlands, Germany, Spain, and Portugal since the reflowering of eloquence with Petrarch.

The theme of the *Ciceronian* limited consideration of the literary revival to the question of classical style and, to that extent, was not typical of Erasmus's mature thought. For to him the fate of good letters was inextricably bound up with that of pure Christianity. The former was necessary to the latter; the two declined and rose together; and both had now the same enemies. Writing to Leo X in 1517, Erasmus hailed the coming of a golden age under the auspices of the humanist pope, an age in which he saw the three greatest blessings of mankind about to be restored: true Christian piety, which had in many ways broken down; the best letters, hitherto neglected and corrupt; and perpetual public peace, which is the source of piety and learning.[55] That hope was to be sadly disappointed. The Erasmian reform was shattered by the waves of dogmatic controversy aroused by the Lutheran Reformation, but Erasmus's conception of a Christian Renaissance survived among the reformers themselves, especially in the semi-Erasmian circle of South German reformers that centered about Zwingli.[56]

It has seemed worth while to analyze Erasmus's view of medieval and Renaissance culture rather fully, partly because his own conceptions were so typical of those held by a large circle of contemporary

---

[53] Compare *ibid.,* line 78 ff with Valla as cited above, p. 28.

[54] Erasmus, *Dialogus cui titulus Ciceronianus sive de optimo genere dicendi* (Basel, 1528), *Opera Omnia,* I, 973 ff. Eng. trans. (New York, 1908). On Petrarch see *Opera Omnia,* I, 1008 E.

[55] Allen, Ep. 566, 31–40; cf. Ep. 967.

[56] Cf. P. Wernle, *Die Renaissance des Christentums im 16. Jahrhundert* (Tübingen, 1904), p. 1 n. Capito, after becoming a Lutheran, still echoed the Erasmian concept in 1523, when he hailed Erasmus as "autorem cum renascentium literarum tum redeuntis pietatis." Allen, Ep. 1368, 28–30.

humanists,[57] and partly because of the unparalleled influence he exerted on the thought of his own and later generations. Perhaps the best example of the extent to which his principal ideas had been absorbed by the younger Christian humanists is to be found in the *Declamation on Correcting the Education of Young People,* delivered by Philip Melanchthon on his entry into the University of Wittenberg in 1518.[58] With the Lutheran revolt scarcely begun, John Reuchlin's precocious grandnephew was still more humanist than reformer, an Erasmian rather than a Lutheran. After recommending good letters "ac renascentes Musas"[59] to his hearers, Melanchthon opened his inaugural address with a vigorous attack on those barbarians who arrogated to themselves the titles and privileges of doctors in the schools. They cried out that Greek was a danger to idle minds and Hebrew a danger to the faith; that philosophy would be neglected. It was a colossal task to struggle against this ignorant herd, but he begged his hearers to join him in recovering letters from sloth and squalor.

Having thus paid his respects to the contemporary barbarians, Melanchthon turned to the past history of learning. His story of the extinction of the Muses through the Gothic and Lombard devastations followed the accustomed formula. Like Erasmus and Biondo he included Bede among the few learned men after the Fathers, though he also noted the literary revival on the continent that followed Charlemagne's importation of Alcuin from England. In this discovery of a Carolingian renaissance, Melanchthon was probably following the lead of the patriotic German historians, but he returned at once to the theme of the *Book against the Barbarians.* After the hopeful beginning of the Carolingian age, learning again degenerated, for men rushed into the study of Aristotle, and that in defective form, so that better studies were neglected, and a new system of education was imposed upon youth. The result was that both Christian morals and

---

[57] Cf., for example, Ulrich von Hutten, *Opera Omnia,* ed. E. Böcking (Leipzig, 1859–70), I, 197; 217; and further examples in H. Weisinger, "The Renaissance Theory of the Reaction against the Middle Ages as a Cause of the Renaissance," *Speculum,* XX (1945), 461–67.

[58] P. Melanchthon, *Declamatio de corrigendis adolescentiae studiis, Opera quae supersunt omnia,* ed. C. G. Brettschneider (Halle, 1834-60), XI, 15 ff.

[59] *Ibid.,* XI, 15. Melanchthon uses phrases such as "literarum renascentium" repeatedly. Cf. his *In laudem novae scholae, ibid.,* XI, col. 110.

the study of literature were destroyed. Had either been left, the other might have been restored. But, as it was, good letters changed to bad, and pure piety to ceremonies, man-made traditions, decrees, capitularies, and glosses. Melanchthon next discussed with scathing condemnation the system of scholastic education and finally presented a program for a complete educational reform along humanist lines. Here Greek and Hebrew occupied a prominent place beside classical Latin, for no one can achieve excellence in either sacred or secular subjects, so Melanchthon averred, without being well trained in "the humane disciplines." [60] Hebrew and Greek, he continued, are especially necessary to the study of theology, for only when we go to the sources in their pure form will we begin to understand Christ. Thus Melanchthon in 1518 at the moment of transition from humanism to the Reformation.

In the following years dogmatic theology and doctrinal controversy gave new direction to a large part of European thought. But along with the conviction that one must return to the sources, the Reformers adopted from the Erasmian humanists two historical conceptions that were to help shape the orthodox Protestant view of the Middle Ages and the Renaissance, not to mention that of later generations whose thought was less consciously orientated by the Reformation. The first of these was that classical literature and evangelical Christianity had declined at the same time and had later been revived together; the second, that it was the monks and schoolmen who were largely responsible for the intervening darkness.

Protestant and Catholic Interpretations

The Reformation turned historiography into a new channel, where it gained in conviction and singleness of purpose what it lost in critical sense and breadth of secular interest.[61] Here *a priori* reasoning indi-

---

[60] *Ibid.,* XI, 22.

[61] For the historiography of the Reformation and Counter-Reformation, see, beside the works of Fueter, Schnabel, and Wegele cited above, P. Polman, *L'élément historique dans la controverse religieuse du XVIᵉ siècle* (Gembloux, 1932); E. Menke-Glückert, *Die Geschichtschreibung der Reformation und Gegenreformation* (Leipzig, 1912); W. Nigg, *Die Kirchengeschichtschreibung* (Munich, 1934).

cated the direction, while dogmatic certainty lent the momentum that drove it relentlessly over all obstacles of inconvenient fact. The men who wrote history under the direct impulse of the Reformation and Counter-Reformation were inspired by motives compared with which those of the secular humanists were but passionless shadows. They spoke as men having authority and not as the scribes and pharisees. From the northern humanists, who were more closely akin to them than the Italians, the Protestant writers took such concepts as suited their purpose, but they firmly rejected the secular attitude inherent in humanist historiography and used the critical method of the humanists only when it served their interests.

The early reformers placed a high value upon history as they conceived it, giving it a secure place in the system of higher education,[62] as well as in confessional literature. Like the humanists they treasured it as an inexhaustible source of *exempla* for ethical and moral instruction,[63] but, since they were theologians as well as moralists, their pragmatic interest did not end there. One of the principal virtues of history in their eyes was the marvelous manner in which it illustrated the working of Divine Providence in human affairs. Sebastian Franck called his universal chronicle a "Historical Bible."[64] The Reformation, in fact, brought a complete return to the divinely motivated conception of history that had prevailed in ecclesiastical tradition from Augustine and Orosius through the Middle Ages. This was true of Catholic as well as Protestant historians. Bishop Bossuet,[65] writing in the late seventeenth century, agreed perfectly on this point at least with the first Protestant reformers. History thus recaptured the dignity of divine inspiration, of which the Italian humanists had deprived it, and became once more the mirror of God's handiwork. At the same time, neither Protestant nor Catholic historians scrupled to use history, thus fortified by supernatural sanction, in the service of confes-

---

[62] Cf. E. C. Scherer, *Geschichte und Kirchengeschichte an den deutschen Universitäten* (Freiburg im Breisgau, 1927).

[63] Cf. Melanchthon, *Opera*, XI, 22 f; III, 217; 880 ff; 1114 f; IV, 929; IX, 532; XII, 712.

[64] S. Franck, *Chronica, Zeitbuch und Geschichtsbibel von Anbeginn bis in dies gegenwärtig 1531 Jahr* (Frankfurt, 1538).

[65] See especially J. B. Bossuet, *Discours sur l'histoire universelle* (Paris, 1681).

sional propaganda and polemic. Indeed, it was as a weapon against Antichrist or as a counterblast against heresy that history was most frequently used in the era of acute religious strife. With rare keenness of vision, the theologians in both camps perceived the hand of God everywhere in history, often working in devious ways and sometimes in the most unlikely places, but always toward the eventual triumph of the true church.

Even literary history might be pressed into the defense of truth. Bishop Bale noted as the chief value of his immense catalogue of British writers, from Dis the grandson of Noah to his own day, that "from it whoever wished might readily learn through whom our country arrived at an understanding of the Christian religion and by whose ministry sacred doctrine was defended and propagated amongst us." [66] But the two forms that especially attracted the theologians were universal history and church history. The appeal of the former was obvious. In no other type of history could the broad sweep of the divine plan be shown so clearly. Here the reformers were at one with the ecclesiastical chroniclers of the Middle Ages, though they borrowed their material more frequently from the German humanists, especially the antipapal Aventinus, who had rescued universal history from the hands of the monks. The purpose of the theological historians, however, was different from that of the patriotic humanists. The Hebrew and Christian saga replaced that of the German people as the *leitmotif* of their work, and they retained the doctrine of the Four Monarchies because of its prophetic, teleological implications rather than for the support it gave to the Empire. Melanchthon, himself, placed the official stamp of Lutheran orthodoxy on the Four Monarchies in his revision of Johannes Carion's *Chronicle* (1532).[67] Under his influence, reinforced by that of Sleidan's popular textbook, *On the Four Empires* (1556),[68] it remained the standard organization

[66] J. Bale, *Illustrium maioris Britanniae scriptorum summarium in quasdam centurias divisium* . . . . (Ipswich, 1548), Dedication. On Bale, see H. C. McCusker, *John Bale, Dramatist and Antiquary* (Bryn Mawr, 1942).

[67] J. Carion, *Chronica* (Wittenberg, 1532); revised ed. in Melanchthon, *Opera*, XII, 712 ff.

[68] Sleidanus (J. Philippi), *De Quattuor summis Imperiis* (Strassburg, 1556).

of history in Protestant schools for nearly two centuries.[69] There was nothing in this scheme to suggest the modern system of historical periodization. Yet the Protestant point of view did provide ample support for the classic conception of the Middle Ages. The prejudices of the Protestant historians colored their whole presentation of medieval history and of medieval culture, especially as the latter appeared in their histories of the Church.

Modern church history was the child of the Reformation as secular history was the offspring of humanism. The medieval chroniclers had felt no need for a history of the Church distinct from that of Christian society, and the secular humanists had ignored the Church as far as possible. The Protestant churches, however, young and self-conscious, naturally desired a historical account of their origins and triumphant growth. Protestant controversialists were also quick to appreciate the value of history as an aid to polemic and propaganda. Indeed, they could scarcely avoid it. The major premise of the reformers, that they were restoring the pure evangelical doctrine of the early Church, which had been deformed by the Church of Rome, demanded historical proof. The early reformers stated the doctrine and in the following generations the historians supplied the data to uphold it. The Protestant interpretation of medieval history was thus oriented by the necessity of demonstrating that the light of the gospel had been progressively obscured under the malign influence of the popes and their agents, with the result that Western Christendom had remained for a thousand years sunk in barbaric ignorance, superstitution, and spiritual sloth.

The date at which the period of darkness began was none too clear. But, in general, the Protestant historians agreed with the Italian humanists and the Erasmian circle in dating the major decline from about the fifth century. Calvin, with his respect for the Church Fathers, was quite definite on this point,[70] as was also the Genevan

---

[69] Many Catholic historians also followed the tradition of the Four Monarchies. It was vigorously attacked by Jean Bodin, *Methodus ad facilem historiarum cognitionem* (1566; 2nd ed. Paris, 1572), pp. 461 ff, but without much immediate effect.

[70] "Principio, si quid nos movet veteris ecclesiae autoritas, meminerimus quingentis circiter annis, quibus magis adhuc florebat religio, et sincerior doctrina vigebat . . . ." J. Calvin, *Institutio Christianae religionis*, I, xi, 13, *Opera Omnia*, ed. W. Baum *et al.* (Brunswick, 1863–1900), II, 84. Cf. *ibid.*, V, 394.

historian, Simon Goulart.[71] The Lutherans tended to observe an earlier deterioration of doctrine, but inasmuch as the human agent chiefly responsible for the "miserable ruin and desolation of the Church of Christ" [72] was the Bishop of Rome, the dark age could scarcely antedate the rise of papal power. Thereafter, the history of the Church was that of the struggle between God and the devil, between Christ and Antichrist, with the pope unhesitatingly cast for the latter rôle.[73] And from the fifth to the fifteenth centuries the devil was evidently winning. This was the burden of the argument presented by that man of wrath, Flacius Illyricus, and his collaborators in the great *Ecclesiastical History* commonly known as *The Magdeburg Centuries* (1560–74).[74] In each century after the fifth Flacius noted with rising indignation the growing tyranny of the papal Antichrist and the successive deformation of true doctrine.[75] *The Magdeburg Centuries* formed a storehouse of historical material from which later Protestant controversialists drew freely, but its thesis was not new. The Protestant interpretation of medieval history was already stereotyped and it remained long unchanged. Toward the end of the seventeenth century, Bishop Burnet, writing of the humanists who revived learning, noted that

> they found a vast difference between the first five ages of the Christian church, in which piety and learning prevailed, and the last ten ages, in which ignorance had buried all their former learning; only a little misguided devotion was retained for six of these ages; and in the last

71 S. Goulart, *Catalogus testium veritatis qui ante nostram aetatem Papae reclamaverunt* (Lyons, 1597), I, 629 f, notes that in the first five centuries truth still triumphed; in the next five it was mixed with lies and superstition; and in the following five idolatry reigned in the Church.

72 J. Foxe, *Acts and Monuments of the Christian Martyrs* (London, 1563; I use ed. J. Pratt, London, 1877), IV, 250; cf. 139 ff.

73 Cf. Calvin, *Institutio, Opera*, II, 776; 842 ff; W. Whitaker, *Thesis proposita . . . , in academia Cantabrigiensi, cujus summa haec: Pontifex Romanus est ille Antichristus* (London, 1582).

74 Flacius Illyricus et al., *Ecclesiastica historia . . . secundum singulas centurias per aliquot studiosos viros in urbe Magdeburgica* (Basel, 1560–74; I use ed. Basel 1624).

75 Even in the fifth century Flacius thought the evil was present in embryo. Cf. *ibid.*, II, 1: "Tamen plus nimio concessum est ut vere in hoc seculo, Antichristus quasi intra viscera receptus videatur, qui posteriori seculo, veluti maturus foetus, est editus."

four, the restless ambition and usurpation of the popes was supported
by the seeming holiness of the begging friars, and the false counter-
feits of learning, which were among the canonists, schoolmen, and
casuists.[76]

The last phrase is reminiscent of the Erasmian condemnation of
scholasticism. The Protestant historians, in fact, took over the whole
Erasmian view of medieval learning and education, with different
motives and emphasis, but with much the same result for the interpretation of cultural history. While centering their attack on the popes,
they did not forget the monks and schoolmen who, they believed, had
prostituted theology in the interest of papal domination and had supplied the learned support for the doctrines of the Roman Church. In
1548, Melanchthon presented the Protestant view of church history in
terms not too far removed from his own humanist interpretation of
thirty years earlier. He now divided church history into five ages.
The third age, in which Augustine purified doctrine after the Origenist
deviation, was cut short by the Gothic and Vandal invasions. Then
followed the fourth age, that of the monks, in which darkness gradually increased. This age was characterized by the learning of the
schoolmen, as Thomas and Scotus. "And what was that," he asked,
"but a barbaric mixture of two evils: ignorant and yet garrulous
philosophy and the cult of idols?" [77] To the reformers even more than
to the humanists, the leaders of medieval learning were barbarians —
altogether "unfruitful and barbarous," as Bishop Bale put it. The good
English bishop, indeed, felt it necessary to call upon all his very considerable powers of invective to do justice to the scholastic doctors,
"out of whom came forth that obscure and ignoble breed of sordid
writers of sentences and *summulae,* the mere recording of whose names
should move generous and well-born minds to nausea." [78] Throughout the first two centuries of Protestant historiography, medieval culture meant scholasticism, and scholasticism meant a peculiarly pernicious state of ignorance.

[76] G. Burnet, *History of the Reformation of the Church of England* (1679–
1714; I use ed. London, 1865), I, 66 f.

[77] P. Melanchthon, *De Luthero et aetatibus ecclesiae, Opera.* XI, 786.

[78] Bale, *Britanniae scriptorum,* fo. 4[vo]; see also his comments on Duns Scotus,
fo. 124[vo]–125.

For the Protestant historians, then, the millenium preceding the beginning of the sixteenth century was an age of both cultural and religious darkness, bounded on the one side by the decline of ancient learning and the early Church, on the other by the Reformation. And, more clearly than the Italian humanists, the reformers conceived of their own time as marking the beginning of a new age. Where the Italians saw only the revival of secular learning, literature, and the arts, the Protestant divines perceived the opening of a new era in which not only culture but also the Christian faith was restored to its ancient purity. In his outline of church history, cited above, Melanchthon characterized the fifth age as that in which God recalled the Church to its origins ("in qua Deus Ecclesiam iterum ad fontes revocavit"). The idea of a rebirth of the primitive Church was inherent in the whole conception of the Reformation. Chiliastic hopes and concepts of rebirth and reformation of the Church had been commonplaces in the thought of the medieval reformers. Erasmus, too, had suggested both the dawn of a new age and the return to the ancient sources in his optimistic faith in a Christian Renaissance. But with the actual occurrence of the Lutheran Reformation, what had been a pious hope became for the Protestant historians a demonstrable historical fact and, therefore, a practical concept in ecclesiastical historiography. It was implied in the numerous histories that began with the founding of the new churches, and even those historians who traced the history of the Christian Church from its beginnings marked a definite turning point with the appearance of Luther.

Though dated quite definitely by the religious revolution, the new age was foreshadowed by events of the preceding two centuries. The Reformation had its forerunners, its pre-reformers as they were to be called in the nineteenth century. The Protestant theologians, indeed, refused to believe that God had at any time permitted the true church to be wholly suppressed by the papal Antichrist, and Flacius Illyricus was at some pains to show that there had always been some witnesses to the truth.[79] The Protestant martyrologists, too, commonly annexed

[79] Flacius Illyricus, *Catalogus testium veritatis, qui ante nostram aetatem reclamarunt papae* (Basel, 1556). Cf. the Calvinist revision by S. Goulart cited above.

to their cause all who had suffered persecution at the hands of the popes in the Middle Ages. But it was not until the progressive tyranny of the pope had reached its height — Foxe dated the "loosing out of Satan" from the year 1294 [80] — that the true forerunners of the gospel made their appearance. Nearly all the Protestant historians were agreed in regarding Wyclif and Huss as men sent from God to prepare the way for Luther. Both Foxe and Crespin [81] dwelt long upon the Lollards and Hussites, and Burnet opened his history of the English Reformation with an account of the former, whose "opinions did very much dispose people to receive the writings which came afterwards out of Germany." [82]

It was in a similar category of those who prepared the way for Luther that the humanists appeared in Protestant historiography. At the same time, the Renaissance — in the form of the revival of learning — was given a new orientation by being interpreted as a movement inspired by Divine Providence in preparation for the acceptance of the gospel. That Erasmus and his circle, in particular, had supplied the reformers with significant materials and had aroused much discontent with the old church was obvious. Summed up in the popular sixteenth century epigram that Erasmus laid the egg that Luther hatched,[83] this aspect of the relation between humanism and the Reformation has remained a constant factor, with various qualifications, in modern historiography to the present time. It was a point on which Catholic and Protestant opinion could meet, though approaching it from different directions.[84] The Protestant historians, however,

[80] Foxe, *Acts and Monuments*, II, 726.

[81] J. Crespin, *Histoire des martyrs persécutés et mis à mort pour la vérité de l'Evangile depuis le temps des Apostres jusque à présent* (Geneva, 1554; enlarged by S. Goulart, 1582; new ed. Toulouse, 1885–89). The first ed. begins with Huss.

[82] Burnet, I, 55 ff; 66; cf. Bale, fo. 154vo.

[83] Cf. Florimond de Rémond, *Histoire de l'hérésie de ce siècle* (Paris, 1605), p. 32vo: "Aussi disoient ordinairement les Allemans: Erasmus innuit, Lutherus irruit; Erasmus parit ova, Lutherus excludit pullos; Erasmus dubitat, Lutherus asseverat."

[84] See the list of sixteenth and seventeenth century writers who regarded Erasmus as the forerunner of Luther, cited in A. Rébelliau, *Bossuet, historien du Protestantisme* (Paris, 1909), p. 203; see also the Jesuit, L. Maimbourg, *Histoire du Luthéranisme* (2nd ed. Paris, 1681), p. 54.

carried the idea much further than was likely to be acceptable to any Catholic apologist. Taking over the Erasmian conception of the close causal relation between the revival of learning and that of religion — as Luther did when he asserted "that there has never been a great revelation of the word of God unless He has first prepared the way by the rise and prosperity of languages and letters, as though they were John the Baptists" [85] — the Protestant historians blandly assumed that any improvement in learning must have led to a clearer perception of the truth and therefore must have aided acceptance of Protestant doctrine.

To the English-speaking world this idea was made thoroughly familiar by John Foxe's *Acts and Monuments of the Christian Martyrs* (1563), popularly known as the *Book of Martyrs,* which more than any other work from the age of the Reformation shaped English conceptions of church history. Foxe dwelt lovingly upon the restoration of learning and furnished it with a definite date by ascribing its origins to the "divine and miraculous invention of printing." [86] He returned repeatedly to this "admirable work of God's wisdom," which came providentially to confound the pope at the moment of his triumph over the Hussites. Shorn of much quaintly attractive verbiage, Foxe's argument was simply that, as the ruin and decay of the Church was caused by ignorance, so to restore the Church "it pleased God to open to men the art of printing" whereby they gained "the instruments and tools of learning, which were good books and authors, which before lay hid and unknown." Then by God's grace "good wits" were stirred up "aptly to conceive the light of knowledge and judgment, by which light darkness began to be espied and ignorance to be detected, truth from error, religion from superstition to be discerned." Among those prominent in this movement Foxe cited Petrarch, Valla, Pico, Poliziano, and other Italian humanists, and among the northern scholars, Wesel, Reuchlin, Grocyn, Colet, Beatus Rhenanus, and Erasmus. "And here began the first push and assault

[85] M. Luther to Eoban Hess, March 29, 1523. Eng. trans. in Preserved Smith, *Luther's Correspondence* (Philadelphia, 1913–18), II, 176 f. For Luther on the rôle of Erasmus, see *ibid.,* 190 f; 228; 469; 481 f.

[86] Foxe, III, 718 ff; IV, 4 ff; 252 ff. On Foxe, see J. F. Moseley, *John Foxe and his Book* (New York, 1940).

to be given against the ignorant and barbarous faction of the Pope's pretensed church." For after these by their learned writings "had opened a window of light unto the world . . . . immediately, according to God's gracious appointment, followed Martin Luther with others after him, by whose ministry it pleased the Lord to work a more full reformation of His church."

Few of the later Protestant writers placed so much weight on the invention of printing, but Foxe's conception of the relation between the revival of learning and the Reformation remained a standard ingredient in English thought. It was echoed in the seventeenth century by Anglican historians like Burnet as well as by Puritan divines.[87] And in 1701, after the humanist movement had been ascribed to a quite different cause, Cotton Mather still took for granted the whole Protestant interpretation of medieval culture, the Italian revival and the Reformation:

> Incredible darkness was upon the Western parts of Europe two hundred years ago: learning was wholly swallowed up in barbarity. But when the Turks made their descent so far upon the Greek churches as to drive all before them, very many learned Greeks, with their manuscripts and monuments, fled into Italy and other parts of Europe. This occasioned the revival of letters there, which prepared the world for the Reformation of Religion too, and for the advances of the sciences ever since.[88]

Meanwhile, the divinely ordained place of the restoration of learning in the scheme of ecclesiastical history had been stated for the French and Swiss Calvinists by no less a person than Théodore de Bèze, upon whom had descended the mantle of John Calvin. The preface and first book of his *Ecclesiastical History* (1580) [89] might, indeed, be regarded as something like a canonical statement of the orthodox Protestant interpretation of history. The preface opened

---

[87] See Burnet as cited above; also J. Sedgwick, *Learning's Necessity to an able Minister of the Gospel* (London, 1658); cf. P. Miller, *The New England Mind* (New York, 1939), I, 97 f.

[88] Cotton Mather, *American Tears upon the Ruines of the Greek Churches* (Boston, 1701), pp. 42 f; quoted in Miller, I, 97.

[89] T. de Bèze, *Histoire ecclésiastique des Eglises Réformées au royaume de France* (1580; new ed. 3 vols., Paris, 1883–89).

with an essay on the importance of history. After bewailing the lack of good church history after Eusebius, Bèze then went on to describe the post-Patristic period, in which "there was nothing but barbarism and horrible confusion." No church history could be expected from the ignorant and worldly monks and churchmen. Nor had it yet been treated adequately, though the authors of *The Magdeburg Centuries* were engaged in a praiseworthy attempt.

> Certainly [he continued] since it has pleased God to renew the world in the past sixty years or so, making the light of His truth to shine beautifully and clearly out of the abyss of ignorance and superstition in which it had so long been plunged, it would be a great shame to fall into the same fault as our ancestors and to keep from posterity the more than marvellous means, by which the Eternal, fulfilling not what the world merited but what He had promised to His church, has done so great a work.[90]

Some modern histories Bèze thought worthy of praise, including those of Sleidan, Foxe, and Crespin. But these were not enough to give full information "of the rebirth (renaissance) and of the government of the churches thus renewed."[91]

Bèze limited the scope of his *Ecclesiastical History* to the history of religion in France from 1521 to 1563, but he devoted most of the first book to a sketch of the revival of learning, which he regarded as a divinely ordained prerequisite to the Reformation.

> The time having come which God had ordained to rescue His elect from the superstitions, which had grown up gradually in the Roman Church, and to restore the splendor of His truth . . . . [here he paused for a parenthetical recognition of the earlier testimony of Wyclif and Huss] He raised up first in Germany a great personage named John Reuchlin . . . . to recover the knowledge of the Hebrew tongue, which had been altogether abolished among Christians.[92]

A brief account of the Reuchlin controversy followed. Bèze took considerable satisfaction in the fact that the theologians who had opposed Reuchlin were finally silenced by papal edict, "showing in this that the Lord, in order to build His church, knew full well how to use even

---

[90] *Ibid.,* I, v f.   [91] *Ibid.,* I, vii.   [92] *Ibid.,* I, 1.

the principal enemies of the same." From Reuchlin's school emerged Conrad Pellican, Oecolampadius, Capito, and many other Germans. Meanwhile, Bèze continued, studies began to flourish even at Louvain. Thence Erasmus came to Paris, and there, too, Lefèvre d'Etaples, "Doctor of the Sorbonne, but worthy of a better company, seeing the University of Paris altogether sunk in a horrible barbarism and sophistry, restored the true study of the arts." [93] Only at this point did Bèze recognize the earlier Italian phase of the revival of learning. Some time before this, he noted, a number of Greek refugees had been received in Florence by the House of Medici and in other Italian cities, and these had greatly advanced the study of Greek in the universities of Italy.[94] There, several Frenchmen had learned Greek and had returned to teach it in Paris, where they were met by the furious opposition of the Sorbonne, "as though the study of Greek and Hebrew were the greatest heresy in the world." Of the many learned French scholars of that period, Bèze praised especially Guillaume Budé. These men, however, did not concern themselves with theology, "so that one may justly say that they prepared a road for others which they themselves would not tread." For these things were but preparations for the goodness and mercy of God which presently appeared. The work of the classical scholars made possible the proper study of the Gospel in which the secrets of God were written, but Bèze made it clear, as a Calvinist theologian should, that God did not employ human learning of necessity. If he had not done so, however, Bèze argued, he would have been forced to bestow the gift of languages upon men miraculously, as he had done for the apostles.

Compared with the Protestants, the Catholic apologists played little more than a negative rôle in shaping the future conceptions of cultural history. They attacked the Protestant arguments at all points, except that they were quite happy to agree in recognizing the medieval heretics as prototypes of Luther. They defended the tradition of the Church and produced learned histories based on the same selective principle of criticism employed by their antagonists. But while they obviously did not share the reformers' interpretation of medieval history, they did not develop the historical cult of the Middle Ages that

[93] *Ibid.,* I, 3.   [94] *Ibid.,* I, 5.

was to be the Romantic Catholic reaction to both Protestantism and rationalism in the early nineteenth century. Nor did they make the use they might have of the argument that the Lutheran revolt had wrecked the hopeful development of northern humanism.[95]

[95] Erasmus, himself, was bitterly aware of the effect of the Lutheran "tumult" on good letters, as were many of his friends. Even Aventinus, sound Protestant though he was, thought the "theological furor" had ruined good letters. Cf. Aventinus, *Werke*, VI, 79.

CHAPTER THREE

The Later Humanist Tradition and the Crystallization of Concepts

UNTIL the eighteenth century the theological preconceptions arising from the religious revival of the Reformation and the subsequent controversies dominated German historiography and to a lesser degree that of the other European countries. Nevertheless, the humanist tradition of secular historical interpretation still survived, especially in Italy and France, and kept alive the classicist's conception of the course of cultural history. Classical education and classical standards in art formed the taste of Western Europe during the sixteenth and seventeenth centuries and guaranteed the continuance of humanist prejudices. And as the various revivals of literature, learning, and the arts gradually receded into the past, the historical conceptions formed by the humanists, and more or less modified by the reformers, tended to crystallize into more definite if not more accurate patterns.

VASARI AND *la Rinascita dell'Arte*

It was the Italian humanists who had first become conscious of the recent revival of art and letters and who worked out the scheme of cultural history since the decline of Rome, which was to form the basis of later conceptions of the Middle Ages and the Renaissance. They saw the whole development of literary and artistic history more clearly than did their northern successors and wrote about it more frequently, because for them it was a relatively simple and unified story replete with patriotic interest. Unlike the northern scholars, they could regard both the ancient Roman civilization and the new aesthetic and intellectual developments as purely national phenomena. The destruction of art and letters had been the work of the barbarians; their restoration had been achieved by the Italian masters. By the end of the fifteenth century this simple pattern had been established as a tradition in numerous essays, individual biographies, and collections of the lives of writers and artists. Italian humanism had by then passed its prime and there was little left for the Italians to add to the history of their classical revival. The center of gravity of humanism was shifting rapidly to the North. Italian art, on the other hand, was just entering upon its golden age. Its history had yet to be written, and could not be written satisfactorily for at least another half century. The middle of the sixteenth century was the logical time for a comprehensive retrospect of Italian artistic achievement, but it was sheer good fortune that produced a masterpiece of art history at precisely that moment.

Giorgio Vasari was peculiarly fitted for his self-appointed task of writing the history of Italian art from its "rebirth" through its period of greatest glory. Born at Arezzo in 1511 and educated in Florence, his youth coincided with the age of the great masters. He was himself a distinguished architect and a very popular painter, who served popes in Rome and Medici princes in Florence. He also traveled to many parts of Italy to fulfill commissions, meanwhile observing everywhere the work of earlier artists with the critical eye of a fellow craftsman. He was personally acquainted with most of the contemporary Italian masters and was a lifelong friend of Michelangelo. His own taste had been shaped by a humanist education and by classical standards in art, so that he was in perfect harmony with the prevailing taste of his age. When in middle life he published the first edition of his *Lives of the Great Painters, Sculptors, and Architects* (1550),[1] the art of the High Renaissance had still the vividness of present reality,

---

[1] G. Vasari, *Le Vite de' più eccellenti architetti, pittori, et scultori italiani da Cimabue insino a tempi nostri* (Florence, 1550; 2nd ed. revised and enlarged, Florence, 1568); I use ed. in Vasari, *Opere*, ed. G. Milanesi (Florence, 1878–85). Eng. trans. in *Everyman's Library*, 4 vols. (London, 1927). On Vasari, see W. Kallab, *Vasaristudien, Quellenschriften für Kunstgeschichte*, N. F., XV (1908). For general discussion of art history in this period, see J. von Schlosser, *Die Kunstliteratur* (Vienna, 1924).

but its greatest achievements were already past. The *Lives* were limited almost entirely to Italian artists and especially those of Tuscany. They followed the traditional biographical form and contained few ideas not already familiar in the fifteenth century. But in total effect they presented a new, rationally organized history of the development of Renaissance art. Their influence upon the criticism and historiography of art was immediate and overwhelming. After nearly four centuries it is still with us.

The charm of Vasari's work is inherent in the narrative of the individual lives. He could tell a story as a good Florentine should, and if he did not always distinguish too critically between the *vero* and the *bene trovato,* the fault has endeared him to generations of casual readers. Yet the *Lives* are much more than a collection of anecdotal biographies. There is much acute, critical judgment in Vasari's appraisal of the work of his predecessors and contemporaries. He strove to classify them under categories of style (maniera) as well as of chronology, and to trace a reasoned system of development from the first revolt against the crudity of medieval art to the culmination of the whole movement in the perfection of Michaelangelo. This was his original contribution. From the fragmentary pattern of the revival of the arts, as it had been drawn by humanist tradition, Vasari created for the first time a conception of Renaissance art as an organic whole, developing by clearly marked stages, each of which was admirable in relation to its place in the steady progression toward the perfect style of his own day. Nor was this merely implicit in the narrative of the lives. It was stated definitely as a thesis in the philosophical introductions to the whole work and to the second and third parts.

The organic conception of art or letters as analogous in their development to natural organisms, which have their periods of growth, maturity, withering, and death, was not original with Vasari. It was a more or less unconscious assumption underlying the historical thought of nearly all the humanists. Vasari made it the conscious basis of his work, and focused it on the moment of rebirth. He presented the historical background of the *rinascita* in the long introduction to the *Lives.*[2] With one eye on Pliny, he traced the rise, perfection, and

[2] Vasari, *Opere,* I, 215–44.

decline of ancient art. The decline was already well begun by the time of Constantine, which he designated as marking the boundary between the antique and the merely old (antico and vecchio), but then continued more rapidly because of the barbarian invasions and the iconoclastic zeal of the Christians. Vasari noted occasional evidences of commendable, though unhappily not classical, architecture throughout the Middle Ages. But on the whole, he presented a dismal picture of medieval art until the middle of the thirteenth century when the great awakening began. After that time, a new generation of Tuscan artists "were able to distinguish the good from the bad, and abandoning the old style, they began to copy the ancients with all ardor and industry." [3] So far Vasari's sketch of the early history of art was conventional enough, but his conclusion went further to elevate the metaphor of rebirth and the analogy of the organic growth of art to the status of a conscious historical scheme.

> Up to the present, I have discoursed upon the origin of sculpture and painting, perhaps more at length than was necessary at this stage. I have done so, not so much because I have been carried away by my love for the arts, as because I wish to be of service to the artists of our own day, by showing them how a small beginning leads to the highest elevation, and how from so noble a situation it is possible to fall to utterest ruin, and consequently, how these arts resemble nature as shown in our human bodies; and have their birth, growth, age, and death, and I hope by this means they will be enabled more easily to recognize the progress of the renaissance (rinascita) of the arts, and the perfection to which they have attained in our own time. [4]

The formal structure of the whole work further emphasized the theme of progressive growth. Vasari divided it into three parts, each corresponding to a definite period or stage of development in modern art. In the introduction to Part II, [5] he explained that he had done this to facilitate discussion of the general characteristics peculiar to each age. The first period (from the middle of the thirteenth century to the end of the fourteenth) was marred by grave imperfections. Yet the artists of that age were worthy of great praise for they made the

3 *Ibid.*, I, 242 [I, 17].   4 *Ibid.*, I, 243 [I, 18]; cf. *ibid.*, II, 96.
5 *Ibid.*, II, 93–107.

beginning. They destroyed the Byzantine manner and replaced it with that of Giotto. The second period (the fifteenth century) showed immense improvement in technique. The childhood of art was now past and it was reaching maturity. In this period, Brunelleschi recovered the measure and proportion of the antique in architecture; Masaccio so improved the art of painting that he may be said to have effected its new rebirth (sua nuova rinascita); and Donatello created figures of such life and reality that his work may be compared to that of either the moderns or the ancients. The outstanding characteristic of this *seconda età* in painting and sculpture was strict adherence to the reality of nature. The masters "sought to reproduce what they saw in nature and no more, and thus they came to consider more closely and understand more fully." [6] Full perfection, however, came only in the third period (the sixteenth century), "of which," Vasari observed, "I may safely say that art has done everything that is permitted to an imitator of nature, and that it has risen so high that its decline must now be feared rather than any further progress expected." [7] The analogy of organic growth had sinister implications that evidently worried Vasari when he thought about the future; but for the most part his pessimistic presentiment that the artistic development of his age was passing its prime was buried under his satisfaction with the present.

In the introduction to Part III,[8] Vasari returned to the discussion of the general characteristics of the three periods and illustrated his thesis with further detail. Here he insisted again that the masters of the second period had made great progress toward perfection. "If they were not altogether perfect, they came so near the truth, that the third category, of whom we are now to speak, profited by the light they shed, and attained the summit of perfection, producing the more valuable and renowned modern works." [9] Vasari evidently regarded progress as the result of a cumulative improvement in technique, handed on from generation to generation. But this natural development of Italian art was not entirely autonomous. Antique models played a secondary but decisive part in the struggle toward ultimate

[6] *Ibid.,* II, 106 [I, 209].   [7] *Ibid.,* II, 96 [I, 203].
[8] *Ibid.,* IV, 7–15.   [9] *Ibid.,* IV, 7 [II, 151].

perfection. It was from them that the architects of the fifteenth century learned "rule, order, and proportion." In the life of Brunelleschi
he had already told how the great Florentine architect measured all
the ancient buildings in Rome, "neglecting to sleep and to eat, his
only concern being architecture, which had been corrupted, studying
the good ancient orders and not the barbarous Gothic style then in
general use." [10] The decisive influence of antiquity came later in
painting and sculpture. The imitation of nature was the dominant
motive in the first two periods, and exact reproduction of the natural
model was at once the glory and the defect of the second age. Too
anxious study led to a "certain dryness and crudeness" of style, which
was overcome only after the Laocoon, the Hercules, Venus, Apollo,
and other examples of the best of ancient art had been discovered and
studied. The artists, Vasari felt, must learn to select ideal beauty and
to improve upon the defects of the natural model, as did the ancient
masters. But this, of course, would have been impossible without the
earlier improvement in technique. The third or modern manner,
which began with Leonardo da Vinci, thus profited by the results of
two centuries of progressive improvement based on the study of nature, plus the example of the best works of antiquity, thereby attaining, as Vasari proudly noted, "that excellence which, by surpassing the
achievements of the ancients, has rendered the modern age so
glorious." [11]

Vasari's conception of the history of Renaissance art has remained
such a vital force in modern thought that he is often criticized as
though he were a contemporary historian. Recent critics, seeking to
reinterpret the aesthetic culture of the Middle Ages and the Renaissance, or to apply more satisfactory methods and criteria to the history
and criticism of art, have frequently underestimated the real magnitude of his achievement in the age in which the *Lives* were written.
The defects of his work from the modern point of view are clear. His
method was "unscientific." He was frequently credulous and prejudiced, though seldom consciously untruthful. He shared the pragmatic,
individualistic tendency of the humanist historians, laying great stress
on the practical and ethical lessons taught by history, and ascribing each

[10] *Ibid.*, II, 337 [I, 275].   [11] *Ibid.*. IV, 7 [II, 151].

step in the progress of art to individual skill or invention. He seemed quite unaware of changes in the spirit of art, and failed to observe the slightest connection between the evolution of art and that of society or of economic life. And he assumed, without question, that the art of antiquity, together with the classical Italian art of his own day, represented the ultimate degree of perfection possible to man. Conversely, the art forms of the Middle Ages, whether Gothic or Byzantine, seemed to him the lowest forms of aesthetic expression. He knew nothing of the Gothic art of the North. What medieval art he had seen in Italy he thought formless, crude, and ugly, almost, one feels, indecent.

Modern critics may question his judgments, but it was by virtue of these very omissions and preconceptions that Vasari was able to construct a co-ordinated historical scheme, which not only crystallized the traditional humanist conception of the revival of Italian art, but threw into sharp relief the relation between the modern manner and the antique on the one hand and on the other the contrast between the new art and the Byzantine and Gothic styles of the preceding centuries.[12] At the same time his enthusiastic portrayal of the art of the High Renaissance, for the glory of which all other ages were but a preparation, left a glowing impression of superhuman grandeur and beauty that has never been forgotten. Finally, it was Vasari who gave to the new age of art the name it still bears — the rebirth, *la rinascita* — though he himself applied the term more specifically to its beginnings.

Despite its familiarity in the field of religious thought, or perhaps because of that, the Italian humanists had generally avoided the metaphor of rebirth in relation to the revival of art or letters. It occurred fairly frequently among the Erasmian humanists of the North, but the earlier Italians used instead almost every possible equivalent: revival, restoration, awakening, reflowering, or return to the light. Vasari chose the more vivid metaphor, and his influence was a powerful factor in gaining universal acceptance for it. He was the first Italian writer to use it in a history of art, but the idea of a rebirth of culture was

[12] Cf. W. Weisbach, "Renaissance als Stilbegriff," *Historische Zeitschrift,* CXX (1919), 262 ff.

evidently becoming familiar in his circle at the time when he was writing the *Lives*. Four years before the publication of the first edition, his friend the journalistic historian, Paolo Giovio, applied the metaphor of rebirth to the history of letters in his collection of *Eulogies of Famous Men of Letters* (1546).[13] Here Giovio introduced Boccaccio as having been born "in that same happy century in which Latin letters are considered to have been reborn (renatae)."[14] Later he said that Trapezuntios was one of the first of the Greeks to achieve a good Latin style "in that century when letters were reborn."[15] Giovio's work was in no way comparable to that of Vasari, being merely a collection of portraits accompanied by brief, journalistic sketches of the lives of famous literary men. It was immensely popular, however, especially in the North, and it may have helped to spread the conception of a renaissance of letters.

During the following century and a half, Vasari's *Lives* served as the foundation for all histories of Renaissance art. The northern historians were left free to do original work in describing the rise of art in their own countries, but they started with Vasari's conception of the Italian movement. The most significant contributions to the history of art during this period were the works of the Fleming, Karel van Manders,[16] and the German, Joachim von Sandrart.[17] Both wrote universal histories of art, depending on Pliny for the ancient artists and translating or paraphrasing Vasari for the Italian; but both added much valuable material on the growth of modern art in the Netherlands and Germany. It may be worth noting in passing that Sandrart translated Vasari's *rinascita* as "Wiedergebuhrt der Mahlkunst in Italien."[18] England produced no histories of art worthy of note, and France none comparable to the Flemish and German, though Félibien des Avaux[19] wrote an extensive, if badly organized,

13 Paolo Giovio, *Elogia virorum literis illustrium* (Venice, 1546; I use ed. Basel, 1577). Eng. trans. (Boston, 1935).

14 *Ibid.*, p. 13.

15 *Ibid.*, p. 46. In his *De vita Leonis decimi Pont. Max. libri iiii* (Florence, 1548), Giovio put the golden age of the Renaissance in the reign of Leo X.

16 K. van Manders, *Het Schilder-Boeck* (Haarlem, 1604).

17 J. von Sandrart, *Teutsche Akademie* (Nuremberg, 1675). On Sandrart, see W. Waetzoldt, *Deutsche Kunsthistoriker* (Leipzig, 1921–24), I, 23 ff.

18 Sandrart, II, 57.

19 Félibien des Avaux, *Entretiens sur les vies et sur les ouvrages des plus excellens peintres, anciens et modernes*, 5 vols. (Paris, 1666–88).

discussion of Italian and French painting, taking his ideas and material regarding the revival of modern art in Italy straight from Vasari. For the metaphor of rebirth, he substituted the words "renouvellé," "se relever," and "remis au jour" most frequently, but in one place at least he referred to the age of Cimabue as that in which "la Peinture commença de renaistre."[20]

The history of art in the North could be written as a continuation or expansion of Vasari's *Lives* all the more readily because the artists of the seventeenth century were still under the spell of the classical art that had spread northward from Italy in the sixteenth century. They were in full agreement with Vasari concerning both the priority of the Italian development and the pre-eminence of the Italian masters of the golden age. If the taste of the seventeenth century challenged Vasari's judgment at any point it was in substituting Raphael for his hero Michelangelo as the supreme example of perfection,[21] and in showing less enthusiasm for the earlier "primitives." As the Italian Renaissance receded into the past, only its highest peak met the view, and the long upward slope on its further side was all but forgotten until the nineteenth century rediscovered the pre-Raphaelites.

Pierre Bayle and *la Renaissance des Lettres*

The literary renaissance was overshadowed in the North by the Reformation, and it was most frequently treated during the sixteenth and seventeenth centuries as a divinely ordained preparation for the religious revolution. This was less true in France than elsewhere, however, and there a secular conception of the *renaissance des lettres* grew up to take its place beside that of the *renaissance des beaux arts*.[22]

Interest in the classical revival seems to have waned somewhat in both France and England toward the end of the sixteenth century, countered by the struggle to place the vernacular on a basis of equality with the ancient tongues. In this struggle, national sentiment and

[20] *Ibid.*, I, 108; cf. 91; 100; 112.
[21] Cf. *ibid.*, I, 249.
[22] For the history of the idea of the Renaissance in the North during the sixteenth century, see the preceding chapter.

Protestant faith were aligned in defense of the modern languages.[23] Then, during the following century, rising interest in the investigation of the natural sciences and Cartesian philosophy introduced into the thought of Western Europe new elements that were essentially antagonistic to both the classical and religious revivals of the preceding period. Bacon and Descartes and their successors challenged the authority of the ancients and thereby, though indirectly, cast doubts upon the ultimate importance of the renaissance of antique letters and learning. An embryonic theory of the progress of knowledge was taking shape among the scientists and philosophers and finally spread into the field of *belles-lettres,* where it stirred up the wordy quarrel of the ancients and the moderns.[24] The seventeenth century was busy evaluating its own achievements and measuring them against the standard of antiquity, in general to its great content, as Mr. Pepys would put it. But if the growing idea of progress and the cultural complacency of the Age of Louis XIV tended to dim the radiance of antiquity and hence the reflected glory of the *renaissance des lettres,* the change was one of relative value rather than of definition.

This was true of even so enthusiastic a champion of the moderns as Fontenelle, who might be accepted as a popular spokesman for late seventeenth century scientific thought. In his *Digression on the Ancients and the Moderns* (1688),[25] Fontenelle admitted that the best argument of the partisans of antiquity was to be found in the history of culture during the ages of barbarism and in the revival that followed the recovery of the classics. To the question, why in those centuries was ignorance so dense and so profound, they reply that it was because men no longer knew the Greeks and the Latins and did not read them. But as soon as they recovered these excellent models, reason and good taste were at once reborn ("on vit renaître la raison et le bon goût"). Fontenelle was forced to agree. The reading of the ancients, he admitted, did dissipate the ignorance and barbarism of the pre-

---

23 Cf. V. Hall, *Renaissance Literary Criticism* (New York, 1945), pp. 82 ff; 153 ff.

24 Cf. J. B. Bury, *The Idea of Progress* (London, 1920), Chaps. II–V; R. Flint, *History of the Philosophy of History* (London, 1893), pp. 210 ff.

25 B. le Bouvier de Fontenelle, *Digression sur les anciens et sur les modernes* (1688), *Oeuvres* (Paris, 1790), V, 296 f.

ceding centuries. It restored in a moment ideas of truth and beauty that it would have taken a long time to recover, but which man would have recovered eventually without the aid of the Greeks and Latins. The last phrase indicates the change in evaluation suggested by the idea of progress. But Fontenelle's conception of the actual historical significance of the classical revival is in the pure humanist tradition.

The seventeenth century produced no historical work of major importance dealing with the Renaissance. The French historians and philologists who in that century were laying the foundations for modern learned historiography devoted their research especially to the Middle Ages. Their work might have altered the interpretation of the Middle Ages and the Renaissance, but it failed to do so, for they were erudite compilers of material rather than interpretive historians. A life time spent in the meticulous study of medieval latinity failed to shake Du Cange's faith in the humanist view of the history of literature.[26] And the chief result of the pious researches of Mabillon and Tillemont seems to have been to supply the rationalists of the eighteenth century with material for their attacks upon medieval civilization.[27]

Among the conflicting interests of the period that preceded the dawn of the Enlightenment, the Renaissance was allowed to sink somewhat into the background, but it was never forgotten. The rebirth of art and letters was taken for granted as part of the tradition of cultural history. The phrase *la renaissance des beaux arts* was included in Furetière's *Dictionary*[28] in 1701 as an accepted usage in the French language; and in 1718 even that official custodian of purism, the *Dictionary of the Academy,* recognized the word *renaissance* with the note: "It is used only in a metaphorical sense" and cited as an example the phrase: "Depuis la renaissance des lettres." Meanwhile,

[26] See Ch. du Cange, *Glossarium ad scriptores mediae et infimae latinitatis,* 10 vols. (1678; new ed. Paris, 1773), I, xlviii.

[27] Cf. E. Fueter, *Geschichte der neueren Historiographie* (Munich, 1936), pp. 307 ff; 311.

[28] A. Furetière, *Dictionnaire universel* (2nd ed. corrected and enlarged. The Hague and Rotterdam, 1701). J. Plattard, " 'Restitution des bonnes lettres' et 'Renaissance,' " in *Mélanges offerts par ses amis et ses élèves à M. Gustave Lanson* (Paris, 1922), p. 131, stresses the fact that the phrase does not appear in this dictionary, a fact true only of the first edition.

toward the end of the century, the traditional interpretations were restated in Bayle's great *Historical and Critical Dictionary* (1695 ff.) [29]
in a formula that was to crystallize the conception of the *renaissance
des lettres* in the minds of innumerable readers for generations to
come.

Pierre Bayle was not a great historian nor, perhaps, a great thinker;
but he had all the virtues of erudition, intellectual independence, and
critical skepticism. His *Dictionary* was a unique achievement. It
brought together an amazing collection of erudite information — a
folio page of notes for every four or five lines of text — the whole
enlivened by anecdotes which were occasionally scandalous but always interesting, and shot through with skeptical *obiter dicta* on the
most cherished beliefs of his day. No writer since Erasmus had made
footnotes such fascinating reading, nor poured the acid of rational
irony on so many traditional preconceptions. The *Dictionary* was republished almost every decade after its first appearance in 1695 and
was soon translated into English and German. It probably did more
than any other single book to shape the rationalist thought of the
eighteenth century.[30]

Bayle's conception of the revival of letters combined the French
humanist tradition with that of the Protestant church historians; but
he deleted from the latter the faith in the directing hand of Divine
Providence and the assurance that the Reformation was the triumphant
result of God's plan for the salvation of mankind, both of which had
been its motivating forces. He agreed with the Protestant theologians
that the literary renaissance had aided the Reformation. In his view,
however, it was a fortuitous aid, due chiefly to the fact that the contemporary form of religion was Catholic and criticism of the Catholic
Church and faith automatically prepared the way for the Reformers.
He attributed Luther's success, where Wyclif and Huss had failed,
not to divine support but to a variety of circumstances: his personal
genius; the fact that he came at an opportune time, treating the illness
at its highest point and therefore gaining credit for the cure; and,

---

[29] P. Bayle, *Dictionnaire historique et critique* (1695 ff; I use 3rd ed., Rotterdam, 1715). Eng. trans. (London, 1735).

[30] Cf. H. Robinson, *Bayle the Skeptic* (New York, 1931), concluding chapter;
and E. Faguet, *Le dix-huitième siècle* (Paris, 1890), Chap. I.

finally, the revival of lay learning which prepared the way. "Learning flourished among the laity, whilst churchmen would not renounce their barbarism, and persecuted the learned and scandalized all the world by unbridled lust. It was said with reason that Erasmus, by his railleries, prepared the way for Luther. He was his St. John the Baptist." [31]

As a Huguenot, who had been driven into exile by the revocation of the Edict of Nantes, Bayle had no love for the Catholic Church; as a rational skeptic, who hated all forms of fanaticism, he had grave doubts about the Reformation and all its works. His thought was essentially irreligious, and he was inclined, as many historians have been since, to read into an intellectual movement that he admired qualities of thought akin to his own. He interpreted Renaissance humanism as an enlightened revolt against barbarism, a basically irreligious movement, comparable to the Cartesian philosophy which in the seventeenth century had laid open the mysteries of the Christian religion to the healthy winds of doubt. He made the comparison in his article on the Arabic philosopher Takiddin.

> Generally speaking the Cartesians are suspected of irreligion, and their philosophy is thought to be very dangerous to Christianity. . . . But irreligion is not only ascribed to the study of philosophy, but also to philology; for it is pretended that atheism never began to discover itself in France till the reign of Francis I, and that the first appearance of it in Italy was when philological learning was revived there. . . . It is certain that most of the wits and learned philologers, who shined in Italy, when the Belles Lettres began to revive there (commencèrent à renaître), after the taking of Constantinople, had but little religion. But, on the other hand, the reformation of the learned languages and polite literature made way for the Reformation; as the monks and their adherents clearly foresaw, who continually inveighed against Reuchlin, Erasmus, and the other scourgers of ignorance.

It was the Italian humanists whom he noted especially as lacking in religion, the northern scholars as aiding the Reformation. But the contribution of the latter was entirely negative, a destructive criticism dangerous to the Catholic faith. In the article on Budé, he again stressed the opposition of Catholic ecclesiastics to the cause of good

[31] Bayle, Article, *Luther.*

letters, "which they labored to smother in their rebirth (dans leur renaissance)," as the mother and nurse of opinions which did not please the court of Rome. Nowhere does he suggest that the northern humanists were more positively religious than their Italian predecessors.

Bayle's conception of the *renaissance des lettres* crystallized the northern tradition as distinct from the Italian. Aside from the emphasis on Erasmus and Reuchlin and the insistence on the relation between the literary revival and the Reformation, which he took from the Protestant historians and restated in terms that would make it acceptable to eighteenth century rationalism, Bayle popularized the quite erroneous theory that the revival of letters in Italy originated with the Greek refugees who fled from Constantinople after the Turkish conquest of 1453. There was no precedent for this theory among the Italian humanist historians. They had reason to know better. But Bayle's account and his citations show that it was familiar in France in the seventeenth century, and we have already found it suggested in Théodore de Bèze.[32] With it went the much sounder theory that the *renaissance des lettres* reached France in the reign of Francis I.[33] This was the point of cardinal interest to French writers. They were prepared to admit that the new movement had come from Italy, but they were not especially interested in its history during the preceding two hundred years. A similar foreshortening of the Italian Renaissance occurred in the history of art, but there, thanks to Vasari, the early origins could not be wholly ignored. The errors in Bayle's theory of the origin of the Renaissance are easily demonstrable. Nevertheless, it had the advantage of supplying a definite date (1453), and a dramatic cause in the fall of Constantinople. And it found support in the current tendency, which lasted throughout the Enlightenment, to attribute historical developments to accidental or cataclysmic events.[34] It was a clear, precise conception, easily grasped and, as the event proved, long to be retained. We shall meet it again and again until the late nineteenth century.

[32] See above, p. 57.
[33] See the quotation from Amyot, above, p. 31; also Joachim du Bellay, *Oeuvres français,* ed. Ch. Marty-Laveaux (Paris, 1866), I, 264.
[34] Cf. Fueter, pp. 343 ff.

CELLARIUS AND THE *Medium Aevum*

As we have seen in the preceding chapters, the idea of a rebirth of art and letters was linked from the beginning with a conception, very vague for the most part, of a middle period between the decline of ancient culture and the modern revival; during the seventeenth century this latter conception also crystallized in definite and lasting form.[35] The two ideas were necessarily connected, for the one presupposes the other. The idea of a revival, rebirth, or restoration of any branch of culture implies that there was a period during which it was feeble, dead, or neglected. For every metaphor of rebirth, reawakening, or return to the light, there was a corollary metaphor of death, sleep, or darkness.[36] The middle age was thus as much a part of the humanist historical scheme as was the revival; but the early humanists referred to the dark intermediate period only in relation to specific forms of culture, artistic or literary. They did not develop the idea into a conscious or explicit periodization of history.

The Protestant historians, in full cry against the medieval church and all its works, added a new content to the conception of the intermediate age. In their view it was not merely the illiterate period between the decline of ancient learning and the modern revival, but the age of popish iniquity between the decline of the primitive evangelical church and its restoration through Martin Luther. The theological scheme of universal history, to which all the reformers were addicted, prevented them from distinguishing the middle age as part of a formal system of periodization, but the whole tenor of their historical writing pointed to the existence of such a period and furnished it with a very definite character.

Within the past generation there has been a good deal of intensive research into the origins not only of the idea of a middle age, but also of the term by which it has been known to modern historiog-

[35] G. Falco, *La polemica sul Medio Evo* (Turin, 1933) furnishes the best account of the historical development of the idea of the Middle Ages.

[36] Cf. L. Varga, *Das Schlagwort vom "finsteren Mittelalter"* (Vienna, 1932); F. Simone, "La Coscienza della Rinascita negli humanisti," *La Rinascita*, III (1940), 163–86; and other works cited above in Chapter I.

raphy.[37] Paul Lehmann has traced the term, in the form *media tempestas,* back to the fifteenth century,[38] and G. S. Gordon has demonstrated, by means of tables showing the results of his own research and that of Lehmann and others, that the application of such terms as *media aetas, media antiquitas,* and *media tempora* to the medieval period was not uncommon in the sixteenth century and became increasingly frequent, with the addition of the more familiar *medium aevum,* in the seventeenth century. The Dutch historian Georg Horn has thus been deprived of the rather doubtful honor, ascribed to him by tradition, of having christened the Middle Ages in his *Ark of Noah* in 1666.[39] But if both the idea of a middle age and its rather invidious name were present at a much earlier date, it was not till after Horn's work that the two were combined to form a practical periodization of history. Nearly all the examples cited by Lehmann and Gordon refer to literary activity and are no more than vague attempts to give a chronological designation to authors who were neither ancient nor modern.

The combination of humanist and Protestant views of the course of European history would seem to have made its formal division into three periods a foregone conclusion. The long delay that preceded the crystallization of the concept was due to limitations inherent in both types of historical thought. The humanists' conception of a dark intermediate age was limited to literature, learning, and the arts, and was partially contradicted by their political histories; the Reformers were bound by the traditional theological scheme of the Four Monarchies; and both humanists and reformers at first thought of the

---

[37] P. Lehmann, *Vom Mittelalter und von der lateinischen Philologie des Mittelalters* (Munich, 1914); "Mittelalter und Küchenlatein," *Historische Zeitschrift,* CXXXVII (1928), 197–213; G. S. Gordon, *Medium Aevum and the Middle Ages* (S. P. E. Tract, No. XIX, 1925); G. L. Burr, "How the Middle Ages got their Name," *American Historical Review,* XX (1914–15), 813–15; J. Huizinga, "Een schakel in de ontwikkeling van den term Middeleeuwen?," *Medeelingen der Koninkl. Akademie van wetenschappen,* Deel LIII, Ser. A, No. 5 (1921).

[38] Lehmann, *Vom Mittelalter,* p. 2, cites Giovanni Andrea in the preface to an edition of Apuleius (Rome, 1469), referring to Nicholas of Cusa as "vir ipse ... historias idem omnes non priscas modo sed *medie tempestatis* tum veteres tum recentiores usque ad nostra tempora memoria retinebat."

[39] G. Horn, *Arca Noae sive historia imperiorum et regnorum a condito orbe ad nostra tempora* (Leyden and Rotterdam, 1666); cf. Gordon, p. 4. For the tradition ascribing the term to Horn, cf. Lehmann, *Vom Mittelalter,* p. 2; Falco, pp. 86 ff.

middle period as simply that between antiquity and their own age, an uncertain conception which could be clarified only by the passage of time. By the second half of the seventeenth century historians were beginning to look back upon the end of the intermediate period and the beginning of the modern age as something that had occurred in the past, and from this longer perspective they were able to form a more definite historical scheme. The revival of learning and the Reformation were still the most significant factors in determining the new scheme of periodization; but the idea of modern scientific progress had called the attention of historians to other phenomena — the invention of gunpowder and printing, the geographical and scientific discoveries, the development of industry and commerce [40] — which reinforced the idea that the modern age had begun about the end of the fifteenth or beginning of the sixteenth century. After the Treaty of Westphalia the political historians, too, were becoming aware that a new organization of the states of Europe had taken place and that the beginnings of the new system coincided in time with the other evidences of the dawn of a new age. Finally, the theological organization of history, though still current till the eighteenth century, was being gradually weakened by the impact of secular and scientific trends of thought, so that the way was more open for the introduction of a new scheme.[41]

The first historian to make practical use of the division of history into three periods, antiquity, the middle age, and modern times, as a principle of organization was the German pedagogue, Christoph Keller, better known as Cellarius.[42] To him must be accorded the credit for introducing this formula into the system of academic instruction, whence it spread to general historiography. Cellarius was not a great historian. He was an indefatigable writer of textbooks, who understood the pedagogical value of a simple, precise method of organization. He began writing historical manuals for classroom use

[40] Jean Bodin, *Methodus ad facilem historiarum cognitionem* (1566; 2nd ed. Paris, 1572), pp. 478 ff, was one of the first to stress these developments as evidence of the superiority of the modern age over earlier times. See also Francis Bacon, *Novum Organum*, I, secs. 78; 84, (London, 1893) pp. 43; 48 ff.

[41] Cf. Falco, p. 84.

[42] See *ibid.*, pp. 89 ff for discussion of Cellarius; also F. X. von Wegele, *Geschichte der deutschen Historiographie* (Munich, 1885), pp. 484 ff.

in 1675 with a synopsis of ancient history, which he followed the next year with one devoted to the Middle Ages, under the title, *Nucleus of Middle History between Ancient and Modern*.[43] In 1685 he began a new series with an enlarged edition of his *Ancient History*,[44] which he extended to the age of Constantine. Then came the crucial *History of the Middle Ages from the Times of Constantine the Great to the Capture of Constantinople by the Turks* (1688).[45] The series was completed by a *Modern History* in 1696.[46] The popularity of these manuals, incredibly dull though they were, is attested by the fact that the *Ancient History* was in its ninth edition in 1734, the *History of the Middle Ages* in an eighth edition in 1732, and the *Modern History* in the ninth edition in 1735.

The dates Cellarius chose to mark the chronological boundaries of the middle age were arbitrary — they could not have been otherwise — and they were not always followed exactly by later historians. They fitted the various trends of traditional interpretation well enough, however, to make his scheme generally acceptable. The reign of Constantine had frequently been noted by both humanists and reformers as the first stage in the decline of the Roman Empire, Latin culture, or evangelical Christianity. To end the following period, which Cellarius described as one of cultural and religious darkness, with the fall of Constantine's city rounded out the age with a touch of dramatic justice. At the same time, the capture of Constantinople connected the beginning of modern history with the revival of learning in Italy, which Cellarius, in accordance with the northern tradition already noted, ascribed to the migration of the Greek refugees.[47] But for Cellarius other events, the inventions and discoveries, political changes, and, above all, the Protestant Reformation, were equally if not more significant as evidences of the dawn of a new age.[48] He apparently

---

[43] Cellarius, *Nucleus historiae inter antiquam et novam mediae* (1675), cited by Gordon, p. 4.

[44] Cellarius, *Historia antiqua* (1685; 9th ed. Jena, 1734).

[45] Cellarius, *Historia medii aevi a temporibus Constantini Magni ad Constantinopolim a Turcis captam deducta* (1688; 8th ed. Jena, 1732).

[46] Cellarius, *Historia nova* (1696; 9th ed. Jena 1735).

[47] Cf. Cellarius, *Hisoria medii aevi*, p. 214 f: "Cadebant litterae in Oriente, surgebant ex diuturna barbarie in Occidente, doctissimo quoque Graecorum, ut Turcos evaderet, in Italiam confugiente." [48] Cf. Falco, p. 91 f.

came to feel that 1453 was too early a date to be entirely satisfactory, for in the introduction to his final work, the *Modern History,* he added an "et paulo ultra" to his earlier description of the middle age as the twelve centuries in which Constantinople was Christian, and stated categorically that the reformation of the Church justifies us in dating modern history, as distinct from that of the middle age, from the beginning of the sixteenth century.[49] Later historians were to agree more generally with this latter date, though not always for the same reason.

The success of Cellarius's scheme is proof that it was in accord with the major trends of historical interpretation not only in his own day but for generations to come. From this point on we can take the Middle Ages for granted as an established ingredient in historical thought. It will, therefore, not be necessary to treat conceptions of it as fully as we have done for the formative period of historical periodization. But the attitude of each school of historians toward the Middle Ages will still be very significant for our problem. In many instances it was the reaction, favorable or unfavorable, to medieval civilization that determined the interpretation of the Renaissance. At the same time, the threefold division of history tended to retard the development of the concept of the Renaissance as an historical epoch, since no independent place was left for it between the Middle Ages and modern times. It long remained merely *la renaissance des lettres et des beaux arts,* one of the phenomena that had heralded the beginning of the modern age.

[49] Cellarius, *Historia nova,* pp. 4; 11.

CHAPTER FOUR

The Rationalist Tradition in the
Eighteenth Century

THE ORIGINAL CONTRIBUTION of the mid-eighteenth century to historical interpretation was made by the men of the Enlightenment, who wrote history *en philosophe*.[1] From the assured heights of the Age of Reason they gazed back upon the history of the human race with a kind of irritable complacency, observing the incomprehensible follies, stupidities, and superstitions that had hindered and interrupted man's progress from savagery and barbarism. The main lines of the picture had been drawn for them by the humanist and Protestant historians, but the point of view was their own. Man had progressed by slow degrees from savagery to a fairly high point of civilization in the great age of antiquity. Thence he had been plunged once more into the depths of barbarism and superstition. After centuries of medieval darkness, the slow process of enlightenment and amelioration of man's lot had begun again, the age of the revival of learning marking the first decisive stage in modern progress. The philosophic historians took the conception of the Renaissance as it had been handed on to them by the various trends of past interpretation, but they saw it in a new light and from a new perspective.

[1] For general discussion of the historiography of the Enlightenment, see E. Fueter, *Geschichte der neueren Historiographie* (Munich, 1936), pp. 334 ff; J. B. Black, *The Art of History, a Study of Four Great Historians of the Eighteenth Century* (New York, 1926); W. Dilthey, "Das achtzehnte Jahrhundert und die geschichtliche Welt," *Gesammelte Schriften* (Leipzig, 1927), III, 209–68; J. W. Thompson, *A History of Historical Writing* (New York, 1942), II, 58 ff; B. Croce, *History, its Theory and Practice* (Eng. trans., New York, 1921), pp. 243 ff; R. Flint, *History of the Philosophy of History* (Edinburgh, 1893), I, 235 ff.

THE HISTORICAL PHILOSOPHY OF THE ENLIGHTENMENT

History had never been so popular as it was in the mid-eighteenth century, and with reason. Seldom has history been at once so well written and so perfectly in accord with the leading ideas of the age. During the two preceding centuries, learned historiography had labored under the weight of theological solemnity or of solid but graceless and often unthinking antiquarianism. The humanist strain, so promising in the work of the great Florentines, had degenerated in the seventeenth century into the trivial eloquence of the court historians, who "neglected nothing but the essential." [2] As written by Voltaire, Hume, Robertson, and Gibbon, on the other hand, history combined literary style with rational thought and an adequate measure of critical exactitude. It appealed to both taste and reason, which was all the eighteenth century asked of any literary form. Above all, it illustrated and supported the "philosophy" that was the dominant intellectual interest of the Enlightenment. History, for the *philosophe,* was "philosophy teaching by examples." [3] And the philosophy of the Enlightenment, in turn, supplied history with a group of leading ideas which made possible, for the first time in secular historiography, a co-ordinated conception of the whole past of the human race.[4] This is not the place for an essay on eighteenth century philosophy, but it may be well to call to mind the principal ideas that made up the intellectual furniture of the age, if we are to understand the historical interpretations that grew out of them.

The rationalism of the eighteenth century represented a new stage in the development of the secular *Weltanschauung* that had begun with the rise of an educated urban laity in the later Middle Ages. Though partially eclipsed by the Reformation and Counter-Reformation and later diverted by Puritanism and Jansenism, the secular attitude had continued to grow with the evolution of bourgeois society. It found expression in the skepticism, the scientific investigation, and the Cartesian philosophy of the seventeenth century, and from these

[2] G. Lanson, *Voltaire* (Paris, 1906), p. 108.
[3] H. St. John, Viscount Bolingbroke, *Letters on the Study of History, Works* (Dublin, 1793), II, 267.
[4] Cf. Dilthey, *Schriften,* III, 222.

it gained an intellectual sanction that had been lacking heretofore. The most characteristic ideas of the Enlightenment stemmed from this age. Picking the ideas that suited them from a wide variety of sources, the *philosophes* constructed a mechanistic conception of the universe, picturing it as a machine which God had designed and set going, but which operated automatically in accordance with unchanging natural laws. By the use of his reason and the empirical method, man could ascertain these laws, as Galileo and Newton had done. The *philosophes* rejected revelation and authority as they denied the supernatural and the transcendental, and placed their faith in reason and the progress of knowledge. And this not only in relation to the physical universe. What applied to it applied also to man. From the psychological theories of Locke, they drew the conclusion that man is a physical mechanism, the essential nature of which is invariable, and that man's ideas result entirely from the experience of his senses. Man thus became a suitable subject for scientific study. In the social as in the natural sciences, reason and natural law were the beginning and end of the rationalists' creed. About them were grouped a whole complex of more or less interrelated ideas, each clear in itself but not always too logically related to the others. Emile Faguet's prejudiced dictum on Voltaire — "This great mind is a chaos of clear ideas" [5] — would apply equally well to the whole philosophy of his age. For our purposes these ideas are significant only as they influenced historical thought, and will therefore be discussed in that connection.

Perhaps the most obvious effect upon historiography of the new rationalism was the complete and positive rejection of the theological conception of history. In this direction the philosophical historians went far beyond the Italian humanists. The latter, who were simply laymen writing secular history from a secular point of view under the influence of classical models, had tacitly ignored the theological tradition with its emphasis on teleology and Divine Providence. But they seemed unaware of any acute conflict between their attitude and that of the Church, which itself had become secular enough. If they thought of the theological interpretation at all, they were content to

---

[5] E. Faguet, *Dix-huitième siècle, études littéraires* (Paris, s. d., Nouvelle bibliothèque littéraire), p. 226.

leave it to the theologians. Paolo Cortese brought up the question of the historical rôle of Divine Providence in his *Dialogue of Learned Men* (1490),[6] and promptly dropped it again as being none of his business. "Let us," he said, "omit this science of men learned in the investigation of heavenly matters."[7] The *philosophes* would leave nothing to the science of men learned in heavenly matters. They were arrayed in positive battle against the supernatural, and to the dogmas of its ministers they opposed a dogma of their own.[8]

Having rejected on dogmatic philosophical grounds the causative action of Divine Providence in history, the historians of the Enlightenment were more consciously concerned with the problem of finding a substitute than the humanists had been. Natural law was the obvious substitute, and was taken for granted. It was assumed that events were the necessary product of universal laws.[9] But it was not easy to determine how these laws actually worked in human affairs, or what were the immediate motivating forces. Montesquieu made the pregnant suggestion that geography and climate exercised a determining influence on laws and institutions. Voltaire asserted that three things constantly influence the human mind: climate, government, and religion. "It is the only way of explaining the enigma of this world."[10] But these factors are changeable, peculiar to time and place. How was their variability to be reconciled with the theory, based on Locke's psychology, of the universal similarity of human nature? A little further on in the same discussion, Voltaire furnished the answer in one of the clearest statements of his historical philosophy:

It follows from this survey [of history] that everything which pertains intimately to human nature is much the same from one end of the world to the other; that everything which depends on custom is dif-

---

[6] P. Cortese, *Dialogus de hominibus doctis* in F. Villani, *Liber de Florentiae famosis civibus,* ed. G. C. Galletti (Florence, 1847), pp. 221–48.
[7] *Ibid.,* p. 223: "Quis enim dubitet cuncta a supremo illo Opifice praeclaro quodam judicio administrari? Sed omittamus istam doctorum hominum in coelestium rerum investigatione scientiam."
[8] Cf. A. von Martin, "Motive und Tendenzen in Voltaires Geschichtschreibung," *Historische Zeitschrift,* CXVIII (1927), 20.
[9] Lanson, p. 117.
[10] Voltaire, *Essai sur les moeurs et l'esprit des nations, Oeuvres complètes* (Paris, 1883–85), XIII, 178.

ferent, and it is mere chance if there is any resemblance. The empire
of custom is indeed much larger than that of nature. It extends over
manners, over all usage; it spreads variety over the universal scene.
Nature spreads unity; it establishes everywhere a small number of
invariable principles: thus the foundation is everywhere the same,
and culture produces diverse fruits.[11]

In short, man is everywhere the same, yet "every man is shaped by his
age." [12] Voltaire thus opened the way for a history of civilization,
which could recognize the peculiar and varying spirit of nations or of
ages, while still denying that these differences are essential or inherent
in the nature of men of different times or different races. Along with
the invariable attributes of human nature, then, such variables as
climate, institutions, religion, custom, opinion,[13] *l'esprit du temps,* and
l'esprit des nations all became recognized motive forces in history.
This was a revolutionary conception, for these were "general causes,"
as Gibbon called them,[14] and the recognition of their existence broadened the scope of history and pointed the way to synthesis.

General causes, however, like universal laws, proved difficult to discover from the inadequate data available to the eighteenth century
historians, and failure to find them led in many cases to a diametrically
opposed tendency. In practice, at any rate, the historians of the Age
of Reason were frequently forced to resort to the alternative solutions
which the humanists, following their antique models, had most commonly adopted: individual reason and chance. Chance seemed to the
philosophes, as it had to Machiavelli, a much more plausible cause
than providential design. It might even be raised to the dignity of a
natural law.[15] Hence the tendency, so often deplored by modern historians, to ascribe great events to petty, accidental causes, and revolu-

---

11 *Ibid.,* XIII, 182.

12 Cf. *ibid.,* XII, 66: "Tout homme est formé par son siècle."

13 On the causative force of opinion, see Voltaire, *Remarques de l'Essai, Oeuvres,*
XXIV, 551 ff.

14 E. Gibbon, *Essai sur l'étude de la littérature* (1761), *Miscellaneous Works,*
ed. Lord Sheffield (London, 1814), IV, 69.

15 Cf. Voltaire, *Essai, Oeuvres,* XII, 258. Referring to the capture of Francis
I at Pavia, he remarked: "Voici un des plus grands exemples des coups de la
fortune, qui n'est autre chose, après tout, que l'enchaînement nécessaire de tous
les événements de l'univers."

tionary changes in general culture to single cataclysmic events. At the same time, conceiving man to be an essentially rational being, the philosophic historians were inclined, wherever possible, to trace events to conscious, rational motives. And, being unwilling to admit that men in the past were in any essential way different from themselves, and being further unable to reconstruct sympathetically the complex emotions and ideas of a radically different society, they frequently accounted for actions which seemed to them quite unreasonable by motives of a rather low and uninspiring sort. As Gibbon observed, they tended "to make all men beings as systematic in practice as in speculation. They find art in their passions, policy in their weaknesses, dissimulation in their inconsistencies; in a word, by trying to do honor to the human intellect, they have often done little honor to the heart." [16] Many of the *philosophes,* in fact, for all their optimistic faith in the power of reason, took a rather gloomy view of human nature, especially in unenlightened ages. Voltaire thought history was composed chiefly of crimes, follies, and misery.[17] The reason of great men was often perverted by passion and greed, that of the mob by ignorance, superstition, and fanaticism. Progress could be hoped for only from the occasional contributions made by the few really great men: the thinkers, the enlightened princes, and the wise law-givers. What has been called "the great man theory" thus took its place as yet another rival to the "general causes" so hopefully sought by Voltaire and Gibbon.[18]

These theories of causation might suggest an explanation of particular events; they could not give order and meaning to history as a whole. Something was needed to take the place of the Christian teleology, which the *philosophes* had rejected together with Divine Providence. They found an acceptable substitute without difficulty, almost without thinking about it, in the theory of progress. Nearly all the eighteenth century historians were convinced that man had made great progress in the past and that the progress of knowledge

---

[16] Gibbon, *Works,* IV, 68.   [17] Voltaire, *Oeuvres,* XIII, 177.

[18] Cf. *ibid.,* XII, 161. Voltaire ascribed the whole movement of Portuguese exploration to the sole initiative of Henry the Navigator, and added: "Il ne s'est presque jamais rien fait de grand dans le monde que par le génie et la fermeté d'un seul homme qui lutte contre les préjugés de la multitude, ou qui lui en donne."

and reason, and the consequent amelioration of man's lot would continue in the future.[19] Many of them shared the optimistic faith in the perfectibility of man which the pre-revolutionary thinkers drew from Locke's psychology. But whether they were prepared to go quite that far or not, the rationalist philosophers, like their scholastic predecessors, saw all history working inevitably, if by devious ways, toward a definite goal: the construction of a "heavenly city." [20]

The theory of progress oriented eighteenth century historiography. The aim of the historian *en philosophe,* however, was not merely to depict the march of human progress, but to aid further advance by instructing and enlightening men. Thanks to the belief in the invariability of human nature, it was thought possible to draw scientifically valid inductions from the observation of historical phenomena. As Hume stated the current theory: "Mankind are so much the same, in all times and places, that history informs us of nothing new in this particular. Its chief use is only to discover the constant and universal principles of human nature." [21] It was assumed that, having discovered these, the philosopher could apply his knowledge to the perfecting of man through instruction and legislation. But the services of history to the cause of progress were not all constructive. It might also help to destroy those institutions which blocked the way to further advance. In France especially, where the apostles of reason were involved in a struggle for practical reform of society, church, and state, the faith of the Enlightenment was a fighting faith; and the rôle of history was to supply ammunition for the children of light. In practice, the "chief use" of history was to furnish the empirical data needed to support the conclusions already arrived at by reason. This was, perhaps, not quite the scientific method, but it was effective. Viewed *en philosophe,* history provided ample proof that the ills of man in the past had been due to ignorance, to superstitious religion with its self-seeking ministers, and to social and political institutions that were both unreasonable and unjust.

The *philosophes* were at one with both the humanists and the

19 Cf. J. B. Bury, *The Idea of Progress* (London, 1920), pp. 144 ff.
20 Cf. C. Becker, *The Heavenly City of the Philosophers in the Eighteenth Century* (New Haven, 1932).
21 D. Hume, *Essays* (1767), II, 94; quoted in Becker, p. 95.

theologians in the practical, didactic value they placed on history. It must teach lessons useful to contemporary society. Melanchthon might have endorsed the dictum of the deist Bolingbroke that "any study that tends neither directly nor indirectly to make us better men and better citizens is at best but a specious and ingenious sort of idleness." [22] Like the reformers, the philosophical historians expected all of human history to furnish proof of the validity of their beliefs, and they were similarly drawn to universal history or large sections thereof. But if the purpose was similar, the end product was very different. The doctrines of the Enlightenment provided the historians of the eighteenth century with a new set of standards for judging the past and gave a new direction to their historical interests. For them history was exclusively the history of mortal man, its central theme the intellectual and social amelioration of the human race. Hence their unprecedented emphasis on social and cultural history and their transference of the halo from the heads of saints and military heroes to the loftier brows of the wise princes, the intellectual giants, and the practical benefactors of mankind.[23] Enlightenment, rationality, tolerance, public order and security, wealth and material comfort, these were the standards by which the Age of Reason assessed the achievements of the past.

To these moral or philosophical criteria the rational historians added new critical standards. They were less inclined than the humanists had been to accept the authority of the ancients in matters of fact, and they rejected revealed authority *in toto*. Assuming the invariability of natural law and of human nature, they rejected all miracles, no matter how well documented, and with them all "fables" [24] which ascribed to men emotions or actions contrary to the principles of human nature — as they knew it. The Italian humanists had, in general, ignored the miraculous on common sense grounds, but their skepticism was a feeble thing compared with the conviction of the rationalists that what was not in accordance with reason could not

---

[22] Bolingbroke, *Works,* II, 245.
[23] Cf. Voltaire to Thieriot, July 15, 1735, *Oeuvres,* XXXIII, 506: "J'appelle grands hommes tous ceux qui ont excellé dans l'utile ou dans l'agréable. Les saccageurs de provinces ne sont que héros."
[24] Cf. *ibid.,* XIII, 173.

have happened. This short cut to historical criticism produced many admirable results, which partially compensated for inadequacy of research, but it also imposed certain limitations. It hindered the sympathetic understanding of irrational motives and of the ideals, faiths, preconceptions, and emotions of radically different societies in the past. To judge the actions of medieval men by the standards of the age of Enlightenment was to make the distortion of history inevitable.

The tendency of the eighteenth century writers to judge the past by the standards of the present was further reinforced by the peculiar rigidity of the contemporary rules of taste. In this century, the classicism that had begun with the Renaissance enthusiasm for antiquity developed into a strict critical orthodoxy. Literary and artistic forms were classified and assessed according to a dogmatic system of "Kinds, Qualities, and Rules." [25] In less technical terms, the eighteenth century demanded of literature and art the virtues of classical form, order, correctness, elegance, restraint, and, above all, common sense. The classical and rational strains ran closely parallel. Taste and reason went side by side in perfect harmony. And in no respect were they more perfectly agreed than in their condemnation of medieval civilization.

The men of the Enlightenment combined in their attitude toward the Middle Ages the humanists' dislike of Gothic art, unclassical Latin, and unliterary learning with a hatred of medieval religion, scholastic philosophy, and ecclesiasticism very similar in effect to that of the Protestants; but they added to the former a more conscious revulsion against the irrationality, eccentricity, and formlessness of medieval art and literature, and to the latter a broader and more rational condemnation of all medieval institutions.[26] Their attitude toward the Renaissance, which they valued in proportion to the unmedieval qualities they perceived in it, was not so clear nor so uniform, but it was shaped by the same set of preconceptions. It can be examined most profitably through a study of the most influential historical works of the period.

[25] G. Saintsbury, *A History of Criticism and Literary Taste in Europe* (London, 1902), II, 409; cf. 211 ff; 407 ff.

[26] For discussion of the interpretation of the Middle Ages in eighteenth century historiography, see G. Falco, *La polemica sul medio evo* (Turin, 1933), I, 101 ff; L. Varga, *Das Schlagwort vom "finsteren Mittelalter,"* (Vienna, 1932), pp. 113 ff.

VOLTAIRE AND THE FRENCH RATIONALISTS

If Voltaire was not the "founder" [27] of the historiography of the Enlightenment — one may doubt if so natural a product of the eighteenth century climate of opinion can be ascribed to the initiative of any one writer — he was certainly the most articulate exponent of its historical philosophy. No other historian so nearly personified the spirit of the Age of Reason. All its leading ideas and its prejudices are to be found in his work, and one need not read between the lines to find them. His general view of the past may be accepted as the norm for rationalist historical thought. But though his stock of basic ideas was taken from the common domain of his age, his application of them to cultural history, and especially to that of the Renaissance, was often brilliantly original and led in directions that were to be followed with greater consequence a century later.

It is probably no exaggeration to say, with Lanson,[28] that Voltaire was the first historian of civilization. The *Century of Louis XIV,* (1752),[29] in which his object was to portray "l'esprit des hommes" in the most enlightened of centuries,[30] would alone be enough to establish his right to that title. But much more significant for our purpose was the *Essay on the Manners and the Spirit of Nations* (1756).[31] Here Voltaire undertook the still larger and more novel task of writing the history of civilization from the age of Charlemagne to that of Louis XIII. Despite all its faults of construction, its sins of omission, its superficial judgments, and its inadequate foundation of research, it was an epoch-making achievement, the pioneer work of modern history of civilization.

Voltaire was well aware that he was breaking with the established traditions of historiography. Indeed, it was his disgust, or that of Mme. de Châtelet, with the traditional forms of history which pro-

---

[27] Cf. Fueter, p. 350. [28] Lanson, *Voltaire,* p. 116.
[29] Voltaire, *Siècle de Louis XIV* (Berlin, 1752), *Oeuvres,* XIV–XV. Eng. trans. (Everyman's Library, New York, 1926).
[30] *Ibid.,* XIV, 155.
[31] Voltaire, *Essai sur les moeurs et l'esprit des nations, et sur les principaux faits de l'histoire, depuis Charlemagne jusqu'à Louis XIII* (Geneva, 1756), *Oeuvres,* XI–XIII. Eng. trans. in Voltaire, *Works* (New York, 1901).

vided the initial impetus to the work. The learned marquise, who wanted to read history *en philosophe*,[32] could find in the available histories of the European nations only a chaos of useless facts, mostly false, "barbarous action under barbarous names," or insipid romances: no knowledge of manners, of government, of laws, or of opinions.[33]

> She sought [said Voltaire] a history that would speak to reason; she wanted the portrayal of manners, the origins of so many contradictory customs, laws, prejudices; how so many peoples have passed one after another from refinement to barbarism, what arts were lost, what conserved, what others born in the shock of so many revolutions.[34]

No such history existed, but M. Voltaire would write one for her. In it there would be few of those wearisome details and dates for which Mme. de Châtelet felt such an understandable aversion. Small facts would enter the plan only when they produced great results. "Il faut voir les choses en grand." Again and again, Voltaire announced a revolutionary program for cultural and intellectual history: "I would discover what human society was at that time, how men lived in their family circle, what arts were cultivated." [35] And again:

> The object was the history of the human mind, and not the detail of facts which are almost always distorted; it was not important to discover, for example, to what family the Seigneur de Puiset belonged . . . but to see by what degrees man has progressed from the barbaric rusticity of those times to the refinement of ours . . . . It is, then, the history of opinions that must be written; and by that the chaos of events, of factions, of revolutions, and of crimes becomes worthy of being presented to the consideration of wise men.[36]

That his achievement fell far short of his aim was inevitable. Generations of research would be needed before his program could be carried out successfully. But as an essay in a new kind of history, it was all that Mme. de Châtelet or the philosophical world of the eighteenth century could have asked.

[32] *Ibid.*, XI, 3.
[33] Voltaire, *Remarques de l'Essai, Oeuvres,* XXIV, 543 f; cf. XI, 157 f.
[34] *Ibid.*, XXIV, 545.
[35] Voltaire, *Essai, Oeuvres,* XII, 53.
[36] Voltaire, *Remarques de l'Essai, Oeuvres,* XXIV, 547; cf. *Essai, ibid.,* XI, 157: "Le but de ce travail n'est pas de savoir en quelle année un prince indigne d'être connu succéda à un prince barbare chez une nation grossière."

Unbiased objectivity was not among the more prominent virtues of the *Essay,* but its lack was not one which the *philosophes* would either notice or greatly deplore. The Age of Reason expected philosophical history to be didactic, to interpret history so as to further the cause of reason and progress. As Voltaire put it, the purpose of history, properly conceived, was to enlighten men and to make them think. "At last," he asserted hopefully, "men will be a little enlightened by this picture of their ills and their stupidities. Society will succeed in time in rectifying its ideas: men will learn to think." [37]

The history of the Middle Ages seemed especially well designed to fulfill this purpose. The evils that the militant French rationalists were fighting in their own society were nearly all legacies from the Middle Ages. In medieval history these could be portrayed in all their pristine irrationality. That, indeed, was the chief reason for studying it. "It is necessary," said Voltaire, "to know the history of that age only in order to scorn it." [38] As Voltaire presented it, medieval history was philosophy teaching by horrible examples. One had only to report the facts, he felt, to make the Middle Ages and all that sprang from them detestable; not that he could resist the temptation to editorial comment. His diatribes against medieval religion [39] and scholastic philosophy [40] were as bitter as any that emanated from the Protestant controversialists, if based on different grounds. Viewed *en philosophe,* Antichrist became *l'Infâme.* His appraisal of medieval culture was as contemptuous as that of any of the humanists. Medieval Latin was a barbaric jargon. The rhyme of the Latin hymns was the seal of barbarism. "It was not thus that Horace sang . . . ." [41] But Voltaire, the political and social reformer, the exponent of a comfortable bourgeois philosophy of reason and material well-being, the lover of civilized manners, was also offended by other aspects of medieval civilization of which his predecessors had scarcely been aware. The political chaos

---

[37] Voltaire, *Remarques de l'Essai, Oeuvres,* XXIV, 548.
[38] Voltaire, *Essai, Oeuvres,* XII, 123.
[39] Cf., for example, *ibid.,* XII, 180.
[40] Cf. *ibid.,* XII, 61: "La théologie scolastique, fille bâtarde de la philosophie d'Aristote, mal traduite et méconnue, fit plus de tort à la raison et aux bonnes études que n'en avaient fait les Huns et les Vandales."
[41] *Ibid.,* XII, 61.

of feudalism, and the poverty, brutality, and insecurity which accompanied it occupied as prominent a place in his picture of "ces siècles grossiers" as did ignorance, superstition, and bad taste.

In contrast to the medieval darkness, the age of the Renaissance was illuminated by the first evidences of modern progress toward rational enlightenment and political and social well-being. Voltaire, it is true, did not treat it as a separate epoch, nor did he commonly use the term *renaissance* except in the traditional form of *la renaissance des lettres et des beaux arts*. But, although he left it undefined as a historical period, his treatment of the age we know as the Renaissance stressed for the first time certain essential elements in the periodic conception later formulated by Burckhardt. Voltaire saw in that age the rebirth of more than literature and the fine arts, though the perception came in fitful flashes. In one place, at least, he characterized the course of European history as that of "the extinction, the *renaissance,* and the progress of the human mind." [42]

With a reiterated insistence that seemed to foreshadow the Burckhardtian thesis, Voltaire dwelt upon the unique character and the relatively early and rapid development of Italian civilization. It was in Italy that human intelligence first began to revive. There, if anywhere prior to the Age of Louis XIV, were to be found those conditions that he regarded as essential to human happiness. Italy, he thought, began to emerge from the "grossièreté" of the Middle Ages about the end of the thirteenth or beginning of the fourteenth century. [43] Thereafter, for two centuries or more it was the exception that proved the rule of European barbarism. In the reign of Louis XI, "barbarism, superstition, ignorance covered the face of the world, except in Italy." [44] The Italians were the most ingenious people in the world. [45] As late as the sixteenth century, "the glory of genius belonged then to Italy alone, just as it had once been the property of Greece." [46]

And of all the Italian cities, Voltaire thought Florence the most truly civilized. Even in the fourteenth century, it was a new Athens. [47]

[42] Voltaire, *Remarques de l'Essai, Oeuvres,* XXIV, 548.
[43] Voltaire, *Essai, Oeuvres,* XII, 53.
[44] *Ibid.,* XII, 123.   [45] *Ibid.,* XII, 179; 180.
[46] *Ibid.,* XII, 250.   [47] *Ibid.,* XII, 61; cf. 168.

It was distinguished by commerce and the fine arts and later by the wise, just, and beneficent rule of the Medici.[48] Cosimo *Pater Patriae* and the magnificent Lorenzo seemed to Voltaire to represent the ideal of the enlightened despot, governing by peaceful means and encouraging all the higher forms of culture. In the introduction to his *Century of Louis XIV*,[49] he declared that of the four periods in human history, which could be accounted happy by a man of thought or taste, the third age was that which followed the capture of Constantinople, when the merchant house of Medici ruled Florence and welcomed the learned refugees. "It was the age of the glory of Italy." The fine arts had already taken on a new life and "everything tended toward perfection." The arts transplanted from Greece to Italy found a favorable soil and at once bore fruit. France, England, Germany, and Spain, in their turn, desired the same fruits, but either they were not imported or they degenerated too soon in these climates. "In a word, the Italians alone had everything, if you except music, which was not yet perfected, and experimental philosophy, which was equally unknown as yet everywhere, and which Galileo finally made known." [50]

This recognition of Italy's cultural priority was not, of course, entirely original. The Italian humanists had certainly suggested as much, and it had been taken for granted by nearly all later writers. But Voltaire made the contrast between the historical development of Italy and that of the rest of Europe more explicit. And he based his assertion of Italy's superiority not merely on her literary and artistic achievement, but on the broader grounds of her general enlightenment, the genius of her people, and her phenomenal commercial and industrial prosperity. More clearly than any of his predecessors, Voltaire perceived the causal relation between the wealth of Italy and her abnormally advanced civilization. While the rest of Europe was poverty-stricken and miserable, "it was not so in the fine commercial cities of Italy: there, one lived in comfort, with opulence; it was only in their bosom that one could enjoy the pleasures of life. There, wealth and freedom finally excited genius, as it had inspired courage." [51]

[48] *Ibid.*, XII, 168 ff.   [49] Voltaire, *Oeuvres*, XIV, 155 f.
[50] *Ibid.*, XIV, 156.
[51] Voltaire, *Essai, Oeuvres*, XII, 57; cf. 187, where he noted that France under Louis XII lacked only "l'industrie du commerce et la gloire des beaux-arts, qui étaient . . . le partage de l'Italie."

But there was also a darker side to Voltaire's picture of the Italian Renaissance. He was one of the first to observe the fantastic contrasts, the brilliant culture combined with moral confusion, the rampant and often criminal individualism, that were to become the distinguishing characteristics of the Italian Renaissance in nineteenth century historiography.

> Poisoning and assassination, combined with superstition, were [he declared] characteristic of the people of Italy at that time; they knew how to avenge themselves, and yet scarcely knew how to fight; one would find many poisoners and few soldiers, and such was the fate of that beautiful country since the time of the Ottos. Intelligence, superstition, atheism, masquerades, poetry, treason, devotion, poison, assassination, a few great men, an infinite number of clever and yet unfortunate scoundrels: that is what Italy was.[52]

Voltaire was familiar with the works of Machiavelli and Guicciardini, both of whom he valued highly,[53] and his conception of Renaissance society may have been colored by their pessimistic view of the contemporary scene. Echoes of Machiavelli's conviction that his fellow-countrymen were peculiarly lacking in public spirit,[54] together with his intense admiration for great men like Francesco Sforza[55] or Cesare Borgia,[56] may be found throughout the chapters of the *Essay* that deal with the Italian history of that age. Voltaire could express a fine moral indignation at the crimes of the great men of the Renaissance, especially when they were popes or the sons of popes, but the moral judgment does not lessen the impression that the period was distinguished by an unusual number of forceful, intelligent, and uninhibited individuals. "Nature at that time produced extraordinary men of all kinds, especially in Italy."[57]

The moral confusion and unrestrained passions of the Renaissance Italians Voltaire ascribed directly to their lack of religion. At first glance, this may seem a little surprising, yet it was not inconsistent

---

[52] *Ibid.*, XII, 167.   [53] *Ibid.*, XII, 246; cf. 188; 191; *et passim.*
[54] Voltaire's comments on the condottieri are especially reminiscent of Machiavelli. Cf. *ibid.*, XII, 174.
[55] Voltaire described Sforza as "bâtard d'un paysan, grand homme et fils d'un grand homme." *Ibid.*, XII, 167.
[56] Cf. *ibid.*, XII, 187 ff.   [57] *Ibid.*, XII, 218.

with his general ideas.[58] It is difficult to reconstruct a coherent interpretation of the Renaissance from his scattered comments upon it, but
the main lines are clear enough. He obviously regarded the Italians as
the most enlightened of the European peoples, thanks to their native
genius and their unusual material prosperity. And, like the Protestant
historians, he assumed that enlightenment would destroy their faith
in medieval superstition. Unlike the reformers, however, he took it for
granted that the awakening of reason would discredit not only the
dogmas peculiar to the Roman Church, but also Christianity itself. He
was quite prepared, therefore, to accept the conclusion, to which the
skeptical Bayle had given a wide circulation, that the men of the
Renaissance "had but little religion." [59] The story of the Pazzi con-
spiracy, he thought, furnished proof of the atheism that reigned in
Renaissance society. While the people adored, the influential classes
mocked: "All the history of the age demonstrates it." [60] The moral
that he drew was one that would have been impossible before the
eighteenth century. The whole tenor of the *Essay* shows that he considered the destruction of Christian "superstition" the first necessary
step in the progress of reason. That was the glorious achievement of
the Renaissance. It was only the first step, however, and being purely
destructive it was fraught with dangerous results. The men of the
Renaissance had rejected Christianity, but in doing so they had also
abandoned the "natural religion" of reason and morality. Hence the
moral chaos. "They all made this detestable argument: men have
taught me lies, therefore there is no God. Thus natural religion was
extinguished in almost all who governed at that time; and no century
was so prolific in assassinations, in poisonings, in treasons, in monstrous debauches." [61] The second essential step in the progress of
reason — the discovery of "true philosophy" — did not begin until the
end of the sixteenth century, with Galileo.[62]

Compared with his fresh interpretation of the character of Italian
society and of the general intellectual development of the Renaissance,
Voltaire's account of the revival of art and letters was conventional,
though enlivened by occasional critical prejudices that were peculiar

[58] Cf. Faguet, *Dix-huitième siècle*, pp. 214 ff.   [59] See above, p. 71.
[60] Voltaire, *Essai, Oeuvres*, XII, 169.   [61] *Ibid.*   [62] *Ibid.*, XII, 249.

to the taste of his age. His story of the artistic renaissance was in the
Vasari tradition. Cimabue, Giotto, and Brunelleschi were the great
original geniuses responsible for it.[63] He reserved his highest praise
for the Italian poets of the sixteenth century, especially Ariosto and
Tasso,[64] but followed the precedent set by the Italian historians in
ascribing the original revival of the national literature to Dante,
Petrarch, and Boccaccio.[65] In dealing with the classical revival, however, he seems to have been more influenced by the later northern
tradition, which Bayle had formulated, than by that of the Italian
humanists. He made no reference to the ancient languages in his
discussion of fourteenth century culture. Even Petrarch appeared
there only as an Italian poet, though elsewhere he included Dante and
Petrarch among those whose genius was cultivated by reading good
Roman authors.[66] In general he attributed the revival of antiquity to
the migration of the Greeks from Constantinople after 1453,[67] but, at
the same time, he made it very clear that both Italian literature and the
fine arts were the original creation of the Italians themselves.

> We owe all these fine innovations to the Tuscans. They caused every-
> thing to be reborn by their sole genius, before the small amount of
> science which remained in Constantinople had flowed into Italy with
> the Greek language, as a result of the Ottoman conquests. . . . It is
> not to the fugitives from Constantinople that the renaissance of the
> arts is due. These Greeks could teach the Italians nothing but Greek.[68]

So far as he suggested causes for the revival of culture in the Italian
Renaissance, the catastrophic event was overshadowed by "general
causes," by national characteristics, and by the genius of great men.

Voltaire's discussion of the Renaissance in France added little to the
conventional interpretation. Francis I was given credit for transplant-
ing the fine arts from Italy to France.[69] Under him France began to
emerge from barbarism. Thanks to the spirit of the king and his
court, the language became more polished, less Gothic.[70] He scarcely

---

[63] *Ibid.,* XII, 60.   [64] *Ibid.,* XII, 246 f.
[65] *Ibid.,* XII, 57 ff.   [66] *Ibid.,* XII, 181.
[67] Cf. Voltaire, *Siècle de Louis XIV, Oeuvres,* XIV, 155 f. In the *Essai* he made
the incredible statement that the barbarous style of the papal *datarie* was abolished
in favor of Ciceronian Latin under Leo X. *Ibid.,* XII, 278.
[68] *Ibid.,* XII, 60 f.   [69] *Ibid.,* XII, 217.   [70] *Ibid.,* XII, 271 f.

mentioned the revival of classical learning in the northern countries, and then only in the traditional relation to the invention of printing, on the one hand, and the revolt against Rome, on the other.[71] Voltaire did not find the unmistakably religious tone of northern humanism congenial, just as he was incapable of understanding the religious issues involved in the Reformation.[72] The causes he found for the religious revolt were petty and materialistic, quite inadequate to explain the fanatical convictions that he thought so unreasonable. On the whole, he approved the effort to reform abuses in the Church and to break the power of the pope, the clergy, and the monks, but he deplored the intolerance and the religious wars which followed. "These quarrels," he said disgustedly, "were but one more malady of the human mind."[73]

Despite the wars of religion, however, Voltaire regarded the sixteenth century as a great age for Europe. The brilliant chapter entitled, "General Idea of the Sixteenth Century,"[74] brief and badly organized though it is, might have been written by Michelet. This century, he noted, saw the discovery of a new world and new trade routes to the Indies. It was an age of opulence, of growing industry and commerce. "Europe saw the birth of good times." It was also an age of great men and of rapidly advancing culture. The genius which had caused the fine arts to flourish in Italy and from there had spread them abroad in Europe softened the manners of men everywhere. The gallantry of the court of Francis I gave to this age a grandeur and *politesse* hitherto unknown. But, as in Italy, it was also an age of crime and violence. "This courtesy glittered in the midst of crime; it was a robe of gold and silk covered with blood."[75]

Eighteenth century France produced no other historian comparable to Voltaire. The *Essay on Manners* remained a unique achievement. The major conceptions of the course of human history incorporated

---

[71] *Ibid.,* XII, 282; cf. 276 n.

[72] Voltaire's definition of the three principal theories of the Eucharist is a masterpiece of epigrammatic blasphemy, but shows no profound understanding: "Ainsi, tandis que ceux qu'on appelait papistes manageaient Dieu sans pain, les luthériens mangeaient du pain et Dieu. Les calvinistes vinrent bientôt après, qui mangèrent le pain, et qui ne mangèrent point Dieu." *Ibid.,* XII, 286.

[73] *Ibid.,* XII, 249; cf. 284.   [74] *Ibid.,* XII, 217–19.   [75] *Ibid.,* XII, 219.

in it, however, became the common property of enlightened society. They were echoed again and again by the *philosophes*,[76] and were finally restated with passionate conviction in Condorcet's *Outline of a Historical Survey of the Progress of the Human Mind* (1793).[77] Writing under the shadow of the guillotine, the last of the Encyclopedists here proclaimed his unshaken faith in reason and human progress, and sketched a universal history that would furnish the proofs. If Voltaire's *Essay* inaugurated the cultural history of the Age of Reason, the *Outline* was its last will and testament. It is worth considering as the most unqualified interpretation of history in the light of the doctrine of reason and natural law and of the theory of progress.

Basing his theory explicitly on Locke's psychology,[78] Condorcet assumed that social progress depends on the progress of knowledge.[79] The latter thus formed the central theme and motive force of human history. He therefore adopted, in place of the old systems of periodization, a new division of history into ten ages, each corresponding to a new stage in the progress of knowledge. The tenth age, like the chiliastic seventh age of the theologians, lay in the future. For our purpose the most interesting are the seventh and eighth ages, entitled respectively, "From the First Progress of the Sciences after their Restoration in the West to the Invention of Printing," and "From the Invention of Printing to the Time when the Sciences and Philosophy threw off the Yoke of Authority." The former period began about the time of the Crusades. It had been preceded by a disastrous epoch of complete darkness, in which "Europe, crushed between sacerdotal tyranny and military despotism, awaited in blood and tears the moment when a new enlightenment would permit her to be reborn to freedom, to humanity, and to virtue."[80] The causes Condorcet found for this rebirth are interesting.[81] Reaction against ecclesiastical authority and abuses aroused a new spirit of free enquiry among heretics

---

[76] See for example, Chastellux, *De la félicité publique; ou considérations sur le sort des hommes dans les différents époques de l'histoire* (Amsterdam, 1772).

[77] Condorcet, *Esquisse d'un tableau historique des progrès de l'esprit humain* (1793; new ed. Paris, 1933). Eng. trans. (London, 1795).

[78] *Ibid.*, p. 1 ff.   [79] Cf. Bury, *Idea of Progress*, p. 209.

[80] Condorcet, *Esquisse*, p. 90.   [81] *Ibid.*, pp. 104 ff.

like those of southern France and skeptics like Frederick II. Kings and
their lawyers began to combat the Church and the nobles and to
revive Roman law. The Crusades brought the people of the West into
contact with Moslem science and religion. Republics were founded in
Italy and free cities elsewhere. Commerce increased and new industries were introduced. Gunpowder and the mariner's compass were
invented with momentous results. In Italy the language was very
nearly perfected in the fourteenth century. The classics were studied
and the example of ancient monuments began to revive artistic genius.
This period was a kind of pre-Renaissance, though Condorcet did not
call it that. "It was the general character of this period to have disposed the human mind for the revolution that the discovery of printing was to bring." [82]

The importance Condorcet attached to the invention of printing is
curiously reminiscent of John Foxe, who had stated with equal vigor
at least half of Condorcet's thesis that printing was the enemy that had
unmasked and dethroned priests and kings.[83] The revolutionary rationalist was also at one with the Protestant martyrologist in his belief that
the coincidental revival of learning was a further factor in destroying
the enemies of truth. The epoch-making effect of printing, Condorcet
noted, was reinforced by two events which coincided closely with it:
the capture of Constantinople and the discoveries of a new world and
a new route to the East. As a result of the former, which drove Greek
scholars in flight to Italy, there came a new, more critical interest in
philosophy, geometry, and physics, "and the anti-Christian opinions
of the philosophers reawakened the almost extinct ideas of the ancient
rights of human reason." [84] Condorcet shared Voltaire's belief in the
irreligious character of Renaissance learning without his doubts about
its moral effect. Among the happy consequences of the geographical
discoveries, Condorcet included the vast increase in knowledge of the
earth and its inhabitants, and the growth of commerce, which stimulated industry and, "as a necessary consequence," all the sciences and
arts.[85] The age thus happily inaugurated witnessed also the qualified
blessing of the Reformation. The religious revolt aroused Europe

82 *Ibid.*, p. 115.   83 *Ibid.*, p. 116; cf. above, p. 54 f.
84 Condorcet, *Esquisse*, p. 121.   85 *Ibid.*, p. 122 f.

from the shameful sleep of superstition and, despite the intolerance of the Protestant sects, opened the road to greater freedom of thought. All through the sixteenth century science made rapid progress, while everywhere reason and authority struggled for domination.[86] The transition to the following period, that of the triumph of reason, was marked by three great men, Bacon, Galileo, and Descartes.[87]

The *Outline,* eloquent though it was, was no more than a prospectus of a world history which Condorcet did not live to write, and probably could not have written in any case. But the very fact that it was stripped of detail, free from the curse of the stubborn fact and the contrary instance, lent its thesis a clarity and convincing force that few more scholarly works have possessed.

THE ENGLISH RATIONALISTS

The character of the Enlightenment in England differed in one significant respect from the French. It was not revolutionary in its attitude toward contemporary social and political, or even ecclesiastical, institutions. The upper and middle classes in England were well satisfied with their government. It guaranteed them all the personal and civil rights, the intellectual and religious freedom, and the political representation they desired. Their complacent assurance of progress thus covered the political as well as the intellectual sphere.[88] As a result, English historiography lacked the violently polemical tone of Voltaire and Condorcet. It was an instrument of instruction rather than a political weapon. In almost every other respect, however, the English historians of the Age of Reason shared the interests, prepossessions, and historical philosophy of their French contemporaries. The doctrines of the Enlightenment determined their point of view and lent coherence to their interpretation of history. But, perhaps because their didactic purpose, though strong, was directed more toward general instruction and entertainment than toward revolutionary pro-

[86] *Ibid.,* p. 137.   [87] *Ibid.,* p. 143.
[88] Cf. D. Hume, *History of England from the Invasion of Julius Caesar to the Revolution in 1688* (1763; I use ed. London, 1864), II, 372. Hume thought that the English "have happily established the most perfect and most accurate system of liberty that ever was found compatible with government."

paganda, Hume, Robertson, and Gibbon laid greater stress on research and wrote, on the whole, sounder history than did the French publicists.

No amount of research, however, could alter the contempt and aversion with which the men of the philosophical century regarded the Middle Ages. For the English historians, as for Voltaire, the period between the fall of the Roman Empire in the West and the beginning of modern times was an age of ignorance, superstition, barbarism, and lawless brutality. With the exception of Gibbon, whose imagination was caught by the grandeur of the theme of Rome's decline and fall — "the greatest, perhaps, and most awful scene in the history of mankind" [89] — they thought the history of the Middle Ages scarcely worth bothering about in detail, save as patriotic sentiment might justify some interest in the past of one's own country.[90] The contemplation of these barbarous centuries could, they felt, be neither entertaining [91] to civilized people nor useful, and usefulness in the eighteenth century was a prime requisite of historical study. A great revolution in the political, intellectual, and religious life of Western Europe, at about the end of the fifteenth century, divided medieval from modern times. Prior to that revolution the conditions of public and private life were so different from those with which the modern reader was acquainted that he could draw from the study of the earlier age few lessons of other than negative value.[92]

This theory was first stated by Bolingbroke in his popular *Letters on the Study of History* (1735). Bolingbroke's knowledge of history was never more than superficial; his thought was disorganized and seldom profound; [93] but he possessed the gift, much prized in the eighteenth century, of being able to give clear and facile expression to

[89] E. Gibbon, *The History of the Decline and Fall of the Roman Empire* (London 1776–88; I use ed. J. B. Bury, New York, 1914), VII, 338.

[90] Cf. W. Robertson, *View of the Progress of Society in Europe* (London, 1769), *Works* (London, 1840), III, v.

[91] Cf. Hume, *History of England*, I, 1.

[92] Cf. *ibid.*, II, 372. Referring to the Middle Ages, Hume said that for English people "an acquaintance with the ancient periods of their government is chiefly useful by instructing them to cherish their present constitution from a comparison or contrast with those distant times."

[93] Cf. Leslie Stephen, *History of English Thought in the Eighteenth Century* (New York, 1876), II, 173 ff.

current trends of thought. As a philosopher, he recognized that the experience of men in all ages might furnish data for ethical and philosophical instruction, though even for this purpose the modern ages were most fruitful.[94] But as a man whose major interests had always been politics and diplomacy, he was inclined to deny any utility to history prior to the end of the fifteenth century. At about that time, he argued, there had occurred such great changes in "the manners, customs, and interests" of the European nations and in "the whole policy, ecclesiastical and civil, of these parts of the world" that the chain of causation with the past was broken. Hence, the history of the preceding ages was largely devoid of interest to the modern citizen or statesman.

> To be entirely ignorant about the ages that precede this aera would be shameful. Nay some indulgence may be had to a temperate curiosity in the review of them. But to be learned about them is a ridiculous affectation in any man who means to be useful to the present age. Down to this aera let us read history: from this aera, and down to our own time, let us study it.[95]

Hume's argument was surprisingly similar. The end of the fifteenth century — the reign of Henry VII — marked the close of one epoch and the beginning of another. The "series of many barbarous ages" then gave way to "the dawn of civility and science."[96] At about that time the growth of strong government together with civil and personal liberties, growing prosperity, "luxury and refinement," inventions and geographical discoveries, the revival of learning, and the Reformation made a "general revolution" in human affairs, so that

> men gradually attained that situation with regard to commerce, arts, science, government, police, and cultivation, in which they have ever since persevered. Here, therefore, commences the useful as well as the more agreeable part of modern annals. . . . Whoever carries his anxious researches into preceding periods is moved by a curiosity, liberal indeed and commendable; not by any necessity for acquiring knowledge of public affairs, or the arts of civil government.[97]

Hume the empirical philosopher, who thought the chief use of history was "only to discover the constant and universal principles of human

---

[94] Bolingbroke, *Letters on the Study of History, Works*, II, 316 f.
[95] *Ibid.*, II, 343.   [96] Hume, *History of England*, II, 365.
[97] *Ibid.*, II, 447 ff; cf. 369 ff.

nature,"[98] and Hume the historian, whose aim was to instruct and entertain the British public, never parted company. Their collaboration is evident on every page of the *History of England*. But they got along together more congenially after they had passed the Middle Ages and had reached the "dawn of civility and science."

William Robertson was equally positive about the relative utility of medieval and modern history. The Voltairian Scots minister had done much more research than either Bolingbroke or Hume into the history of Europe during the Middle Ages. Nevertheless, he thought that a "general knowledge" of the period before the reign of Charles V, that is, before "the political state of Europe began to assume a new form," was all that was useful either for "those who are called to conduct the affairs of nations" or for "such as enquire and reason concerning them."[99] Robertson's chief interest in modern history was concentrated on the state system which, since the sixteenth century, had maintained a balance of power in Europe. And when he turned to medieval history, as he did in the *View of the Progress of Society in Europe from the Subversion of the Roman Empire to the Beginning of the Sixteenth Century* (1769), which served as an introductory volume to his *History of the Reign of Charles V*, it was merely to trace in general outline "the great causes and events" that had made this state system possible and that had brought "order, regularity, and refinement" out of "confusion and barbarism."[100] Beginning with the Crusades, to which he attached a cataclysmic importance, and the rise of the cities, the significance of which he appreciated even more fully than Voltaire had done, Robertson here sketched the first systematic study of the dynamic elements in medieval civilization. Yet, despite the signs of progress he observed, the Middle Ages remained for him dark and confused until the dawn of the modern age with the reign of Charles V.

These historians obviously regarded the period that has since been called the Renaissance as one of revolutionary change in the condition of Western Europe, and they greatly enriched the conception of the nature and extent of that change by adding a new emphasis to the

[98] See above, p. 84.   [99] Robertson, *Works*, III, v f.
[100] *Ibid.*, III, vi; 20.

political and, in lesser degree, the economic and social factors involved in it. In a word, it was at the end of the fifteenth century or beginning of the sixteenth that the Middle Ages ended and the modern era began. And, given the eighteenth century view of medieval civilization, nothing could be much more revolutionary than that. Despite its epoch-making significance, however, they made little attempt to isolate the transitional age or to characterize it by itself. One misses in the sober English historians those flashes of imaginative insight that added freshness and originality to Voltaire's depiction of Renaissance society. When they took cognizance of the intellectual changes of the age, they either spoke vaguely of a growing "refinement" or repeated the conventional account of the revival of learning, with the characteristic rationalist implication that the rediscovery of the classics encouraged the development of reason and hence tended to unmask the superstitions of medieval religion.

Bolingbroke's comments on the literary renaissance would scarcely be worth noting were they not so typical of the current trend of historical interpretation. Mentioning the "resurrection of letters" among the circumstances that had aided the success of the Reformation, he ascribed its progress to the newly discovered art of printing and its origins to the fall of Constantinople. In Italy the newly imported learning had been encouraged by the misguided policy of the popes, who thereby destroyed their own power.

> The magicians themselves broke the charm by which they had bound mankind for so many ages . . . . As soon as the means of acquiring and spreading information grew common, it is no wonder that a system was unravelled, which could not have been woven with success in any ages, but those of gross ignorance and credulous superstition.[101]

One might have expected something more profound from the learned and philosophical Hume, but his few comments on the intellectual history of the Middle Ages and the Renaissance are meagre and conventional. In a brief retrospect at the end of the chapter on the reign of Richard III,[102] he summarized the decline of Roman culture,

[101] Bolingbroke, *Works,* II, 345 f.
[102] Hume, *History of England,* II, 366 f.

laying the original blame, in the manner of Leonardo Bruni, on the despotism of the emperors. The decline continued until the eleventh century, at which time "the people of Christendom were the lowest sunk in ignorance, and consequently in disorders of every kind." Thereafter "the sun of science, beginning to reascend, threw out many gleams of light, which preceded the full morning, when letters were revived in the fifteenth century." For this upward movement no cause is suggested save that "there is a point of depression, as well as of exaltation, from which human affairs naturally return in a contrary direction." He returned to the revival of learning again in the chapter on Henry VII as a part of the general revolution that distinguished that age.[103] Here he ascribed the recovery of Greek learning directly to the flight of the refugees from Constantinople in 1453, and added that "about the same time, the purity of the Latin tongue was revived, the study of antiquity became fashionable, and the esteem for literature gradually propagated itself throughout every nation of Europe." In this instance the only cause suggested is the catastrophic event. Later he suggested that familiarity with ancient literature made Leo X aware of "the ridicule and falsity of the doctrines, which, as supreme pontiff, he was obliged by his interest to promote," [104] and finally he completed the Protestant-rationalist picture by including the revival of learning, with printing, among the reasons for the success of the Reformation.[105]

Robertson was oddly silent about the classical renaissance in his *View of the Progress of Society*. Perhaps he did not consider it a medieval phenomenon. He did note the "progress of science and literature" in the twelfth and thirteenth centuries, however, with some astute comments on the influence of the growing commerce, public order, and personal security.[106] While deploring its deviation into the sterile and restricted paths of scholasticism, he included it among "the great causes which contributed to introduce a change of manners into Europe." When he finally mentioned the humanist revival, in the *History of Charles V*,[107] as one of the causes of the Reformation, he made no similar suggestion concerning the influences that had brought

---

[103] *Ibid.*, II, 448 f.   [104] *Ibid.*, II, 503.   [105] *Ibid.*, II, 506.
[106] Robertson, *Works*, III, 68 ff.   [107] *Ibid.*, IV, 50 ff.

it about. As was natural for a Presbyterian minister, Robertson was more sympathic toward the Reformation than were the other rationalist historians. His account of the relation of Reuchlin, Hutten, and Erasmus to the Lutheran Reform is in the old Protestant tradition. At the same time, his emphasis on "the bold spirit of enquiry which the revival of learning excited in Europe" is in close accord with the tendency of the Enlightenment to correlate the recovery of the classics with a general awakening of human intelligence and reason. There is a touch of Voltaire's "renaissance de l'esprit humain" in Robertson's observation: "Mankind seem, at that period, to have recovered the powers of enquiring and of thinking for themselves, faculties of which they had long lost the use; and fond of the acquisition, they exercised them with great boldness upon all subjects." [108]

Both Hume and Robertson were widely read for generations. In lasting influence, however, their work cannot compare with Gibbon's masterly *Decline and Fall of the Roman Empire* (1776–88). Edward Gibbon, too, was a child of the Enlightenment. The philosophy of the age furnished the basis of his historical thought, but it did not dominate his work as it did that of Voltaire and Hume. He shared the faith of his century in human progress,[109] but the theme of his history, the disintegration of Roman civilization, tended to emphasize the decay of the ancient rather than progress toward the modern. The perspective from which he viewed the Middle Ages was thus the reverse of Robertson's, and from that point of view they appeared, if possible, more dark and barbarous. The one indication of approaching dawn upon which he dwelt at any length in the concluding chapters of the *Decline* was the revival of classical learning. This was a natural corollary of the love for antique culture that had led him to undertake the history of Rome from the great age of the Empire. In his treatment of Renaissance culture the classicist took precedence over the rationalist, though with Gibbon, as with all the men of the Enlightenment, there was no possible quarrel between the two.

Gibbon's account of the revival of learning was a return to the humanist tradition in content as well as in emphasis. In the youthful *Essay on the Study of Literature* (1761), he had accepted the catastro-

108 *Ibid.,* IV, 50.   109 Cf. Black, *Art of History,* p. 173.

phic theory which ascribed the revival of learning in the West to the fall of Constantinople,[110] but when he reached the final volume of the *Decline* he was better informed. He had become more familiar with Italian humanist literature, and had read Humphrey Hody's *Famous Greeks* (1742) [111] and Tiraboschi's *History of Italian Literature* (1772–82).[112] The former work had been available to the earlier eighteenth century historians. Had they read it, it would have changed their conception of the classical renaissance. It was a very learned work, if more than ordinarily uninspired, and may claim to be the first systematic modern history of the revival of Greek in the West. Hody made it abundantly clear that the recovery of Greek in Italy was well advanced before the fall of Constantinople. He hailed the fourteenth century as the happy century in which polite letters began to be reborn in Italy,[113] and devoted more than half of his book to the period prior to 1453, beginning his account with Boccaccio's teacher, Leontius Pilatus, and Chrysoloras.

Following Hody, Gibbon laid the major stress in his sketch of the humanist movement on the introduction of Greek into Italy from the time of Boccaccio.[114] At the same time, he was careful to note that the revival of classical Latin preceded the importation of ancient Greek and that it was the zeal of the Italians themselves which was primarily responsible for the latter development. The Greeks could do no more than transmit what they had preserved. Their services would have accomplished nothing had not the Italians been so eager to seize every opportunity of learning from them. Greek society was "stationary or retrograde." The Western peoples, on the other hand, were now actively progressive, thanks to the acquisition of political independence and emancipation from feudal servitude, for "freedom is the first step to curiosity and knowledge." Latin of a sort had been preserved "by superstition" throughout the Middle Ages, and there were thousands of students in the universities whose "misguided ardour might be directed to more liberal and manly studies." All that was needed was

---

[110] Gibbon, *Miscellaneous Works*, IV, 17.

[111] H. Hody, *De Graecis illustribus linguae graecae literarumque humaniorum instauratoribus, eorum vitis, scriptis, et elogiis, libri duo* (London, 1742).

[112] See below, pp. 110 ff.   [113] Hody, p. 1.

[114] Gibbon, *Decline*, VII, 119–37.

the study and imitation of the ancient Roman writers. From Cicero and Virgil, they would be led to their Greek masters. And in this "resurrection of science, Italy was the first that cast away her shroud; and the eloquent Petrarch, by his lessons and his example, may justly be applauded as the first harbinger of day." [115] Among the patrons of the classical renaissance, Gibbon extolled Nicholas V, though with an approving note to Bolingbroke's comment on the misguided policy of a pope who favored learning. His most enthusiastic praise, however, was reserved for the Medici, "whose name and age are almost synonymous with the restoration of learning." [116]

Gibbon's feeling for the value of the classics and his conviction of the epoch-making importance of their restoration was in full accord with the humanist point of view. But a longer historical perspective, together with the eighteenth century tendency to identify antiquity with reason and the rediscovery of antiquity with progress, enabled him to state the significance of the classical renaissance in the history of European intellectual progress as the humanists could not have done. While recognizing the unfortunate effects of servile imitation and deploring the temporary abandonment of the vernacular, Gibbon considered the recovery of the ancient literatures a necessary stage in the "education" of the Western peoples. His concluding remarks summarized the classical-rationalist interpretation of the Renaissance with the ponderous authority that only Gibbon could achieve:

> Before the revival of classic literature, the barbarians in Europe were immersed in ignorance; and their vulgar tongues were marked with the rudeness and poverty of their manners. The students of the more perfect idioms of Rome and Greece were introduced to a new world of light and science; to the society of the free and polished nations of antiquity; and to a familiar intercourse with those immortal men who spoke the sublime language of eloquence and reason . . . . As soon as it had been deeply saturated with the celestial dew, the soil was quickened into vegetation and life; the modern idioms were refined; the classics of Athens and Rome inspired a pure taste

---

[115] *Ibid.,* VII, 122.

[116] *Ibid.,* VII, 134; cf. J. Murray, ed., *The Autobiographies of Edward Gibbon* (London, 1897), p. 197. Gibbon had at one time contemplated writing a history of Florence under the Medici.

and a generous emulation; and in Italy, as afterwards in France and England, the pleasing reign of poetry and fiction was succeeded by the light of speculative and experimental philosophy.[117]

THE GERMAN RATIONALISTS

The *Aufklärung* in Germany was largely a reflection, in the field of historiography a not very brilliant reflection, of the Enlightenment in France and England. A century after the Thirty Years' War German scholars were still conscious of cultural inferiority and were therefore peculiarly open to foreign influences. Throughout the middle of the eighteenth century German historians borrowed their ideas from the French and English rationalists. They were particularly indebted to Voltaire, though unfortunately not for their style. Most of them were pedagogues, primarily interested in supplying students with historical texts in harmony with the views of the Enlightenment.[118] It is not surprising then that they offer little that is new or interesting for the interpretation of the Renaissance.

The German historians of the mid-eighteenth century had been prepared by a long Protestant tradition to accept the rationalist picture of medieval darkness and the subsequent revival of learning. The Protestant tradition now drifted over into the Voltairian hatred of medieval ecclesiasticism, scholastic philosophy, and feudal anarchy without perceptible change, save as a philosophical tone replaced the theological and the conception of social misery and political insecurity took its place beside that of spiritual and intellectual degradation. They had also been prepared to accept the eighteenth century condemnation of the literary and artistic forms of the Middle Ages by an unbroken tradition of classical education, to which Protestantism had added a note of moral indignation. An exception to the classical-Protestant view, if of minor importance, may be found in the essay, *Concerning the Supposed Barbarism of the Middle Ages especially in Latin Poetry* (1719) [119] of Polykarp Leyser. But that this was the exception that proved the rule is indicated by the storm of opposition

---

[117] Gibbon, *Decline*, VII, 135 í.   [118] Cf. Fueter, p. 371.
[119] Polykarp Leyser, *De ficta medii aevi barbarie inprimis circa poesim Latinam* (Helmstedt, 1719). See also his *Historia poetarum medii aevi* (1721).

it aroused among his contemporaries, who regarded his defense of
medieval Latin poetry as a "monstrosa opinio."[120] A generation later
the humanist and Protestant strains had merged with the rationalist
in J. J. Brucker's massive *Critical History of Philosophy* (1742–57),[121]
which for our purpose is significant only because it applied the scheme
of medieval decline and the later revival specifically to the history of
philosophy. Brucker denied to scholasticism any true spirit of philosophy, regarding it as merely an instrument of papal tyranny,[122] and saw
the first faint dawn of modern philosophy in the fourteenth century
revival of learning.[123] The Greeks who introduced Plato and the
genuine Aristotle to Italy in the fifteenth century gave a further
stimulus to the rebirth of philosophy, and finally the Protestant Reformation by freeing both religion and philosophy from the yoke of
ecclesiasticism, cleared the way for the full growth which began with
Francis Bacon.[124]

Universal history had long been a favorite theme with Protestant
historians, so that here, too, the transition to philosophical considerations of world history on the model of Voltaire's *Essay on Manners*
was an easy one. One example of this type may suffice: Isaak Iselin's
On the History of Humanity (1764).[125] Iselin was the complete historian *en philosophe,* a "friend of humanity," inspired by faith in the
progress of mankind and seeking in history the proofs of his faith.
Ignoring the externals of political history, he concentrated his attention
on the general character of the successive ages. He had no patience
with Rousseau's cult of the noble savage and had some very positive
things to say about the barbarous stages in human development, including the medieval. Like Voltaire, he saw in the Middle Ages little
more than lawless despotism, crudity, and ignorance, with a low state
of morals maintained by superstition and superstition maintained by
the self-seeking policy of the clergy.[126] The nobles were as bad as

---

120 J. F. Bertram, *De vera medii aevi barbarie* (1722), in his *Meletemata
literaria* (Brunswick, 1731); cf. P. Lehmann, *Aufgaben und Anregungen der
lateinischen Philologie des Mittelalters* (Munich, 1918), p. 3 f.
121 J. J. Brucker, *Historia critica philosophiae,* 6 vols. (Leipzig, 1742–57; I use
2nd ed. Leipzig, 1766–68).
122 *Ibid.,* IV, 3 ff.   123 *Ibid.,* IV, 77 ff.   124 *Ibid.,* V, 3 ff.
125 I. Iselin, *Über die Geschichte der Menschheit* (1764; I use 2nd ed. 2 vols.,
Zurich, 1768).   126 *Ibid.,* II, 265 ff.

their dependents, for they hated city life, without which neither taste nor social intercourse could be improved.[127] The founding of cities and the beginnings of municipal freedom in the twelfth and thirteenth centuries marked for Iselin the first faint signs of progress. In this movement Italy led the way, her cities attracting both noble and servile classes from the land and offering them richer opportunities for the expression of every virtue, talent, or taste.[128] Progress was endlessly slow, however, until the invention of printing and the flight of the Greek refugees from Constantinople opened a new era.[129] Even then the ancient literature was not fully absorbed, but was merely collected, edited, and purified. The taste for true beauty was first revived in the golden days of Pope Leo X, when poetry, painting, and sculpture rose all at once to a wonderful fulfillment. For this, Europe had Leo X and the Medici to thank. It was through this merchant family that Italy was raised to heights equal to Greece in the age of Pericles and more lofty than ancient Rome had reached in her greatest age.[130]

During the last half of the eighteenth century there were increasing evidences in Germany, as in England, of a radical change in historical thought, in aesthetic values, and in the general *Weltanschauung*. But these early signs of an intellectual revolution were more in harmony with the dominant tone of the early nineteenth century than with that of the eighteenth and may profitably be left for consideration in the two following chapters.

THE HUMANIST TRADITION CONTINUED IN ITALY

The Italian historians of the eighteenth century were in general less influenced by the thought of the Enlightenment than were their Northern neighbors, and their view of the past was untouched by Protestant prejudice. But though they lacked the rationalist and Protestant motives for abhorring the Middle Ages, they were far from the positive evaluation of medieval culture that came later with the Romantic movement. The humanist tradition still ran strongly

[127] *Ibid.*, II, 284.
[129] *Ibid.*, II, 307 ff.

[128] *Ibid.*, II, 297 ff.
[130] *Ibid.*, II, 313.

through Italian learning and determined many of its value judgments, if not its historical methods. For the latter, the most decisive influence in this period was the example of learned research and compilation set by the industrious Benedictines of St. Maure. In contrast to the *philosophes,* these pious and indefatigable French scholars had made the critical examination and publication of sources and the annalistic recording of facts their chief concern, with small concession to the demands of literary presentation or synthesis.[131] Thanks to their example, the two most important works produced in Italy in the eighteenth century were monuments of scholarship, and are still valuable. Muratori's *Annals of Italy* (1744–49)[132] was an adaptation of the method of Mabillon to secular political history, and Tiraboschi consciously modelled his massive *History of Italian Literature* (1772–82)[133] on the Benedictine *Literary History of France* (1733 ff.), founded by Rivet de la Grange. Both works were landmarks in Italian historiography, but only the latter demands attention in a history of the interpretation of the Renaissance.

In Girolamo Tiraboschi, the learned librarian of Modena, the traditions of early Italian humanism and the later Catholic erudition met without apparent conflict. His great contribution was the accumulation and critical examination of a vast amount of material on the history of Italian culture, including every branch of literature and learning, whether in Latin or the *volgare,* together with a running commentary on the history of the fine arts and periodic resumés of the political state of Italy and its effects on the progress of letters. If in the end the work remained less a cultural history than a mine of information in which the reader is forced to do his own mining, the fault was inherent in the erudite method rather than in any narrowness of interest. Nevertheless, Tiraboschi did occasionally permit himself the luxury of an interpretive opinion, and it is in these that the

[131] Cf. Fueter, p. 308 ff.
[132] L. Muratori, *Annali d'Italia del principio dell'era volgare sino all'anno 1749,* 12 vols. (Venice, 1744–49). He also published the great collection of *Rerum italicarum scriptores ab anno Chr. 500–1500,* 25 vols. (Milan, 1723–51).
[133] G. Tiraboschi, *Storia della letteratura italiana,* 11 vols. (Modena, 1772–82; I use ed. Rome, 1782 ff).

humanist point of view emerges clearly, particularly in that part of the work devoted to letters and learning in what he called "the fortunate centuries of their *risorgimento*." [134]

Like his humanist predecessors, Tiraboschi was a patriot in the peculiarly Italian manner. He was proud of his country's primacy in the growth of European culture. "There is not a single impartial or sincere writer" he boasted, "who does not willingly concede to Italy the glorious name of mother and nurse of learning and the fine arts." [135] The glory of Italy runs as a constant theme through the whole work, but, at the same time, the characteristic local patriotism of the Italian appears in his grudging attitude toward the Tuscan masters. [136] Tiraboschi was still closer to the humanist tradition, however, in his conception of the whole course of European intellectual history and in his acceptance of classical standards in literature. He saw a disastrous decline in letters and learning with the decline of the Roman Empire, a slight revival in the age of Charlemagne, but little real improvement until the Peace of Constance (1183), which marked the achievement of Italian freedom. [137] Thereafter he gave the most important place among the causes for the progress of culture to the cities and princes. The thirteenth century marked a decided, if slow, advance in learning, letters, and the fine arts despite civil turmoil and, indeed, largely because of the emulation and rivalry of cities and princes. [138] In the fourteenth century progress was greatly accelerated by the collection and study of ancient manuscripts. [139] It was in this century, "when *belle lettere* and learning in Italy had turned after so many centuries from the squalor in which they had lain so long," that Greek was first "recalled to life and made familiar to the learned." [140] Tiraboschi gave due weight to the revival of Italian poetry in the fourteenth century, but it was the restoration of the ancient forms that aroused his greatest enthusiasm. He hailed Petrarch as the restorer and father of Italian literature, but in the list of his achievements the humanist and patriot was given precedence over the Italian poet. Indeed, Tiraboschi insisted that Petrarch would still

[134] *Ibid.*, I, ix.   [135] *Ibid.*   [136] Cf. *ibid.*, IV, 433.
[137] Cf. *ibid.*, III, 247 ff.
[138] *Ibid.*, IV, 424 ff. On the service of princes to letters, cf. IV, 13 ff.
[139] *Ibid.*, V, 82 ff.   [140] *Ibid.*, V, 391.

have been one of the greatest Italians if he had never written a word in the *volgare*.[141]

The clearest statement of Tiraboschi's conception of the classical renaissance appears in his eloquent preface to the volume dealing with the fifteenth century.[142] It is in the pure humanist tradition, with the addition of a longer historical perspective than the men of the *Quattrocento* themselves could have possessed. The fifteenth century, he declared, was "the most glorious in the history of Italian literature." The sixteenth century produced more learned and eloquent writers, but that new Augustan age owed its glory to the work of the preceding century. During the fourteenth century, he continued, Italy had already been rescued in large part from her former crudity (*oridezza*) and was filled with enthusiasm to complete the task. Then, with the beginning of the fifteenth century "the whole of Italy turned ardently to the restoration of learning and to recalling the fine arts from their long exile." They hunted codices in every corner; made long and dangerous voyages to find them; and corrected and copied them. The cities summoned famous Greek teachers at public expense. Soon there was scarcely a learned man who did not know Greek. Scholars formed academies, held erudite meetings, propagated literary combats, collected medals, diplomas, inscriptions, and statues, and "everything breathed antiquity and erudition." New light was thrown on all the sciences. Princes, ministers, generals, magistrates, and nobles cultivated or patronized learning. Every court welcomed learned men. And "in the meantime the fine arts, painting, sculpture, and architecture rose again to new life and returned at last to their ancient perfection." It was indeed a glorious century, Tiraboschi concluded, "in which so many great men seemed to conspire together .... to disperse the darkness from everything, to restore Italy to the splendor and fame of the first centuries, and to make her the marvel of the whole world."

141 *Ibid.*, V, 443.   142 *Ibid.*, VI, iii ff.

CHAPTER FIVE

The Romantic Reaction

THE AGE OF ROMANTICISM brought a major revolution in the inter-pretation of both the Middle Ages and the Renaissance. It was natural that this should be so. For Romanticism, to use the term in its most gen-eral historical sense, was itself an intellectual revolution which left its mark on every aspect of European culture, and nowhere more signifi-cantly than on the writing and interpretation of history.[1] It was "a com-prehensive reaction against the eighteenth century," [2] but by no means in an entirely negative sense. Romanticism implied also the positive affirmation of human qualities and of emotional and aesthetic values that had been neglected by the Age of Reason. The Romantic his-

[1] The terms "Romantic" and "Romanticism" have been so variously used and misused that they have become almost meaningless. Cf. A. O. Lovejoy, "The Meaning of Romanticism for the Historian of Ideas," *Journal of the History of Ideas*, II (1941), 257–78. But though Romanticism may be impossible to define, as Lovejoy argues, because there is no single idea or coherent system of ideas shared by all those who are commonly denoted as Romantic, there was, neverthe-less, a fund of more or less interrelated ideas which were widely held in the half century c. 1780–c.1830 and were strongly opposed to those most commonly held during the preceding century. These ideas and the period of which they are characteristic are commonly referred to as Romantic, and there is no other generally accepted term for them. It is in this sense, as applied to a specific historical phenomenon, that the term "Romanticism" is used here. For general studies of the historiography of the Romantic age, see E. Fueter, *Geschichte der neueren Historiographie* (Munich, 1936), pp. 415 ff; G. P. Gooch, *History and Historians in the Nineteenth Century* (London, 1935); G. von Below, *Die deutsche Geschichtschreibung von den Befreiungskriegen bis zu unsern Tagen* (Munich, 1924), pp. 4 ff; T. P. Peardon, *The Transition in English Historical Writing, 1760–1830* (New York, 1933); R. Flint, *History of the Philosophy of History* (Edinburgh, 1893), I, 340 ff; L. Halphen, *L'histoire en France depuis cent ans* (Paris, 1914); J. W. Thompson, *A History of Historical Writing* (New York, 1942), II, 132 ff.

[2] Von Below, p. 6.

torians reversed the value judgments of their predecessors. At the same time, they created a new philosophy of history and recalled the past to life with a pious enthusiasm hitherto unknown. Few of the great historians of the "historical century" were doctrinaire Romanticists, but still fewer were untouched by Romantic ideas.

THE HISTORICAL PHILOSOPHY OF ROMANTICISM

The Romantic movement and the historical philosophy that grew out of it were the products of too many diverse tendencies, emotional, literary, artistic, philosophical, political, to be safely characterized in the limited space at our disposal. Yet any discussion of the Romantic influence upon Renaissance historiography would be dangerously unstable without such a foundation. There seems no alternative, therefore, but to risk the certain dangers of over-simplification, and to attempt a brief characterization of the main lines of Romantic thought in so far as they bore on the writing and interpretation of history.

To trace the roots of Romanticism one must work down deep into the eighteenth century. The first signs of the new growth appeared in mid-century as an incipient revolt, confined at first largely to literature, against the rigidity of eighteenth century rules of taste and the aesthetic limitations imposed by the pseudo-classicism that was the literary counterpart of rationalism. Here the English led the way with a "Gothic revival" [3] which awakened a new appreciation of the unclassical forms of English poetry and particularly the early folk literature. The publication of Thomas Percy's *Reliques of Ancient Poetry* (1765) and James MacPherson's *Ossian* (1760 ff.) were literary events of the first magnitude, with important repercussions in Germany and elsewhere on the continent.

Closely associated with this early literary Romanticism, but much broader in its implications, went an analogous rebellion against the emotional inadequacy of rationalist thought and against the maddening complacency with which the Age of Reason regarded its own civilization. In this, as in many other respects, Rousseau was the

---

[3] Cf. H. A. Beers, *A History of English Romanticism in the Eighteenth Century* (New York, 1898), pp. 221 ff.

grandparent of Romanticism.[4] From him stemmed a new emotional-
ism in literature, a warmer feeling for irrational human sentiments, and
a tendency to idealize what he thought the more natural, and therefore
purer and more noble, morality of less civilized ages. Translated
through Herder and the young Goethe, the Rousseauian strain found
expression in the immoderate rebellion against all artificial rules and
in the anti-rational "philosophy of feeling" of the *Sturm und Drang*.[5]
The Romanticists were, on the whole, less rebellious than the young
men of the period of the *Sturm und Drang;* but they shared many of
their predilections. Life was for them an endless striving, in which
the struggle was more important than the unobtainable goal. They
valued originality, imagination, and spontaneity above imitation and
rules, and creative genius above technical perfection. They prized
sentiment more than reason, and the instincts more than the conscious intellect. They were drawn toward the infinite, the unbounded,
rather than the precisely finite. When necessary they would sacrifice
clarity to the vaguely sublime, and even when not necessary they
preferred eccentricity to conventionality. They found inspiration in the
far away and strange, even the macabre, and were more attracted by
the mysterious gloom of primeval forests than by the ordered perfection of formal gardens.

The men of the late eighteenth century were beginning to lose faith
in the utilitarian and mechanistic philosophy of the Enlightenment,
with its exclusive emphasis on reason and natural laws, even before
the failure of the French Revolution proclaimed the bankruptcy of
rationalism; but that event turned the Romanticists, a bewildered generation, to a more earnest search for a substitute.[6] They found what
they sought, according to their various characters, in idealistic philosophy, in religion, in a more profound feeling for subjective morality,
in personal identification with the state, the nation, the church, or
some other corporate social group, or in the nostalgic study of their

[4] Cf. I. Babbitt, *Rousseau and Romanticism* (Boston, 1919).
[5] G. Salomon, *Das Mittelalter als Ideal in der Romantik* (Munich, 1922), pp.
20 ff, argues that the *Sturm und Drang* movement, like Romanticism, was also in
part a national reaction against foreign ideas.
[6] Cf. E. N. Anderson, "German Romanticism as an Ideology of Cultural Crisis,"
Journal of the History of Ideas, II (1941), 301–17.

national past. Convinced that reason was not enough, the Romanticists were thrown back upon instinct and faith, upon "the higher logic of sentiment." A corollary of this rebellion against reason, of particular importance for historiography, was a rejection of the rational individual as the consciously directing force in history. The Romantic feeling for instinctive, irrational, and unconscious forces led them to place a new emphasis above all on the corporate action of the whole national group, the folk.

Johann Gottfried Herder was the early apostle of the Romantic philosophy of history. He rejected both the rational individualism of the Enlightenment and the cosmopolitanism that was its counterpart. In place of the Lockian conception of the universal similarity of human nature, he set up the diametrically opposed conceptions of national peculiarity and development.[7] In his *Ideas on the Philosophy of the History of Humanity* (1784–91) [8] and in numbers of essays and articles, Herder poured forth a confused mass of ideas that were in various ways to exert a profound influence on nearly all Romantic thought.[9] Herder saw in history a divinely ordered teleology, the end of which was the development of "humanity." [10] But, unlike Rousseau, from whom nevertheless he drew much of his inspiration, Herder proclaimed the national group rather than the individual the agent of this development. Here, for the first time, appeared the pregnant idea, not clearly worked out but expressed in emotionally potent iteration, that the nation is a natural organic unit, which "bears in itself the standard of its perfection, totally independent of comparison with that of others." [11] Inherent in this organic body there is a directing soul which is the creative force that produces and regulates all culture.[12] Like Divine Providence this "genetic spirit" moves in a mys-

[7] Cf. R. R. Ergang, *Herder and the Foundations of German Nationalism* (New York, 1931), pp. 82 ff; R. G. Collingwood, *The Idea of History* (Oxford, 1946), pp. 90 ff.

[8] J. G. Herder, *Ideen zur Philosophie der Geschichte der Menschheit*, 2 vols. (1784–91), *Sämtliche Werke* (Berlin, 1877–1913), XIII–XIV. Eng. trans. (London, 1803).

[9] Cf. Ergang, pp. 193 ff.

[10] On the theological orientation of Herder's thought, see Fueter, pp. 408 ff.

[11] Herder, *Werke,* XIV, 227.

[12] Cf. K. Borries, *Die Romantik und die Geschichte* (Berlin, 1925), pp. 128 ff, for discussion of the influence of this idea on Romantic thought.

terious way, but Herder saw evidence of its activity everywhere. "It is inexplicable and ineradicable; as old as the nation, as old as the country it inhabits."[13] Language, literature, religion, art, science, and law are all products of this *Volksgeist* and are inter-related parts of the organic whole of national culture, reflecting throughout the peculiar personality of the nation. Herder rejected the idea of a classic norm of perfection in literature or art. The nation produces the culture that is right for it at each stage in its development. It follows, therefore, that any attempt to impose alien rules upon the national culture or to imitate the culture of other peoples can result only in checking real progress by hindering the natural development of the national organism. The function of the individual poet, artist, philosopher, or statesman is merely to give expression to the soul of the nation. The more spontaneous his work, the less it is hampered by imitation or by cold rationality, the more it will be in harmony with the unconscious creative spirit of the *Volk* and the more perfectly it will express the peculiar character of the nation.

The reaction against the French Revolution and Napoleonic aggression gave ideas such as these a wider circulation and made Romantic nationalist philosophy a European phenomenon. The patriotism aroused by the Wars of Liberation swept away the cosmopolitan individualism of the pre-revolutionary era. The failure of the French attempt to impose foreign laws and institutions upon the conquered peoples seemed to demonstrate the futility of conscious efforts to interfere with the natural growth of a nation.[14] And, finally, the excesses of the Terror and fear of Napoleon combined to inspire a strong anti-revolutionary and anti-despotic sentiment that found positive comfort in the doctrine of organic development and the sanctity of national tradition. This conservative, nationalist reaction was formulated into a political philosophy by Edmund Burke, whose influence worked even more powerfully in Germany than in his own country.[15] For the cult of individual reason, self-evident rights, and natural law, Burke substituted that of the national community, patri-

[13] Herder, *Werke*, XIV, 38.   [14] Cf. Fueter, p. 415 f.
[15] Adam Müller wrote in 1806: "The weightiest epoch in the history of German political science was the introduction of Edmund Burke to German soil: the greatest, most deep-thinking, most powerful, and most human statesman of all

otic sentiment, idealized history, and tradition.[16] Regarding the growth of national tradition with a reverence akin to religious piety, Burke insisted that only those institutions that grow naturally out of the manners and characteristic traits of a people can have lasting value. To attempt to change them arbitrarily at the dictates of anything so frail and ephemeral as individual reason is not only disastrous but impious. Savigny, Eichhorn, Niebuhr, and others of the German "historical-legal school" promptly applied this conception to the study of national law, while philologists like the brothers Grimm carried the doctrine of organic national development and unconscious historical growth over into the field of language and folk literature.

For the Romantic generation history, and particularly national history, thus acquired a new and deeper significance.[17] Its use was no longer merely to instruct or entertain, to teach moral lessons or to prove a scientific theory. It became the sole means of obtaining a true understanding of contemporary national culture, since contemporary culture was the product of an unbroken development, beginning far back in the past, in which each stage was a necessary part of the organic growth. It became also a guide for practical action in a new sense, since only action that harmonized with the historical development of the nation could be ultimately beneficial. For the Romanticists, history was philosophy in a sense very different from that held by the rationalists. As Fueter puts it: "Men believed that in history lay hidden a secret wisdom of a higher sort than any human ingenuity."[18] Every aspect of civilization must, therefore, be studied historically and in relation first of all to the national unit. The doctrine of national development or evolution, thus formulated, was a new conception of revolutionary significance for historical thought. It shifted attention

ages and all peoples . . . . I say it with pride, he belongs more to us than to the British . . . ." A. Müller, *Vorlesungen über die deutsche Wissenschaft und Literatur* (Munich, 1920), p. 165 f. On Burke's influence in Germany see also F. Braune, *Edmund Burke in Deutschland* (Heidelberg, 1917).

16 Cf. G. H. Sabine, *A History of Political Theory* (New York, 1937), pp. 607 ff.

17 For full discussion of the historicism that accompanied the Romantic movement, see F. Meinecke, *Die Entstehung des Historismus,* 2 vols. (Munich, 1936); E. Rothacker, *Einleitung in die Geisteswissenschaften* (Tübingen, 1920); F. Engel-Janosi, *The Growth of German Historicism* (Baltimore, 1944).

18 Fueter, p. 416.

from the universal similarities of human nature to what was peculiar to the nation or the age. It bound the present to the past as never before. It implied a new theory of historical causation, finding in the unconscious working of the national spirit the fundamental motive force of history. And from this there followed a new conception of the importance of "general causes," unconscious, irrational, and, all too often, unintelligible. At the same time, the great individuals of history were saved from oblivion by the Romantic cult of the hero, who personifies the spirit of his people, and the genius, whose spontaneous creative power, always in harmony with the folk spirit, defies all rules and reason.

When to this philosophy of history was added a social and religious nostalgia, rebellion against the recently current standards of taste, an all-pervasive sentimentality, and a love of the far away and strange, it is small wonder that the Romanticists should sink themselves in the past with unprecedented zeal, striving not only to understand it sympathetically but also to portray it in all its colorful idiosyncrasy. To this end the historical novelists contributed as effectively as did the historians. Few historians did more to shape contemporary ideas of the past than did Sir Walter Scott, to whom, indeed, many of the Romantic historians owed the original inspiration for their work.[19] There was in all Romantic historiography a warmly human tone and a love of local color for its own sake, very different from the judicial detachment with which the great rationalists had surveyed the major trends of human history.

THE ROMANTIC REHABILITATION OF THE MIDDLE AGES

The Romanticists, as we shall see, added new colors to the traditional picture of the Renaissance, but the most significant change they made was to provide it with a new background peopled with the idealized figures of benevolent lords, courtly knights and Crusaders, saintly monks, and pious laborers. They filled the cultural void between antiquity and the rebirth of art and letters with sentimentalized

[19] Halphen, pp. 17 ff; cf. L. Maigron, *Le roman historique à l'époque romantique, Essai sur l'influence de Walter Scott* (Paris, 1898).

Christian faith, Gothic art, folk poetry, and chivalrous romances.[20] Against this background the classical Renaissance still remained a contrasting phenomenon, but colored with new tones of value judgment. Medieval civilization attracted the Romanticists by those very qualities that had repelled their predecessors. They idealized what the rationalists and humanists had condemned, and with equal exaggeration. They gloried in the eccentricity, formlessness, and naïveté of medieval art. They loved the childlike simplicity and piety of medieval painting and, like the young Goethe,[21] they found in the Gothic cathedrals a "titanic" quality of vital originality, free from the cramping effects of classical rules. Where the rationalists had seen only ignorant and superstitious barbarism, the Romanticists perceived noble simplicity, pure, uncomplicated emotions, and intuitive faiths. Their bards, knights, and peasants were close kin to Rousseau's noble savage, but with national and religious over-tones.[22] Friedrich Schlegel, who did much to formulate the Romantic literary dogma, thought medieval men more naturally poetic than those of later ages in which criticism and artifice had interposed their chilling breath between the inspiration and the expression.[23] "Chivalry," he wrote, "was in itself the poetry of life; what wonder that that life of the imagination should have opened a new fountain of poetry in the traditional songs, the fairy lays, the varied minstrelsy, and knightly narratives of Germany, France, Spain, and England?" [24] Schlegel envisaged the medieval poet as living in an enchanted society and composing his poetry spontaneously, as a bird sings. Even the archaic idiom of medieval speech — Voltaire's *grossièreté* — being unfamiliar, seemed to the Romanticists the product of an especially poetic imagination. Narrative

20 On the Romantic interest in medieval history see R. Stadelmann, "Grundformen der Mittelalterauffassung von Herder bis Ranke," *Deutsche Vierteljahrsschrift für Literaturwissenschaft und Geistesgeschichte*, IX (1931), 45–88; G. Salomon, *Das Mittelalter als Ideal in der Romantik* (Munich, 1922).

21 Cf. Goethe, *Von deutscher Baukunst* (1771), *Werke* (Stuttgart and Tübingen, 1850–51), XXV, 1–8.

22 Cf. Babbitt, *Rousseau and Romanticism*, pp. 97 ff.

23 Cf. F. Schlegel, *Geschichte der alten und neuen Literatur* (1815), *Sämtliche Werke* (Vienna, 1846), I, 195 f. Eng. trans. (Philadelphia, 1818).

24 F. Schlegel, *Philosophie der Geschichte* (1828), *Werke*, XIV, 123. Eng. trans. (New York, 1841), II, 166.

historians of the "local color school," like Johannes von Müller,[25] Barante,[26] and Augustin Thierry,[27] took particular delight in the quaintness of medieval speech and manners. As Chateaubriand remarked in one of his more lucid moments, "the further those times are removed from us, the more magical they appear." [28]

The revival of poetic religious feeling and especially of an aesthetic Catholic piety, which was one aspect of the Romantic revolt against rationalism, furnished a more specific motive for the sympathetic reinterpretation of the Middle Ages.[29] That much abused era now became the Age of Faith, a kind of golden age of innocence, of child-like trust and emotional security, now lost forever. Even in Protestant Germany many of the Romanticists — including such leaders as Wackenroder, Tieck, Novalis, Friedrich Schlegel, and Adam Müller — turned to Catholicism and found in the medieval church a spiritual home toward which they could direct their religious, aesthetic, or social nostalgia. The Romantic historians rescued medieval civilization from the long-standing charges of religious and moral decline, of clerical tyranny and feudal anarchy. They saw in the Age of Faith a social as well as intellectual security, which had since been shattered by the disruptive forces of rational liberalism. There was a close connection, in fact, between the Catholic revival, with its accompanying idealization of the Middle Ages, and the conservative or anti-revolutionary strains in Romantic political thought.[30] The latter found strong support in Catholic traditionalism and authoritarianism. But still more, the medieval functional theory of society, which subordinated the interests of the individual to those of the whole community, served

[25] J. von Müller, *Geschichten schweizerischer Eidgenossenschaft* (Leipzig, 1786–1808).

[26] P. Brugière, Baron de Barante, *Histoire des ducs de Bourgogne de la Maison de Valois,* 12 vols. (Paris, 1824–38).

[27] A. Thierry, *Histoire de la conquête de l'Angleterre par les Normands* (Paris, 1825); *Récits des temps mérovingiens* (Paris, 1840).

[28] F.–R. de Chateaubriand, *Le génie du Christianisme* (1802), *Oeuvres* (Paris, 1861), II, 293.

[29] A. von Martin, "Das Wesen der romantischen Religiosität," *Deutsche Vierteljahrsschrift für Literaturwissenschaft und Geistesgeschichte,* II (1924), 367–417, furnishes a keen analysis of the sentimental aesthetic and poetic quality of Romantic religiosity.

[30] Cf. Flint, pp. 366 ff.

as a bulwark against the tendency of rational liberalism to regard the individual as the primary value, and the state and society as existing solely for his convenience and protection. Thus, Friedrich Schlegel contrasted the moral soundness and social stability of the age of Christian principles with the pagan individualism and anarchy of the late Middle Ages and modern times.[31] Novalis, too, praised the Middle Ages as the great age of Christian unity, when all men, princes and workers alike, lived in loving harmony under the benign jurisdiction of the universal Church.[32] And Adam Müller, the political philosopher of German conservatism, proclaimed the necessity of founding economic and political life on a basis of religion, as had been true in the Middle Ages.[33] Müller portrayed medieval society, not as a feudal anarchy, but as an organic, corporate commonwealth (Gemeinschaft), held together by bonds of service, in which each class performed a divinely ordained function necessary to the good of the whole community.[34]

Christian sentiment also furnished one of the most effective bases for the re-evaluation of medieval literature and art. In this respect the eloquent special pleading of Chateaubriand's *The Genius of Christianity* (1802)[35] was an event of epoch-making significance. The genius of Christianity, as François-René de Chateaubriand envisaged it, was purely Catholic, and its true home was in the Middle Ages. Chateaubriand's great contribution to aesthetic criticism was a fundamental attack on the dogma of classical perfection and an assertion of the absolute superiority of Christian art and letters. This was a long step beyond Herder's relative and historical defense of medieval Christian culture as the organic and therefore perfect expression of the people and the age. Chateaubriand labored to prove, with a wealth of examples and impassioned rhetoric, that the spirit of

[31] Schlegel, *Philosophie der Geschichte, Werke*, XIV, 114 ff.
[32] Novalis, *Die Christenheit oder Europa* (1799), *Sämtliche Werke* (Munich, 1924), II, 5–27.
[33] A. Müller, *Von der Notwendigkeit einer theologischen Grundlage der gesamten Staatswissenschaft und der Staatswirtschaft insbesondere* (Leipzig, 1819).
[34] Cf. A. Müller, *Die Elemente der Staatskunst* (Berlin, 1809). For discussion of Müller and conservative Romantic theory, see G. A. Briefs, "The Economic Philosophy of Romanticism," *Journal of the History of Ideas*, II (1941), 279–300.
[35] Cited above, n. 28.

Christianity is more poetic than any other, that it furnishes a deeper insight into human character and passions, gives more emotional value both to nature and to the supernatural, and is, therefore, the most perfect inspiration for literary or artistic achievement. "Without religion one may have wit, but it is difficult to have genius." [36] Christianity, he thought, had accomplished a revolution in social life by changing the foundations of morality.[37] It changed, among other things, the brutal valor of the warrior into the magnanimity and poetic generosity of the knight. It created a new "beau idéal moral," and "it was this that made the beauty of the chivalrous ages, and gave them superiority over the heroic centuries as much as over those entirely modern." [38] It was this moral revolution that made Christianity "the true philosophy of the fine arts," and to it the modern age must return for inspiration.[39]

Strong as were the religious and other motives, however, the most potent incentive to the historical study of the Middle Ages came from the patriotic nationalism, combined with a philosophical *Historismus,* that formed so important a strain in Romantic thought. In its simplest form this was merely a patriotic interest in the national past, not unlike that of the humanist historians, save that the national sentiment was now infinitely stronger. But what gave the Middle Ages a new significance for the Romantic historians was the theory, stemming from Herder and held more or less consciously by most of them, that the nation is a growing organism with a peculiar spirit, which develops but never changes its fundamental character and which is the source of all culture and all institutions. The nation's history is thus a continuous story, all parts of which are important; but a particular importance attaches to the history of the Middle Ages as the formative period in the nation's growth. As Sharon Turner put it in his *History of England from the Norman Conquest to 1509* (1814–23), the Middle Ages were "that period which has been the least studied and the most negligently written, but within which our political relations, our religion, literature, language, manners, laws, and constitution have been chiefly formed." [40] Further, the Romantic historians thought of the

[36] Chateaubriand, *Génie, Oeuvres,* II, 319.
[37] *Ibid.,* II, 194 ff.   [38] *Ibid.,* II, 190.   [39] *Ibid.,* II, 206.
[40] S. Turner, *History of England from the Norman Conquest to 1509* (London, 1814–23), II, iii.

Middle Ages as the period in which the national spirit could be studied in its purest form, the period in which it was least adulterated by foreign influences. For this was the springtime of the national spirit, when the genius of the people formed customs and institutions in perfect because unconscious accord with the national character, and when the folk soul spoke through the unsophisticated utterances of bard and *Minnesinger* to create a national literature.

This approach to the Middle Ages not only gave the period a new value, but also exerted a strong influence on the interpretation of its history and civilization. It led the Romantic historians to stress the unconscious and irrational, the typical and corporate qualities in medieval society at the expense of the conscious, rational, and individual. They tended to portray medieval men as members of a nation, class, or corporation rather than as autonomous personalities. At the same time, the Romantic theory led historians, philologists, and legal theorists to place the major emphasis on the national strains in medieval civilization, the vernacular in literature, and the customary in law and institutions, ignoring or depreciating the alien classical heritage in medieval learning and law. There was a definite "Germanist" trend to Romantic history, not only in Germany but also in England, where the Romanticists tended to idealize the Anglo-Saxons and to trace the best characteristics of English society, government, and language to the manly vigor and love of freedom inherent in the Germanic Saxon character.[41] And even in France, Romantic Germanism, combined with the religious aestheticism of Chateaubriand, was developed by Mme. de Staël into a racial interpretation of Western European civilization.

Thanks to her years of exile during the Napoleonic régime, Mme. de Staël had acquired an acquaintance with German culture rather rare among Frenchmen. In her affectionate study, *Of Germany* (1813),[42] she introduced German Romantic thought into France and, incidentally, to English and American readers who were more conversant with French than with German literature.[43] But she did more

---

[41] See, for example, S. Turner, *The History of the Anglo-Saxons from the Earliest Period to the Norman Conquest,* 3 vols. (London, 1795–1805).

[42] G. de Staël, *De l'Allemagne* (1813, 5th ed. Paris, 1818).

[43] Cf. E. G. Jaeck, *Madame de Staël and the Spread of German Literature* (New York, 1915).

than merely adopt the ideas of her German friends. She extended the idea of the peculiar character of the nation to the larger unit of the race. Her major premise was that European civilization springs from three racial roots, Latin, German, and Slav.[44] The Italians, French, and Spaniards are of the Latin race, having received their civilization and their language from the Romans; the Germans, English, Swedes, Danes, and Dutch are Teutonic peoples. The Latin nations, having a more ancient civilization of pagan origin, are more practical, more given to worldly pleasures and interests; the Germanic peoples, having been civilized later and having passed directly from barbarism to Christianity, are more profoundly influenced by chivalry and by the religious spirit of the Middle Ages. This theory ignores such troublesome problems as the intermixture of racial stocks during the barbarian migrations, the later spread of Latin culture through the Church, and, indeed, the entire validity of a racial theory based on language groups; but it possessed a surface plausibility which recommended it to generations of historians. Mme. de Staël developed it in a number of directions, but chiefly in relation to literature. The evolution of European letters, she thought, can be understood only in the light of the contrasting Latin and German racial characteristics, which she qualified further in a series of antitheses as paganism and Christianity, south and north, antiquity and Middle Ages, Greek and Roman institutions and chivalry.[45] From this remarkable premise she drew the equally remarkable conclusion that the only hope for modern literature (even that of the Latin French apparently) was to return to the Germanic, Christian, and chivalrous sources of inspiration, foreswearing the imitation of classical models.[46] The superiority of Romantic literature over the classical lay not in absolute standards, but in the natural, historical relation of the former to the spirit of the northern peoples.

> The poetry of the ancients is more pure as art, that of the moderns causes one to shed more tears; but the question for us is not between classic poetry and romantic poetry, but between the imitation of the one and the inspiration of the other. The literature of the ancients is, among the moderns, a transplanted literature; romantic or chival-

---

[44] De Staël, I, 1 ff.   [45] Ibid., I, 260.   [46] Ibid., I, 266.

rous literature is indigenous with us; it is our religion and our institutions that have made it flourish.[47]

This is more than a defense of the medieval, Christian, Germanic
forms of literature. It implies also a positive devaluation of the imitative classical forms introduced by the Renaissance, while at the same
time identifying the latter with both paganism and Latin race.

THE ITALIAN RENAISSANCE IN ROMANTIC *Belles Lettres*

Absorbed as they were in the rediscovery of the Middle Ages and
their own national past, the Romantic historians for the most part
ignored the Italian Renaissance. Their influence upon its interpretation was, therefore, largely indirect. Nevertheless, the historical
philosophy, the literary theories, the tastes, prejudices, and predilections
of the Romantic movement implied a new interpretation of the
familiar story of the rebirth of culture in Italy. For the Romanticists,
the age of rebirth was still the antithesis of the Middle Ages, but the
antithesis was no longer that of light and darkness, reason and superstition, good taste and barbarism, but rather that of paganism and
Christianity, antique and chivalrous culture, Latin and German
spirit. The effect of this conception on the history of Renaissance art
and letters, reinforced, opposed, or modified as it was by the contemporary current of neo-classicism, is a tangled story, which must be
left for fuller discussion in the following chapter. But we can scarcely
leave this general discussion of the Romantic movement without
noting the new coloring it gave to the popular idea of the nature of
the Italian Renaissance. Here we will have to deal less with the work
of the historians than with that of the men of letters: the novelists,
poets, and dramatists.[48]

Antithesis and dramatic contrast were part of the stock in trade of
every Romantic writer. They were drawn to what was foreign and
unfamiliar only slightly less than to what was native and filled with
nostalgic memories. They loved to depict noble virtues, but they

[47] *Ibid.,* I, 264.
[48] See E. Schaeffer, "Das moderne Renaissance-Empfinden," *Die neue Rundschau,*
XVI (1905), 769–84, for discussion of the idea of the Renaissance in Romantic
belles-lettres.

found vice equally picturesque, and pleasantly shocking. Their villains were very villainous, though usually endowed with a single surprising virtue to furnish dramatic relief. Tales of black magic, witchcraft, and unnatural vice could give them a *frisson esthétique* that would have seemed incomprehensible, if not faintly disgusting, to an eighteenth century deist. The pious and chivalrous Middle Ages appealed to the major interests of the Romanticists, but it was inevitable that they should also feel the unholy attraction of the antithetical phenomenon. Nearly all the leading Romantic writers visited Italy and were enchanted by the dangerously sensuous atmosphere of the southern land, by the sinister charm of Venice, by the irresponsible passions of the Italian people, and by the art of the classical Renaissance, an art that they felt to be foreign, cold, and unchristian, yet flawless in its pagan beauty. The historical philosophy of Herder, Schlegel, and Mme. de Staël had prepared them to find in Italy a national soul radically different from their own. And, like all romantic tourists, they found what they sought, though they had to turn back to the past to find it in its most perfect form. They discovered the Italy of the later Medici, of Benvenuto Cellini, and the Venetian "Council of Ten"; Italy, the land of beauty, blood, and lust.

The Romantic littérateurs were aided in their imaginative recreation of the Italian society of the Renaissance by such narrative histories as Marshal Daru's *History of the Republic of Venice* (1819),[49] Heinrich Leo's *History of the Italian States* (1829-37),[50] or Sismondi's great *History of the Italian Republics in the Middle Ages* (1807-18),[51] all of which fitted the Romantic point of view. They found more of the local color they sought, however, in the literary sources of the Renaissance itself, and not only in such fairly reliable, if disillusioned, chroniclers of contemporary life as Machiavelli and Guicciardini, but also in the scandalous *novelle,* diaries, memoires, and satires, in which Renaissance Italy abounded. Taken at their face value, these furnished stimulating material for the Romantic imagination. Even Voltaire who, though a dramatist, was no Romantic, had been moved by Re-

---

[49] P. Daru, *Histoire de la République de Venise,* 7 vols. (Paris, 1819).
[50] H. Leo, *Geschichte der italienischen Staaten,* 5 vols. (Hamburg, 1829-37).
[51] J. C. L. Simonde de Sismondi, *Histoire des républiques italiennes au Moyen Age,* 16 vols. (Zurich and Paris, 1807-18).

naissance chronicles to picture the age as one of contrasting intellectual brilliance and vice. Since then the Romantic school of historians had given a new *kulturgeschichtlich* importance to all literary sources indiscriminately, as expressions of the national soul at a given stage in its development.[52] And if the historians were none too critical, the historical novelists were enthusiastically credulous.

The picture of Renaissance Italy developed by the Romantic imagination stressed two characteristics that were new, at least in the exaggerated form they now assumed. The conception of Italian society of that age as one marked by irreligion, violence, passion, and unnatural crime had been suggested by contemporary writers and reiterated in passing by Voltaire, but it had never before been the dominating note. Similarly, the conception of Renaissance men as personalities of remarkable force and genius had been suggested by the tradition of the great masters of art and letters without being generalized as a characteristic of the society of the age. The Romantic cult of genius gave a deeper emotional value to the latter tradition while, at the same time, the Romantic tendency to think in terms of national character led to unprecedented generalization. The worship of genius ran through all shades of Romantic thought, from the "titanism" of the *Sturm und Drang,* through the silly aestheticism of the later German school which thought of the artist as accomplishing his masterpieces by sheer inspiration without thought or effort, to the robust hero-worship of Carlyle. But there was also a minor strain or cross-current in Romanticism that went a step further to admiration, not only for genius, but for all strong, untrammeled, even amoral personalities. This attitude was not characteristic of the pious, patriotic, conservative majority, but rather of the discontented rebels against the restrictions of contemporary bourgeois society. And it was these who took the lead in the idealization of the Renaissance man, combining the cult of genius with that of free, egoistic personality, an idealization which the more conservative Romanticists accepted, but with a kind of fascinated horror.

The earliest prototype of the Romantic picture of the Italian Renaissance is to be found in Wilhelm Heinse's once popular novel,

[52] Cf. Fueter, p. 463 f.

Ardinghello and the Fortunate Islands (1787).[53] Heinse was one of the wild young rebels of the *Sturm und Drang,* who found in Italy a new spiritual home. Like his contemporary Goethe, he felt himself reborn in that "land of beauty." But whereas Italy made Goethe a classicist, it made Heinse a sensual hedonist. He perceived in the Italian people a peculiar character, very different from that of the stuffy German burghers among whom he had grown up — pure sense experience and passion, uninhibited by reflection. And what charmed him in contemporary Italian society he found most perfectly expressed in the Italy of the sixteenth century. Heinse was attracted not only by the beauty of Renaissance art but by the strong personality and will to power of such Renaissance figures as Cesare Borgia and by the ruthless ethic of Machiavelli. Under the combined spell of Italian art, history, and fiction Heinse evolved an ethical doctrine of "aesthetic immoralism." [54] The story of *Ardinghello* was designed to illustrate that doctrine. The hero represented Heinse's ideal, the superman of fully developed personality, artist and adventurer, combining in perfect harmony beauty and strength, aesthetic enjoyment and uninhibited action. The first part of the story is set in the court of the Medici about the year 1576. It is full of picturesque detail taken from chronicles and *novelle.* There are scandals, murders, and artistic revenges, and not a moral inhibition in the whole rambling story. The book is less a portrayal of Renaissance society than of an ideal, and in the end Ardinghello founds his peculiar Utopia in the "fortunate isles" of the Greek archipelago. Yet the picture of sixteenth century Italy that Heinse painted was unforgettable. It might shock the Romanticists, but many of the generation who read his book saw the Renaissance through Heinse's eyes, as later Neo-romanticists would see it through the very similar vision of Nietzsche.

Heinse's conception of Renaissance society, or one very much like it, was given wider popularity a generation later through the works of Henri Beyle, the prolific French littérateur who wrote under the name

[53] W. Heinse, *Ardinghello und die glückseligen Inseln* (1787), *Sämtliche Schriften* (Leipzig, 1887), I; cf. W. Rehm, *Das Werden des Renaissancebildes in der deutschen Dichtung vom Rationalismus bis zum Realismus* (Munich, 1924), pp. 61 ff.

[54] Cf. W. Brecht, *Heinse und der ästhetische Immoralismus* (Berlin, 1911).

of Stendhal.[55] Writing in the midst of the Romantic movement, Stendhal was a Romanticist after his own fashion. He disliked the pathos and the lush style of Rousseau and Chateaubriand, and he had no patience with the timid conservatism of the era of reaction. Like Heinse, he found a freer and more stimulating life in Italy than he had at home. Renaissance art impressed him so deeply that he began collecting material for a history of Italian painting, part of which he published in 1817, but he was less interested in the art of the Renaissance for its own sake than in the people and the age that had produced it. He felt that there was a direct connection between the genius of the great masters and the society of the age in which they lived. "It was in this century of passions, in which the souls of men could raise themselves freely to the highest exaltation, that so many great painters appeared." [56]

Aside from the love of beauty, the keynote of Stendhal's thought was admiration for strong personalities, for the talented egoists who translate every passion into ruthless action. The ex-cavalry officer had never lost his hero-worship for Napoleon. And in Renaissance Italy, as nowhere else, he found men worthy to be compared to the great Corsican: Julius II, Cesare Borgia, the Sforzas, Alexander VI — "ce grand homme qui savait tout et pouvait tout," [57] — Lorenzo and Cosimo de' Medici, and all the great captains.[58] These men, "whose force and variety of talent one cannot but admire," were not, he thought, isolated phenomena, but characteristic of their age and nation. Cesare Borgia he called "the representative of his century," and he cited Benvenuto Cellini and Machiavelli's *Mandragora* as proof that the same qualities were to be found in private life as among princes.[59] The introduction to the *History of Painting in Italy* (1817), in which he sketched the social background of Renaissance art, is filled with anecdotes of the crimes and passions of the Borgias and the Medici.[60]

[55] Cf. F. Blaschke, "Stendhals Begriff der Renaissance," in his *Kulturgeschichte und Universalgeschichte* (Leipzig, 1927), pp. 201–12; C. Simon, "Le sillage de Stendhal en Allemagne," *Revue de littérature comparée*, VI (1926), 608–37.
[56] Stendhal, *Histoire de la peinture en Italie* (1817), *Oeuvres* (Paris, 1927–37), XXI, 35 f.
[57] Stendhal, *Chroniques italiennes, Oeuvres*, XX, 15.
[58] Stendhal, *Histoire de la peinture, Oeuvres*, XXI, 17 f.
[59] *Ibid.*, XXI, 20 ff.   [60] *Ibid.*, XXI, 17 ff.

Passion, "that is to say, the passion that seeks to satisfy itself," [61] Stendhal thought to be the peculiar characteristic of the Italian people throughout most of their history, and he wrote numbers of short stories, based on old chronicles, to illustrate his point. These *Italian Chronicles* range in scene from the sixteenth to the eighteenth century, but Stendhal evidently preferred the earlier period. It was then that Italian passion was to be found at its best. "That passionate manner of feeling," he noted, "which reigned in Italy about 1559, desired actions and not words." [62] This was Stendhal's ideal, and like all the Romanticists, he found his ideal embodied in the past.

Among the English Romanticists, Byron seems nearest to the rebellious egoism of Heinse and Stendhal, and he was attracted in much the same way by the strong personalities and the dramatic atmosphere of Renaissance society. It was Byron, indeed, who discovered the Romantic Venice, the Venice of inhuman pride and sinister beauty. "Everything about Venice," he wrote in 1820, "is, or was, extraordinary — her aspect is like a dream, and her history is like a romance." [63] In the two historical tragedies in verse, *Marino Faliero* (1820) and *The Two Foscari* (1821), Byron developed the themes of undying vengeance and of the strong man driven by relentless pride and iron will into conflict with the secret powers of the implacable oligarchy. Both dramas were based on historical incidents drawn from Marino Sanuto's *Lives of the Doges,*[64] with supplementary material from Daru and Sismondi.

With Victor Hugo we return to the more common norm of Romanticism. The picture of Renaissance Italy presented in his two astonishingly popular plays, *Lucretia Borgia* (1833) and *Angelo, Tyrant of Padua* (1835), is the very quintessence of Romantic exaggeration. Hugo's primary interest was in the moral lesson and the pathos of the dramatic situation, but he also underlined the historical significance of the plays. It was his purpose, so he wrote in the preface to *Angelo,* "to paint, in passing . . . . not only man and woman, not only these

[61] Stendhal, *Chroniques italiennes, Oeuvres,* XX, 11.
[62] *Ibid.,* XX, 14.
[63] Byron, *Marino Faliero* (1820), Preface, *Works* (London, 1901), IV, 331.
[64] M. Sanuto, *Vitae Ducum Venetorum,* in L. A. Muratori, *Rerum italicarum scriptores* (Milan, 1823–51), XXII.

two women and these three men, but a whole century, a whole climate, a whole civilization, a whole people." [65] And how he painted them! The scene is Byron's Venice with its spies, assassins, and the secret "Council of Ten," but it is equipped with an apparatus of secret passages, trapdoors, and improbable poisons that Byron would have scorned. The story of *Lucretia Borgia* is equally replete with vengeance and strange poisons, with incest as an added attraction. Hugo describes his heroine as a monster of the most hideous moral deformity who is also a mother — if by way of incest — a fact which, he thought, should make the monster interesting and cause one to weep. [66] But, however much he labored the pathos of the situation, it is the picture of the monster as type of her age that remains. The very sight of her palace moves her (unwitting) son to a burst of tautological rhetoric, which sums up Hugo's impression of the age: "Voilà donc son exécrable palais! palais de la luxure, palais de la trahison, palais de l'assassinat, palais de l'adultère, palais de l'inceste, palais de tous les crimes, palais de Lucrèce Borgia!" [67]

Of the numbers of men of letters who depicted Renaissance society in the days before Burckhardt, one more name must be mentioned, if only to end this chapter on a note of sanity. During the two middle decades of the century Robert Browning achieved the perfect synthesis of Romantic and neo-classical conceptions. In "My Last Duchess," in "The Bishop Orders his Tomb at Saint Praxed's Church," in "Pictor Ignotus," "Fra Lippo Lippi," and "Andrea del Sarto," Browning presented all the facets of Renaissance character as the mid-nineteenth century saw them, and made them human and believable. From Browning it is but a short step to Burckhardt.

[65] V. Hugo, *Angelo Tyran de Padoue, Oeuvres complètes: Drame* (Paris, 1882), II, 285.
[66] V. Hugo, *Lucrèce Borgia, Oeuvres*, III, 4 f.
[67] *Ibid.*, III, 55.

CHAPTER SIX

Conflicting Trends and the Beginnings of a
Periodic Concept

FROM THE GREAT HISTORIANS of the eighteenth century, who viewed the revival of art and letters in the light of rational philosophy and traditional classicism simply as the beginning of modern progress, to Burckhardt's formulation of an integrated periodic concept, there was a long period of conflicting and interacting tendencies in the interpretation of the Renaissance. The Romantic movement, as we have seen, provided the Renaissance with a new medieval background and regarded Renaissance society from a new point of view. At the same time neo-classical enthusiasm revived the humanist tradition, but in an altered form, attaching a new significance to the reborn spirit of antiquity. Nineteenth century liberalism, Hegelian teleology, Romantic nationalism and piety, and the habit of thinking historically that grew up with the Romantic movement, each in its own way exerted an influence on men's attitudes toward the Renaissance. Finally, the phenomenal growth of historical research and writing which characterized the nineteenth century not only added greatly to knowledge of the Renaissance but stimulated efforts toward periodization.

THE RENAISSANCE IN THE HISTORY OF ART

The conflict of interpretations and the tendency toward periodization appeared earlier and more clearly in the history of art than elsewhere.[1] Both Romanticists and neo-classicists were strongly, though

[1] For the art historians from Winckelmann to Burckhardt, see L. Venturi, *History of Art Criticism* (New York, 1936); W. Waetzoldt, *Deutsche Kunsthi-*

133

diversely, interested in Renaissance art. To many it seemed the essential characteristic of the age, and for both schools its evaluation had a vital bearing upon their contemporary cultural aims. Until the middle of the eighteenth century there had been little change in the classical tradition of art history formulated by Vasari, except that with the passage of time the early development of Italian art had dropped into the background, with more recent artists taking a proportionately more important place. That tradition still dominated the following century, but it was no longer unchallenged, and even when accepted it was subject to significant modifications.

The first modification of the Vasari tradition came from the neo-classical school. Like the Romantic movement, neo-classicism sprang from rebellion against the arid, rational classicism that was all that remained in the eighteenth century of the Renaissance aesthetic. Both movements turned from an uninspired present to seek a reawakening of creative spirit in return to the past. But whereas the Romanticists sought inspiration in a thoroughly revolutionary return to the national and Christian culture of the Middle Ages, the neo-classicists strove merely to infuse the old ideal with new life by rediscovering the pure and perfect classicism of ancient Greece.

Johann Joachim Winckelmann was the founder and high priest of the new cult of Greek beauty. In the midst of an age that regarded art as a pleasant ornament of civilized life, he wrote of ancient sculpture with the devout fervor of a prophet. It was he who made Rome, the city of ancient monuments, once more the artistic capital of Europe.[2] There he spent the last twelve years of his life (1755–68) and there cast the spell of his personal, almost "romantic," enthusiasm over a whole generation of aesthetic pilgrims. Meanwhile, his ideas were disseminated throughout Europe by his widely read *Reflections on the Imitation of the Greek Works in Painting and Sculpture*

storiker, 2 vols. (Leipzig, 1921–24); for special discussion of the interpretation of Renaissance art, see R. Kaufmann, *Der Renaissancebegriff in der deutschen Kunstgeschichtschreibung* (Basel, 1932); M. Deetz, *Anschauung von italienischer Kunst in der deutschen Literatur von Winckelmann bis zur Romantik* (Berlin, 1930); W. Rehm, *Das Werden des Renaissancebildes in der deutschen Dichtung vom Rationalismus bis zum Realismus* (Munich, 1924).

[2] Cf. L. Hautecoeur, *Rome et la renaissance de l'antiquité à la fin du XVIIIe siècle* (Paris, 1912).

(1755) [3] and finally by the great *History of Ancient Art* (1764).[4] The cardinal point of Winckelmann's aesthetic theory, belief in the absolute perfection of ancient art and in the necessity of imitating it, was not, of course, entirely new, but he gave it a new meaning. The art of ancient Greece, he thought, owed its perfection to a unique combination of circumstances, of climate, manners, temperament, religion, and social organization. These produced an almost unimaginable physical beauty and at the same time gave the artist the freest possible opportunity to observe the most perfect human forms and to "enjoy nature without a veil." [5] Given such unrivalled opportunities, the Greek masters learned to form general ideas of beauty and proportion and to create ideal types, "brain-born images" of beauty never found in the imperfect forms of actual nature.[6] From this it followed that for the modern artist the shortest, if not the only, path to the achievement of ideal beauty lay in the imitation, not of imperfect nature, but of the Greek models.[7] Winckelmann thought of nature primarily in terms of the human form, so that the ideal norm established by the Greeks was valid for all humanity, for all times and all peoples. Yet he held out little hope that even the most faithful imitation would enable the moderns to equal the perfection of the ancients, for Greek art possessed qualities of "noble simplicity and quiet grandeur" which had their origins in a state of mind peculiar to Greek society. In short, the art of Greek antiquity was inimitable, yet the only hope for modern art lay in imitating it.

Winckelmann's historical method was still more original than his aesthetic theory, if not so immediately influential. His aim was to explain the development of Greek art according to natural laws determined by the physical and social environment. Here the influence of Montesquieu and the *philosophes* is apparent, but Winckelmann broke with the rationalists by denying the dogma of modern progress and foreshadowed the later Romantic historical theory by portraying art as

[3] J. J. Winckelmann, *Gedanken über die Nachahmung der griechischen Werke in der Malerei und Bildhauerkunst* (Friedrichstadt, 1755). Eng. trans. (London, 1765).

[4] J. J. Winckelmann, *Geschichte der Kunst des Alterthums*, 2 vols. (Dresden, 1764). Eng. trans. (Boston, 1872–73).

[5] Winckelmann, *Gedanken, Werke* (Dresden, 1808–34), I, 13 [p. 9 f].
[6] *Ibid.*, I, 16 ff.   [7] *Ibid.*, I, 7 f; 20 ff.

a developing organism, changing by itself without the conscious or reasoned guidance of the individual artist. The result was something new in the history of art, as he himself realized: the history of art rather than of artists.[8] Winckelmann's historical method was scarcely appreciated and certainly not imitated till the nineteenth century, but the effect of his enthusiasm for pure classical art was immediate. It aroused a new interest in everything pertaining to Greek antiquity, including the classical art of the Italian Renaissance. For in Winckelmann's view the art of the early sixteenth century represented the sole brief rebirth of the antique form through a uniquely successful imitation of the ideal beauty of Greek sculpture.[9]

Neo-classicism reached its full development, contemporaneously with the high tide of Romanticism, at the end of the eighteenth century and in the first part of the nineteenth, and found its most persuasive exponent in Goethe. After his youthful participation in the emotional and aesthetic revolt of the *Sturm und Drang,* during which he learned to appreciate the titanic originality of Gothic architecture, Goethe found in Rome among Winckelmann's disciples an ideal more suited to his mature taste. The Greek ideal of beauty, with its harmony, clarity of form, and serenity of spirit, appealed to him profoundly and made a permanent impression on his own work. But his interests were broader than those of Winckelmann and he added a corresponding breadth to the classical ideal. To Goethe, as to many of his generation, ancient Greece represented not merely the perfection of artistic form, but also the perfection of humanity, the purest, noblest, and most natural expression of ideal man. And it was this human as well as artistic ideal that he found reflected in the artists of the classical Renaissance. Goethe had carried from his stormy poetic youth too profound a conviction of the value of originality to accept Winckelmann's doctrine of imitation in its strictest form. He could never forget that the letter killeth but the spirit giveth life. To recreate the beauty of antiquity, if that be possible, the artist must, therefore, create from within himself. He must not imitate the Greeks, but must think and act like a Greek.

[8] Cf. Winckelmann, *Geschichte* (Preface), *Werke,* III, i ff.
[9] Cf. Winckelmann, *Gedanken, Werke,* I, 7; *Geschichte, Werke,* V, 279.

Taught by Winckelmann to see in art an expression of the society that produces it, and urged by his own poetic turn of mind to seek in an individual the concrete expression of a type, Goethe found in the personality of Benvenuto Cellini, whose autobiography he translated in 1796, the essence of Renaissance culture. "The translation of Cellini," he wrote, "is of the greatest usefulness to me, since I can grasp nothing without an immediate image to contemplate; I see the whole century more distinctly through the confused individual than in the exposition of the clearest historian." [10] In choosing Cellini rather than Raphael as "the representative of his century," [11] Goethe approaches Heinse and Stendhal, but there was more of Greek *humanitas* and less *"ästhetischer Immoralismus"* in Goethe's conception.

A comparison of Goethe's general views of art with those of Winckelmann demonstrates the extent of the latter's influence and also the repercussion of other contemporary trends in shaping neo-classical opinion. Goethe had a much more sympathetic appreciation of early German and Flemish art; [12] he was more aware of the importance of those artists who since the days of Giotto had prepared the way for the perfection of Raphael; [13] but he was at one with Winckelmann in feeling that only the idealized classical art of the sixteenth century had independent or absolute value. Thus did the neo-classicists preserve the Vasari tradition, but narrowed by Winckelmann's exclusive classical norm and further altered by a new emphasis on the classical spirit of the Renaissance artists.

The tendency to criticize art in terms of its spirit was even more evident among the Romanticists, but their interpretation of Renaissance art was not merely a deviation from tradition. It was a direct reversal, and as such deserves somewhat fuller treatment. Romantic criticism was much more subjective than that of the neo-classical school: less

[10] Goethe in Schiller's journal *Die Horen* (1796), quoted in Waetzoldt, I, 170.
[11] Goethe, *Anhang zur Lebensbeschreibung des B. Cellini, Werke* (Weimar, 1887–1919), I Abt., XLIV, 350.
[12] Cf. Goethe, *Kunst und Altertum am Rhein und Main* (1814–15), *Werke,* I Abt., XXXIV, 170 ff.
[13] Cf. Goethe, *Anhang zur Cellini, Werke,* I Abt., XLIV, 304 f; and *Tagebücher,* Oct. 19, 1786, *Werke,* III Abt., I, 305: "In order to know him [Raphael] and to evaluate him correctly, and also not to think of him as a god who like Melchisedech was born without father or mother, one must regard his forerunners as his masters. These laid the broad foundation on a firm basis of truth . . . ."

interested in objective beauty or technical skill and more in the intention of the artist and the feeling evoked by his work. Further, where Winckelmann's disciples sought in art universal, ideal human types, the Romanticists were drawn especially to what was characteristic, whether individual or national. Above all, the most purely Romantic critics tended to identify artistic inspiration with religion and to make moral earnestness and Christian piety the primary criteria in evaluating medieval and modern art.

This latter tendency received a decisive impetus from Wilhelm Heinrich Wackenroder's *Outpourings from the Heart of an Art-loving Friar* (1797).[14] It is rather difficult to classify this strange little book which exerted such an apparently disproportionate influence. It is set in fictional form and composed mostly of emotional effusions and sentimental tales. It contains little formal criticism, little systematic thought of any kind; yet in total effect it presented a new attitude toward art. Ignoring aesthetic rules and technical considerations, Wackenroder threw all his emphasis on the divine inspiration of the artist and on the necessity of viewing his work with the devout humility of a believer before a sacred shrine. Christian piety, Wackenroder thought, was indispensible to the true artist or the true critic. He saw nothing but religious feeling in either the Italian or the Northern Renaissance. His two major saints, Raphael and Albrecht Dürer, whom he once beheld in a dream hand in hand in friendly converse,[15] were alike in their childlike faith, and therein lay their glory. They created as they felt, almost unconsciously, and their deepest feelings were rooted in religious devotion. It is characteristic that he explained Raphael's ideal conception of the Madonna by a rather unlikely tale of the Mother of God posing for the artist in a vision.[16] Wackenroder's insistence on the artist's way of feeling rather than on his technical skill helped open the way for the Romantic appreciation of national as well as religious art, though here the fundamental preparatory work had already been done by Herder. Wackenroder refused to bewail the fact that Dürer could not have visited Rome and

---

14 W. H. Wackenroder, *Herzensergiessungen eines kunstliebenden Klosterbruders* (Berlin, 1797), *Werke und Briefe* (Berlin, 1938), pp. 1–131.
15 *Ibid.*, p. 65.   16 *Ibid.*, pp. 13 ff.

have learned ideal beauty from Raphael, for had he done so he would not have remained himself. "His blood was not Italian blood," and the art-loving friar rejoiced that in Dürer Germany had gained an *echt-vaterländischen* painter.[17]

Wackenroder was evidently little read outside of Germany, but his basic ideas, in slightly more systematic form, were given a wide European circulation by the brothers Schlegel. A. W. Schlegel wrote an enthusiastic expository review of his work at the time of its appearance,[18] and Friedrich Schlegel further developed Wackenroder's attitude in his popular *Descriptions of Paintings from Paris and the Netherlands* (1802–1804)[19] and other works of criticism. Christian piety was Friedrich Schlegel's primary standard for all evaluation of art. "I have little taste," he confessed, "except for the earlier schools of Christian art."[20] Like Wackenroder he saw a deep religious feeling in the work of both the Italian and northern artists of the early Renaissance, but he was more aware of an alien, pagan spirit in the classical period and hence encountered difficulties which Wackenroder, with his slight historical knowledge, had ignored. This led him to make a distinction between the old and new schools of Italian painting, between "the devout, pious, deeply significant style of the former and the florid pomp of the latter."[21] The new school, which began with Raphael and others of his generation, reached the highest summit of art, "yet bore within it the seeds of premature decay." Schlegel could be enthusiastic about the religious feeling in the work of Raphael whom he thought most closely akin of his generation to the genius of the old masters;[22] but in general he seemed to feel that the magnificent technical perfection of the sixteenth century was not sufficient compensation for the loss of that "poetic view of things,"[23] which the old masters of the fourteenth and fifteenth centuries had imbibed from religion, and which declined with the growth of a

[17] *Ibid.*, pp. 63 ff.
[18] A. W. Schlegel in *Allgemeine Literatur-Zeitung* (1797), No. 46.
[19] F. Schlegel, *Gemähldebeschreibungen aus Paris und den Niederlanden in den Jahren 1802–1804, Sämtliche Werke* (Vienna, 1846), VI. Eng. trans. in Schlegel, *Aesthetic and Miscellaneous Works* (London, 1848; new ed. London, 1900).
[20] *Ibid.*, VI, 13 [p. 5].
[21] *Ibid.*, VI, 60 f [p. 49].
[22] Cf. *ibid.*, VI. 107 ff.
[23] *Ibid.*, VI, 83 [p. 70].

more pagan feeling and a more exclusive appeal to the senses.[24] Later, in the *Philosophy of History* (1828),[25] he again noted the age of Raphael as forming the dividing line between early Christian art, which "displayed the profoundest import and most masterly power" and the art of that "second period of European culture" which was affected by enthusiasm for the pagan antique.[26] The influence of classical antiquity he thought equally fatal to the art of the North after it was imported from Italy in the sixteenth century.[27] Prior to that time the art of Germany and the Netherlands had followed an entirely independent organic development from the Van Eycks, through Dürer, to Holbein along lines marked out by Christian piety and the national spirit. Schlegel's interpretation of Renaissance art was polemical rather than scholarly. It was consciously designed to effect a regeneration of contemporary culture by a return to the past: "to lead back the taste of modern times and to form it in some degree on the model of the old masters." [28] But that made it a no less potent influence on the historical and critical thought of the Romantic generation.

Following Schlegel the Romantic movement brought about a rehabilitation of the Italian primitives, the "Pre-Raphaelites," as well as of the older German and Flemish painters, which was very similar in motive to the Romantic rediscovery of medieval architecture and sculpture. Here religious and national sentiments were combined in much the same way with rebellion against the intellectualism and coldness of eighteenth century criticism and an emotional feeling for all that was simple, childlike, and naïve. Indeed, it was to all intents and purposes part of the same process, for to Schlegel and most of the Romantic critics the Christian painting of the fourteenth and fifteenth centuries, though regarded as a rebirth of art in something like Vasari's sense, was in reality a continuation of the medieval religious and national spirit and belonged essentially to the Middle Ages.

24 Cf. *ibid.*, VI, 88.
25 F. Schlegel, *Philosophie der Geschichte* (1828), *Werke*, XIV. Eng. trans., 2 vols. (New York, 1841).
26 *Ibid.*, XIV, 127 [II, 171].
27 Cf. Schlegel, *Gemähldebeschreibungen*, *Werke*, VI, 140.
28 *Ibid.*, VI, 76 [p. 64].

The early art of the Netherlands and Germany was thus freed from dependence upon Italy and the antique. F. G. Waagen, in particular, made the continuity of independent national tradition and of medieval religious spirit in the fifteenth century the themes of his scholarly study of the Van Eycks (1822),[29] which is, incidentally, one of the best examples of the adaptation to Romantic ends of Winckelmann's historical method. The Germanic national interest did not, of course, apply to the Italian primitives, and in that field Schlegel's most characteristic successors were to be found abroad. In the following generation Rio and Ruskin became the most influential champions of the religious school of Romantic criticism as applied to Italian art.[30]

Alexis-François Rio combined the conservative orthodoxy of the French ultramontanist with a religious sentimentality and mystical fervor that enabled him to draw inspiration from the earlier German Romanticists. His rebellion against rational criticism and the classical aesthetic sprang from the same religious and emotional sources as that of Wackenroder and Schlegel, but his appreciation of art was even more narrowly Catholic. Rio's *History of Christian Art* (1836–51) [31] was a declaration of faith, of the belief that true art is impossible without religion, that is, without Catholic piety and mysticism. In a sense more absolute than Schlegel's he took Christian morality and religious inspiration as the sole criteria for the evaluation of the artist and his work, and he had a keener eye for signs of pagan influence or any deviation from the medieval Christian spirit. Thus he had unqualified praise for the century following Giotto, but noted that already in the fifteenth century there were symptoms of decadence and of a dangerous tendency toward naturalism, caused by the revived interest in pagan antiquity. For Rio's discriminating judgment, to be a Pre-Raphaelite was not enough. He found Filippo Lippi's madonnas intolerably vulgar, and damned the genial friar as a libertine who

[29] F. G. Waagen, *Ueber Hubert und Johann van Eyck* (Breslau, 1822), pp. 63 ff; 73 ff; 139 ff; cf. Preface, p. v.

[30] Cf. C. von Klenze, "The Growth of Interest in the Italian Masters," *Modern Philology*, IV (1906), 207–74; cf. T. Borenius, "The Rediscovery of the Primitives," *Quarterly Review*, CCXXXIX (April, 1923), 258–71.

[31] A.-F. Rio, *De la poésie chrétienne, dans son principe, dans sa matière et dans ses formes* (Paris, 1836); *De l'art chrétien* (Paris, 1851); both later published together under the latter title. Eng. trans. (London. 1854).

"could not possibly rise to the height of those religious painters who in the preceding century gave to art so great a destiny." [32] His favorites in the *Quattrocento* were the mystical Fra Angelico and Perugino. In general he preferred the pious Umbrian painters to the semi-pagan Florentines, and he hailed the divine Raphael as "the crown and completion of the Umbrian school, who had the glory of carrying Christian art to its highest point of perfection." [33] But it was only the early Raphael of the Madonnas that met with Rio's unqualified approval. He discerned signs of decay in Raphael's later work, and he had neither interest nor understanding for any of the other artists of the classical period.

Rio was not alone among his countrymen, but the classical aesthetic was too firmly rooted in France for the general revolution of taste that he hoped to achieve. His ideas were more warmly received in England where the Oxford Movement and Pugin's Romantic-religious enthusiasm for late Gothic architecture [34] had created a favorable atmosphere. His ideas are clearly reflected in Lord Lindsay's *Sketches of the History of Christian Art* (1847). Rio's influence was also largely responsible for the translation of Schlegel's *Descriptions of Paintings from Paris and the Netherlands* into English in 1848. His own work was translated in 1854.

It was John Ruskin, however, who first established the Romantic school of criticism firmly in England. He has been called with some justice "the true continuer of Wackenroder, even if he had never read him." [35] He had read Rio and the event marked an epoch in his thought. He was as convinced as Rio or Schlegel that true art cannot be separated from religion, and he was equally suspicious of intellectualism or purely technical skill. But he was more profoundly concerned than either with the moral aspects of art. His vehement defense of the "Pre-Raphaelites" — those before Raphael and those of his own day who had taken the name — was based on moral rather than aesthetic grounds, though Ruskin would admit no distinction between

[32] Rio, *De la poésie*, p. 115 f.   [33] *Ibid.*, p. 274 f.
[34] Cf. A. W. N. Pugin, *Contrasts; or a Parallel between the Noble Edifices of the Fourteenth and Fifteenth Centuries and Similar Buildings of the Present Day, Shewing the Present Decay of Taste* (London, 1836).
[35] Venturi, *Art Criticism*, p. 182.

the two. It was his thesis that art had undergone a complete transformation at the beginning of the sixteenth century, a change not only from Christian to unchristian art, or from the religious to the profane, but from moral to immoral art.[36] Until the end of the fifteenth century the old masters had put truth before beauty. Thereafter the relation was reversed, whence the decadence of modern art. Ruskin could designate the precise moment in Raphael's career when the change occurred, the moment at which he began to paint the "School of Athens."[37] Nor was the moral difference between the earlier art and that of what he called "the Renaissance" a matter of more or less. It was a distinction as firm as that between light and darkness.[38] Few critics have been as arbitrary as Ruskin, but still fewer have been gifted with such eloquence or such explosive emotional force. His critical standards were narrow, but they were probably better designed to attract the attention of Victorian England than was Rio's Catholic mysticism or his "poetry of Christian art."

One of Ruskin's primary tenets was that we cannot consider art properly "until we consider it in its relation to the inner spirit of the age in which it exists,"[39] and this belief led him beyond the mere criticism of art to rash generalizations about the whole complex of Renaissance culture. He regarded the spirit of the Renaissance in general as "evil,"[40] though there were noble exceptions in its early stages: Raphael, Leonardo, and Michelangelo, all of whom were taught by masters of the old school who "knew the true ends of art" and were "imbued with the old religious and earnest spirit."[41] Pride and infidelity he thought the chief characteristics of the Renaissance, and of the subdivisions of the former the most dangerous was pride of science.[42] Ruskin loved the old masters who were "simple and unlearned men," and he blamed the later corruption directly on the study of classical letters or, as he put it, the sciences of words and methods, "into which the whole energy of men during the Renaissance period was thrown."

[36] J. Ruskin, *Lectures on Architecture and Painting* (1854), *Works* (London, 1903–12), XII, 145; cf. 137 ff.
[37] *Ibid.*, XII, 148.   [38] Cf. *ibid.*, XII, 143.   [39] *Ibid.*, XII, 137.
[40] Cf. Ruskin, *Stones of Venice*, III (1853), *Works*, XI, 18.
[41] *Ibid.*, XI, 70.   [42] *Ibid.*, XI, 46 ff.

They discovered suddenly that the world for ten centuries had been living in an ungrammatical manner, and they made it forthwith the end of human existence to be grammatical. And it mattered thenceforth nothing what was said, or what was done, so only it was said with scholarship, and done with system. Falsehood in a Ciceronian dialect had no opposers; truth in patois no listeners.[43]

This is a view of humanism that has been echoed frequently, though seldom so felicitously, in the present century.

Ruskin's use of the term *Renaissance* to denote a definite epoch in the history of art reminds us that a decisive advance in periodization had been made since the beginning of the nineteenth century. The neo-classicists and the Romanticists, approaching the problem from opposite points of view, were yet agreed in observing an epoch-making change in the character of Italian art at about the beginning of the sixteenth century and in regarding the period following the golden age as one of decline. The age of the classical Renaissance was thus isolated more definitely than in the tradition of Vasari and his successors down to the eighteenth century. Controversy over its character also encouraged critics and historians to consider the Renaissance as a distinct phenomenon, rather than as simply the beginning of modern art after the hiatus of the Middle Ages. As a result the old qualifying phrase, *renaissance des beaux arts* gradually gave way to the more definitely periodic term *la Renaissance,* which was also used adjectivally to denote a type or style of art. In normal usage it was applied only to the first half of the sixteenth century, though there was no general agreement on chronological limits. By about 1830 the use of the term was apparently well established in France.[44] From there it spread without benefit of translation to Germany during the following decade,[45] and by the middle forties it had become naturalized in England.[46] From recognizing the Renaissance as a period in the his-

---

43 *Ibid.,* XI, 69.

44 Cf. J. Huizinga, "Das Problem der Renaissance," in his *Wege der Kulturgeschichte* (Munich, 1930), p. 100 f; A Philippi, *Der Begriff der Renaissance* (Leipzig, 1912), pp. 99 ff.

45 Cf. E. Heyfelder, "Die Ausdrücke 'Renaissance' und 'Humanismus,' " *Deutsche Literaturzeitung,* XXXIV (1913), 2245–50; W. Goetz, "Mittelalter und Renaissance," *Historische Zeitschrift,* XCVIII (1907), 36; 46.

46 Cf. *New English Dictionary,* ed. J. A. H. Murray (Oxford).

tory of art, it was but a step to the application of the term to other aspects of the culture of the age, and suggestions of such a concept were already numerous before the middle of the century.

The achievement of a more definite periodization was only a part, however, and not the most important part, of the effort made during the first half of the nineteenth century to place the art of the Renaissance in its historical setting. So far we have been dealing chiefly with critics whose aesthetic or religious bias helped to color the historical thought of the age, but who were less interested in the history of Renaissance art than in its relation to their own aesthetic doctrines. But contemporary with them there was also a great advance in the purely historical treatment of art, which by itself added greatly to both the knowledge and the interpretation of the Renaissance. Here again the influence of Winckelmann coincided with that of the Romantic movement. Both placed a new emphasis on historical development and on the indispensability of historical background for the understanding of any form of culture, though the historical feeling of the Romanticists ran deeper and was much more fundamental to their thought. Most of the art historians of the first half of the nineteenth century followed the classical rather than the Romantic aesthetic, but they were more and more profoundly influenced by the historical method that had grown up with Romanticism.

The foundations for the scholarly study of art history were laid in the last decade of the eighteenth century and the first two decades of the nineteenth by careful historians in Italy, France, and Germany, all men of discriminating taste and encyclopedic knowledge, who yet added but little to the classical interpretation.[47] The first decisively new note, reflecting the Romantic current of thought, appeared rather belatedly with the *Italian Researches* (1827-31) [48] of Karl Friedrich von

[47] See, for example, L. Lanzi, *Storia pittorica della Italia dal risorgimento delle belle arti fin presso al fine del XVIII secolo* (Bassono, 1795-96); L. Cicognara, *Storia della scultura dal suo risorgimento in Italia fino al secolo di Napoleone* (Venice, 1813); J. B. Seroux d'Agincourt, *Histoire de l'art par les monuments, depuis sa décadence au IVe siècle jusqu'à son renouvellement au XVIe*, 6 vols. (Paris, 1809-23); Eng. trans. (London, 1847); J. D. Fiorillo, *Geschichte der zeichnenden Künste von ihrer Wiederauflebung bis auf die neuesten Zeiten*, 5 vols. (Göttingen, 1798-1808). Note the various equivalents of the term "Renaissance."

[48] K. F. von Rumohr, *Italienische Forschungen*, 3 vols. (1827-31; critical ed. Frankfurt a/M., 1920).

Rumohr. In his rigorous objectivity, exhaustive archival research, and critical examination of sources, Rumohr was in close harmony with contemporary developments in other fields of historiography where the Romantic influence had been felt, but these very qualities mark a deviation from the current Romantic treatment of art. He had taken from the Wackenroder-Schlegel school a keen interest in the simple, naïve Christian art of the Middle Ages and early Renaissance, but he rejected the emotional subjectivity and extreme religious bias of the Romanticists as decidedly as he did Winckelmann's narrow concept of the classical norm of beauty. This rare independence enabled him to view the successive stages of Italian art from the Middle Ages through the High Renaissance with a consistently sympathetic yet critical eye. What resulted was the material for a history of Italian art rather than a history, for Rumohr restricted himself to the philological examination of sources and to technical or stylistic criticism. Nevertheless, his work demonstrated the error of the traditional idea that art had been resurrected from the grave by the late thirteenth century artists, and by implication at least it presented the growth of Italian art as a continuous, natural development, which owed relatively little to the imitation of the antique. Rumohr's influence worked in a variety of ways. His method set a new standard of critical exactitude for the history of art. His sympathetic treatment of early Christian art furnished Rio with the inspiration and much of the material for his quite uncritical work. And his research forced even those historians who showed a marked leaning toward classical aesthetic to give unprecedented attention to the art of the Middle Ages.

Franz Kugler's widely read *Handbook of the History of Painting from Constantine the Great to the Modern Age* (1837)[49] provides ample evidence of Rumohr's influence in this direction. Kugler's own tastes were classical, but he admitted the necessity of a more thorough treatment of medieval art, to which the Romanticists and Rumohr had called attention, than was common among the older historians.[50] And sympathetic appreciation of pre-Renaissance art became still more evi-

[49] F. Kugler, *Handbuch der Geschichte der Malerei von Constantin dem Grossen bis auf die neuere Zeit,* 2 vols. (Berlin, 1837; 2nd ed. revised and enlarged by J. Burckhardt, Berlin, 1847). Eng. trans. of part on Italian art (London, 1855).

[50] Cf. *ibid.,* I, v f.

dent in the second edition of the *Handbook* (1847), which was revised and considerably enlarged with the aid of Jacob Burckhardt. Kugler's work also showed some less consciously admitted influences of Romantic historical thought, particularly in the emphasis he placed upon the national element in the growth of Italian culture. On the whole, his compromise with Romanticism resulted in a solid gain in historical understanding. He noted the growth of an independent style in Italy following the dawn of an epoch of national prosperity at the end of the eleventh century, and characterized it as the metamorphosis of antique tradition in the spirit of the newly created nationality.[51] The progress of Tuscan art in the second half of the thirteenth century, he thought, must be understood in relation to "the renovation which marked the intellectual life of Italy at that time," [52] a renovation which he ascribed to the beginnings of a national culture as exemplified by the contemporary vernacular literature, and also to the glowing religious devotion inspired by St. Francis. The fourteenth and fifteenth centuries contributed respectively the subjective liberation of the individual artist and the correct delineation of form guided by the study of nature.[53] Finally, the first quarter of the sixteenth century combined all the qualities developed during the preceding centuries to create the most perfect art of modern times. There is no doubt that in Kugler's mind this golden age represented in a sense a rebirth of antiquity. "Here was reborn that wonderful age of Greek antiquity, in which beauty was revealed to the eyes of mortals, the divine idea was incorporated in perfect form, and the highest values of humanity were clearly portrayed in art." [54] But Kugler (or Burckhardt) was closer to Goethe than to Winckelmann in his insistence that the classical Renaissance did not spring from laborious imitation of the ancients.

> The period of Raphael [he asserted in the second edition] was not indebted in the first instance to the antique, but rather felt itself marvellously inspired by its spirit, and borrowing from it not the merely national and accidental, but the immutable and the infinite, was itself enabled to reproduce the immutable and the infinite likewise.[55]

[51] *Ibid.,* I, 268 f.   [52] *Ibid.,* I, 288 f [I, 108].   [53] Cf. *ibid.,* I, 392 f.
[54] *Ibid.,* (1st ed.) II, 84.   [55] *Ibid.,* (2nd ed.) I, 494 f [II, 276].

The interaction of classical and Romantic points of view, together with reaction on positivist grounds against the extreme positions of both, was more consciously expressed by the distinguished art critic, Eduard Kolloff, in a thoughtful article, "The Evolution of Modern Art out of the Antique to the Epoch of the Renaissance" (1840).[56] Though apparently not very influential in its own day, this article is of special interest for our purpose as the first methodical attempt to investigate the whole problem of the Renaissance and its relation to both antiquity and the Middle Ages. Kolloff was almost unique among art critics in his realization of the dangers involved in absolute systems and of the difficulty of reconciling historical continuity and variety with the demands of periodization. Herein, he thought, lay the major weaknesses of the exclusive systems set up by Winckelmann's disciples and by the Romanticists, both of which he dismissed with a finely malicious turn of phrase. A German living in Paris, Kolloff was unusually aware of the conflicting trends of historiography and criticism in both countries. His attitude toward them was certainly more independent than that of most. He insisted that it was the primary duty of the critic to bring an open mind to the appreciation of all types of art. Yet, like all critics, even the most objective, he had his preferences in taste, and they were decidedly classical. He reserved the bitterest edge of his irony for the Catholic Romanticists, who envisaged a rebirth of art by divine revelation in the late thirteenth century, which was followed shortly by a fall from grace, and he described their contemporary aspirations in terms that must have made him some enemies: "Thus he who finds in himself the desire or vocation to raise art from its decline, let him bow his head humbly to the earth and strew it with ashes: To him who prays and chastises himself will the artistic heaven of the thirteenth and fourteenth centuries be opened. Hallelujah!" [57]

The greater part of Kolloff's essay was concerned with disproving

---

[56] E. Kolloff, "Die Entwicklung der modernen Kunst aus der antiken bis zur Epoche der Renaissance," *Historisches Taschenbuch*, N. F., I (1840), 275–346. For discussion of Kolloff as a positivist historian, see Waetzoldt, *Kunsthistoriker*, II, 95–105.

[57] Kolloff, "Entwicklung der modernen Kunst," *Historisches Taschenbuch*, I, 284 f.

the erroneous assumption on which both the neo-classical and Romantic schools based their historical systems, namely, that art had been destroyed with the decline of the Roman Empire and resuscitated only in the thirteenth century or, as Winckelmann would have it, in the sixteenth. The decline of ancient art he admitted and explained by the indifference and spiritual apathy of the late Roman world. But the rise of Christianity and the barbarian invasions had neither destroyed the art of antiquity nor, as some of the Romanticists thought, replaced it with an entirely new form. Once the fear of paganism was past, Christian artists made what use they could of the antique heritage. The tradition of art was thus altered but remained unbroken, and after the time of Charlemagne the practice of art increased steadily, especially in Italy. Medieval art, Kolloff argued, was neither as incoherent as the classicists thought, nor had it the marvellous harmony which the Romanticists saw resulting "from a high morality and priestly wisdom." There was neither a unified, symbolical Christian art nor much study of the antique principles of harmony, for the men of the Middle Ages, though not ignorant, were yet indifferent to rules or principles. They "knew no other impulse than necessity, no other inspiration than instinct, and no other rule than chance." [58] Only such indifference could explain why the medieval artists did not learn more from the available remnants of antiquity. The Middle Ages were content with preserving the elements and monuments of ancient art. And this, Kolloff thought with a touch of Hegelian teleology, was providential, since the apathetic spirit of antiquity had to be outlived and men long enough impregnated with the Christian idea so that the Renaissance could restore reverence for the noble heritage of the ancient world without sharing its evils and futilities.

"It is now time," Kolloff continued, "to investigate the question, what have we to understand by the Renaissance and in what epoch must we put it?" [59] The first part of the question he answered by defining the Renaissance as "the return of order, not theocratic or academic order, which suppressed individuality and held self-consciousness in restraint, but the order that mingled all tendencies, all

[58] *Ibid.*, I, 322.   [59] *Ibid.*, I, 328.

talents, and all faculties harmoniously and led them to the highest development, in that it set aside all restrictions." [60] Later he defined it again more precisely as "the new manner of art founded on free imitation and use of the antique models and materials." [61] To the second part of the question — which he restated in phrases all too familiar to the present generation: "Where do the Middle Ages end and where does the Renaissance begin?" — Kolloff found no arbitrary answer possible, though he thought the question a vital one and too long neglected. The facts of history and the variety of works of art do not fit clear-cut divisions. If one looks closely one may discern contrary styles and principles of art in the same school, the same work, or the same artist. In any age the most vigorous works of art are the offspring of old custom and inspired innovation. Kolloff thought, therefore, that we must recognize an intermediate period between the full bloom of medieval art and the time when the clearly recognizable art of the Renaissance had gained an indubitable preponderance, a period characterized by a "neutral interim art" which showed traces of both periods.[62] He saw elements of the Renaissance in medieval art as far back as the period immediately following Gregory VII, and was convinced that the first movement of the Renaissance proper went back at least to the end of the thirteenth century. By the time of Cimabue and Giotto art had reached the point where it had all it needed for further advance. These artists "commonly called Christian" helped themselves greatly by study and imitation of the antique. From their time on there was an unbroken progress to the sixteenth century. Kolloff thus disagreed with both the classical and Romantic schools who would limit the Renaissance to the sixteenth century. To do so he thought "a serious error and gross misuse of words." [63] Briefly stated, Kolloff's conception of the Renaissance was that of a movement in art, neither entirely classical nor entirely Christian, but growing gradually out of the Middle Ages, aided by increased use of the antique and inspired by "the feeling of human pride and the striving for freedom and independence" of the Italian artists. It is a conception that would have seemed less original three generations later.

60 *Ibid.*, I, 328 f.   61 *Ibid.*, I, 342.
62 *Ibid.*, I, 330 ff.   63 *Ibid.*, I, 342.

THE RENAISSANCE IN THE HISTORY OF LITERATURE

The histories of Renaissance literature and learning during the half-century before Burckhardt show the same conflicting and interacting trends of Romanticism and neo-classicism as were to be found in art historiography, with a similar increasing tendency toward purely historical study and periodization. Yet the picture is not quite the same, for the literary historians were necessarily more concerned with the thought of the Renaissance, and many of them had inherited from their Protestant or rationalist predecessors, whose attitude toward the fine arts had been either indifferent or conventionally classical, conceptions of the revival of learning as a liberation from medieval superstition and scholasticism, as a prelude to the Reformation or to modern rational thought, conceptions from which the history of art was largely free. Finally, the literary history of the Renaissance lacked the unity of the artistic. Both Romanticists and classicists tended to treat the Latin and Greek writings of the humanists and the literature in the vernacular as two separate literatures.

This distinction was fostered on the Romantic side by the doctrine of organic national development, reinforced by the strong current of medievalism that ran through Romantic thought. From the Romantic point of view, only the literature written in the national tongue seemed an integral part of the national literary history. The vernacular literature of the Renaissance could be fitted into the picture of national growth as a natural continuation of medieval Christian and national traditions, while the classical writing of the humanists seemed an alien phenomenon, imitative rather than original, and therefore no true product of the developing folk soul. In his very popular lectures on the *History of Ancient and Modern Literature* (1815),[64] Friedrich Schlegel mentioned the restoration of classical learning only as an unfortunate occurrence fraught with evil consequences for all Europe, but especially for Italy. It checked originality by inspiring imitation, and it set the fashion of writing in Latin, through which many poets in Germany and Italy "were lost to their language and nation."[65]

---

[64] F. Schlegel, *Geschichte der alten und neuen Literatur, Vorlesungen gehalten zu Wien im Jahre, 1812* (1815), *Werke*, I–II. Eng. trans. (Philadelphia, 1818).
[65] *Ibid.*, II, 14 f [II, 23 f].

Limiting his discussion of Renaissance writers to those who used the vernacular, he further reserved his enthusiasm for the poets who showed signs of the old religious and chivalrous spirit. Dante naturally stood highest in his esteem, as he did with most of the Romanticists. Schlegel deplored Petrarch's absorption with the classical tongue and his consequent failure to understand the true nature of modern poetry, but admired his Italian love songs, which he thought expressed the very spirit of the Middle Ages. He also found a revival of chivalry in Boiardo and Ariosto, but considered the Italians in general to be lacking in true feeling for the romantic.[66] German literature, too, he felt was corrupted by the rage for latinity, and this he thought had even more pernicious effects than the tumult of the Reformation.[67] What Schlegel objected to was not the classics themselves, which he held in high regard, but their misuse, that is, imitation in modern times. Not all Romantic historians adhered to the strict Schlegelian orthodoxy, but their exclusive interest in the national languages was strong enough to prevent most of them from writing a comprehensive history of both the Latin and vernacular forms of Renaissance literature.

The history of the classical revival was left, therefore, in large part to men who rejected the Romantic theories and who saw in the restoration of the ancient literature one of the foundations of modern culture. This was a long established point of view, but in this generation it gained a new significance from the current trend of neo-classical enthusiasm for the ancient Greek ideal of life and culture, a significance reflected clearly in the opening pages of A. H. L. Heeren's *History of the Study of Classical Literature since the Revival of Learning* (1797–1801).[68] If the ancient literature was not the foundation of German culture in particular, Heeren wrote, it was at least "the foun-

---

66 *Ibid.*, II, 11.   67 *Ibid.*, II, 14 f.

68 A. H. Heeren, *Geschichte des Studiums der classischen Literatur seit dem Wiederaufleben der Wissenschaften mit einer Einleitung welche die Geschichte der Werke der Classiker im Mittelalter enthält*, 2 vols. (Göttingen, 1797–1801), *Historische Werke* (Göttingen, 1822), IV–V. Heeren was primarily an economic historian of the school of Adam Smith, and his interpretation of the classical revival is unusually materialistic for his age, yet he shared the new-humanist enthusiasm for the "inner worth" of the ancient literature, which he thought the chief reason for its survival. Cf. *ibid.*, V, 4 ff.

dation of that higher and nobler culture, which since it belongs to no nation, to no time or place, but is grounded in the inner core of our nature, we call the pure human culture (die rein menschliche Bildung)" [69] We have already noted the new cult of the Greek ideal in the field of art. It was also one of the most vital forces in the literary activity of Goethe's generation. This "Romantic Hellenism," as it has been called, was a European phenomenon, though more potent in Germany than elsewhere.[70] It owed much to Winckelmann, but much also to French archaeology. The Abbé Barthélemy's *Voyage of the Young Anacharsis in Greece* (1789) [71] presented an idealized picture of Greek antiquity that charmed the imaginations of men for more than half a century. Ancient Greece, thus romantically conceived, became a symbol of freedom for Romantic liberals like Shelley and Byron, a symbol of serene beauty for troubled aesthetes like Keats, but above all it furnished an ideal of universal human culture to all who found themselves in revolt against the objective rationalism of the Enlightenment and the materialism that accompanied the industrial revolution on the one hand, and against the religious preoccupations and narrow nationalism of the Romantic movement on the other.

A new conception of humanism was one of the significant byproducts of the cult of Greek antiquity.[72] The age of Goethe and Wilhelm von Humboldt revived the Ciceronian concept of *humanitas* and applied it, as Cicero had done, especially to Greek culture. In this sense *humanitas* was still inseparably connected, as it had been in Renaissance usage, with the study of ancient letters, but this was now more consciously regarded as a means to an end, the ultimate goal being a philosophy or view of life centering about man and a culture that would express man's highest intellectual potentialities. The new

---

[69] *Ibid.*, IV, 2.

[70] For the influence of the new Hellenism on literature, see L. Bertrand, *La fin du classicisme et le retour à l'antique* (Paris, 1897); E. M. Butler, *The Tyranny of Greece over Germany* (Cambridge, 1935); W. Rehm, *Griechentum und Goethezeit, Geschichte eines Glaubens* (Leipzig, 1936); B. H. Stern, *The Rise of Romantic Hellenism in English Literature 1732–86* (New York, 1940).

[71] J. J. Barthélemy, *Voyage du jeune Anacharsis en Grèce* (Paris, 1789). Eng. trans. (London, 1790–91).

[72] Cf. A. W. Livingstone, *Greek Ideals and modern Life* (Cambridge, Mass., 1935).

humanist view of man was more subjective than that of the rationalists, more intellectual than that of the Romanticists. It was closely associated in many ways with the contemporary trend of German philosophical idealism. Where the rationalist viewed man objectively as a mechanism operating according to natural laws, and the Romanticist saw in man the unconscious reflection of the folk soul, the new humanists proclaimed man to be an autonomous personality whose highest attribute was his cultivated intellect, a being peculiar to himself, not only the measure of all things but the creator and master of all things. This view of man they believed to have been most perfectly expressed in the culture of Greek antiquity. It was the major contribution of ancient Greece to modern civilization.

Enthusiasm for the Greek ideal ran strongly through much of the thoughtful writing of the nineteenth century. Inevitably it colored the interpretation of the age in which men believed that Greek antiquity had been rediscovered and brought back to life. The renewed interest in the revival of classical letters was reflected about the beginning of the century in a number of literary histories that were devoted primarily to the classical Renaissance.[73] We need not pause over these, however, except to extend them the courtesy of a footnote. The story they tell is familiar; what is new in their attitude is implied rather than consciously worked out. Time was needed to crystallize the new conceptions before they could be applied historically to the interpretation of the Renaissance. In this process the Romantic movement played an active rôle as *agent provocateur*. By emphasizing the national, religious, and chivalrous elements in medieval literature and the corporate quality of medieval life, the Romantic historians helped unwittingly to clarify the issue, pointing by implication to the opposite characteristics in the Renaissance as products of the revived spirit of antiquity. The phrase "renaissance of antiquity," which began to appear in the fourth decade of the century, suggested a broader yet more specific concept than the familiar *renaissance des lettres* or

[73] See, for example, Heeren, *op. cit.;* C. Meiners, *Lebensbeschreibungen berühmter Männer aus den Zeiten der Wiederherstellung der Wissenschaften*, 3 vols. (Zurich, 1795–97); W. Shepherd, *Life of Poggio Bracciolini* (Liverpool, 1802); H. A. Erhard, *Geschichte des Wiederaufblühens wissenschaftlicher Bildung*, 3 vols. (Magdeburg, 1827–32).

"revival of learning." At about the same time, the general adoption of the term "humanism" (from the German *Humanismus*)[74] in an historical sense to designate the intellectual movement associated with the revival of the ancient languages and literature provided modern historiography with a new linguistic tool that left its mark on all later interpretations of the Renaissance. Though applied specifically to the study of antiquity, its abstract form carried connotations that were not always consciously realized but were none the less effective.[75] It suggested an intellectual attitude that included a new interest in man, a new consciousness of individual personality, a more secular culture, all reflecting the ancient Greek rather than the medieval Christian spirit.

Around the year 1840 three works appeared which showed a deepening consciousness of historical problems and which cannot be passed over as mere repetitions of the classical literary tradition. The first of these, Henry Hallam's great *Introduction to the Literature of Europe in the Fifteenth, Sixteenth, and Seventeenth Centuries* (1837–38) was unique in its apparent disregard of both Romantic and neo-classical enthusiasms. A rationalist in the sense that he trusted reason rather than emotion or intuition, a classicist by education and temperament, an unimpassioned liberal, Hallam seems to belong more to the eighteenth century than to his own age, but his conscientious historical research belongs to a newer tradition. His work had unusual virtues, with their corresponding defects. He recounted the literary history of all the major European countries in both the national and ancient languages with a broad, cosmopolitan interest and magnificent good sense. Sound judgment marks every page of the book, but the total result is not a coördinated synthesis. His austere refusal to be carried away by current theories and enthusiams led to philosophical negation and left the whole work formless and pointless. It should have acted as a corrective to many contemporary trends, but the time for that had not yet come.

If Hallam's work was judicial to the point of theoretical nullity, no

[74] Cf. E. Heyfelder, "Die Ausdrücke 'Renaissance' und 'Humanismus'," *Deutsche Literaturzeitung*, XXXIV (1913), 2245–50.

[75] Hegel (see below, p. 173) was partly responsible for the erroneous notion that *humanitas* or *studia humaniora* connoted the literature in which man is stressed.

such criticism could be made of J. P. Charpentier's *History of the Renaissance of Letters in Europe in the Fifteenth Century* (1843).[76] Charpentier was a thorough classicist, in conscious reaction against the Romanticism of the previous generation. It was his contention — and this is a contentious book — that antiquity was the principle source of all that was best in modern literature and thought. "The modern nations," he asserted, "have no original traits nor a physiognomy peculiar to themselves; in their manners, their laws, their institutions, their literatures, one finds the vestiges and, as it were, the seal of antiquity."[77] The Middle Ages had abhorred the literature of pagan antiquity and, as a result, had lacked the sense of form and "the secret of art."[78] Its learned and its popular literature were alike sterile and formless. Then came "the renaissance and cult of antiquity and in that cult the awakening of thought."[79] Charpentier saw a "first renaissance"[80] in the fourteenth century with Dante, Petrarch, and Boccaccio, but the true "renaissance of antiquity" or, as he frequently called it, "the renaissance" did not come till the fifteenth century. This renaissance was more than the restoration of literary form and feeling for art; it was a violent revolution in language, ideas, and beliefs which made the fifteenth century and the Middle Ages two different worlds.[81] The study and imitation of the ancients caused not only the birth of the modern national literatures but also the restoration of the antique state of mind, which at its worst led to paganism, at its best to the humane and skeptical tolerance of an Erasmus or a Montaigne.[82] Charpentier's work is interesting chiefly for his unqualified statement of the revolutionary significance of the rebirth of antiquity. His historical treatment of the humanist movement is superficial and generally disappointing. For a more thoughtful analysis we must turn to a contemporary German work.

Karl Hagen's study of *Germany's Religious and Literary Relations in the Age of the Reformation* (1841–43)[83] was primarily an attempt

---

[76] J. P. Charpentier, *Histoire de la renaissance des lettres en Europe au quinzième siècle,* 2 vols. (Paris, 1843).

[77] *Ibid.,* II, 184.   [78] *Ibid.,* I, 23; II, 172 ff.   [79] *Ibid.,* I, 5.

[80] *Ibid.,* I, 157.   [81] *Ibid.,* I, 1.   [82] Cf. *ibid.,* I, 20 f; II, 176 ff.

[83] K. Hagen, *Deutschlands literarische und religiöse Verhältnisse im Reformationszeitalter,* 3 vols. (1841–43; I use ed. Frankfurt a/M., 1868).

to analyze the interrelated trends of opposition to the system of medieval religion which led to the Reformation. He dealt with humanism as merely one of the tendencies of the pre-Reformation period, if one of the most important. This point of view was significant, for it forced Hagen to treat humanism as a distinct intellectual movement and to gauge its relation to other contemporary developments. He was, incidentally, one of the first historians to use the term "humanism" consistently in the now accepted historical sense.[84] Like many previous writers, Hagen contrasted the spirit of the Middle Ages with that of antiquity, but there is a new note in his selection of their diametrically opposed attitude toward nature as the essence of the antithesis.[85] It was a harmonious inner relation to nature that caused the perfection of ancient art and literature, while at the same time it left ancient morality devoid of other than natural motives. The spirit of the Middle Ages, on the other hand, as most perfectly expressed in asceticism, was opposed to nature, to both the natural inclinations of man and to the natural element in the external world. This antagonistic attitude toward nature, Hagen thought, was chiefly responsible for the decline of art and poetry and of all intellectual activity that required consideration of nature or was essentially concerned with external form. At the same time, the Middle Ages made the positive contribution of a deep religious experience and substituted a higher principle for natural motives. To the modern age was left the task of reconciling the antithesis of these two worlds in a harmonious synthesis.[86] There is more than a touch of Hegel's philosophical method here.

Hagen ascribed the gradual disruption of the medieval system partly to the decline of what was best in it after it had passed its prime, but also to the rise of new tendencies: growing national consciousness, heretical movements, the appearance of a new burgher class with a "sound, sensible, and cheerful outlook on life,"[87] and, finally, humanism. What Hagen called the "popular tendency" which accompanied the growth of the bourgeoisie and found expression in their satirical literature was based entirely on natural feelings.[88] It was

---

[84] Cf. K. Brandi, *Das Werden der Renaissance* (Göttingen, 1908), p. 15.
[85] Hagen, I, 2 ff.   [86] *Ibid.*, I, 8 f.
[87] *Ibid.*, I, 17.   [88] *Ibid.*, I, 34 f.

opposed to anything contrary to man's nature and good sense. Humanism, in turn, was a necessary result of this development. As men revived the natural element, they were led by themselves to ancient literature in which nature had been so admirably expressed.[89] The mystical and heretical movements were also related to the popular tendency by their desire for a simpler, less ecclesiastical religion, and to humanism by a common interest in Platonic philosophy. The three tendencies, though separate in form and spirit, were thus inter-related and in Germany they tended toward an increasingly close co-operation.[90]

The chief service of humanism, in Hagen's view, was to give a new direction to learning in both form and content. The humanists re-covered the clarity, simplicity, and beauty of ancient literature; ex-tended the scope of knowledge; and destroyed scholasticism.[91] Hagen saw in Italian humanism, in which the spirit of antiquity was most fully reborn, a force essentially opposed to Christianity. Some hu-manists like Petrarch and Ficino tried to reconcile Christianity with ancient philosophy, "but in general one may assert that humanism in Italy toward the end of the fifteenth century had taken a direction indifferent to Christianity, that, indeed, indifference had passed over into depreciation and frivolity." [92] This, however, brought no change in belief. The Italians lacked the moral vigor for a serious religious reform. Reverting to the Romantic conception of the continuity of national character, Hagen declared that the Italian people had always lacked moral strength. They were weaker than ever during the Renaissance because with the spirit of antiquity had been revived the egoism that was one of its prime motives. The full victory over the medieval system required the contribution of a nation in which great moral force was combined with enlightenment, and enthusiasm for lofty ideas with the courage to act.[93] The author was referring to the Germans.

In Hagen's interpretation of the classical revival, the familiar Protest-ant, rationalist, and classical traditions had been altered by historical theories stemming from the Romantic movement and from Hegel's

89 *Ibid.*, I, 37.   90 *Ibid.*, I, 377.   91 *Ibid.*, I, 37 f.
92 *Ibid.*, I, 59.   93 *Ibid.*, I, 63.

philosophy of history to form something like a new synthesis. His whole work was oriented by the Reformation rather than the Renaissance. Nevertheless, he was the first historian to throw into strong relief two aspects of the Renaissance, in so far as it can be identified with humanism: its relation to the spirit of the rising burgher class, and its naturalistic reaction to the other-worldliness of the Middle Ages.

The next significant contribution to the characterization of humanism, and a much more influential one, came nearly two decades later in Georg Voigt's *The Revival of Classical Antiquity, or the First Century of Humanism* (1859).[94] In this youthful work, fresh, vigorous, and intuitive, Voigt sketched the pattern for the delineation of Italian humanism that was to be followed by the majority of historians for two generations. Later (1880–81) he filled in the gaps in this early study with a mass of illustrative material taken from more authentic sources, and thereby made it a book for scholars rather than for the lay public. In neither form did the book receive the wide acclaim of Burckhardt's contemporary essay, but generations of readers have absorbed his ideas at second hand. Anyone who has read Philippe Monnier's *The Quattrocento* (1900)[95] will find Voigt strangely familiar.

The son of Johannes Voigt, the distinguished Prussian historian, young Georg had been raised in an atmosphere of historical research, and had early come under the invigorating influence of Ranke and Niebuhr. His approach to the Renaissance was that of a Protestant with a high respect for the classics, but above all it was that of an historian. He was first attracted to the history of humanism by his interest in Pius II, the humanist pope, whose correspondence he collected and whose biography he wrote in three large volumes.[96] And it was the personality of the humanists that continued to hold his attention. He took for granted the *weltgeschichtlich* significance of the revival of antiquity in Italy. In the philosophical phraseology of his generation, it was Italy's task "to recapitulate antiquity and the bloom of Christian-

---

[94] G. Voigt, *Die Wiederbelebung des classischen Altertums, oder das erste Jahrhundert des Humanismus* (Berlin, 1859).

[95] P. Monnier, *Le Quattrocento, Essai sur l'histoire littéraire du XVe siècle italien,* 2 vols. (Paris, 1900). See below, p. 244.

[96] G. Voigt, *Enea Silvio de' Piccolomini,* 3 vols. (Berlin, 1856–63).

Romantic life, to unite the form and sensible beauty which was the heritage of the ancient peoples with the spirit of the Romantic in art." [97] But in his study of early humanism, which he recognized to be merely one aspect of the Renaissance, he limited his attention to the immediate historical problem of discovering the form actually taken by the revival of antiquity and its psychological effects on the humanists, and through them on the rest of Italian society. Yet, limited though his aim may have been, the effect of his work as a whole was to identify the rebirth of antiquity indissolubly with the Renaissance as the dominant characteristic of its culture.

The humanists, as Voigt portrayed them, formed a new class of lay men of letters and represented a new type of individualistic personality. Their learning and their literary activity were anthithetical to those of the schoolmen, and one of their most significant achievements, he thought, was their comprehensive attack on all forms of scholastic learning. Voigt analyzed the opposition of humanism to scholasticism as that of aesthetic, literary wit to coherent but dull and painful study, of a brilliant, universal, human culture to pedantic schoolroom erudition, of artistic instinct to hard, ingrained method. Each had its disadvantages. "While exclusive learning collected masses of unfruitful erudition, its rash rivals spread abroad in the world a quantity of unripe knowledge, of misunderstood truth and rapidly grasped half-truths." [98] On the positive side, the early humanists of the first century of humanism made an invaluable contribution to the modern world by restoring antique culture and by giving a new form to learning, but, as the preceding quotation suggests, Voigt had no great respect for their own intellectual achievements. Disparaging comments on their accomplishments occur frequently throughout his work. "They produced scarcely anything independent and nothing that was not surpassed in the following century. The humanists believed they had created a new Augustan age; in reality they had merely prepared the ground and planted the seed for the future." [99] Over-praised in their own day, their writing is now almost forgotten. Reverence for antiquity put upon them the curse of imitation. Their perception of antique values

[97] Voigt, *Wiederbelebung*, p. 3.
[98] *Ibid.*, p. 446.   [99] *Ibid.*, p. 445.

was often childish and uncritical. Their attempt to shape the modern world on the ancient model was unrealistic and futile. Their philosophy was without philosophical method or original ideas.

> In opposition to the scholastics, the humanists boasted that they had taken philosophy out of the schools into the world; actually they had merely taken it into another school . . . . What they called philosophy was not much more than reiteration and variation of classical commonplaces on the uncertainty and inevitability of death and on the transitoriness of all things earthly, on virtue and vice, on fortune and the highest good, on youth and age . . . . and the like.[100]

After Petrarch there was no earnest religious thought to be found in them.[101] Their playing with paganism and their criticism of the Church were alike frivolous. On the other hand, the critical method which resulted from their philological and historical studies was of immeasurable importance, while their exclusive concentration on form produced a style that, with all its rhetorical faults, was vastly superior to the crabbed forms of scholastic writing or the obscurantism of the mystics.[102]

Criticism of the humanists' literary production was, however, only a small part of Voigt's work. He was much more interested in their personal characteristics. He was aware that this was an odd attitude for a literary historian, but justified it on the ground that their activity and example was as important as their writing, that, in fact, their personality was in itself a human achievement of the highest significance.[103] That Voigt should place his emphasis thus was in keeping with his whole conception of the psychological influence of the revival of antiquity. As Hagen had seen the essential contrast between humanism and the medieval system in the return of the former to the antique attitude toward nature, Voigt saw it in the recovery of the antique consciousness of individual personality which had been lost during the Middle Ages.

> Nothing [Voigt wrote] penetrated and distinguished the Christian Middle Ages so decisively as the corporative tendency. After the chaos of the folk migrations, the renewed humanity crystallized in

100 *Ibid.*, p. 438.　　　　　101 *Ibid.*, p. 454 ff.
102 *Ibid.*, pp. 444 f; 428 ff.　　103 *Ibid.*, p. 428.

groups, orders, systems. Hierarchy and feudalism were merely the largest formations. Even learned and artistic life . . . . accommodated itself to the general trend. . . . When great men arose, they seem so only as representatives of the system in which they lived, only as the first among their peers, like the heads of the feudal states and the church. Their greatness and power depended, not on the accidental and peculiar in their person, but rather on the energy with which they expressed the ideal essence of their system.[104]

To this corporate consciousness the individual self-consciousness of the humanists stood out in glaring contrast.

It was from this point of view, as the powerful personality "who first broke through the bonds of corporation" and "made his ego the mirror of the world" that Voigt hailed Petrarch as "the prophet of the new age, the ancestor of the modern world." [105] There was nothing new in regarding Petrarch as the founder of the classical revival. The Renaissance writers had done so as had all serious historians since Tiraboschi, though many textbooks still dated the revival from the fall of Constantinople. But there was much that was new in Voigt's penetrating psychological analysis of the first humanist and in his perception of the quality of Petrarch's originality.

> In him for the first time individuality and its rights stood forth strong and free with a claim to the highest significance. . . . Even his unmeasured thirst for fame and his petty vanities belonged as essential parts thereto. Everything that he read or learned, everything that he did or experienced, he related to his own person; the whole external world served him simply as material for his personal education. How differently he learned from books! Not only did his memory acquire knowledge, not only did his understanding exert itself in distinctions and judgments; his whole self entered into communication with the great men who had lived before him. He searched in the books of Cicero and Augustine for experiences comparable to his own; he sought men in books. Petrarch did much for classical learning; he gave the strongest impulse to the destruction of scholasticism; but the greatest, most arduous, and most serviceable of his achievements was himself.[106]

Voigt devoted nearly a quarter of his book to Petrarch and thereafter continued to use him as a standard by which to measure his suc-

---

[104] *Ibid.*, p. 80 f.   [105] *Ibid.*, p. 81.   [106] *Ibid.*, p. 81 f.

cessors, seldom to their advantage. The later humanists followed faithfully in Petrarch's footsteps and shared most of his traits of character; but in none of them did Voigt find the depth of consciousness, the introspective searching, nor the absorbing conflict between old and new cultural elements, that made Petrarch the prototype of the modern individual man. What seemed excusable, if unfortunate, attributes of greatness in Petrarch often degenerated in the later humanists into pettiness and childish egocentricity. In them the conflict between ideal and reality, between what they wrote and how they lived, seldom led to soul struggle. Masters of self-deception, they took the word for the deed, and believed themselves to be high-principled antique sages because they had learned to write about morality as Cicero and Seneca had done.[107] Voigt called them "mouth philosophers" and "pen Stoics." He dwelt on their struggle for place and their literary feuds, their shameless flattery and more shameless invective. He could characterize Poggio and Filelfo as "slanderous big-mouths." But he found them endlessly interesting none the less and immensely significant in their self-conscious individualism.

THE RENAISSANCE IN CULTURAL HISTORY — THE LIBERAL AND IDEALIST TRADITIONS

The Renaissance made its appearance relatively late in general history or was included only in the limited form of the traditional revival of art, learning, and letters. During the first half of the nineteenth century, most general history was political, and the majority of historians were more interested in archival research than in cultural synthesis.[108] They accepted the conventional division between the Middle Ages and the modern period at about 1500 and either ignored the culture of the Renaissance or merely echoed the contemporary specialists in the history of art and literature.[109] Neither Ranke

[107] *Ibid.*, p. 410.

[108] For the general historiography of this period see the authorities cited above, p. 113.

[109] See, for example, H. Leo, *Geschichte der italienischen Staaten* (Hamburg, 1829–37), IV, 284. Leo took his treatment of Italian art admittedly from Rumohr.

nor Guizot, despite their unusual interest in the underlying ideas of
the age, added anything significant to the conception of the Renaissance as such, though Guizot did note a universal tendency toward
centralization of peoples, cultures, and governments as the dominant
trait of the fifteenth century.[110]

One of the few historians of the early nineteenth century to attempt
a *Kulturgeschichte* of the Renaissance period was that strangely
erudite Liverpool attorney, William Roscoe. His work deserves mention in any history of Renaissance historiography, not only for the immense stimulus it gave to Italian studies,[111] but also for the direction it
gave to many later interpretations. Roscoe conceived the whole cultural
revival of the Renaissance in Italy as centering about the Medici family,
as indeed largely the product of that family's intelligent direction and
liberal patronage.[112] He, therefore, undertook to write a general cultural and political history of Italy in the late fifteenth and early sixteenth centuries, the period between those covered by Gibbon and
Robertson, in the form of biographies of the two most influential members of the Medici clan. The result was the famous *Life of Lorenzo
de' Medici, Called the Magnificent* (1796) and the only slightly less
popular *Life and Pontificate of Leo the Tenth* (1805). Both works
enjoyed an immediate and lasting success. They ran rapidly through
numerous editions and were translated into all the principle European
languages. There was good reason for the enthusiastic reception of
Roscoe's work. It was the first of its kind and remarkably good considering the difficulties of research "in a remote part of this remote
kingdom." [113] Yet it was not without its faults. Roscoe was completely lacking in sympathetic understanding of the religious element
in the thought of the age. His account of the revival of art and letters,

---

110 F. Guizot, *Histoire de la civilisation en Europe* (1829–32; new ed. Paris,
1846), pp. 292 ff. On lack of a *Renaissancebegriff* in Ranke, see C. Neumann,
"Ende des Mittelalters?," *Deutsche Vierteljahrsschrift für Literaturwissenschaft
und Geistesgeschichte*, XII (1934), 50 f.
111 Cf. R. Marshall, *Italy in English Literature, 1755–1850* (New York, 1934),
pp. 271 ff.
112 Voltaire and Iselin had suggested as much (see above, pp. 91 and 109), but
Roscoe gave to "the age of the Medici" a much more literal meaning.
113 W. Roscoe, *Life of Lorenzo de' Medici, Called the Magnificent* (1796; new
ed. London, 1846), p. xlii.

though thorough and stimulating, and more closely integrated with political history than was customary, was otherwise unoriginal, following the rational-classical tradition. Roscoe's whole conception of history, in fact, seems more nearly that of Voltaire's generation than of his own. He tended to exaggerate the personal influence of enlightened princes and to ignore general causes. His interpretation of the political policies of the Medici was much too consistently favorable,[114] and his estimate of their effect was out of proportion to the cause. His judgment in this respect was reversed by many nineteenth century liberals, but his conviction that the influence of the Medici was of vital importance was to become almost a constant factor in Renaissance historiography. In the present century Roscoe's apologia for the Medici has been repeated with little essential modification in Colonel G. F. Young's study of the family.[115]

The first attack upon Roscoe's conception of the golden age of Italy and the rôle of the Medici came little more than a decade later from the liberal Swiss historian, Simonde de Sismondi. The two men had much in common. They were both immensely industrious, both were Protestant by tradition, and both had inherited their dominant ideas from the liberal rationalism of the Age of Enlightenment. But whereas Roscoe's historical philosophy stemmed from Voltaire and was not incompatible with faith in a beneficent and enlightened despotism, Sismondi was a romantic apostle of liberty from the school of Rousseau. For him political freedom was the highest possible achievement of a people, and was in turn the source of all other achievements of the human will or intellect. It was the standard by which he judged all history, and he was no lenient judge. His most influential work, *The History of the Italian Republics in the Middle Ages* (1807-18),[116] was one long hymn to liberty followed by a funeral ode. It was also the first, and the last, attempt to write a full, detailed history of all the Italian states from the rise of the communes to the beginning of the sixteenth century. It has been superseded in almost every part, but not yet as a

[114] *Ibid.*, pp. 192 ff.
[115] G. F. Young, *The Medici*, 2 vols. (London, 1909).
[116] J. C. L. Simonde de Sismondi, *Histoire des républiques italiennes au Moyen Age*, 16 vols. (Zurich and Paris, 1807-18; I use ed. Paris, 1826). Eng. trans., condensed (London, 1832).

whole, and its comprehensiveness, combined with a very respectable degree of accuracy, has maintained its usefulness down to the present time.

Sismondi opened his history with a statement of historical philosophy that sprang directly from the eighteenth century and was an equally direct denial of the current Romantic theories.

> One of the most important conclusions that we can draw from the study of history [he wrote] is that government is the prime cause of the character of peoples; that the virtues or vices of nations, their energies or their weaknesses, their talents, their enlightenment or their ignorance, are almost never the effects of climate or the attributes of a particular race, but the work of laws; that everything has been given to all men by nature, but that government takes from or guarantees to men who are subjected to it the heritage of the human species.[117]

Working from this premise, Sismondi ascribed the decline of Roman civilization to the tyranny of the emperors, and the rebirth of Italian vigor, virtue, and culture to the recovery of freedom by the communes. So far his thesis is curiously similar to that of Leonardo Bruni's *History of the Florentine People,* but he added a third act to the drama, that of the decline of Italian morality and culture with the failure of republican government.

Sismondi traced the origins of all that was great in Italy to the twelfth and thirteenth centuries, to the age of the communes with their united, homogeneous, and virtuous citizenry and their "énergie de liberté."[118] It was in the thirteenth century that literature, learning, and the arts awoke and caused centuries of taste to succeed those of barbarism.[119] The fourteenth century was more brilliant. "In no time have letters been cultivated with more ardor or scholars been honored with more enthusiasm, or greater light acquired and generally spread among men."[120] But it was not a happy period, for virtue and morality were already being corrupted by tyrannous government and the example of the despotic courts. The fourteenth century, Sismondi thought, lacked the definite character of the two preceding

117 *Ibid.,* I, v.
119 *Ibid.,* IV, 70 ff.
118 *Ibid.,* VIII, 2.
120 *Ibid.,* VI, 1.

centuries. It had no unified purpose. Individuals detached themselves from the crowd, distinguished themselves by great deeds, great talents, and great crimes, but did not advance their nation in any direction.[121] Florence alone retained the spirit of liberty, and even she fell under the tyranny of the Medici in the following century.[122] In general the fifteenth century presented to Sismondi's view a gloomy picture. The progressive destruction of liberty was accompanied by the ruin of all energy and all public and private morality. Even literature was losing its vigor and imagination. In any case the literary and artistic achievements of the fifteenth and sixteenth centuries were but the delayed fruits of a freedom that was fast perishing. Earlier historians had called attention to the revitalizing influence of the free communes on medieval culture, but this corollary emphasis on the pernicious effect of the loss of liberty was relatively new. It made a strong appeal to many liberals throughout the nineteenth century, especially in Italy. It formed the theme of Cesare Balbo's *History of Italy* (1844) and *Life of Dante* (1839),[123] and of the works of such champions of the Risorgimento as Gino Capponi and Carlo Troya.[124]

Second only to political liberty, Sismondi stressed the predominant rôle of the cities in shaping Italian social and cultural life. And not only because they formed the communes. Sismondi always admired the well-to-do burgher class and had small respect for the chivalrous nobility.[125] He noted as a very significant factor in the development of Italian society that the nobles were early drawn into the cities and that the new lords were not feudal but were children of the cities. "This predominant influence of the cities," he declared, "is the true origin of the distinctive character of the Italians." [126] The early urban life of Italy gave the Italians a more active spirit and developed more talent, more patriotism, and more *habilité*. It accumulated more riches

[121] *Ibid.*, VIII, 2 f.
[122] *Ibid.*, VII, 394; cf. IX, 33 ff; 358 ff; X, 167 ff; XI, 257 ff.
[123] C. Balbo, *Sommario della storia d'Italia* (1844, new ed. Bari, 1913–14); *Vita di Dante* (Turin, 1839). Eng. trans. (London, 1852).
[124] Cf. B. Croce, *Storia della storiografia italiana nel secolo decimonono* (Bari, 1921), I, 130 ff.
[125] Cf. Sismondi, *De la littérature du Midi de l'Europe* (Paris, 1813), I, 88 ff. Eng. trans. (London, 1823).
[126] Sismondi, *Républiques*, V, 3.

and caused a more rapid flowering of art, letters, and learning. In short, "the Italians were formed in the bourgeois school." [127] This too was an emphasis that would be frequently repeated by later historians.

Although Sismondi in the main rejected the Romantic historical theories and attitudes, he was not entirely immune from their influence. He became a member in good standing of the literary court of Mme. de Staël, and as his work progressed he showed an increasing tendency to talk in terms of the national spirit. Of the Florentine people, whom he compared to the ancient Greeks, he wrote: "One must seek in the very character of a nation the motives of the habitual conduct of its government," a theory oddly at variance with his original premise.[128] In his treatment of Italian literature he reflected the Romantic view that the revival and imitation of the classics had had a pernicious effect.[129] This theory he developed further in his history of *The Literature of the South of Europe* (1813). Here he definitely excluded the men "to whom we owe the revival of Greek and Latin literature" from his discussion on the ground that they "do not properly belong to Italian literature." [130] Here, too, he accepted Mme. de Staël's distinction between the Latin and Teutonic nations. Finally, Sismondi was in full accord with the Romanticists, if not always for the same reasons, in his conviction of the moral superiority of the twelfth and thirteenth centuries and in the picture he presented of the irreligion, immorality, crimes, passions, and irresponsible egotism of Renaissance society.[131]

The growing interest in periodization and the philosophical construction of history, which we have already noted in the history of art and literature toward the middle of the nineteenth century, received a powerful stimulus from the spread of Hegelian philosophy. Hegel's influence was already great before his death in 1831, but his historical philosophy was first widely disseminated by the posthumous publication of his lectures on *The Philosophy of History* (1837) [132] and *The*

127 *Ibid.*, V, 4.   128 *Ibid.*, V, 166; cf. V, 1 ff; VI, 163 ff.
129 *Ibid.*, VI, 166 ff; VIII, 4 ff; X, 1 ff.
130 Sismondi, *De la littérature*, II, 28 [II, 27]; cf. I, 1 ff; 23 ff.
131 Cf. Sismondi, *Républiques*, VI, 2 ff; VII, 2 f; VIII, 51 f; 230 f.
132 G. W. F. Hegel, *Vorlesungen über die Philosophie der Geschichte* (Berlin, 1837), *Werke* (Berlin, 1832–87), IX. Eng. trans. (London, 1857). The critical

History of Philosophy (1833–36).[133] The effect of these was to introduce a way of thinking about history that has exerted an incalculable influence on the historiography of the past century. Relatively few historians, it is true, were strict Hegelians. Perhaps no good historian could be. Yet great numbers drew from Hegel such ideas as suited their purpose, while still more utilized fragments of his philosophy of history without being aware of the source. It is thus extremely difficult to determine the extent of Hegel's direct influence in individual cases, the more so that Hegel himself represented a synthesis of ideas stemming from nearly every trend of thought in the preceding century. Hence, ideas that have a suspiciously Hegelian ring may in fact be either the result of independent currents of thought or merely the expression of a climate of opinion saturated with the Hegelian miasma.

One decided effect of Hegel's philosophy was to revive the habit of thinking in terms of teleological world history, as the theologians and rationalists had done. But for the Divine Providence of the former and the latter's faith in progress based on individual reason, Hegel substituted the metaphysical concept of a world spirit that works through history by a logic of its own toward the realization of its Idea. The goal of this teleological process, in Hegel's mind, was the modern state, specifically the Prussian state, though he confused the issue by talking of it as the drive of the spirit toward consciousness of freedom. It was not necessary, however, to accept the ultimate purpose of Hegel's scheme to be charmed by a theory that seemed to give a rational meaning to history and that was equipped with the philosophical terminology and apparently scientific method needed to make it intellectually respectable. Like the Romantic historical philosophers,

work on Hegel is very extensive, but the best explanation of his philosophy of history is still that in his own introduction. As Hegel's language is unusually difficult, I give alternate references to the English translation for all citations. See also summary in R. Flint, *La philosophie de l'histoire en Allemagne* (Paris, 1878), pp. 260–334. There is an excellent discussion of Hegel in R. G. Collingwood, *The Idea of History* (Oxford, 1946), pp. 113–22, which I did not see till my own work was in galley proof. Particularly interesting is Collingwood's discussion of the historical philosophy of Hegel's predecessors, Herder, Kant, Fichte, and Schelling (*ibid.*, pp. 88–113) and his analysis of Hegel's indebtedness to them.

[133] Hegel, *Vorlesungen über die Geschichte der Philosophie,* 2 vols. (Berlin, 1833–36), *Werke*, XIII–XV. Eng. trans. (London, 1892).

with whom he had much in common,[134] Hegel dealt with large, unconscious, abstract forces. To quote George Sabine, who has an unusual aptitude for making sense out of Hegel's "formidable terminology":

> In Hegel's interpretation of history, it is the nation, rather than the individual or any grouping of individuals, that forms the significant unit. The genius or spirit of the nation (Volksgeist), working through individuals but largely in independence of their conscious will and intention, is the true creator of art, law, morals, and religion. Hence the history of civilization is a succession of national cultures in which each nation brings its peculiar and timely contribution to the whole human achievement.[135]

Thus the national spirit is the creative force, as with the Romanticists, but it operates under the direction of the world spirit and is constantly changing through development. At any given point in history the world spirit makes itself manifest through the national spirit, at its particular stage of development, as the spirit of the age. The historians must, of course, select for mention only those nations, and those events in their history or aspects of their culture, that demonstrate the working of the world spirit, that is, that have world-historical significance. Ideas such as these, even if not strictly adhered to, led easily to much loose generalization about the *Zeitgeist* or *Volksgeist,* about the "task" of a nation, its rôle in world history, or its destined contribution to civilization.

Much the same kind of loose generalization was fostered by Hegel's habit of characterizing a nation or an age by a few abstract qualities. This was a natural part of his system since each national civilization represented an aspect of the world spirit in process of development. To cite an example not without relevance to our subject, he characterized the ancient Greek spirit as "Individuality conditioned by Beauty," [136] and explained Greek civilization by "the several radiations which this idea throws out in realizing itself."

134 Cf. G. von Below, *Die deutsche Geschichtschreibung von den Befreiungskriegen bis zu unsern Tagen* (Munich, 1924), pp. 29 ff.

135 G. H. Sabine, *A History of Political Theory* (New York, Henry Holt and Company, 1937), p. 261.

136 Hegel, *Philosophie der Geschichte, Werke,* IX, 292 [p. 248].

All issue in works of art, and we may arrange under three heads: the subjective work of art, that is, the culture of man himself; the objective work of art, that is, the shaping of the world of divinities; lastly, the political work of art — the form of the constitution and the relations of the individuals who compose it.[137]

This is a generalization that might easily be adapted to the Renaissance, regarded as the rebirth of the Greek spirit.

In Hegel's own thought the conception of the world spirit was inseparable from the method through which it achieved its ends in actual history, that is, the dialectic, the peculiar logic of history. They were not, however, necessarily inseparable. Many historians accepted Hegel's idealism, in part at least, without the dialectic. Karl Marx, on the other hand, adopted the dialectic while rejecting the spirit. And in a less conscious fashion many historians who could not follow the whole Hegelian philosophy yet found in his dialectic an instrument that could be adapted to their use. In its simplest form the dialectic served to lend an apparent clarity to the interaction of traditions or cultural tendencies. It taught historians to look for the logical succession of thesis, antithesis, synthesis, to assume a causal relation between the full development of one tradition, the resultant rise and completion of its opposite, and the ensuing amalgamation of what was most permanent in both to form a new and "higher" tradition. We have already noted Hagen applying this method to the Renaissance in the formula of medieval otherworldliness, Renaissance return to nature, and the modern synthesis of both produced by the Reformation. The Hegelian dialectic might easily strengthen the long-standing conception of the Renaissance as both the antithesis of the Middle Ages and the forerunner of the Reformation by lending it the authority of logical necessity.

Such was, in fact, Hegel's own interpretation of the Renaissance. In both *The Philosophy of History* and *The History of Philosophy* he labored to demonstrate that during the Middle Ages feudalism and the Church had combined to destroy freedom and to barbarize and debase the spirit. Scholastic thought and the sacramental system despiritualized religion by binding it to externalities.[138] But this,

[137] *Ibid.*, IX, 293 [p. 250].
[138] *Ibid.*, IX, 457 ff; cf. 497 ff [pp. 392 ff; 429 ff].

when fully developed, brought reaction. At the end of the Middle
Ages the national states replaced feudalism and assumed many of the
functions together with the divine sanction of the Church. At the
same time, men turned from the exclusive contemplation of the
"supersensuous world," which had been robbed of its spiritual content,
to interest in the present world, "this hither side," to "man's inner life
and to external nature." The gap between the secular and the ecclesiastical was closed and "the secular element spiritualized itself in
itself." [139] This Hegel interpreted as the return of the spirit to consciousness of freedom, that is, to itself.

> Thus men came to the point of knowing that they were free, and
> insisting on the recognition of that freedom, and having the power
> of exercising their activity for their own objects and interests. Thus
> spirit came again to itself. . . . This new birth is pointed out as the
> revival of the arts and sciences which were concerned with present
> matter, the epoch when the spirit gains confidence in itself and its
> existence, and finds its interest in its present. It is in reality reconciled
> with the world.[140]

The "return of the spirit to itself" is a concept of dubious meaning
to anyone who is unaccustomed to thinking in Hegelian terms, but the
connotations he attached to it are by no means unfamiliar. Wherever
the influence of German idealism has made itself felt, the Renaissance
has been identified, more or less, with the ideas of reaction against
medieval transcendentalism and of the reassertion of man's self-consciousness, his moral and intellectual autonomy, and his spiritual reconciliation with this present world. The Renaissance thus became a
necessary phase of man's destined progression toward freedom, as
that term was understood by idealist philosophy.

Hegel saw the new birth of the spirit working through three specific movements.[141] The first of these was the rise of art, which partially spiritualized medieval religion by lending beauty and sentiment
to the material objects of adoration. The second was the study of

---

139 Hegel, *Geschichte der Philosophie, Werke*, XV, 177 ff [III, 95 ff].
140 *Ibid.*, XV, 189 [III, 106 f].
141 *Ibid.*, XV, 190 [III, 108]; *Philosophie der Geschichte, Werke*, IX, 493 ff
[pp. 425 ff].

antiquity or *studia humaniora*. "The name *humaniora*," Hegel added, "is very expressive, for in those works of antiquity honor is done to the Human and to the development of Humanity: through this study the West became acquainted with the true and eternal element in the activity of man."[142] And again, "Men turned to the works of the ancients . . . . as *studia humaniora,* where man is recognized in what concerns himself and in what he effects . . . . Men, because they are men, found it interesting to study men as men."[143] This is a distortion of the original meaning of the term, but one which, as we have already noted, gained increasing acceptance during the nineteenth century.[144] Hegel ascribed the revival of antiquity essentially to the "awakening of the self-hood of the spirit," but noted incidentally that its outward occasion was the fall of the Byzantine Empire which introduced Greek literature to the West, a tradition that had long been abandoned by nearly all historians of literature. On the philosophical side he interpreted it as pure return to Greek philosophy, the spirit of which he had already noted as antithetical to that of medieval scholasticism.[145] As the third characteristic of the period, Hegel pointed to "that urging of the spirit outward — that desire on the part of man to become acquainted with his world" which resulted in the explorations and discoveries. "These three events," he concluded, "may be compared with the blush of dawn, which after long storms betokens the bright and glorious day."[146] The next step in the dialectic process was, of course, the Protestant Reformation.

From Hegel, the progression to Jules Michelet's brilliant if erratic synthesis, the first attempt to isolate and characterize the Renaissance so called as a period in general European history, seems a very natural one. Yet it is difficult to establish any direct connection between the German philosopher and the French historian. Certainly one would hesitate to classify Michelet as Hegelian. He is, indeed, a hard man to fit into any ready-made category. Fueter treats him under the heading

---

[142] *Ibid.,* IX, 494 [p. 427].
[143] Hegel, *Geschichte der Philosophie, Werke,* XV, 190 [III, 108].
[144] See above, p. 155.
[145] Hegel, *Geschichte der Philosophie, Werke,* XV, 191 ff; cf. 179 [III, 109 ff; cf. 96].
[146] Hegel, *Philosophie der Geschichte, Werke,* IX, 496 [p. 428].

of the "lyrical-subjective school," [147] Gooch under the "Romantic school," [148] and Robert Flint under the "democratic historical school," [149] while Louis Halphen places him at the head of his chapter on "the return to synthetic history." [150] There is reason for each of these classifications. Michelet's reconstruction of history was both lyrical and subjective to the highest degree. He shared the Romantic love of the national past and its local color as well as the Romantic theory of the national spirit. He was the first great democratic historian by virtue of his feeling for the people and his hatred of all tyranny. And he was forever seeking to find in any event or personality that struck his impressionable imagination a deep significance, the characteristic expression of an age or a race, and to construct an historical synthesis therefrom. Always avid for ideas, he was admittedly influenced by such diverse thinkers as Vico, Voltaire, Rousseau, Herder, Kant, Sismondi, and Guizot. He had also absorbed a good deal of the contemporary German idealistic philosophy of history, probably through the mediation of his friends Cousin and Quinet. He was, indeed, one of the principal exponents in France of what Augustin Thierry called "that method, come from Germany, which sees in each fact the symbol of an idea and in the course of human events a perpetual psychomachy," [151] and it was this tendency, deplorable though it seemed to Thierry, that lent to Michelet's interpretation of the Renaissance its special significance.

Michelet's epoch-making characterization of the Renaissance appeared in the introduction to the seventh volume of his great *History of France* (1833–62).[152] Twelve years had passed between the publication of the sixth volume on the end of the Middle Ages and the seventh on the sixteenth century, to which he gave the title, *La Renaissance* (1855). In the meantime he had written the history of

147 E. Fueter, *Geschichte der neueren Historiographie* (Munich, 1936), pp. 452 ff.

148 G. P. Gooch, *History and Historians in the Nineteenth Century* (London, 1935), pp. 175 ff.

149 R. Flint, *History of the Philosophy of History* (New York, 1894), pp. 531 ff.

150 L. Halphen, *L'Histoire en France depuis cent ans* (Paris, 1914), pp. 81 ff.

151 A. Thierry, *Récits des temps mérovingiens, précédés de considérations sur l'histoire de France* (Paris, 1856), p. 181.

152 J. Michelet, *Histoire de France* (1833–62; ed. définitive, Paris, 1898). Eng. trans. (New York, 1845 ff).

the French Revolution and had become disastrously involved in the democratic and anticlerical agitation that led to the Revolution of 1848. He had lost his professorship in the struggle and had lost also the last vestige of his early Romantic love for the Middle Ages. The retrospective discussion of medieval civilization which took up the greater part of the introduction to the seventh volume was motivated by an unrelenting antagonism, intensified by personal bitterness, toward the aristocracy, the clergy, and the Church. It was a very different picture from that presented in the earlier volumes.

Like Hegel, Michelet weighed medieval civilization in the scale of the spirit and found it wanting. It was based on fundamental error. As Hegel had written of "that infinite falsehood which rules the Middle Ages and constitutes their life and spirit," [153] so Michelet could write of "the bizarre and monstrous condition, prodigiously artificial, which was that of the Middle Ages." [154] His conception of the antithetical spirits of the Middle Ages and the Renaissance is, indeed, curiously similar to Hegel's, though his symbols were concrete and personal rather than abstract, and his argument depended more upon passionate statement and colorful portrayal than upon logic. He, too, saw in feudalism and the Church the enemies that had destroyed human freedom and that had combined with scholasticism to debase the spirit. His sections on scholastic philosophy were eloquently entitled: "Concerning the creation of a people of fools," and "The proscription of Nature." [155] But Michelet could not find hope, as Hegel did, in the growth of the monarchial state at the end of the Middle Ages, though he did note the beginning of "a revolution, obscure, but great and holy" in the rise of national languages and of feeling for the *patrie*. [156] In a phrase reminiscent of Hegel, he declared that the monarchy had become in the late Middle Ages a kind of church with a divine character, [157] but he deplored the fact that it had been raised on the ruins of municipal freedom. Michelet was too democratic to put his trust in princes and, as Sismondi had done, he

[153] Hegel, *Philosophie der Geschichte*, *Werke*, IX, 444 [p. 380].
[154] Michelet, *Histoire de France*, VII, 9.
[155] *Ibid.*, VII, 27 ff; 36 ff.   [156] *Ibid.*, VII, 53 ff.
[157] *Ibid.*, VII, 14; cf. Hegel, *Geschichte der Philosophie*, *Werke*, XV, 188 [III, 106].

idealized the democratic communes, which had created "all the arts and forms of civilization." [158] As a result, he regarded the fourteenth and fifteenth centuries, in which the communes had lost their freedom and had become undemocratic, as a period of spiritual decline. Even the upper bourgeoisie, for whom he did not share Sismondi's admiration, had sunk to the lowest spiritual level. With them dominant in all Europe, even in Italy under the Medici, "the Renaissance could not come by a popular revolution." [159] Michelet could find no more than a single evidence of rebirth in *Quattrocento* Italy, the calculating genius of Brunelleschi, and the whole spirit of the age was against him.

> Never was there an age less favorable to these high tendencies. Italy had entered into a profound prose, the living materialism of the tyrants and the bands of mercenaries, the bourgeois platitude of the men of finance and money. A religion began in the banks of Florence having in gold its real presence and in letters of exchange its eucharist.[160]

Michelet's Renaissance was thus not the traditional Italian revival of the fourteenth and fifteenth centuries. What then was it?

> The amiable word, Renaissance, [he wrote] recalls to friends of beauty only the coming of a new art and the free play of imagination. For the scholar, it is the renovation of the study of antiquity, for the legists, the day which began to shine on the discordant chaos of our old customs. Is that all?

And he answered that those who think so forget two things:

> the discovery of the world and the discovery of man. The sixteenth century . . . . went from Columbus to Copernicus, from Copernicus to Galileo, from the discovery of the earth to that of the heavens. Man refound himself. While Vesalius and Servetus revealed life to him, his moral mysteries were penetrated by Luther, by Calvin, by Dumoulin and Cujas, by Rabelais, Montaigne, Shakespeare, and Cervantes. He plumbed the profound depths of his nature.[161]

In this great movement the revived antiquity took its place as one of the foundations of "the new faith." It "recognized itself as identical

[158] Michelet, VII, 23 f; cf. 15.   [159] *Ibid.*, VII, 77; cf. 25.
[160] *Ibid.*, VII, 62.   [161] *Ibid.*, VII, 7 f.

at heart with the modern age." Art, too, was part of the Renaissance. "Art and Reason reconciled, that is the Renaissance, the marriage of the beautiful and the true." [162] Its spirit was forecast by Abelard and Joachim of Flora, by Brunelleschi and Jan van Eyck, but not again developed until Leonardo da Vinci. The source of the new art was a spiritual reconciliation with nature. "The Middle Ages had stood in trembling timidity in the presence of nature." Da Vinci, on the contrary, "felt that he himself was also nature." [163] One is reminded of Hegel's more abstract phrase: "In the contemplation of nature the spirit begins to have a sense of being present therein." [164] Michelet's Renaissance lacked the dialectic foundation of Hegel's construction, and it included the Reformation which Hegel made a resultant step in the progress of the spirit. But it had the same essential ingredients: art and the rebirth of antiquity, reconciliation with nature, the rediscovery of man's inner nature and his external world. It was above all a rebirth of the human spirit. For Michelet a spontaneous rebirth without antecedent causes. "It started from nothingness. It was the heroic outburst of an immense will." [165]

With Michelet we come at last to the Renaissance conceived as a period in the history of European civilization, a period with a distinctive spirit, sharply contrasted with that of the Middle Ages. The term was no longer limited to the revival of art, literature, or the classics, but was applied to the age as a whole and had meaning only as the age was conceived as having a characteristic spirit expressing itself in all forms of activity. For this the historians of literature and art had undoubtedly prepared the way by their increasing emphasis on the spirit of Renaissance culture. Hegel and his disciples (Hagen *et al.*) had made what seems an essential contribution by relating history philosophically to spiritual or idealistic causation and by giving to historical periods a special character as aspects of the life of the spirit. Michelet's great achievement was to take the conception of spiritual rebirth or renewal out of the sphere of the special disciplines on the one hand and of philosophical abstraction on the other, to make it at

[162] *Ibid.*, VII, 66.   [163] *Ibid.*, VII, 68 ff.
[164] Hegel, *Geschichte der Philosophie, Werke*, XV, 189 [III, 107]; see also Hagen, above, pp. 157 ff.
[165] Michelet, VII, 13.

once universal and concretely human. Yet his conception of the Renaissance was in one respect essentially unsatisfactory. Limited as it was to the sixteenth century, it fitted a long-standing tradition in French history, but not the more generally recognized tradition of Italian precedence. To make the Renaissance a universally acceptable period it would have to be thrust further back in time and be identified primarily with Italy. It must also be developed much more fully. An unforgettable epigram would have to be expanded into a great book. That was the work of Jacob Burckhardt.

CHAPTER SEVEN

Burckhardt and the Formation of the Modern Concept*

"Our conception of the Renaissance is Jacob Burckhardt's creation." [1] Thus Karl Brandi opened his eloquent sketch of the Italian Renaissance in the *Propyläen Weltgeschichte*. That sentence may stand as a text, to be demonstrated or modified, for the remainder of this book. It is true, as the preceding chapters have attempted to show, that nearly all the separate materials for the creation of Burckhardt's synthesis were already present by the middle of the nineteenth century. The early humanists, the new humanists and classicists of Goethe's generation, Protestants, rationalists, and liberals, Romanticists, Hegelians, and the disciples of *Historismus,* historians of art and letters, and the pioneers of *Kulturgeschichte* had all made essential contributions. Yet Burckhardt's Italian Renaissance was nonetheless, in its integrated entirety, an original creation, the masterpiece of a great historical artist. Accepted almost without question by the majority of historians for more than fifty years, it still remains the classic conception around which the storms of revisionism rage with increasing violence. Its unique place in the history of Renaissance historiography is attested today by the virulence of its opponents no less than by the more moderate defense of those who still find in it an essential verity.

* This chapter first appeared as an article in the *Bulletin of the Polish Institute,* and is reproduced with their permission.

[1] W. Goetz, ed., *Propyläen Weltgeschichte,* IV (Berlin, 1932), p. 157.

Burckhardt's Ideological Background and Historical Method

As is true of most artistic creation, Burckhardt's work reflected both his own personality and the tendencies and prejudices of at least a part of his generation. There is much in it that was the product of his own peculiar character, but it would not have been so generally accepted had it not appealed to men of a wide variety of temperament, who were yet children of their century. In every age since the Renaissance itself, men have viewed that phenomenon from the perspective of their own time and through the astigmatic lenses of contemporary interests and presuppositions. This was no less true of the period following the middle of the nineteenth century. The time was ripe for a new idealization of the Renaissance analogous to the neo-classical idealization of ancient Greece or the Romantic rehabilitation of the Middle Ages. Like these movements, it sprang in part from discontent with present civilization and the desire to find in the past a model for contemporary aspiration. But it was also in part an affirmation of faith in the spirit of the modern world. The favored sons of this prosperous age were on the whole well content with their material well-being, their personal freedom, and the advance of scientific knowledge. The idea of progress had never been so generally accepted.[2] Yet there were many who felt that contemporary civilization, despite essential progress, suffered from serious ills and that in the growth of bourgeois materialism, industrial mechanization, and democracy there were inherent dangers to the life of the spirit. It was from this combination of faith in modern progress with revulsion against certain of its attributes that men turned to the Renaissance as a cultural ideal. To the vogue of Hellenism and Romanticism there thus succeeded something like a new intellectual movement, to which the German historians have given the barbarous name of *Renaissancismus*.[3]

The primary motive of Renaissancism was in most instances aesthetic. As always, the Renaissance was regarded from one side as the antithesis of the Middle Ages. It thereby profited from the growing reaction

[2] Cf. J. B. Bury, *The Idea of Progress* (London, 1920).
[3] The term seems to have originated with F. F. Baumgarten, *Das Werk C. F. Meyers: Renaissance-Empfinden und Stilkunst* (Munich, 1917), Chap. I.

against the nationalist, religious, and sentimental medievalism of early nineteenth century Romantic criticism. At the same time, viewed from the other direction, the Renaissance appeared as the beginning of the modern age, but distinguished from the present, as had been the general view since Winckelmann, by an artistic decline in the intervening period. It therefore profited also from revulsion against contemporary bourgeois taste and philistinism. Aesthetes of the later nineteenth century were frequently inclined to feel that industrial production was destroying beauty and vulgarizing taste, that the reign of the money-grubbing businessman was forcing the artist into a position of unappreciated isolation, and that the general run of contemporary art was formless and superficial. The same reaction that led men like Ruskin and the Pre-Raphaelites back to the late Middle Ages turned to the Renaissance those whose inclinations were classical and who set the highest value on form. In either case it was the nostalgic reconstruction of an age in which art had been an integral part of life and in which the artist had been universally appreciated.

But the present discontent and the corresponding appeal of the Renaissance extended beyond the field of pure aesthetics, though seldom entirely disassociated from it. Intellectual aristocrats tended to cast a pessimistic eye upon the growing democratization of all branches of culture, while humanists of Goethe's type saw in the increasing uniformity and materialism that were the social results of industrialization a threat to both intellectual and human values. The former found in the Renaissance a culture of the élite; the latter perceived in it a highly developed *humanitas* lacking in their own day. Finally, all who found themselves cramped by the narrow moral standards and timid conventionality of middle class society were prone to seek in the Renaissance the heaven of all their wish. They had been taught by Heinse, Stendhal, Byron, Browning, and a host of Romantic novelists to think of the Italian Renaissance as the happy hunting ground of uninhibited, forceful, and passionate personalities.

Romantic escape from the present to an ideal past was, however, only one aspect of Renaissancism, its negative side. It was as the birth hour of the modern world that the Renaissance acquired its positive historical significance and also the justification for its excesses.

The closely associated currents of liberalism, new humanism, and German idealism in nineteenth century thought had combined to establish as essential attributes of modern progress the growth of individual freedom of thought and expression, the full development of self-conscious personality, and the evolution of moral autonomy founded upon a high conception of the dignity of man. Faith in the progress of these qualities was not incompatible with fear lest they be threatened by other factors in modern life. Such fear, indeed, merely emphasized their importance. At the same time, the growth of the natural sciences and of a rational, secular *Weltanschauung* since the Enlightenment had pointed to a worldly positivism as an equally distinctive trait of modern civilization and one of the most potent forces for progress. Finally, the unbroken tradition of classicism had never ceased to emphasize the fundamental rôle of antiquity in shaping modern culture. And by the middle of the nineteenth century, a long series of interpretations, approaching the problem from various angles, had taught men to see in the Renaissance, bounded on one side by the Middle Ages and on the other by the Reformation and Counter-Reformation, the age in which all these traits of the modern world had first appeared and had flourished with youthful vigor. Burckhardt's decisive contribution was to gather all these trends of interpretation together into one coherent synthesis, based upon a respectable foundation of historical research.

Jacob Burckhardt was in many ways peculiarly fitted for the rôle he was to play in crystallizing the incipient Renaissancism of the late nineteenth century.[4] Born in Basel in 1818 of a patrician family with a long tradition of cultural and religious leadership, he inherited the cosmopolitan individualism of the Swiss,[5] together with the prejudices of the intellectual aristocrat. He was a sensitive aesthete for whom

---

[4] There is a vast literature on Burckhardt. The best biography is that by K. Löwith (1937); that by Carl Neumann is tendentious. See also R. Stadelmann, "Jacob Burckhardt und das Mittelalter," *Historische Zeitschrift*, CXLII (1930), 457–515; W. Kaegi's introduction to *Die Cultur der Renaissance in Italien* in Burckhardt, *Gesamtausgabe* (Stuttgart, 1930–34), V; and R. Marx's *Nachwort* to his edition of Burckhardt, *Weltgeschichtliche Betrachtungen* (Leipzig, 1935).

[5] Cf. F. Ernst, "La tradition médiatrice de la Suisse," *Revue de littérature comparée*, VI (1926), 586–606; K. Jöel, *Jacob Burckhardt als Geschichtsphilosoph* (Basel, 1918), pp. 18 ff.

beauty of form was almost a religion, a humanist trained in classical philology and deeply impregnated with the new-humanist feeling for the dignity of man, a cultivated worldling who yet possessed an ascetic integrity of character and retained a firm foundation of Protestant morality. He hated the aggressive power politics and the subordination of individual freedom that he saw developing in the Bismarckian state, but he also feared the rising tide of industrial democracy.[6] He was by nature a dispassionate and somewhat skeptical observer rather than a man of action, and he was always the complete individualist. He refused to take part in the political controversies of his age and sought only to be left undisturbed to live his own private life. Until the pessimistic crisis of his later years, he retained a hopeful faith in the progress of modern civilization through free individual development, which he always considered the indispensable condition of culture.[7] Nevertheless, there was much in contemporary society that irked his aesthetic, humanist soul and drove him, a modern Petrarch, to seek escape from it in fellowship with men of a more congenial age.[8]

The Renaissance, it is true, furnished an ideal asylum for only a relatively short period of Burckhardt's mature life. But it was the most fruitful period. As a student at Berlin in the 1830's he had been strongly influenced by the Romantic enthusiasm for the Germanic Middle Ages. His early works reflect a strong attraction to medieval Gothic art.[9] With greater maturity, however, he rejected the patriotic and religious mania of his Romantic friends and also the subjective sentimentalism of Romantic art criticism.[10] Two trips to Italy in 1846 and 1853–54 achieved his conversion from Romanticism to classicism. This is a familiar pattern. We have met it before in the life of Goethe, whom Burckhardt always considered a kindred spirit. Like his great predecessor from Weimar, Burckhardt discovered in Italy a new home

---

[6] Cf. E. Dürr, *Freiheit und Macht bei Jacob Burckhardt* (Basel, 1918); H. Bächtold, "J. Burckhardt und das öffentliche Wesen seiner Zeit," in *Deutscher Staat und deutsche Parteien*, Festschrift for F. Meinecke (Munich, 1922), pp. 96 ff; and "Der Geist des modernen Wirtschaftslebens im Urteil J. Burckhardts," *Schweitzerische Monatshefte für Politik und Kultur*, III (1923), 321 ff.

[7] Cf. Dürr, p. 10 f. [8] Cf. Marx, p. 288 ff.

[9] J. Burckhardt, *Kunstwerke der belgischen Städte* (1842); *Conrad von Hochstaden* (1843); both in *Gesamtausgabe*, I.

[10] Cf. J. Burckhardt, *Cicerone* (Leipzig, 1925), p. 91.

in a land consecrated to the ageless beauty of harmonious form and left behind him forever the Storm and Stress Romanticism of his youth. It is significant that he approached the Renaissance first as an amateur of art. His reworking of Kugler's *Handbook* (1847) [11] and his masterly analysis of the decline of ancient culture, *The Age of Constantine the Great* (1853) [12] occupied the transitional period. Then followed some fifteen years of full preoccupation with the Italian Renaissance, during which he wrote that ever-popular guide to Italian art, the *Cicerone* (1855),[13] and the crucial essay on *The Civilization of the Renaissance in Italy* (1860), and planned to complete the latter by a comprehensive history of Renaissance art of which only a fragment on architecture was published (1867).[14] This was his last work on the Renaissance. His enthusiasm for the dawn of the modern age was dimmed by a growing pessimism concerning its fruits, a pessimism stimulated by melancholy observation of the Prussian wars and the mass barbarism of the Paris Commune of 1870. When, in 1889, Ludwig von Pastor asked him for a criticism of his *History of the Popes Since the Close of the Middle Ages,* Burckhardt replied that he was "unfortunately now estranged from that age." [15] He never published another book. The philosophical lectures on world history (1868-71),[16] which reflected his growing pessimism about the modern world, and his *History of Greek Civilization* [17] were not published till after his death at the age of eighty.

Recent critics of Burckhardt are perhaps too prone to stress the motives that led to his idealization of the Renaissance and to explain its success in terms of its appeal to the desires and prejudices of the following generations. These are, indeed, of fundamental importance. But it must not be forgotten that Burckhardt was also an unusually

11 F. Kugler, *Handbuch der Geschichte der Malerei* (Berlin, 1837; 2nd ed. revised and enlarged by Burckhardt, Berlin, 1847). See above, p. 146 f.

12 J. Burckhardt, *Die Zeit Constantins des Grossen* (Basel, 1853).

13 J. Burckhardt, *Der Cicerone, eine Anleitung zum Genuss der Kunstwerke Italiens* (Basel, 1855). Eng. trans. (London, 1873).

14 J. Burckhardt, *Die Renaissance in Italien*, in F. Kugler, *Geschichte der Baukunst* (Stuttgart, 1867), IV.

15 Stadelmann in *Historische Zeitschrift*, CXLII, 500, n. 1.

16 J. Burckhardt, *Weltgeschichtliche Betrachtungen*, ed. J. Oeri (Basel, 1905). Eng. trans. *Force and Freedom, Reflections on History* (New York, 1943).

17 J. Burckhardt, *Griechische Kulturgeschichte*, 4 vols. (Stuttgart, 1898–1902).

gifted historian, a literary artist, and one of the most significant founders of modern *Kulturgeschichte*. *The Civilization of the Renaissance* was not only the decisive formulation of the modern conception of the Renaissance; it was also the first masterpiece in a new genre, and it carried conviction, in part at least, because of its intrinsic merits. Earlier essays in the history of civilization had been made by Voltaire, Winckelmann, the Romanticists, Guizot, Buckle, Riehl, Freytag, and others. Voltaire had stated the *desiderata* with his wonted clarity. But no one had come close to achievement of the ideal till Burckhardt. The influence of his example has extended far beyond the field of Renaissance historiography. To quote one of the most distinguished of present day historians of civilization, and no friendly critic of Burckhardt's Renaissance: "*Kulturgeschichte* today faces in many respects the task of freeing itself from Burckhardt, yet this does not in the least cloud his greatness nor lessen the debt we owe him." [18]

Burckhardt's historical method was highly original and was largely responsible for the distinctive quality of his essay on the Renaissance. Though not the first to rebel against the tyranny of political history, he was a pioneer in breaking away from the narrative form. Even Voltaire had not freed himself entirely from the conventional method of chronological narration, and his successors had usually been content to string their observations on general civilization along the main thread of the political story. Burckhardt's method, on the other hand, was entirely topical. He would treat a whole civilization as a unit in a series of parallel discussions, each approaching the central problem of its essential character from a different point of view. The result for which he labored was a coherent, if static, picture, in which every feature fitted into place because all had been selected to illustrate his conception of the spirit of the age and of the nation. He himself recognized that his forte was neither narrative nor philosophical construction of the Hegelian type, but description and intuitive interpretation. Problems of origins and causation held little interest for him. Though undoubtedly influenced by Hegel, perhaps more than he knew, he was repelled by Hegel's abstract rationalization of world history, not only because he disliked its teleological end, but because it

[18] J. Huizinga, *Wege der Kulturgeschichte* (Munich, 1930), p. 140.

was a chronological construction which at no point paused long
enough to give a concrete picture of the human scene.[19] Burckhardt
preferred to think of his approach to history as that of an artist rather
than of a philosopher.[20] Having identified the philosophy of history
with Hegel, he took a perverse satisfaction in disclaiming all capacity
for philosophical thought. "I have never in my life thought philosophically," he once wrote to a friend.[21] And again, discussing his
purpose in the *Observations on World History:* "Further, we renounce
all system; we make no claim to 'world historical ideas,' but are content
with observation and give cross sections through history, from, indeed,
as many directions as possible; we give above all no philosophy of
history." [22] It was in this tendency to "give cross sections through
history," which he did superbly, that Burckhardt's greatness lay, and
also his fundamental weakness as an historian. It made possible a
remarkable combination of analysis and synthesis of a given period,
but it was essentially "unhistorical," for it ignored the factor of historical development. In this he departed decisively from the theory
of the Romantic historians, from whom, however, he had learned a
great deal, particularly in regard to the organic character of a national
culture and the unifying concept of the *Volksgeist.*

Despite his wry disclaimer of historical philosophy and system,
Burckhardt had devoted a good deal of thought to formulating the
aims and methods of *Kulturgeschichte.* He was quite aware of what
he was doing, and he summarized his ideas on the subject in the introduction to *The History of Greek Civilization.*[23] They are worth
noting for they apply equally well to the essay on the Renaissance,
written a decade earlier. To begin with, he was careful to distinguish
between his aims and those of the antiquarians and political historians
who had hitherto monopolized the field. Where they are content with

---

19 Cf. Burckhardt, *Weltgeschichtliche Betrachtungen, Gesamtausgabe,* VII, 2 f.
See also for general discussion, K. Löwith, "Burckhardts Stellung zu Hegels
Geschichtsphilosophie," *Deutsche Vierteljahrsschrift für Literaturwissenschaft und
Geistesgeschichte,* VI (1928), 719 ff; and G. von Below, *Die deutsche Geschicht-
schreibung von den Befreiungskriegen bis zu unsern Tagen* (Munich, 1924),
p. 70.
    20 Marx, pp. 277 f.   21 *Ibid.,* p. 278.
    22 Burckhardt, *Gesamtausgabe,* VII, 1.
    23 Burckhardt, *Griechiche Kulturgeschichte, Gesamtausgabe,* VIII, 1 f.

establishing "facts" and the sequence of "events," the historian of civilization must devote his research to discovering the mentality of the people and the spirit of the age. And all of Burckhardt's thought was based on the tacit assumption that there was a peculiar mentality, character, or spirit, a *Volksgeist,* common to the whole nation in a given age.

> Our task, as we understand it, is to give the history of the Greek way of thinking and of looking at things, and to strive for perception of the living forces, constructive and destructive, that were active in Greek life. Not by narrative, yet historically . . . we must consider the Greeks in their essential peculiarity. . . . To this, to the history of the Greek spirit, must the entire study be directed. The particular fact and, above all, the so-called event can be valued here only as evidence of the common, not for its own sake; for the data we seek are the ways of thinking, which are also facts. But the sources, if we consider them from this point of view, will speak very differently than in mere research for antiquarian material.

Burckhardt was conscious that his use of sources differed from the critical-historical method he had learned in Ranke's seminar, but he thought that to be a necessary result of the aims of *Kulturgeschichte,* which "lives chiefly on what the sources and monuments indicate unintentionally, without self-interest, despite themselves." He was interested in the point of view expressed by the sources rather than in their accuracy. "If a recounted action did not in reality happen or did not happen so, yet the point of view which set it forth as having happened in such a way has its value because of the typical quality of the account." Here Burckhardt was rationalizing the practice, common among the Romantic historians, of treating all literary sources as authentic expressions of the national spirit,[24] and forgetting, as they did, that a novel may be as misleading as a state paper. Since what he sought was the constant and typical in a civilization, it followed that "a characteristic appears greater and more instructive than an action; for actions are only the single expressions of the corresponding inner capacities . . . What is willed and planned is therefore as significant as anything actually done." On the basis of this argument,

[24] Cf. E. Fueter, *Geschichte der neueren Historiographie* (Munich, 1936), p. 463 f.

Burckhardt was optimistically convinced that *Kulturgeschichte* has greater certainty than ordinary history, which can never establish its data beyond question. It has "primum gradum certitudinis." Yet he recognized certain difficulties. "How does one know what is constant and typical, what is a force and what is not?" And to this question the only answer he could find was a wide reading of the available source material. In the long run, Burckhardt's perception of the inner spirit of a civilization, which was at once the chief aim of his research and his sole guide to the selection and evaluation of sources, was based on nothing more than his own intuition and his undoubted familiarity with the literature of his chosen fields.

The Civilization of the Renaissance in Italy

The Civilization of the Renaissance in Italy,[25] Burckhardt's master-piece, was planned as an investigation of the inner spirit of Italy during the Renaissance along the lines thus formulated. Its subtitle, *An Essay*, was not merely the product of his accustomed ironical modesty. He did not intend it to be a comprehensive history nor a reference book, as Geiger later made it. Even in the use of illustrative material he practiced perpetual restraint. He congratulated himself that he had not made it "three times as thick," as he might easily have done. But he wanted nothing to confuse the essential thesis or mar the artistic form of the work. As a result, the architectural design stands out clearly and leaves the impression of a perfectly integrated synthesis.

To outline the argument of a book so well known may seem an unjustifiable waste of space, yet in no other way could one do justice to the organic construction which is one of its most effective features. Moreover, it is not impossible that there may be scholars whose familiarity with Burckhardt's interpretation of the Renaissance is based on something less than a complete reading of his work. The

25 J. Burckhardt, *Die Cultur der Renaissance in Italien: Ein Versuch* (Basel, 1860). The third (1877) and later editions were expanded by Ludwig Geiger until the original text was almost submerged. It was restored by W. Goetz in the thirteenth edition. Eng. trans. 2 vols, (London, 1878). I use the first German edition and the eighth English edition (London, 1921).

book is divided into six parts, each viewing the civilization of Italy from the beginning of the fourteenth to the beginning of the sixteenth century from a different angle. The first part establishes the general political background. Here Burckhardt approached most nearly to the narrative tradition, though even here narrative is strictly subordinated to topical discussion of a prevailing condition. The peculiar character of Italian politics he ascribed in general to the conflict between the emperors and the popes. But causation was not his major interest. The principal thesis of this part is indicated in the title: "The State as a Work of Art," a phrase reminiscent of Hegel's characterization of Greek civilization. There is just enough narrative to illustrate his conclusion that in the Italian states "the modern European state-spirit appeared for the first time, free to follow its own inclinations," and that with them "a new factor enters history, the state as a calculated, conscious creation, the state as a work of art."[26] Interwoven with this major theme is the secondary one of the character of the Renaissance man as illustrated and conditioned by his political activity. The illegitimacy of despotic government and the party strife in the republics bred a new type of individual, wholly dependent on his own resources and therefore developing them to the fullest extent, seeking only egocentric ends, and uninhibited by sentimental or traditional standards. "The conscious calculation of all means, of which no prince outside of Italy had at that time any idea, combined with an almost absolute power within the limits of the state, produced here men and modes of life that were altogether peculiar."[27]

From this Burckhardt proceeded naturally to the second part, devoted to the most significant thesis of the book: "The Development of the Individual," which he thought resulted in large part from the unique political condition of the Italian states.

> In the character of these states, whether republics or despotisms, lies not the only but the chief reason for the early evolution of the Italian into the modern man. That he became the first-born among the sons of modern Europe hangs on this point.
>
> In the Middle Ages both sides of human consciousness — that which turned outward toward the world and that which turned inward

[26] *Ibid.*, p. 2 f [p. 4].   [27] *Ibid.*, p. 6 [p. 8]; cf. p. 132 f.

toward man himself — lay dreaming or half awake beneath a common veil. The veil was woven of faith, illusion, and childish prepossession, through which the world and history were seen clad in strange hues. Man was conscious of himself only as a member of a race, people, party, family, or corporation — only through some general category. In Italy this veil first melted into air; there developed an *objective* consideration and treatment of the state and of all things of this world; at the same time the *subjective* asserted itself with full power; man became a spiritual *individual* and recognized himself as such. In the same way the Greek had once distinguished himself from the barbarian. . . .[28]

There are echoes of Hegel in this and a remarkable similarity to Voigt's analysis of the corporate spirit of the Middle Ages and to his perception of Petrarch's consciousness of individual personality as the distinguishing trait of the "ancestor of the modern world."[29] Yet Burckhardt had not read Voigt until his own work was almost through the press,[30] and he need not have actually read Hegel. That individualism was the dominant trait of modern civilization and that it had first appeared during the Renaissance were ideas which had been in the air for some time.[31] And the Romanticists had emphasized the unselfconscious, corporate qualities of medieval society *ad nauseam*. But no one had developed the concept of Renaissance individualism so fully in relation to every aspect of the culture of the age. Burckhardt made it the central point about which his whole synthesis was constructed. Perhaps for this reason, it remained a very protean concept. At times Burckhardt applied it to the individual's conscious dependence on his own resources for power and success in a hazardous society that had lost its traditional sanctions. Or again, it might denote the self-centered interests of "the private man, indifferent to politics and busied partly with serious pursuits, partly with the interests of a dilettante."[32] In many instances it evidently meant a new moral autonomy or emancipation from inherited standards and authorities. Cosmopolitanism was

[28] *Ibid.,* p. 131 [p. 129].
[29] G. Voigt, *Die Wiederbelebung des classischen Altertums* (Berlin, 1859), p. 81.
[30] Cf. Burckhardt, *Cultur,* p. 564.
[31] Cf. R. Koebner, "Zur Begriffsbildung der Kulturgeschichte," *Historische Zeitschrift,* CXLIX (1933), 253–93.
[32] Burckhardt, *Cultur,* p. 134 [p. 131].

still another of its occasional traits.[33] In this section, where he developed the idea most specifically, Burckhardt stressed above all the stimulating consciousness of personality, and the resulting urge to give full expression to every talent and every facet of character. Leo Battista Alberti, the many-sided man and artist, is here the prototype. From this awareness of personality in oneself and in others resulted the modern idea of fame and its counterpart, the spiteful wit and satire of the humanists. Egotism was an ever-present ingredient in the compound, but more significant is the constant suggestion of a liberation, a new consciousness of spiritual freedom.

In the third part, and not till then, Burckhardt took up the "Revival of Antiquity," "the 'rebirth' of which has been one-sidedly chosen to sum up the whole period." And he began with the notable assertion that, though the influence of the ancients colored the civilization of the Renaissance in a thousand ways, it was not essential to its evolution. "The essence of the phenomena might have been the same without the classical revival."

> We must insist upon it [he added] as one of the chief propositions of this book, that it was not the revival of antiquity alone, but its union with the genius (Volksgeist) of the Italian people, which achieved the conquest of the Western World.[34]

Here Burckhardt was running counter to a powerful tradition, though Hegel, Hagen, and, *mutatis mutandis,* Jules Michelet had already suggested that the classical revival was only one part of the Renaissance. Burckhardt went further than they, however, in demonstrating its relation to the major tendencies of the age as a result rather than cause.

> For this [the Italian enthusiasm for antiquity] a development of civic life was required, which took place only in Italy, and there not till then [the fourteenth century]. It was needful that noble and burgher should first learn to dwell together on equal terms, and that a social world should arise which felt the want of culture and had the leisure and means to obtain it. But culture, when it first tried to free itself from the fantasies of the Middle Ages, could not find its way to knowledge of the physical and intellectual world by mere empiricism.

[33] Cf. *ibid.,* p. 135 f.   [34] *Ibid.,* p. 171 [p. 171].

It needed a guide, and found one in the ancient civilization with its wealth of objective, evident truth in every intellectual sphere.[35]

For the rest, Burckhardt's account of the revival of antiquity is noteworthy chiefly for his description of the humanists as a new class in society and one marked by the modern traits of individualism and secularity. Their frequent character defects he ascribed to the hazards of their social position as well as to the influence of pagan antiquity.

Having thus established the bases of Renaissance civilization in the political situation, the emergence of the individual, and the revival of antiquity, Burckhardt devoted the remainder of the book to an analysis of the ways in which these factors operated in the cultural, social, and moral life of the age. Under the title, "The Discovery of the World and of Man," he expanded the concept and filled in the content of Michelet's famous phrase with a quantity of variegated illustrative material. To geographical exploration of the world, he added the discovery of natural beauty and progress in all the physical sciences. The greater part of this section, however, is devoted to the discovery of man, and the delineation of personality in the literature of the age. Here the development of the individual and consciousness of individuality is once more the keynote, conditioned in its expression by the influence of ancient literature. "But the power of perception lay in the age and in the nation." [36]

In the fifth section, "Society and Festivals," Burckhardt proceeded to place the individual in his social setting. Here the prime factor is again the mingling of noble and burgher in an urban society founded on wealth and culture rather than on birth.[37] As a result of this "the individual was forced to make the most of his personal qualities, and society to find its worth and charm in itself. The demeanor of individuals, and all the higher forms of social intercourse, became a free, consciously created work of art." [38] Burckhardt's illustration of this theme is a veritable model for social *Kulturgeschichte*.

Finally, in the last part, "Morality and Religion," Burckhardt turned, hesitatingly and with qualifications which his successors too frequently

35 *Ibid.*, p 175 [p. 175].   36 *Ibid.*, p. 304 [p. 308].
37 *Ibid.*, pp. 355 ff.   38 *Ibid.*, p. 365 [p. 369]; cf. pp. 379 ff.

ignored,[39] to judgment of the men of his favorite age. The tone of this part is set by Machiavelli's dictum: "We Italians are irreligious and corrupt above others." And Burckhardt concluded that "Italy at the beginning of the sixteenth century found itself in the midst of a grave moral crisis."[40] With no moral supports left except the sense of personal honor, the upper classes gave free reign to imagination and passion, with results that were frequently deplorable. Burckhardt's conception of Renaissance morality was in the tradition of Heinse and Stendhal, with qualifications, but he did not idealize egotism and uninhibited passion. He may have felt unconsciously the fascination of forces of character which he himself lacked, but his Swiss Protestant morality was too firmly grounded to permit the suspension of moral judgment. He was far indeed from Nietzsche's positive approbation of the amoral superman.[41] Burckhardt's apologia for the Renaissance man was based on purely historical grounds:

> The fundamental vice of this [the Italian] character was at the same time a condition of its greatness, namely excessive individualism. . . . But this individual development did not come upon him through any fault of his own, but rather through an historical necessity. It did not come upon him alone, but also, and chiefly by means of Italian culture, upon the other nations of Europe, and has constituted since then the higher atmosphere which they breathe. In itself it is neither good nor bad, but necessary; within it has grown up a modern standard of good and evil, which is essentially different from that which was familiar to the Middle Ages. But the Italian of the Renaissance had to bear the first mighty surging of a new age. . . .[42]

This was as far as he could go in excusing the immorality of the Renaissance men, or their indifference to religion, for, like Pierre Bayle and Voltaire, he was convinced that they had but little religion, though he did note frequent signs of true piety. The irreligious tone of Renaissance society he thought was partly the fault of the Church, partly of reverence for pagan antiquity, but mostly it was the natural result of that same individualism that made the Renaissance Italian in all things the forerunner of the modern world.

[39] *Ibid.*, p. 427 f.   [40] *Ibid.*, p. 429 f [p. 433].
[41] Cf. Stadelmann in *Historische Zeitschrift*, CXLII, 493 f.
[42] Burckhardt, *Cultur*, p. 455 f [p. 454 f].

These modern men . . . were born with the same religious instincts as other medieval Europeans. But their more powerful individualism made them in religion as in other things altogether subjective, and the intense charm which the inner and outer universe exercised upon them rendered them markedly worldly. In the rest of Europe, religion remained till a much later period something given from without.[43]

Thus, to the end, individualism and modernity remained for Burckhardt the twin keys to the interpretation of the Renaissance.

After generations of revisionism it is easy to discern the faults in Burckhardt's synthesis. It was too static, too sharply delimited in time and space, the contrast with the Middle Ages and the other European countries too strong. It was limited moreover, as Burckhardt himself was at times aware,[44] to the upper classes of Italy. It omitted the economic life of Italy almost entirely and underestimated the effect of economic factors. It overstressed the individualism, and with it the immorality and irreligion of Renaissance society, as well as its creative energy. Finally, the whole synthesis was built upon an insecure foundation, upon the doubtful assumption that there was a specific spirit common to Italian society for a period of two hundred years, that it was born of the mystical cohabitation of the antique spirit with the Italian *Volksgeist,* and that it was essentially modern, the prototype of the modern world. Yet for all its faults of exaggeration, it contained much brilliantly penetrating analysis, and a great deal of evident truth. And it was no more one-sided than many of the later revisions.

[43] *Ibid.,* p. 494 [p. 490].   [44] *Ibid.,* p. 428.

CHAPTER EIGHT

The Burckhardtian Tradition in the Interpretation of the Italian Renaissance

BY FAR THE GREATER PART of Renaissance historiography for more than half a century followed, in general conception, the Burckhardtian tradition. Yet, with the exception of John Addington Symonds, Burckhardt had no real successors. No one else attempted to do what the master had done so brilliantly. That no other full length history of the Italian Renaissance appeared during these years was certainly due to no lack of interest in the subject, for this was the high tide of Renaissancism. But historians, daunted perhaps by the harmoniously integrated perfection of Burckhardt's outline, were long content to illustrate it, to amplify it in detail, or to remodel some particular feature of it without abandoning its guiding principle.

HISTORICAL TRENDS OF THE HALF-CENTURY AFTER 1860

The half-century following the publication of Burckhardt's masterpiece was an age in many ways unsuited to works of historical synthesis in the grand manner.[1] The heroic period of the early and mid-century was past, during which the giants of historiography had staked out for themselves great quarter-sections of virgin ground and had cultivated them with an unflagging enthusiasm that could spring only from unshaken confidence and the stimulus of perpetual dis-

---

[1] The general histories of historiography cited above, p. 113, treat the late nineteenth century rather slightly and offer little guidance to the student of more recent trends in historical writing. For the historians discussed in the remainder of this book, the most valuable treatments will be found in specialized articles or monographs.

covery. The first age of Hegelian philosophy, too, was passing in which historians could leave the ground entirely and construct their synthetic castles in the air. And the time had not yet come for the large-scale co-operative enterprises that are the characteristic products of twentieth century industry. Nor had the time come for that self-conscious absorption in the abstract problems of historiography — periodization, historical concepts, or methodology — that were to make the Renaissance the subject of endless and acrimonious debate.

In general, the half-century after 1860 was an age of increasing specialization in all branches of historiography. The prevailing tendency, in Carl Becker's memorable phrase, was to learn more and more about less and less. To this end several factors contributed. Academic research was becoming more thoroughly institutionalized under the influence of the German seminars and their French and American imitators, though British historians still maintained some vestige of the literary freedom of the amateur tradition. The search for academic reputation drove scholars deeper and deeper into the archives. It became increasingly necessary to unearth new material, however slight its intrinsic value. And this tendency was further reinforced by the current reverence for the natural sciences and the resulting effort to apply their methods to the study of history. This might lead, as with Taine, to a kind of synthesis, but for the majority of historians it meant simply a closer and more unthinking application to the task of establishing facts with all the objective accuracy of a naturalist observing biological phenomena. Thus considered, all facts might be regarded as of equal value, including those that could be observed only through a microscope. It was tacitly assumed that when all the facts had been exposed to light the history of mankind would be complete. The facts would speak for themselves and would not even need an interpreter. Finally, specialization was an inevitable product of the vast expansion in the scope of history through the inclusion of every aspect of the life of humanity, of *Kulturgeschichte* in its broadest sense. "No one would now dare to maintain with Seeley that history was merely the biography of states, and with Freeman that it was merely past politics." [2] At the same

2 G. P. Gooch, *History and Historians in the Nineteenth Century* (1913; new ed. New York, 1935), p. 573.

time, every field of history was being worked over more and more intensively. The amount of available material increased in a kind of geometrical progression. Confronted by ever more numerous fields of history, each producing an increasing crop of learned monographs, it is small wonder that the average historian abandoned the hope of harvesting so vast a domain and was content to cultivate his own particular plot.

Specialization added immensely to the sum of our knowledge of all periods of history, including the Renaissance, but that, as Louis Halphen has remarked, was attended by certain inconveniences. "And first of all, though science gains thereby, the 'great public' complains that this science renders the work of professional historians inaccessible to it. The very complexity of problems examined in these works frightens it and leaves it defenseless against those who understand how to amuse and flatter its tastes." [3] This dilemma might be applied with special aptitude to the history of the Renaissance. Its infinite complexity invited endless monographs, scholarly editions of sources, detailed criticisms, and all the bewildering minutiae of labored research. At the same time, the Renaissance held for the reading public an unequalled romantic interest, a glamor that would assure a ready sale for the works of those "who understood how to amuse and flatter its tastes." The result was a regrettable tendency for popular history and specialized research to lose contact with one another. And from neither could any significant reinterpretation of the Renaissance be expected. It was not the business of the researcher, working on his own particular tree, to view the whole woods with a critical eye, nor that of the popular writer to flout accepted ideas. If the latter departed from Burckhardt's conception, it was only in the pernicious way of exaggeration, romanticizing, and vulgarization.

Fortunately, there were some historians who combined the better while avoiding the worse qualities of both extremes. Even among these, however, we shall have to ignore almost entirely one whole category, and that the largest. One of the outstanding features of Renaissance historiography in this period was the prevalence of the biographical form. This was to be expected from the very nature of the Burckhardtian view of the

[3] L. Halphen, *L'Histoire en France depuis cent ans* (Paris, 1914), p. 172 f.

Renaissance as an age characterized primarily by individualism and typified by powerful, fully developed, and immensely variegated personalities. More than of any other period, the history of the Renaissance seemed the history of its great men: scholars, artists, and poets, condottieri, popes, and princes. In sum the innumerable biographies made up a very large and valuable part of the work that may be included under the Burckhardtian tradition, but their individual scope was too limited to merit notice here. We can consider only those works that dealt with a larger segment of the Renaissance, and especially with those that in some degree altered the Burckhardtian conception while still adhering to it in the main.

GENERAL INTERPRETATIONS OF THE ITALIAN RENAISSANCE
IN THE HALF-CENTURY AFTER 1860

John Addington Symonds was the one outstanding exception to the general rule of specialization, and his immense *Renaissance in Italy* (1875–86) [4] is still the only history of Renaissance civilization by a single author that can be compared to Burckhardt's. It was Symonds with his vital enthusiams, his nervous and frequently overwrought prose, his flair for the dramatic, his love of Browningesque contrasts, and his keen aesthetic appreciations, all saved, if only at the eleventh hour, by a persistent sanity, who achieved the thorough naturalization of Renaissancism in the English-speaking world. From his seven volumes generations of students have drawn the material with which to fill out the careful economy of Burckhardt's outline. Symonds belonged to the great school of nineteenth century historians who wrote history as literature. And like the best of them he succeeded in reaching a wide public without losing the respect of the learned. His driving urge was the *maladie d'écrire* rather than that more profound malady which drives scholars to self-immolation in the archival dust. But

---

[4] J. A. Symonds, *Renaissance in Italy*, 7 vols. (London, 1875–86; I use 3rd ed. London, 1897). It was first published in separate volumes: I. *The Age of the Despots* (1875); II. *The Revival of Learning* (1877); III. *The Fine Arts* (1877); IV–V. *Italian Literature* (1881); VI–VII. *The Catholic Reaction* (1886). For critical discussion, see E. M. Bräm, *Die italienische Renaissance in dem englischen Geistesleben des 19. Jahrhunderts* (Zurich, 1932), pp. 44 ff.

if his research was sometimes sketchy and much of his work produced in a Swiss health-resort where books were scarce, his erudition was still broad enough to bear the weight of a general history. The most serious criticism that can be made of him in this respect is that he depended almost entirely on literary sources or on secondary works. He used the best of these, however, and they served him well by providing the kind of material that interested him. Unfortunately, they gave him little information concerning the economic activity of the age, or the more obscure aspects of social life. Of the civilization of the Middle Ages he remained profoundly ignorant. Inevitably he saw the Renaissance through the eyes of its men of letters or through the medium of those more recent historians whom he found congenial.

Symonds' view of the Renaissance was a product of those currents of thought that had produced Burckhardt's synthesis and that Burckhardt, in turn, had so decisively crystallized. He was a contemporary of the great Swiss historian, remarkably similar to him in education, interests, and temperament. He had been trained in Greek philology, had become an art critic, and enjoyed some reputation as a minor poet. He was a cosmopolitan intellectual, well read in all the leading European languages. His approach to the Renaissance was primarily aesthetic and humanistic, and his view of it had been colored by the same authors — Voltaire, Goethe, Stendhal, Sismondi, and Michelet — though he quoted Hegel and Browning more frequently than did Burckhardt and he had not studied under Ranke. Like Burckhardt, too, he was a man much withdrawn from active life, but he lacked the magnificent health of the Basel professor. Frequently ill and always more or less neurotic, alternating between bursts of imaginative creation and skeptical criticism, at once enthusiastic and disillusioned, he suffered from the *mal du siécle* that was the curse of so many self-conscious aesthetes of his generation. "Je suis venu trop tard dans un monde trop vieux." [5] Yet for all the personal maladjustment that made him seek a happier world in the Renaissance, he had the English liberal's faith in humanity and in progress through the growing freedom of individual personality and reason, and this faith had been

[5] H. F. Brown, *John Addington Symonds, a Biography compiled from his Papers and Correspondence* (London, 1895), I, 320 f.

strengthened for him by German idealism. He also shared the faith of his age in the progress of the physical sciences. And, unlike many of the intellectual aristocrats who admired the Renaissance, he was not frightened or repelled by the growth of "the democratic idea." To an even greater degree than was true of Burckhardt, he was inclined to see in the Renaissance — and to exaggerate — that double significance that was the essence of Renaissancism. Two quotations from the introduction to the first volume illustrate this so aptly that they are worth quoting despite their length.

> Thus what the word Renaissance really means is new birth to liberty — the spirit of mankind recovering consciousness and the power of self-determination, recognizing the beauty of the outer world, and of the body through art, liberating the reason in science and the conscience in religion, restoring culture to the intelligence, and establishing the principle of political freedom. The Church was the school-master of the Middle Ages. Culture was the humanizing and refining influence of the Renaissance. The problem for the present and the future is how through education to render knowledge accessible to all — to break down that barrier which in the Middle Ages was set between clerk and layman, and which in the intermediate period has arisen between the intelligent and ignorant classes. Whether the Utopia of a modern world, in which all men shall enjoy the same social, political, and intellectual advantages, be realized or not, we cannot doubt that the whole movement of humanity from the Renaissance onward has tended in that direction.[6]

The Renaissance, in brief, marked for Symonds the beginning of modern progress, the first stage in a movement which was continued by the French Revolution and through the nineteenth century. It was the *fons et origo* of all that he valued in the present or hoped for in the future. But at the same time it had a significance, a charm, of its own, for it possessed qualities of youthful energy that have since been lost, however much may have been gained in other ways.

> No ages of enervating luxury, of intellectual endeavour, of life artificially preserved or ingeniously prolonged, had sapped the fibre of the men who were about to inaugurate the modern world. Severely nurtured, unused to delicate living, these giants of the Renaissance were like boys in their capacity for endurance, their

6 Symonds, I, 22.

inordinate appetite for enjoyment. No generations, hungry, sickly, effete, critical, disillusioned, trod them down. Ennui and the fatigue that springs from scepticism, the despair of thwarted effort, were unknown. Their fresh and unperverted senses rendered them keenly alive to what was beautiful and natural. They yearned for magnificence, and instinctively comprehended splendour. At the same time the period of satiety was still far off. Everything seemed possible to their young energy; nor had a single pleasure palled upon their appetite. Born, as it were, at the moment when desires and faculties are evenly balanced, when the perceptions are not blunted nor the senses cloyed, opening their eyes for the first time on a world of wonder, these men of the Renaissance enjoyed what we may term the first transcendent springtide of the modern world. Nothing is more remarkable than the fulness of life that throbbed in them. Natures rich in all capacities and endowed with every kind of sensibility were frequent. Nor was there any limit to the play of personality in action.[7]

Such a conception of the Renaissance might have been possible without Burckhardt, but that Symonds owed much, directly or indirectly, to the "creator of the Renaissance" is obvious throughout the entire work, even if we had not his express admission of indebtedness. True, the first volume, Symonds noted, "had been planned and in great measure finished" before *The Civilization of the Renaissance in Italy* fell under his notice. "But," he added, "it would be difficult indeed for me to exaggerate the profit I have derived from the comparison of my opinions with those of a writer so thorough in learning and so delicate in his perceptions as Jacob Burckhardt, or the amount I owe to his acute and philosophical handling of the whole subject."[8] Difficult indeed! The influence of Burckhardt, by that time so widely diffused that it need not be direct or conscious, is evident not only in Symonds' whole treatment of the Renaissance, but also in his conception of *Kulturgeschichte*. He was nowhere more clearly Burckhardt's successor than in his determination "to write neither a constitutional nor a political history, but a history of culture in a certain epoch"[9] and in his constant effort to relate all aspects of Renaissance civilization to "the spirit of the age."[10]

[7] *Ibid.*, I, 9 f.   [8] *Ibid.*, I, viii f.
[9] *Ibid.*, I, 36.   [10] See especially *ibid.*, chap. I, "The Spirit of the Renaissance."

Symonds' work was not as coherently organized as Burckhardt's; the proportions allotted to the various aspects of the subject were very different; but the treatment followed a somewhat similar sequence, based on a similar logic. The first volume, *The Age of the Despots*, was a topical treatment of the political state of Italy from the fourteenth to the early sixteenth centuries, roughly comparable to the first section of Burckhardt's essay. Both men found the origins of the peculiar Italian genius in the unique political history of the communes and the illegitimate despotic states, which bred a new political skill, "more methodic in its use of means to ends," [11] and also an unprecedented degree of individualism and self-reliance in both princes and subjects. [12] Individualism was a constant theme here, while the second volume opened with a chapter on "The Men of the Renaissance" that was almost a rewriting of Burckhardt's second section, "The Development of the Individual."

Then followed, as with Burckhardt, the treatment of the *Revival of Learning,* to which the second volume was devoted. Much of the material for this volume was drawn from Voigt; but Symonds was in full accord with Burckhardt in the place he assigned to the revival of antiquity in the general scheme of the Renaissance. It was only a part of the Renaissance,[13] a directive rather than causative force, but an exceedingly important part nonetheless, "the most important achievement of the fifteenth and sixteenth centuries." [14] True, it interrupted the natural development of the national literature, [15] but with what immense profit to posterity! "What the modern world would have been if the Italian nation had not devoted its energies to the restoration of liberal learning, cannot even be imagined." [16] And this restoration could have taken place only in Italy and only at the time when the character of the Renaissance man was ripe for it. But there was more of Hegel than of Burckhardt in Symonds' definition of humanism. "With unerring instinct the men of the Renaissance named the voluminous subject-matter of scholarship 'Litterae Humaniores' — the more human literature, or the literature that humanises." [17] And again: "The essence

---

[11] *Ibid.,* I, 60.   [12] Cf. *ibid.,* I, 65; 78; 80 f.   [13] Cf. *ibid.,* I, 1; 11.
[14] *Ibid.,* II, 37.   [15] *Ibid.,* II, 40.   [16] *Ibid.,* II, 7.
[17] *Ibid.,* I, 16; cf. Hegel as cited above, p. 173.

of humanism consisted in a new and vital perception of the dignity of man as a rational being apart from theological determinations, and in the further perception that classic literature alone displayed human nature in the plenitude of intellectual and moral freedom." [18]

With the determining factors thus established, Symonds devoted the next three volumes to *The Fine Arts* and *Italian Literature* which illustrated the way these factors worked out in the culture of the age. Except for the much longer treatment, especially of the arts which Burckhardt omitted with the intention of treating them elsewhere, these volumes correspond to Burckhardt's fourth section entitled, "The Discovery of the World and of Man." The major themes are: the unique Italian perception of individual personality and enjoyment of nature, the growing secularization of thought and emancipation from ecclesiastical control, and the innate tendency of the Renaissance Italians "to invest every phase and variety of intellectual energy with the form of art." [19] The last two volumes on the Counter-Reformation are in the nature of an epilogue tracing the decline of Renaissance culture.

Symonds did not devote separate sections as Burckhardt did to "Society and Festivals" or "Morality and Religion," but treated them at intervals throughout the work and especially in the first volume, all very much in the Burckhardtian tradition. There is much emphasis on the pagan spirit of the Renaissance men and their indifference to religion, noted here with small evidence of disapproval, for Symonds himself had little religion. The moral chaos of the age, too, is an ever-recurrent theme. Perhaps the lusty sinners of the Renaissance appeal-ed to the frustrated and disease-ridden man of letters who had spent most of his life in books. "I verily believe," he once wrote, "that a ro-bust vice, an energetic state of sinning, if it conspires to confidence in some reality, is better than the condition of negation." [20] Yet he never condoned the flagrant immorality he saw everywhere in the Renais-sance, except on the ground of historical necessity. It was the inevitable

[18] Symonds, II, 52.
[19] *Ibid.*, III, 1; cf. III, 3: "The speech of the Italians at that epoch, their social habits, their ideal of manners, their standard of morality, the estimate they formed of men, were alike conditioned and qualified by art."
[20] Brown, *Symonds*, I, 403.

product of the vigorous enthusiasms and energies that made the age great, of "the fermentation of a new age coming to life," combined with "the contrast between medieval Christianity and renascent paganism — the sharp conflict of two diverse principles, destined to fuse their forces and to recompose the modern world." [21]

To conclude, Symonds' Renaissance was in all essentials the same as Burckhardt's. Yet there were differences, subtle, difficult to isolate or define, but significant in general effect. What we have here is the Burckhardtian Renaissance exaggerated, vaguely distorted, and, above all, dramatized. Symonds had not the temperament for cool analysis or careful qualification. Writing "with time and death at his heels," [22] he never gave his mind time to digest the fruits of his voracious reading, and the sense of driving strain and excitement that burned fitfully throughout his work heightened its dramatic quality. In his presentation, far more than in Burckhardt's, the Renaissance appeared as an age of violent contrasts, of high lights and deep shadows. [23] His Renaissance man derived from Browning as well as from Burckhardt. And his conception of the spirit of the Renaissance owed more than did that of Burckhardt to Michelet and Hegel. Causation was never Burckhardt's strongest point, but he never descended to explaining the Renaissance as "a spontaneous outburst of intelligence," [24] nor as the fulfillment of Italy's appointed rôle in the "drama of liberty" that is modern history. [25] Burckhardt would not have written without qualification that the Renaissance "was the attainment of self-conscious freedom by the human spirit manifested in the European races," [26] nor that "it was the emancipation of the reason of the modern world." [27] It might have been better had Symonds too eschewed all claims to philosophical thought. These are perhaps mere differences of tone or shading, yet they are by no means insignificant. For it was through Symonds, more than through any other author, that the Burckhardtian Renaissance came to life in the minds of generations

[21] Symonds, I, 293; cf. II, 12 f.
[22] Van Wyck Brooks, *John Addington Symonds, a Biographical Study* (New York, 1914), p. 133.
[23] See, for example, Symonds, I, 292 f.
[24] *Ibid.*, I, 3.　　　　　　　　　[25] *Ibid.*, I, 7.
[26] *Ibid.*, I, 3.　　　　　　　　　[27] *Ibid.*, I, 5.

of students. Many a mature scholar today, should he reread both works, might be surprised to find how much of what he remembers as Burckhardt's Renaissance was actually gleaned from the pages of John Addington Symonds.

Any tendency toward exaggeration or distortion of the Burckhardtian tradition that we may note in Symonds pales to insignificance, however, when we turn to two of his contemporaries, Joseph Arthur Comte de Gobineau and Friedrich Nietzsche, who also did much to mold popular conceptions of the Renaissance. Though the ideas of these two men were by no means identical on all points, there was a close affinity between them. Gobinists, at any rate, have claimed that Gobineau was "the chief inspirer of Nietzsche's conception of the Superman"; [28] while orthodox Nietzcheans have claimed him as "a Nietzschean before Nietzsche." [29] Gobineau is remembered today principally as the author of a racial theory, which, incidentally, inspired among his later disciples some very odd interpretations of the Renaissance. [30] But of that more hereafter. For Gobineau himself the Renaissance held an appeal based on other grounds, and for once he was content to neglect his theory of the decisive importance of race. As one of his more sober critics has noted, his Renaissance "is the one work in which his talents as an artist and a historian are not dominated by his ethnological system." [31] They are dominated instead by Gobineau's scarcely less pernicious enthusiasm for the great egotists, the amoral heroes who manipulate the common herd and shape the events of history according to the dictates of their own unbridled will. Gobineau was at all times a self-conscious aristocrat. He hated the egalitarian doctrine of the Revolution, the democracy of his own day, and all their varied works. For him, the culture of the Renaissance was, above all, a culture of the élite. Its essence was expressed in personalities of superhuman force, free, fully developed, many-sided, and ruthless in their egotism.

[28] G. M. Spring, *The Vitalism of Count de Gobineau* (New York, 1932), p. 169.

[29] Cf. Oscar Levy's introduction to the English translation of Gobineau, *The Renaissance* (London, 1913), p. xix.

[30] See below, pp. 323 ff.

[31] A. H. Rowbotham, *The Literary Works of Count de Gobineau* (Paris, 1929), p. 94.

The form of Gobineau's masterpiece, *The Renaissance* (1877),[32] was
dictated by this conception of the age. It is not strictly a work of history but rather a series of historical scenes in dramatic form, in which
the principal characters are Savonarola, Cesare Borgia, Julius II, Leo X,
and Michelangelo, though almost every other outstanding personality
of the period appears sooner or later. Gobineau admired especially
the princes, popes, and condottieri whose versatile characters combined what Nietzsche would have called the Will to Power with a
refined appreciation of literature and the arts. He loved to show
them in familiar discourse with poets, artists, and scholars — little
groups of superior persons, enjoying one another's company in isolation
from the world of common men. Even more frequently the scenes
reveal the coldly rational handling of diplomacy and politics, which
Burckhardt had hinted at under the heading: "The State as a Work
of Art." Machiavelli acts as a kind of Greek chorus throughout the
drama.

The elements of his conception were certainly to be found in
Burckhardt, but the whole tone of Gobineau's Renaissance belonged
rather to the older tradition of Heinse and Stendhal, reinforced by the
Romantic exaggeration of the picturesque vices of Renaissance society.
His credulous acceptance of all the Borgia legends of treachery, in-
trigue, and esoteric poisons is reminiscent of Victor Hugo. Of all his
precursors he was closest to Stendhal, but he was an aristocratic Stendhal, a Nietzschean before Nietzsche, with an aggravated contempt for
common men, their petty souls, and their petty morality. The consola-
tion offered by Alexander VI to Lucrezia Borgia after Cesare had
murdered her husband is almost a complete summary of the "master
morality."[33]

If Gobineau's *Renaissance* is not strictly a history, nor even within
its limits good history, Nietzsche's scattered references to the Renaissance are scarcely historical at all. In his saner moments he could
characterize the Renaissance in the normal manner of contemporary

---

[32] J. A. de Gobineau, *La Renaissance, scènes historiques* (Paris, 1877). Eng. trans.
(London, 1913). For critical discussion, see Rowbotham, pp. 95 ff; E. Schuré,
Précurseurs et révoltés (Paris, 1920), pp. 263 ff.

[33] Gobineau, *Renaissance,* pp. 97 ff.

historians;[34] but his interest in the age was not historical. There is no suggestion in his work of a serious effort to understand the Renaissance. He simply used it as a symbol of what he wanted for the present and the future. It was a myth to be realized.[35] It is sometimes difficult, as one of his most recent biographers has pointed out,[36] to discover just what Nietzsche did want for the future. Perhaps it is too much to expect blueprints of Zarathustra. But whatever it was, he could always find a precedent for it in the myth of the Renaissance. The material basis for the myth was undoubtedly furnished in large part by Burckhardt, one of his earliest friends and sometime colleague at Basel. But the myth itself is one that could never have been accepted by that gentle, if melancholy, apostle of civilization. Nietzsche's Renaissance was the great age of the Superman, the reign of Antichrist. It was the antithesis of the weak, negative, humanitarian, Christian civilization of the nineteenth century. "Will anybody at last understand what the Renaissance was? *The transvaluation of Christian values,* the attempt undertaken with all means, all instincts, and all genius to make the *opposite* values, the *noble* values, triumph."[37]

This is the key to Nietzsche's deviation from the Burckhardtian tradition: "The transvaluation of values." What Burckhardt and Symonds had alike deplored as a blemish on the age or had partially condoned as a necessary by-product of the Renaissance spirit, Nietzsche raised aloft as an ideal toward which men must strive if they would enter into the Valhalla of the Supermen. Even the lush criminality of the Renaissance was a sign of health.

A criminal is at all events a man who has set his life, his honor, his freedom at stake; he is therefore a man of courage. The fact that in our society the criminal happens to be a badly nourished and stunted animal is simply a condemnation of our system. In the days of the

[34] Cf. F. Nietzsche, *Menschliches Allzumenschliches* (1878), No. 237. Editions of Nietzsche are so numerous that it seems most convenient to cite by the number of the aphorisms, which are the same for all editions, rather than by page. Quotations are all taken from the standard English translation, edited by Oscar Levy.

[35] F. Nietzsche, *Unzeitgemässe Betrachtungen* (1873–76), II, "Vom Nutzen und Nachteil der Historie für das Leben," No. 2: "What is the use to the modern man of this 'monumental' contemplation of the past. . . . It is the knowledge that the great thing existed and was therefore possible, and so may be possible again."

[36] Cf. C. Brinton, *Nietzsche* (Cambridge, Mass., 1941), pp. 118 ff.

[37] F. Nietzsche, *Götzendämmerung* (1889), No. 61.

Renaissance the criminal was a flourishing specimen of humanity and acquired his own virtue for himself — virtue in the sense of the Renaissance — that is to say, *virtù*, free from moralic acid.[38]

Above all, Nietzsche emphasized the Renaissance man's positive affirmation of life — and characterized it as anti-Christian. It was a commonplace that the artists of the Renaissance had become more worldly, irreligious, perhaps even pagan, that they had a more joyful acceptance of this world, a commonplace that had been overstated before, but never by such a master of overstatement. Thus spoke Nietzsche: "There is no such thing as a Christian who is also an artist. Let no one be so childish as to suggest Raphael or any homeopathic Christian of the nineteenth century as an objection to this statement: Raphael said Yea, Raphael *did* Yea — consequently Raphael was no Christian." [39]

It is doubtful if any sober historian of the Renaissance took the interpretations of Gobineau and Nietzsche very seriously. But even sober historians are susceptible to popular impressions in their youth and sometimes retain them as an unconscious bias. And certainly both men were widely read and exerted a considerable influence around the turn of the century. The nineteenth century seemed to end as it began, on a note of Romanticism, with Nietzsche substituted for Byron. "The old line of romantic heroes was dying out, and some new touch was needed to renew the popularity of the wicked, defiant rebel, the picturesque egotist, the scorner of convention, the eternal Artist crucified in a world of Business Men." [40] Both Gobineau and Nietzsche made a strong appeal to maladjusted adolescents of both the temporary and permanent varieties, and their vogue was generally accompanied by a cult of the wicked Renaissance. It was taken up by D'Annunzio, Stefan George, Hofmannsthal, the young Emil Ludwig, and a host of other poets, novelists, and popular historians.[41]

That the significance of the Renaissance was primarily a moral one, though in a very different sense, was also the opinion of Pasquale

---

38 F. Nietzsche, *Der Wille zur Macht* (1909–10), No. 740.
39 Nietzsche, *Götzendämmerung*, No. 9.
40 Brinton, p. 194.
41 Cf. W. Rehm, "Der Renaissancekult um 1900 und seine Ueberwindung," *Zeitschrift für deutsche Philologie*, LIV (1929), 296–328.

Villari, one of Italy's most distinguished historians, the only Italian historian of the nineteenth century, indeed, who "has gained not only a European reputation but a European public." [42] At a time when most Italian historians, even more than those of other countries, were chiefly engaged in editing documents and in factual research in local history, Villari sought to reach a wide audience with popular history based on sound scholarship. Villari was an ardent social and political reformer who loved his newly united country with a love that did not hesitate to chasten. Through a long and influential career, he served as "the conscience of Italy." [43] His aim in writing popular history was not to amuse and flatter the popular taste, but to instruct and edify. And to this aim the history of the Renaissance seemed particularly suited. His earliest work in the field was the very successful *Life and Times of Girolamo Savonarola* (1859–61). [44] Here he studied the Renaissance in the person of one of its great men, whose significance consisted in being exceptional rather than typical of the age, who, though "no enemy of the Renaissance" yet "saw and felt the inherent defects which were leading to its decay." [45] Popular as this work was, however, there is greater interest for our purpose in his later study of a man who was in many ways the perfect type of the Renaissance as Villari conceived it. *The Life and Times of Niccolò Machiavelli* (1877–82) [46] is a critical history of the period, introduced by an analytical study of the Renaissance in Italy long enough to have been published as a separate work. It therefore merits fuller consideration than can be accorded to most biographies.

Villari's conception of the Italian Renaissance was in the pure Burckhardtian tradition, but with a difference in emphasis derived partly from his own character and interests, but partly, too, from the influence of Francesco de Sanctis. [47] His approach to the Renaissance was that of

[42] Gooch, *History and Historians,* p. 441.

[43] Cf. E. Armstrong, "Pasquale Villari," *English Historical Review,* XXXIII (1918), 203.

[44] P. Villari, *La storia di Girolamo Savonarola e de' suoi tempi,* 2 vols. (Florence, 1859–61). Eng. trans. (London, 1888).

[45] Ibid., Preface to 2nd ed., Eng. trans. (London, 1889), p. xxvii.

[46] P. Villari, *Niccolò Machiavelli e i suoi tempi,* 2 vols. (Florence, 1877–82). Eng. trans., revised ed. 2 vols. (London, 1892).

[47] See below, pp. 240 ff.

an Italian patriot much concerned with moral problems in their relation to the life of his people and to the newly unified Italian state of his own day. The Renaissance held for him a double attraction. It was the most glorious period in the history of his nation, when "the world seemed renewed and rejuvenated by the splendid sun of Italian culture." [48] But at the same time it presented a problem, the solution of which might be of immense value to his own generation. For Villari thought that, despite its intellectual brilliance, Renaissance Italy was socially and politically corrupt, and that corruption doomed it to foreign conquest and the extinction of its national culture. The primary question he posed, therefore, was "how Italy could become so weak, so corrupt, so decayed, in the midst of her intellectual and artistic pre-eminence." [49]

The answer to this problem Villari, like Burckhardt, found first of all in the excessive individualism of the age, which both thought was caused chiefly by the peculiar political situation in Italy. But Villari was more impressed by the moral perils resulting from the fact that Italy was then caught in a transitional stage between the medieval corporate organization of society and the modern unified state. "The period of change and transition was beset by a thousand dangers; old institutions fell to pieces before new arose; each individual, left to his own guidance, was solely ruled by personal interest and egotism; hence moral corruption became inevitable." [50] The construction of a strong national state, Villari thought, would have brought about a restoration of morality and, in fact, Italy or "the national idea" — good Hegelian phrase — was moving in that direction when foreign conquest halted all national life.[51] The corruption of Italy, the contrast between her intellectual and her moral strength, was not, he was convinced, permanent or inherent in the Italian character.[52] But Renaissance Italy lacked the essential basis of public and hence of private morality, and even the ability to conceive it. "The idea of a public conscience and morality," he asserted, "is intelligible only to one already having that conception of social unity and personality which

48 Villari, *Machiavelli*, I, 2 [I, 2].
49 *Ibid.*
51 *Ibid.*, III, 382.
50 *Ibid.*, I, 9 f [I, 7].
52 *Ibid.*, II, 34.

clearly teaches us that for nations as for individuals true government is self-government, with the inevitable accompaniment of responsibility." [53] Lacking any firm foundation for morality in either religion or the state, the Italians of the Renaissance were left with nothing to guide them but reason, and reason, thus devoid of moral content, Villari felt was not enough. Princes and condottieri might manifest the highest degree of individuality and talent, but they lacked the moral strength "which alone can give true stability to the works of man." [54] Even the literature of the age was sapped by this moral weakness.[55] Villari's final judgment on the man of the Renaissance was that "he suffered from the want of harmony and balance between the emptiness of his heart and the feverish activity of his brain." [56]

It had been suggested before, especially by Protestant and Hegelian historians, that lack of moral strength or religious conviction had vitiated the Italian Renaissance and had prevented the fulfillment of its early promise; [57] but there can be little doubt that Villari's widely read work deepened and strengthened that tradition. It became a common judgment upon the age by historians whose natural bent was moral or philosophical. One might cite as typical the opinion of Robert Flint, the distinguished historian of the philosophy of history:

> But the glory soon began to fade away. The renewal of learning, of art, and of science in Italy came unaccompanied by moral earnestness and religious conviction. Where externally fair, it was often internally foul; it was consequently devoid of the seed and sap of an enduring and fruitful life. A civilization rooted mainly in contempt for ignorance and in appreciation of intellectual freedom and of aesthetic refinement, but almost wholly cut off from reverence for the divine, devotion to duty, and love of country, however it may be laden with promise in the spring, will produce little save disappointment in the autumn. Such a civilization was to be seen in the Italian Renaissance.[58]

The Burckhardtian tradition continued to dominate the interpretation of the Renaissance well into the twentieth century. Throughout

[53] Ibid., I, 519 [I, 406].   [54] Ibid., I, 20 [I, 15].
[55] Ibid., I, 28 f; 88–235.   [56] Ibid., I, 233 [I, 178].
[57] See, for example, Hagen, above, pp. 156 ff.
[58] R. Flint, Vico (Edinburgh, 1884), p. 5 f.

the first two or three decades, it furnished the basic assumptions of most general histories touching upon the period. It was inherent in the point of view — wherever the learned collaborators so far forgot their factual objectivity as to express a point of view — from which the first volume of the *Cambridge Modern History* (1902) [59] was conceived. Thousands of American students absorbed it from Edward Maslin Hulme's popular college text (1914).[60] Innumerable special studies amplified one aspect or another of Burckhardt's thesis, often modifying it in detail but not departing from its fundamental conception. William Boulting's treatise on the status of women in the Italian Renaissance (1910),[61] for example, was simply an extensive treatment of a subject on which the master had touched in passing. The fuller detail presented here modified considerably Burckhardt's rather one-sided picture of Renaissance women, but Boulting's conception of the character of Renaissance society, as expressed in the introduction to his book, was entirely orthodox. Nowhere has Burckhardt's influence lasted more persistently than in the genre of historical biography; but that is a field too vast to be touched upon here. Despite growing criticism, the Burckhardtian tradition does, in fact, still retain many adherents among students of every branch of Renaissance history, literature, art, or thought. Most recent scholars, however, have been forced to some degree of re-examination or qualification of his interpretation. This process is aptly illustrated by a comparison of Karl Brandi's charming essay on *The Renaissance in Florence and Rome* (1899) [62] with his later contribution to the fourth volume of the *Propyläen Weltgeschichte* (1932).[63] The former reflected Burckhardt's conception without question, almost unconsciously; the latter still adhered to it in the main, but Brandi was by that time distinctly aware that the Renaissance was something created by Burckhardt,

---

59 *The Cambridge Modern History,* Vol. I: *The Renaissance* (Cambridge, 1902).
60 E. M. Hulme, *The Renaissance, the Protestant Revolution, and the Catholic Reformation* (New York, 1914).
61 W. Boulting, *Woman in Italy from the Introduction of the Chivalrous Service of Love to the Appearance of the Professional Actress* (New York, 1910).
62 K. Brandi, *Die Renaissance in Florenz und Rom* (Leipzig, 1899).
63 W. Goetz, ed., *Propyläen Weltgeschichte,* IV (Berlin, 1932), Chap. IV: "The Renaissance," pp. 157–276.

and the awareness had led him to a more thoughtful examination of his premises and of his general conclusions.

THE LATER BURCKHARDTIAN TRADITION AS ALTERED BY INTELLECTUAL, SOCIAL, AND ECONOMIC HISTORY

Since the turn of the century, the most notable alterations in the Burckhardtian tradition have come from historians whose interest lay in fields that Burckhardt had slighted or ignored in his synthesis of the Renaissance. For all his interest in the mentality of the Renaissance man, Burckhardt had relatively little to say about the ideas of the age. One of the weakest portions of his work, in keeping with his own wary attitude toward formal philosophy, was his treatment of the philosophical or metaphysical thought of the Renaissance. Indeed, he scarcely treated it at all. And, while convinced that this was an age of great activity in the natural sciences, he freely confessed his own ignorance of its scientific achievements or even of the recent literature on the subject.[64] He did much less than justice to the humanist historians, and he drew his conclusions concerning the political, social, and religious thought of the period far more from concrete examples of action than from the theoretical treatises in which the Renaissance men expressed their conscious and considered ideas. Burckhardt was fully aware of the importance of wealth as the economic foundation of Renaissance culture, and he stated with admirable force the significance of the social revolution involved in the urbanization and intermingling of the Italian upper classes.[65] But these were brilliant intuitions, based upon no systematic study of the economic and social structure of Renaissance Italy.

Research in these comparatively new fields would be less worth noting if it had merely filled in the gaps left in Burckhardt's synthesis. It has, however, done much more than that. New knowledge and, more important, new methods of research and new points of view have served to correct errors, shift the emphasis, and alter the interpretation in fundamental ways. Those historians who were led there-

[64] Cf. J. Burckhardt, *Die Cultur der Renaissance in Italien* (Basel, 1860), pp. 283; 297.
[65] Cf. *ibid.*, pp. 142; 175; *et passim.*

by to sweeping reaction against the Burckhardtian conception will be discussed later. For the present, we have to consider those who, while making significant alterations in the traditional interpretation, still maintained the essential elements of Burckhardt's thesis: the conviction that the Renaissance marked a break with the Middle Ages — however much of medieval tradition might survive in it — and that the Italians of that age were in some sense "the first born among the sons of modern Europe." Most of them, though with somewhat less conviction, have also maintained that individualism, in one form or another, was one of the essential characteristics of the age. Unfortunately, a good deal of the most original work of this kind is scattered in articles or in monographs of limited scope, far too numerous to be cited here. We can do no more than mention a few examples of the major trends.

The work of Wilhelm Dilthey furnished the inspiration for a number of the most significant reinterpretations of the Renaissance in a sense not antagonistic to Burckhardt, but with new fields of interest and a different methodological approach. Due to the fragmentary nature of his written work and the somewhat elusive quality of his thought, Dilthey exerted little influence even in his native land until the last years of his life, and at the time of his death in 1911, he was still almost unknown outside of Germany. His historical relativism and his rejection of the methods of the natural sciences for the study of history ran too strongly contrary to the intellectual tendencies of a generation imbued with reverence for the physical sciences to meet with immediate approval. Before his death, however, he had been recognized in Germany as the founder of a new school of the *Geisteswissenschaften,* a term variously translated as "the intellectual sciences," the "mental sciences," the "human sciences," or simply "the humanities." Since then his ideas have come to seem more reasonable to men whose own intellectual tendencies had developed along somewhat similar lines. His disciples include some of the outstanding German historians of the past generation. During the last two decades, Dilthey has also received increasing attention in Italy, England, and the United States, though the peculiar quality of his philosophical thought is still rather foreign to the mind of English-speaking peoples, and his terminology persistently defies translation into adequate English equivalents. [66]

Dilthey was primarily a philosopher who was led by the nature of his philosophy to the study and writing of history. Like Kant, he was interested chiefly in epistemology and the problems of scientific method. But it was precisely that interest which led him into rebellion against the Kantian theory of cognition and the scientific methodology prevailing in his day. Convinced that these were inadequate for the study of man's thought and behavior, Dilthey sought to replace them by a new system of knowledge and an independent method of study founded upon the full experience of life, that is, upon introspection and history. "The task he set himself was a counterpart of Kant's enterprise. Parallel to the critique of pure (that is, physical) reason, Dilthey proposed a critique of historical reason." [67] Unhappily, Dilthey himself never gave coherent expression to his theories. His written legacy remained a vast collection of scattered fragments, much of it unpublished, the full import of which could scarcely be discerned until the posthumous publication of his collected works.[68] Of even his cardinal methodological work, the *Introduction to the Intellectual Sciences* (1883),[69] only the first volume was published. And nowhere in it was his whole doctrine clearly stated. It is rather difficult, therefore, to discover precisely what Dilthey meant. Perhaps the clearest brief exposition of his fundamental idea is that formulated by Julius Goebel:

> While the theory of cognition of the English empiricists, Locke and Hume, as well as that of Kant, had explained experience and knowledge as facts belonging to mere thinking, Dilthey interprets the

[66] For recent discussion of Dilthey in English, see H. A. Hodges, *Wilhelm Dilthey, an Introduction* (London, 1944); J. Ortega y Gasset, *Concord and Liberty* (New York, 1946), pp. 129–82; see also, M. Mandelbaum, *The Problem of Historical Knowledge* (New York, 1938), pp. 58–67; B. Tapper, "Dilthey's Methodology of the *Geisteswissenschaften*," *Philosophical Review*, XXXIV (1925), 333–49; and R. G. Collingwood, *The Idea of History* (Oxford, 1946), 171–76.

[67] Ortega, p. 154.

[68] W. Dilthey, *Gesammelte Schriften*, ed. B. Groethuysen, 11 vols. (Leipzig, 1921–36).

[69] W. Dilthey, *Einleitung in die Geisteswissenschaften, Versuch einer Grundlegung für das Studium der Gesellschaft und der Geschichte* (1883), in *Gesammelte Schriften*, I.

process of knowing as resulting from the totality of human nature, which consists not only of intellect but of the feeling and the will as well. It is, in other words, the whole living man, the living entities of individuals, out of whom the historical world is built up and who therefore form the object of the study of the mental sciences as opposed to the study of the phenomena of nature in the natural sciences.[70]

Elusive as the relation between Dilthey's epistemology and his historical method may be, his work was filled with pregnant suggestions which gave a new impetus to the historical study of philosophy, literature, art, society, and indeed all aspects of man's thought and behavior. All thought Dilthey regarded as the product of the total complex of individual personality, including much that was irrational, which in turn is conditioned by the total cultural configuration of the age in which he lives. It follows from this that philosophy and all other activities of the human mind must be studied historically, that, indeed, philosophy is the history of philosophy. Further, the history of philosophy must be something drawn directly out of the life of the past, out of living experience, not a system to be imposed in Hegelian fashion upon it. All this gave a new importance to the history of ideas, for the one thing incontrovertibly true about an idea is that someone has thought it, and under circumstances that may be studied historically. It also bound the history of ideas more closely to sociology and psychology, and other kindred disciplines. And, incidentally, since the historian's ideas, like those of other people, are conditioned by the total complex of his personality and that of his time, Dilthey's philosophy gave an added impetus to the study of historiography as a necessary prelude to the study of history. Dilthey's conception of the history of ideas was always dynamic, for the past lives on as part of the living experience of the present, and ideas have therefore a historical development. But at the same time, his insistence upon the relation of ideas to the total cultural structure of the age in which they originate was a stimulus to the construction of periodic syntheses. Finally, the inclusion of the irrational elements of will,

---

[70] J. Goebel, "Wilhelm Dilthey and the Science of Literary History," *Journal of English and Germanic Philology*, XXIV (1926), 145 f.

emotion, and desire in the total *Gestalt,* or *Strukturzusammenhang,* as Dilthey preferred to call it, of human consciousness in which ideas arise, tended to shift the emphasis in intellectual history from the rational systems of formal philosophy to the less conscious "visions of the world" which we know as *Weltanschauung.*[71] Springing from the always peculiar consciousness of living individuals, *Weltanschauung* must always be inherently personal and particular, and Dilthey always tended to concentrate his study upon the great exponents of the ideas of an age. At the same time, however, he opened the way to generalization by grouping the isolated phenomena into "types of *Weltanschauung,*" several of which, unlike the unified *Geist* of Ranke or Burckhardt, might coexist within the intellectual structure of a given society, and to trace the development of these in modern civilization became the major purpose of his own historical writing.

It is clear that the whole bent of Dilthey's philosophy of history tended toward an inescapable relativism.[72] Yet he always maintained that positive historical knowledge was possible, that we may achieve an "understanding"[73] through the intuitive reliving of the experience of men in the past, aided by our own experience of life and by our reconstruction of the total cultural complex, different from our own, in which they lived. The extent to which such understanding is objectively valid may be open to question, but the methodological concept furnished the inspiration for much penetrating historical insight.

Dilthey's influence was most effective when he taught by example rather than by precept. And his historical writing, fragmentary though it remained, was the medium through which his methodological doctrine spread most widely. His projected *magnum opus,* an intellectual history of modern Europe, was never written, but a number of articles discussed its most important phases. Of these the most influential was the lengthy study of Renaissance thought entitled, *Intuition and Analysis of Men in the Fifteenth and Sixteenth Centuries* (1891–92).[74] Here, against a cultural historical background that was

[71] Cf. Dilthey, *Gesammelte Schriften,* V, xii ff.

[72] Cf. Mandelbaum, p. 58 f.

[73] Dilthey made a distinction between the "understanding" (Verstehen), which is the aim of the mental sciences, and the "explanation" (Erklärung), which is the function of the physical sciences. Cf. *Gesammelte Schriften,* V, 172.

[74] W. Dilthey, "Auffassung und Analyse des Menschen im 15. und 16. Jahrhundert," *Gesammelte Schriften,* II, 1–89.

largely Burckhardtian, he portrayed the Italian Renaissance as the period when the synthesis of ideas, shaped by religion, by the Greek concept of a rational universe, and by the Roman conceptions of law and the dominant will, which he called "the European metaphysic," began to break up into its component parts. "With the Renaissance the Epicurean, the Stoic, the nature-intoxicated Pantheist, the skeptic, and the atheist made their appearance once more."[75] Beginning with the semi-stoicism of Petrarch, Dilthey traced the various types of Renaissance *Weltanschauung* through Valla's epicureanism to Machiavelli's revival of the amoral Roman will to power. From all these changes in attitude toward life there came a new and rich literature devoted to man's inner character and passions, which turned attention toward the differentiation of individual personality and heightened men's enjoyment of life through a new consciousness of their purely human powers.[76]

Brilliant as Dilthey's analysis was, there were aspects of Renaissance thought which he ignored, perhaps because they were uncongenial to his own way of thinking. One of these was made a central theme in Ernst Cassirer's study of the philosophy of the fifteenth and sixteenth centuries, *Individual and Cosmos in the Philosophy of the Renaissance* (1927).[77] Cassirer was one of the closest followers of Dilthey's method, and the only one of his disciples to attempt a comprehensive analysis of Renaissance philosophy. What seemed to him most characteristic of the *Weltanschauung* of the age was the sense of mathematically conceived, objective causation in the physical universe, which was accompanied by a new conception of man's ability to create a unified cosmos by virtue of the unity of his own subjective perception of external reality. Where Dilthey had found in Renaissance men the beginnings of modern religious, political, and historical thought, Cassirer thus ascribed to them the origins of the modern scientific view of the world and also of the subjective Kantian epistemology. In accordance with Dilthey's practice of studying the *Weltanschauung* of an age in the persons of its great representatives, Cassirer centered his attention

[75] *Ibid.*, II, 17.   [76] Cf. *ibid.*, II, 18.
[77] E. Cassirer, *Individuum und Kosmos in der Philosophie der Renaissance* (Leipzig, 1927). See good review by H. Baron, "Literaturbericht: Renaissance in Italien," *Archiv für Kulturgeschichte*, XXI (1930–31), 112 ff.

first of all upon the somewhat ambiguous figure of Nicholas of Cusa. "Any study which is directed toward the comprehension of the philosophy of the Renaissance," he asserted, "must take its point of departure from the doctrine of Nicholas of Cusa." [78] In him Cassirer found all the elements, mathematical, philosophical, and humanistic, of what he regarded as the peculiar contribution of the *Quattrocento* to modern thought, including that "deepening of the problem of the individual" which, in agreement with Burckhardt, he thought to be one of the principal goals of the intellectual forces of the age.[79]

Following an analysis of the speculative system of Nicholas of Cusa, Cassirer proceeded to an estimate of his influence upon Italian thought, and finally to an illuminating study of some of the basic questions posed by Renaissance philosophy: freedom and necessity, the subject-object problem, and so forth. The great Cusan's influence, he found, was stronger among the practical technicians, engineers, and artists of the lay world than among the formally learned classes.

> Cusanus became to a certain extent the exponent of the intellectual circle, which in Italy of the fifteenth century represented, alongside the declining scholastic and the rising humanistic culture, a third specifically modern form of knowledge and direction of research. . . . Here everything was directed toward a concrete, technical, artistic purpose, for which a theory was sought. In the midst of creative artistic activity, the demand arose for a deeper understanding of the nature of that activity. And it could not be fulfilled except by a return to the fundamental basis of knowledge, especially of mathematical knowledge.[80]

But while thus assigning to the practical laymen a primary part in the shaping of modern science, Cassirer was far from depreciating the contribution of humanism. On the contrary, he considered the humanists' conception of the creative power, the intrinsic dignity, and the intellectual freedom of man to be an essential ingredient in the new vision of the world. [81] It was this that "led necessarily to a new notion of human perception as a creative activity and thereby to a new theory of cognition, which regarded the world of experience as a creation of the

---

[78] Cassirer, p. 7.
[80] *Ibid.*, p. 53 f.

[79] *Ibid.*, p. 37.
[81] Cf. *ibid.*, pp. 62 ff; 125 f; *et passim.*

human mind and thus postulated the unity of the world of experience."[82]

There can be no doubt that Cassirer thought the Renaissance to be a period of significant innovation. Not long before his death he restated his belief in its essential originality, reasserting the fundamental novelty and lasting influence of both the humanist doctrine of the freedom and dignity of man and the mathematical interests of the practical technicians.[83] Of the latter he wrote:

> Mathematics had been an *element* in culture long before the Renaissance; but in the Renaissance, with thinkers like Leonardo and Galileo, it became a new cultural *force*. It is the intensity with which this new force fills the whole intellectual life and transforms it from within that we should regard as what is significantly new.[84]

At the same time he came once more to the defense of Burckhardt's "individualism" in the sense of a general shift in emphasis from the universal to the particular. Finally Cassirer reasserted his conviction that the Renaissance represented a new age on the broader ground that within it the whole relation of the elements of civilization to one another was changing radically.

> From the beginning of the fifteenth century [he concluded] the *balance* between the particular forces — society, state, religion, church, art, science — begins to shift slowly. New forces press up out of the depths and alter the previous equilibrium. And the character of every culture rests on the equilibrium between the forces that give it form.[85]

It was no small part of the achievement of Cassirer's synthesis that it reconciled elements in the intellectual history of the Renaissance that had already been studied in isolation but had been regarded as mutually antagonistic. Credit for discovering the important rôle played by practical technicians and artists in the genesis of modern science belongs rightly to Leonardo Olschki, whose massive *History of Scientific Literature in the Modern Languages* (1919–27) [86] is one of the

82 Baron in *Archiv für Kulturgeschichte*, XXI, 113.
83 E. Cassirer, "Giovanni Pico della Mirandola," *Journal of the History of Ideas*, III (1942), 123–44; 319–46; "Some Remarks on the Question of the Originality of the Renaissance," *ibid.*, IV (1943), 49–56.
84 *Ibid.*, IV, 51.   85 *Ibid.*, IV, 55.
86 L. Olschki, *Geschichte der neusprachlichen wissenschaftlichen Literatur:* I, *Die Literatur der Technik und der angewandten Wissenschaften vom Mittelalter*

landmarks in the history of science. Here Olschki undertook to trace the development of scientific thought through a philological study of the works of those lay scientists who wrote in the vernacular. His basic assumption was that ideas and modes of expression necessarily develop together in constant interaction and that, therefore, the history of scientific prose is the history of science.[87] A second assumption, and for the interpretation of Renaissance thought a more important one, was that the beginnings of that great renewal of experimental science and of mathematical thought that culminated in the work of Galileo and Descartes found contemporaneous expression principally in the vulgar tongues. The vernacular was the language of the men who had to meet the practical problems of life, and "the inner significance of these [vernacular] writings is evident above all in the effort toward a systematic application of mathematics to the problems of technology in its most varied forms."[88] Renaissance science, Olschki insisted, was "no emanation from antique or medieval methods of research,"[89] but an independent movement arising from the practical activity of technicians, engineers, and artists, who did not share the "official" book-learning of the universities nor the humanists' preoccupation with classical rhetoric. Given his rather narrow definition of what constituted the germ of modern philosophy and science, it was natural that Olschki should find both late scholasticism and humanism sterile. Both, he thought, had become ends in themselves, entirely divorced from reality. Schoolmen and humanists alike had developed "a guild spirit which barred the way to any breath of fresh life."[90] There was, indeed, no real difference between them, except the quality of their Latin, and Olschki was prepared to dismiss them with a curse on both their houses. Certainly, he felt, the thought of Galileo and Descartes could not have originated with either scholasticism or humanism, for it "arose out of principles and premises which were as foreign to one as to the other, namely immediate observation of nature and mathematical abstraction."[91] And these were the contributions of men who were forced by the character of their occupation to deal directly

bis zur Renaissance (Heidelberg, 1919); II, Bildung und Wissenschaft im Zeitalter der Renaissance in Italien (Leipzig, 1922); III, Galilei und seine Zeit (Halle a. S., 1927). [87] Ibid., I, 3 ff. [88] Ibid., I, 7. [89] Ibid., I, 6. [90] Ibid., I, 28. [91] Ibid., I, 30.

with nature. Working in complete independence of the professional learning of their day, these practical men found it necessary to cultivate simultaneously science and practice, idea and fact.

The second component of Cassirer's synthesis of Renaissance philosophy, the idea of the inherent worth and intellectual autonomy of man, was a less recent discovery. It had long been recognized by idealist philosophers as the essence of humanism, and it had recently been studied in detail by Giovanni Gentile. Standing at the opposite end of the ideological spectrum from Olschki, Gentile was the heir to a tradition of historical philosophy older than Dilthey, though in its later phases somewhat influenced by him. German idealism in its Hegelian form had been introduced into Italy in the mid-nineteenth century by Bertrando Spaventa and had there enjoyed a longer dominance over historical thought than in its native land.[92] The Hegelian strain in Italian historiography focussed attention particularly upon the Renaissance, in which Spaventa saw that fulfillment of the freedom and self-consciousness of the spirit, which Hegel had ascribed to the Reformation. For Spaventa, the Renaissance was the birth-hour of modern philosophy, and it was born out of dialectical reaction to medieval transcendentalism. "Our philosophy," he wrote, "began as criticism and negation of that of the Middle Ages: of scholasticism." [93] From Spaventa the idealist interpretation of the Renaissance progressed, with some shifts of emphasis, through the works of Francesco de Sanctis,[94] and the scattered comments of Croce, to Gentile, under whose brilliant leadership it became the orthodox dogma of the most influential group of younger Italian historians during the high tide of *Fascismo*.

Gentile's interpretation of Renaissance philosophy was expressed in a series of essays, collected under the titles, *The Problem of Scholasticism and Italian Thought* (1912), *Giordano Bruno and the Thought of the*

---

92 B. Spaventa, *La filosofia italiana nelle sue relazioni con la filosofia europea* (1862; new ed. Bari, 1926); *Rinascimento, riforma, controriforma* (1867, new ed. Venice, 1928). Cf. C. Licitra, *La storiografia idealistica dal "programma" di B. Spaventa alla scuola di G. Gentile* (Rome, 1925); D. Cantimori, "Sulla storia del concetto di Rinascimento," *Annali della R. Scuola normale superiore di Pisa*, S. II, I (1932), 234 ff; 255 ff.

93 Spaventa, *La filosofia italiana*, p. 65.

94 See below, pp. 240 ff.

Renaissance (1920), and *Studies on the Renaissance* (1923), and was summarized briefly in 1931 in an article on "The Humanist Conception of the World."[95] The preconceptions underlying the whole are those of Hegel and Spaventa. Briefly stated, the transcendental philosophy of the Middle Ages denied to man and to life in this world all reality and all inherent value.[96] To this philosophy, humanism was the dialectical antithesis, which restored the spirit to itself by reaffirming the validity of worldly existence and the worth of man, and by replacing transcendence by immanence. In an analysis of the works of the most influential humanists of the fifteenth and sixteenth centuries, Gentile found evidence everywhere of the self-consciousness and self-confidence, the faith in the dignity of man and his life and in the creative power of the human mind, which were, he believed, the forces that destroyed medieval transcendentalism and laid the foundation for the immanent philosophy of scientific idealism.[97] The humanists sought for the sense of life more and more in life itself. And from their realization of the unlimited potentialities of the self-conscious, willing, and creating individual there grew a new, autonomous relation to revealed authority. Together, these tendencies created the scientific spirit which established man's dominance over nature. The humanists' *Weltanschauung* thus led directly to the philosophy of Bruno and Campanella and to the scientific achievements of Galileo. This is a very different interpretation from that of Olschki, but, as Cassirer had shown, the two could be combined. And, in any case, they were both agreed in supporting, in their various ways, the Burckhardtian formula which had hailed the Italians of the Renaissance as the "first born among the sons of modern Europe." Further, they both restated Burckhardt's formula of "the discovery of the world and of man" in terms which he could not possibly have conceived.

[95] G. Gentile, *I problemi della scolastica e il pensiero italiano* (Bari, 1912); *Giordano Bruno e il pensiero del Rinascimento* (Florence, 1920); *Studi sul Rinascimento* (Florence, 1923; new enlarged ed. 1936); "La concezione humanistica del mondo," *Nuova antologia,* CCLXXVII (1931), 307–17. For criticism, see A. Janner, "Individualismus und Religiosität in der Renaissance, *Deutsche Vierteljahrsschrift für Literaturwissenschaft und Geistesgeschichte,* XIII (1935), 368 ff; H. Baron, "Literaturbericht: Renaissance in Italien," *Archiv für Kulturgeschichte,* XVII (1927), 251 ff.

[96] Cf. the dogmatic summary of this thesis in Spaventa, *La filosofia italiana,* p. 66.   [97] Cf. Gentile, *Giordano Bruno,* pp. 111 ff; 265 ff.

The anti-clerical, Hegelian tradition represented by Gentile was the most characteristic Italian interpretation of Renaissance philosophy in the period between the world wars. In exaggerated form it was applied to the history of humanist education by Guiseppe Saitta (1928).[98] And it was the major theme, though with modifications drawn from Dilthey, Cassirer, and Konrad Burdach, of Guido de Ruggiero's comprehensive, two-volume history of Renaissance philosophy (1930).[99] It was not, however, accepted by historians of more orthodox Catholic faith. We may ignore for the moment those Catholic historians who rejected the Burckhardtian interpretation or simply condemned the Renaissance so conceived. But the most systematic Catholic study of Renaissance philosophy and *Weltanschauung,* Francesco Olgiati's imposing treatise, *The Spirit of Humanism and the Renaissance* (1924)[100] belongs decidedly to the present discussion. It was a direct challenge to the Hegelian interpretation, yet it fitted the major outline of Burckhardtian tradition by recognizing the essential novelty and modernity of the Renaissance and its tendency toward individualism, though at the same time maintaining that there was no fundamental break with medieval faith.

One of the most distinguished of recent Italian Thomists, Monsignor Olgiati was concerned with the problem of assessing the significance of his country's most brilliant era in the light of scholastic philosophy, which, as he noted, posits the action of Providence in history and "forbids the summary condemnation of several centuries."[101] He was prepared to admit with the idealists and positivists, whose interpretation he analysed at some length,[102] that man and nature occupied a larger place in the thought of Renaissance men than had been true in the Middle Ages, and also that there was a stronger tendency toward immanence as well as some examples of a pseudo-pagan morality. Yet he was convinced that there was throughout the period a strong current of honest Catholic faith. In his view, however, these

[98] G. Saitta, *L'educazione dell'umanesimo in Italia* (Venice, 1928).
[99] G. de Ruggiero, *Storia della filosofia,* Parte III: *Rinascimento, riforma, e controriforma,* 2 vols. (1930; new ed. Bari, 1937).
[100] F. Olgiati, *L'anima dell'umanesimo e del rinascimento* (Milan, 1924). For critical discussion, see W. W. J. Wilkinson, "The Meaning of the Renaissance," *Thought,* XVI (1941), 444–56.
[101] Olgiati, p. 22.   [102] *Ibid.,* pp. 30 ff; 45 ff.

characteristics of Renaissance thought were irrelevant to the problem of its essential relation to the spirit of the Middle Ages, the latter being for him best represented by the philosophy of St. Thomas. Summarizing his own interpretation, Olgiati argued that medieval thought was characterized by two easily distinguishable tendencies: on the one hand, "the full triumph of abstraction, of the great Greek achievement which has immortalized the names of Socrates, Plato, and Aristotle," and, on the other hand, the desire "to know and to systematize to the utmost that which is." [103] But though the Middle Ages did not depreciate concrete knowledge nor the sciences of observation, these were subordinated to philosophy. "Hence the spirit of abstraction, proper to metaphysics, tended to carry over into the sciences whose nature demanded concreteness." The result was degeneration into a "fantastic abstractism (astrattismo)." Humanism and the Renaissance had "a most vivid, most profound, and most acute sense of such an error. Against abstractism . . . . was raised the banner of concreteness." This "panting after concreteness" was for Olgiati the essence of the spirit of the Renaissance, evident in every aspect of its culture: its literature, art, political theory, science, and its tendency toward individualism. It was the unifying spirit that made the Renaissance a new age, yet it was not in conflict with true Thomist philosophy in any fundamental way. "Regarded in itself, it did not exclude either the antique abstraction nor the transcendental, but was solely a correction of the old abstractism. And in that everything is explained, including the physiognomy of the believers and saints of that epoch . . . ."

Except for Cassirer's brilliant synthesis, the German scholars of the *Geisteswissenschaften* produced no studies of Italian philosophy comparable in scope to the work of Gentile, de Ruggiero, or Olgiati. They did, however, contribute a number of brief studies of the *Weltanschauung* of the Italian Renaissance, which taken together form a major amplification and modification of the Burckhardtian tradition. We can mention only a few. Ernst Troeltsch was one of the most stimulating, if not provocative, members of that group, but his rather hasty generalizations concerning the Renaissance were so closely related to his major thesis regarding the character of the Reformation that dis-

[103] *Ibid.,* pp. 848 ff; cf. p. 92 *et passim.*

cussion of him may well be left to a later chapter. [104] For Italian studies, the influence of Walter Goetz was considerably more important,
though it was exercised principally in his capacity as editor and director of research. The admirable series entitled *Beiträge zur Kulturgeschichte des Mittelalters und der Renaissance,* the *Propyläen Weltgeschichte,* and the *Archiv für Kulturgeschichte* stand as monuments
to his sane, liberal point of view and his penetrating grasp of the problems in intellectual history.

Walter Goetz was one of the first scholars to perceive clearly that
the Renaissance represented a double problem in the field of intellectual history. Though there is little evidence of his direct connection
with Dilthey, he seems to be carrying Dilthey's methodology to its
logical conclusion in his assumption that, while the Renaissance had
an objective existence in actuality, the historical conceptions of the
Renaissance were the products of their own time and were subjective
to the extent of being colored by the interests, prejudices, and preconceptions of their authors. His article entitled, "Middle Ages and
Renaissance" (1907),[105] which traced the historical evolution of the
Renaissance concept, was thus one of the earliest of those innumerable
studies that treat the Renaissance as a problem in modern *Ideenges-
chichte.* The historical relativism inherent in this approach could not
but shake faith in the absolute authenticity of Burckhardt's interpretation, though it also gave no stronger support to his opponents. The
moral that Goetz seemed to draw from his study was that subjective
and prejudiced conceptions, friendly or unfriendly, of the Renaissance
as a whole had exaggerated the contrast between the Middle Ages and
the Renaissance. What was needed, he felt, was further detailed research which would demonstrate both the development of tradition
from age to age and the diversity of ideas within each period. On the
whole, Goetz remained convinced that, despite necessary qualifications,
Burckhardt's conception of the Renaissance was basically sound. In
one place he called it "a new and great historical view, the deepest
perception of the spirit of the age." [106] But there were questions which

[104] See below, pp. 287 ff.
[105] W. Goetz, "Mittelalter und Renaissance," *Historische Zeitschrift,* XCVIII
(1907), 30–54.
[106] *Ibid.,* XCVIII, 39.

it did not answer. "Whence came the growing emancipation of the individual from the yoke of tradition in these three centuries? And wherein lay in particular — concretely expressed — what was new?" [107] These questions, Goetz insisted, would be answered only when the development of Italian culture from generation to generation was made clear. This was the program he attempted to put into effect as a director of research. His personal contributions were fragmentary, but one very significant one was a thoughtful essay on the relation of the Renaissance to antiquity (1914). [108] Here, using art and historical writing as touchstones, he demonstrated that the cultural movement of the Renaissance had not been called forth originally by a new understanding of antique culture, but had been progressively influenced by it. Goetz thus reaffirmed Burckhardt's thesis that the culture of the Renaissance resulted from the combination of national and antique traditions, but at the same time he gave the formula a more historically realistic character by showing how the proportionate influence of the latter varied from generation to generation and from one aspect of culture to another.

In much the same way, Paul Joachimsen's occasional researches into the intellectual history of the Italian Renaissance were devoted mainly to breaking down Burckhardt's generalized and timeless formulae into characterizations specifically applicable to different stages of development or types of thought. One of the best examples of this process is to be found in his study of the Renaissance *Weltanschauung* in an article entitled, "From the Evolution of Italian Humanism" (1920). [109] Here as in his later parallel study of German humanism, [110] Joachimsen made significant distinctions between the various types of humanist thought — moral, aesthetic, political, hedonistic, and critical — and demonstrated the successive phases of development in what had commonly been regarded as a unified intellectual movement. In so doing, he also analysed the concept of individualism into its component parts,

---

[107] *Ibid.*, XCVIII, 53.
[108] W. Goetz, "Renaissance und Antike," *Historische Zeitschrift*, CXIII (1914), 237–59.
[109] P. Joachimsen, "Aus der Entwicklung des italienischen Humanismus," *Historische Zeitschrift*, CXXI (1920), 189–233.
[110] See below, pp. 280 ff.

and showed how Burckhardt's formula, thus related to the varied ideas of the age, might still be considered valid.

That the shift in method during the past three or four decades from Burckhardtian search for the spirit of the Renaissance to study of the ideas of the age should lead to an increasing awareness of diversity was to be expected. Ideas are intractable things and do not lend themselves so readily to generalization as do intuitively perceived mental qualities. The tendency to note differences and to distinguish stages of development was also characteristic of those historians who extended the scope of intellectual history to include the relation of ideas to the specific social, economic, and political developments of the Renaissance. Since Burckhardt's time, intensive cultivation of the field of economic history, the study of political theory and historiography as sub-categories of the history of ideas, and the methodology of the relatively young science of sociology have combined to make many of his generalizations appear inadequate, brilliantly intuitive though they were. The combination of the history of ideas with analysis of the evolution of political, social, and economic institutions has been particularly fruitful among those historians who were more or less directly influenced by Dilthey, and who carried into broader fields his conviction of the inter-connection between *Weltanschauung* and the total structural pattern of contemporaneous life.

To work out these inter-relations in detail in the history of Renaissance Florence has been the life work of Hans Baron. While recognizing in Burckhardt's conception the beginning of the road along which the interpretation of the Renaissance might be pursued most profitably, Baron devoted his attention for the most part to analysis of the relations between humanism and the civic life of Florence at different times and under varying economic, social, and political conditions. The result thus far has been a series of articles, too numerous to be listed here in full. [111] Among the most noteworthy were his early study of the peculiar character of Florentine "burgher humanism" de-

[111] Baron is at present engaged in a comprehensive study tentatively entitled, *Renaissance Liberty: Politics, Economics, Citizenship, and the Growth of Political Thought in the Florentine Commonwealth,* and he has almost completed a companion volume of literary and chronological investigations of the work of the Florentine humanists and publicists of the *Quattrocento.*

signed as an introduction to Leonardo Bruni's works (1928); an article on "The Awakening of Historical Thought in the Humanism of the Quattrocento" (1932), in which he traced the growth of a new historical outlook in the Florentine burgher milieu; an analysis of the part played by Florentine civic experience in shaping a new idea and theory of human nature (1935); and two systematic appraisals of the influence of Cicero and Aristotle on the moral philosophy of men engaged in active civic life (1938). [112] Taken together, these studies have helped to answer for at least one part of Renaissance Italy Walter Goetz's pertinent question "wherein lay in particular — concretely expressed — what was new."

While Baron was thus engaged in establishing in detailed studies the relation between the ideas and the social and political conditions of fifteenth century Florence, Alfred von Martin undertook to trace in one sweeping sociological synthesis the whole "curve of development" of Florentine burgher society. Like Baron, Martin entered the field of social history from the direction of the *Geisteswissenschaften,* but he was carried further by his implacable conceptualism and his restless interest in new methodologies. During what must have been an intellectually exciting life, he ranged the field of cultural history from the Middle Ages to the Romantic movement, reinterpreting, striving to define periodic concepts, and seeking to isolate the spiritual essence of the age which at the moment attracted his attention, with results of somewhat uneven value. Martin's earliest research in the field of the Renaissance, carried out in the conventional manner of the historian of ideas, led him to emphasize the continuation of medieval attitudes in the humanist *Weltanschauung.*[113] Later, under the influence of Eugen Wolf's psychological study of Petrarch, [114] he

---

[112] Leonardo Bruni Aretino, *Humanistisch-philosophische Schriften,* ed. H. Baron (Leipzig, 1928); H. Baron, "Das Erwachen des historischen Denkens im Humanismus des Quattrocento," *Historische Zeitschrift,* CXLVII (1932), 5–20; "La rinascita dell'etica statale romana nell'umanesimo fiorentino," *Civiltà moderna,* VII (1935), 1–31; "Cicero and the Roman Civic Spirit in the Middle Ages and the Early Renaissance," *Bulletin o; the John Rylands Library,* XXII (1938), 72–97; "Franciscan Poverty and Civic Wealth as Factors in the Rise of Humanistic Thought," *Speculum,* XIII (1938), 1–37.

[113] See below, p. 346 f.

[114] E. Wolf, *Petrarca, Darstellung seines Lebensgefühls* (Leipzig, 1926).

abandoned the methods of the history of ideas for those of psychology, and at the same time reversed his judgment of the relation of humanism to the Middle Ages. In two articles in 1927 and 1928,[115] he developed the thesis that Petrarch and the humanists who followed him were essentially modern in their psychic attitudes and subjective *Lebensgefühl,* however much their objective ideas might still bear a formal resemblance to those of the Middle Ages. He was thus able to dismiss the medieval element in the great humanist's religious thought, which has been the favorite theme of those who would deny the modernity of this "first modern man." [116]

> Although Petrarch [he asserted] never achieved an individual religion of his own creation, but held to the traditional forms of medieval Catholic religiosity, nevertheless the way in which he held it was altogether unmedieval, and in his confession itself his modern soul everywhere breaks through the inherited external forms.[117]

From psychology Martin moved on into the adjacent territory of sociology and adopted with wholehearted enthusiasm its concepts, methods, and hyphenated terminology. The somewhat mixed spiritual ancestry of his *Sociology of the Renaissance* (1932) [118] is evident from the dedication to Karl Mannheim, the frequent mention of Max Weber, Sombart, and Simmel, and the avowed conviction that "Burckhardt's fundamental work is still, despite everything, by no means obsolete." [119] Martin's first premise was his old conviction that periodization is of basic importance to the historian, since it involves the posing of his most fundamental question, that regarding the spirit

---

115 A. von Martin, "Peripatien in der seelischen Entwicklung der Renaissance," *Deutsche Vierteljahrsschrift für Literaturwissenschaft und Geistesgeschichte,* V (1927), 456–84; "Petrarca und die Romantik der Renaissance," *Historische Zeitschrift,* CXXXVIII (1928), 328–42.

116 Cf., for example, D. Bush, *The Renaissance and English Humanism* (Toronto, 1939), pp. 49 ff.

117 Martin in *Deutsche Vierteljahrsschrift,* V, 456 f.

118 A. von Martin, *Soziologie der Renaissance, zur Physiognomik und Rhythmik bürgerlicher Kultur* (Stuttgart, 1932). The English translation (New York, 1944) appeared after my discussion of the book was written. It would have made the problem of translating Martin's difficult terminology easier.

119 *Ibid.,* p. viii. Martin also drew much material to illustrate the social ideology of the Renaissance from F. Engel-Jànosi, *Soziale Probleme der Renaissance* (Stuttgart, 1924).

or essence of an age. From there he proceeded to the sociological thesis that the spirit of an age is essentially that of its dominant class, and that the character of that class may be reduced to an "ideal type." Aiming then at an analysis of what was "in a sociological sense typical" of the Renaissance, Martin felt it necessary to restrict his study to those spheres of activity "in which the bourgeois and specifically modern tendencies appeared most sharply and could best be seized upon." [120] And for that purpose, fifteenth century Florence presented the paradigmatic scene. The selection of the capitalist bourgoisie of Florence as the ideal type of the Renaissance, presupposed, of course, a broader sociological interpretation of the Renaissance as a whole. As Martin stated it: "The center of gravity of medieval society rested on the land, on the soil and property; with the Renaissance the economic center of gravity, and therewith also the social, shifted to the city: from the 'conservative' to the 'liberal' pole, for the city is a changeable and changing force." [121] But city life was not enough in itself to destroy the ordered, corporative civilization of the Middle Ages. The artisans and small shopkeepers could adjust themselves to the medieval scheme of things. The great merchants and capitalist entrepreneurs, however, could not. It was the capitalist burghers, then, whose spirit destroyed the old world and created the new, a world in which community was replaced by society, and religiously sanctioned political power by intellectually supported economic power. This new world was individualistic, rational, realistic, and disenchanted. In short, it was a prototype of the modern world. As Martin summed up his thesis, "the typological significance of the Renaissance consists in the fact that it was the first social and cultural transition from the medieval to the modern age, and as such a typical early stage of modern civilization." [122]

It is impossible to summarize Martin's work, with its intricate interweaving of social and cultural trends, in the brief space available here. There is little padding of specific fact or event. It is all pure analysis and synthesis. The first third of the book, devoted to "The New Dynamic," is perhaps the most generally fruitful. Here Martin

[120] Martin, *Soziologie der Renaissance*, p. vi.
[121] *Ibid.*, p. 1. [122] *Ibid.*, p. 4.

worked out with keen insight the ways in which early capitalism made revolutionary changes in the structure of social classes, created a new type of individualistic entrepreneur, new modes of secular thought, the birth of the natural sciences, new movements in art, and finally a dominant class whose position depended upon wealth and intellect. Thereafter the curve of development follows through a period of increasingly conservative stasis to decline, as the bourgeoisie deteriorated into a courtly society under despotic princes. Despite his new methodology, Martin's Italian Renaissance still bears a marked resemblance to that of Jacob Burckhardt. But if it is in many ways the same Renaissance, it is seen from a different angle, and the result is a picture different in more than its superficial aspects. The artists, humanists, and men of letters, for example, when considered as a social class, bearing a functional relation to a predominantly capitalist society, lose much of their halo of enchantment.

One obvious criticism of Martin's thesis is that, in his search for what was sociologically typical of the Renaissance, he placed a too exclusive emphasis on capitalism and the bourgeois entrepreneur. Overemphasis in that direction was, however, an almost inevitable result of the economic historians' relatively recent discovery of the early development of capitalism and of its far-reaching effects upon the whole economic and social organization of Renaissance Europe. At the same time sociologists and economists, like Max Weber and Werner Sombart, who had been touched by the influence of the *Geisteswissenchaften* were concentrating attention on the "spirit of capitalism." [123] These were new elements, of which nineteenth century historians had scarcely been aware, to be fitted into the traditional pattern. It was natural then that historians seeking a socio-economic genesis for Renaissance culture should look first to the influence of capitalism.

An article on "The Problem of the Origins of the Renaissance" (1924) [124] by the distinguished Norwegian historian, Halvdan Koht,

---

[123] Cf. M. Weber, "Die protestantische Ethik und der Geist des Kapitalismus," *Archiv für Sozialwissenschaft und Sozialpolitik*, XX (1904), 1–54; XXI (1905), 1–110. Eng. trans. (London, 1930); W. Sombart, *Der Bourgeois: zur Geistesgeschichte des modernen Wirtschaftsmenschen* (Munich, 1913). Eng. trans., *The Quintessence of Capitalism* (London, 1913).

[124] H. Koht, "Le problème des origines de la Renaissance," *Revue de synthèse historique*, XXXVII (1924), 107–16.

presents an unusually clear example of this tendency. While accepting Burckhardt's thesis that the essential characteristic of the Renaissance was the emancipation of the individual, Koht rejected his theory that this individualism originated in the peculiar political condition of Italy. The Renaissance, Koht admitted, began in Italy, but it was a European phenomenon and must have grown out of conditions common to all countries in Europe. On the same grounds he rejected all racial or national theories, and in the search for a cause that was both common and fundamental, he turned finally to the rise of capitalism. Economic individualism, Koht argued, was the essential characteristic of capitalism, so that capitalism produced not only the material but also the psychological conditions necessary for the emancipation of the spirit in all fields. With it appeared a burgher class filled with love of personal liberty and of free thought and action. And it was these capitalist burghers who were the creators of the new culture, replacing the nobles and clerics as the bearers of the progress of civilization. Like Martin, Koht thought Florence the best place to study the origins of the Renaissance, and "in Florence the Renaissance appeared through the intermediation of capitalism." [125] But what was true of Florence became true of the rest of Europe. Everywhere the Renaissance followed hard upon the development of capitalism. Koht was, of course, aware that a comprehensive interpretation of the Renaissance must include consideration of many other factors.

> But [he concluded] for the essence of the Renaissance, for the great current of new individualism, I have found no other explanation which is at the same time founded upon specific facts and applicable to the general movement. I cannot, therefore, but assert that the new spirit of the Renaissance, the emancipation of the individual, was the final result of an economic transformation of society. The Renaissance was basically the intellectual life of a new society.[126]

Combining sociology with economic and intellectual history, Edgar Zilsel, in an article on "The Sociological Roots of Science" (1942),[127] ascribed the origins of that particular branch of Renaissance culture

[125] Ibid., p. 114. [126] Ibid., p. 116.
[127] E. Zilsel, "The Sociological Roots of Science," The American Journal of Sociology, XLVII (1942), 544–60.

also to conditions resulting from the rise of capitalism. Zilsel adopted Olschki's thesis that it was neither the humanists nor the scholastic doctors but rather the practical technicians and engineers who laid the foundations of modern science during the Renaissance. They were "the real pioneers of empirical observation, experimentation, and causal research." [128] But Zilsel was interested primarily in the conditions that had produced this social class and determined their manner of life and ways of thought. And the fundamental change that preceded the growth of the natural sciences he thought was the transition from feudalism to early capitalism. This involved a shift in the milieu and in the protagonists of culture from country to city, from knights and clergy to the urban classes. Aside from his conviction that natural science could not develop in a feudal or clerical society, Zilsel argued that capitalism contributed a number of specific prerequisites to its growth. It precipitated a rapid progress in technology and invention, and thereby furthered causal thinking; it dissolved collective organizations and destroyed the collective-mindedness of the Middle Ages, and so gave rise to a new individualism which was a presupposition of scientific thinking; and, finally, it broke away from tradition and custom and proceeded rationally: "It calculated and measured, introduced book-keeping, and used machines." This Zilsel felt was the most important point of all. "The rise of economic rationality furthered the development of rational scientific methods. The emergence of the quantitative method, which is virtually non-existent in medieval theories, cannot be separated from the counting and calculating spirit of capitalist economy." [129]

The socio-economic interpretation of the Renaissance, illustrated in rather extreme form by the work of Martin, Koht, and Zilsel, altered the traditional pattern in two ways, both of decisive importance. In the first place, while recognizing the Renaissance to be a new age in European civilization, marked by many of the familiar characteristics of the Burckhardtian conception, it gave unprecedented emphasis to elements in the life of the age that had hitherto been generally neglected. In the second place, it suggested a new theory of causation and offered a new solution to the problem of the origins of Renaissance

[128] *Ibid.,* XLVII, 551.   [129] *Ibid.,* XLVII, 546.

civilization regarded as a European phenomenon. Although in its extreme form it erred in the direction of underestimating the importance of intellectual traditions, religious beliefs, and other ideal factors, it nevertheless served as a valuable corrective to the long established tradition that interpreted the Renaissance almost exclusively in terms of immaterial forces. Burckhardt and many of his successors in the field of *Kulturgeschichte* had, it is true, been aware of the genetic importance of social change, but they lacked the knowledge or the methodological tools to define it precisely. For more than half a century after Burckhardt, the interpretation of the Renaissance remained, in fact, almost entirely untouched by the results of the rapidly growing research in economic and social history. One potent reason for this was that the Renaissance had commonly been regarded as a concept applicable primarily to the history of intellectual and aesthetic culture. Thanks to Burckhardt, the Italian Renaissance had acquired a more comprehensive epochal significance, but in the northern countries the Renaissance remained pretty largely what it had always been, an intellectual, literary, or artistic movement, an aspect of the life of the age rather than an inclusive periodic concept. [130] As a result, economic and social historians as a rule did not consider the Renaissance their concern, [131] while the historians who did concern themselves with it were equally indifferent to the prosaic discoveries of their materialistic colleagues.

After the beginning of the twentieth century, however, with the growing volume of economic and social history and the development of new historical interpretations, this departmentalization of Renaissance studies tended to break down. And during the period of economic distress and social uncertainty between the two World Wars, certain tendencies in the climate of opinion became increasingly favorable to an economic and social approach to the problem of the interpretation of history — though there were also strongly opposed idealistic trends. What resulted was most frequently a suggestion of a possible causal relation between economic and social change and the evolution

[130] See discussion in the following chapter.
[131] Cf. F. L. Nussbaum, "The Economic History of Renaissance Europe," *The Journal of Modern History*, XIII (1941), 527.

of the higher forms of culture, rather than a genuine synthesis of the two. Academic specialization has, indeed, made comprehensive synthesis for large periods like the Middle Ages and the Renaissance an almost impossible aspiration for the individual historian. Even so widely learned and philosophical an historian as Henri Pirenne, whose life work was probably the greatest single inspiration to the economic and social reinterpretation of these periods, could offer no more than brilliant intuitions as to the relation between economic development and a rather conventionally conceived Renaissance.[132] Economic historians have, as was perhaps natural, been more apt than their fellows in the intellectual and aesthetic disciplines to ascribe the cultural development of the Renaissance primarily to the results of economic and social change. Strongly worded statements of such an interpretation may be found, for example, in Henri Sée's *Modern Capitalism, its Origins and Evolution* (1916)[133] and Alfred Doren's masterly *Italian Economic History* (1934).[134] But they do not regard it as their business to analyze the Renaissance. They are content rather to take it for granted in pretty much the traditional form, with special emphasis upon the Burckhardtian conception of individualism.

Next to the economic historians, the tendency to interpret the Renaissance from an economic point of view has been most common among general historians who have no special vested interest in particular disciplines. In his brilliant synthesis of the history of Europe during the period of the early Renaissance, *The Dawn of a New Era, 1250–1453* (1936), E. P. Cheyney gave the primary place to the expansion of trade. The keynote of the whole work was established at the very beginning in the sentence: "The most fundamental of the changes that marked the passage from medieval to modern times was the increase of wealth, and the principal cause of the increase of wealth was the extension of commerce."[135] Ferdinand Schevill, too, in the *His-*

---

[132] See, for example, H. Pirenne, *Histoire de Belgique,* III (Brussels, 1907), 285 ff.

[133] H. E. Sée, *Les origines du capitalisme moderne* (Paris, 1916), p. 47. Eng. trans. (New York, 1928).

[134] A. Doren, *Italienische Wirtschaftsgeschichte* (Jena, 1934), pp. 156; 304 f.

[135] E. P. Cheyney, *The Dawn of a New Era, 1250–1453* (New York, 1936), p. 2.

tory of Florence (1936) and the brief but more explicitly interpretive essay on "The Society of the Italian Renaissance" (1929) [136] consistently presented the culture of the Renaissance as the product of an urban economic and social development. Both, however, took their actual description of the intellectual and aesthetic movements of the age largely from standard secondary works, and offered little that was new beyond the general interpretative thesis, but that in itself is sufficiently noteworthy to merit their inclusion in this discussion.

As has been suggested already, historians whose field of interest concentrated their attention primarily upon the intellectual and aesthetic aspects of culture have been slower to give consideration to the causative influence of basic economic and social changes, or have denied entirely their causative effect. Still, there has been increasing evidence that thoughtful historians in these fields have become aware of the importance of the material considerations which, while lying beyond the confines of their own disciplines, might yet have a significant effect upon their interpretation. Writing for the fourteenth edition of the *Encyclopaedia Britannica* in 1929, Preserved Smith suggested, indeed, that this interpretative revolution had already been achieved.

> Our view of the Renaissance [he declared in a note appended to the original article by John Addington Symonds] has been greatly modified by the economic historians, who have stressed the material antecedents of the great political and intellectual movements of the fourteenth, fifteenth, and sixteenth centuries. Symonds, like nearly all his contemporaries, wrote as if the change in the mental habits of the race were a first cause, unexplained by any alteration in social conditions. But it is now generally accepted that the intellectual change was but the natural result of material conditions, altered by the growth of wealth, commerce, and city communities.[137]

A review of recent interpretations, however, suggests that "generally accepted" was rather too strong a term, or at least premature. In any case, although both economic and intellectual historians have undoubtedly become more conscious of the interrelations between their re-

---

[136] F. Schevill, *History of Florence from the Founding of the City through the Renaissance* (New York, 1936); J. W. Thompson, F. Schevill, G. Rowley, G. Sarton, *The Civilization of the Renaissance* (Chicago, 1929), pp. 45–72.

[137] *Encyclopaedia Britannica* (14th ed., 1929), article, "Renaissance."

spective fields, no adequate synthesis has as yet emerged.[138] Perhaps the most satisfactory solution to the problem so far is to be found in those co-operative works, like the *Propyläen Weltgeschichte*[139] and the series entitled *Peuples et civilisations*,[140] in which specialists in the various fields have contributed with a fair degree of harmony to form a kind of synthesis. In the former the contributions of Jacob Strieder, Alfred Doren, and Fritz Rörig, and in the latter those of Henri Pirenne and Henri Hauser have given due emphasis to the economic and social aspects of the Renaissance.

THE BURCKHARDTIAN TRADITION IN THE HISTORY OF LITERATURE AND ART

From its earliest beginnings the idea of the Renaissance was bound up in a very special way with the history of literature and art, and this remained largely true even after Burckhardt had carried the concept of the Italian Renaissance over into the field of *Kulturgeschichte*. The results of Burckhardt's work were nevertheless revolutionary. Whereas in the past the idea of the Renaissance had been determined by that of the rebirth of art and letters or the revival of learning, each of which was regarded as an autonomous movement, the situation was now reversed. Historians tended rather to interpret the literary and artistic achievements of the age in accordance with the conception of the Renaissance as a definite and unified period in the history of civilization, characterized by a peculiar spirit. To a greater or less degree throughout the half-century following 1860, the histories of the separate disciplines were conceived, not as isolated phenomena, but as interrelated members of a general cultural history. Scholarly research and scientific objectivity might concentrate the major attention upon factual detail, but the basic assumption remained that the developments

---

138 My contribution to the *Berkshire Studies, The Renaissance* (New York, 1940), attempted a comprehensive synthesis of the civilization of the Renaissance, based upon the fundamental changes that had taken place in the economy of Western Europe in the period following the High Middle Ages, but in far too brief a form to be other than suggestive.

139 W. Goetz, ed., *Propyläen Weltgeschichte*, IV (Berlin, 1932).

140 L. Halphen and P. Sagnac eds., *Peuples et civilisations:* Vol. VII, H. Pirenne, A. Renaudet, E. Perroy, M. Handelsman, and L. Halphen, *La fin du Moyen Age* (Paris, 1931); Vol. VIII, H. Hauser and A. Renaudet, *Les débuts de l'âge moderne* (Paris, 1929).

in literature and art were aspects of a more comprehensive civilization, their character determined by the general spirit or *Weltanschauung* of the age.

One noticeable result of this reversal in the relation of the concepts was an extension of the chronological limits of the Renaissance as a period in the history of art. Rigid classicism in the manner of Winckelmann, as well as the Romantic classification of the artists before Raphael as masters of medieval Christian art, had led most early nineteenth century historians to limit the term Renaissance to the first half of the sixteenth century. It now became the more common practice to identify all art falling within the Burckhardtian period, or at least that of the *Quattrocento,* as Renaissance art. That many critics, including Burckhardt himself,[141] could not extend the style period back to Giotto, as Vasari had done, was undoubtedly due to the increased knowledge of the nature of medieval art which resulted from nineteenth century research. But Vasari's second and third styles, the fifteenth and sixteenth centuries, were now commonly classified as Early and High Renaissance respectively. In literary history such a chronological extension was less necessary, yet even here the influence of the periodic conception of the Renaissance was apparent in a stronger tendency to treat vernacular and humanist literatures together as common products of the age.

The renewed interest in the Renaissance during the half-century after Burckhardt was reflected in an impressive crop of full length histories of Italian art and literature "in the period of the Renaissance." With the development of a scientific *expertise* in art criticism, much research was devoted to verifying factual information and to establishing the authenticity and ascription of works of art. Many of the histories of art were indeed scarcely more than "written museums."[142] There were also, however, innumerable collections of critical essays intended for a more popular audience. The finest of these, Walter Pater's *The Renaissance* (1877), has achieved the permanent status of a minor classic and has served to introduce generations of readers to the culture of the age. Add to these the countless biographies of the great

[141] Cf. J. Burckhardt, *Cicerone* (4th ed., Leipzig, 1879), II, 79.
[142] Cf. L. Venturi, *History of Art Criticism* (New York, 1936), p. 223.

artists and writers of the Renaissance, and the result is a vast mass of literary material, which testifies eloquently to the attraction that brilliant age held for readers of every gradation of scholarly or popular taste. We can mention here only a few of those works which strove toward a definite interpretation of Renaissance culture, within the general tendencies of the Burckhardtian tradition.

For the history of Italian literature, the first such work was one that in reality belonged to the period before Burckhardt. Though not published till 1870–71, the *History of Italian Literature*[143] of Francesco de Sanctis was conceived in the years between 1839 and 1848, when De Sanctis was teaching at Naples, and was largely written during the following years of his imprisonment and exile as an opponent of the Bourbon régime. It was in fact a product, and one of the most distinguished, of the Romantic-idealist school of literary history which flourished in the mid-century. Published after that school had been somewhat discredited by the positivist reaction, it attracted surprisingly little attention outside of Italy. In his own country, however, De Sanctis' personal influence as one of the champions of the Risorgimento was very great, and his work, with its Hegelian emphasis upon the indispensable rôle of the state in the shaping of a sound culture or public morality, was never entirely forgotten. It was revived at the beginning of the present century by the pious enthusiasm of Benedetto Croce, and has since become the inspiration of one of the most active schools of Italian literary history.

De Sanctis' conception of the Renaissance differed in essential features from that of Burckhardt; yet in other ways it was not dissimilar.[144] It might, indeed, be combined with the Burckhardtian tradition, as was done in Villari's *Life of Machiavelli*. That there should be many similarities was natural, for Burckhardt was himself influenced, rather more than he would admit, by Romantic and idealistic trends of thought. For both men the primary interest in cultural history was analysis of the spirit of the age and the nation. It is this that makes

---

143 F. de Sanctis, *Storia della letteratura italiana*, 2 vols. (Naples, 1870–71). Eng., trans., *History of Italian Literature*, 2 vols. (New York: Harcourt, Brace, 1931).
144 Cf. A. Janner, "Individualismus und Religiosität in der Renaissance," *Deutsche Vierteljahrsschrift für Literaturwissenschaft und Geistesgeschichte*, XIII (1935), 357 f.

De Sanctis' book more than a literary history. Croce has called it "an intimate history of the Italian people." [145]

As De Sanctis analyzed it, the Italian spirit in the age of the Renaissance was bourgeois, secular, and individualistic in the sense of caring little for public life or communal welfare, indifferent to religion, morality, or patriotism, devoted to art and giving artistic form to every aspect of life, conditioned by the study of classical antiquity, but not determined by it. Though developing steadily, this spirit remained constant in its primary characteristics from about the middle of the fourteenth century to the middle of the sixteenth. But that is as far as the resemblance to Burckhardt's conception goes. De Sanctis' Romantic nationalism, his Hegelian philosophy, and his moral earnestness furnished him with a set of values different from those of the Swiss individualist and aesthete. They made him see the Renaissance primarily as a period of decadence, superficially brilliant, but empty. The virile spirit of the communes, filled with religious ecstasy, deep moral feeling, and political fervor, did not outlive Dante, its last great exponent. The new spirit of the next generation was best exemplified by Boccaccio, "Giovanni della tranquillità," with his superficial view of life, his sensuous love of beauty, his empty erudition, and his serenely comic spirit.[146] Even Petrarch had shown signs of the changing spirit.

> Moral, religious, political feelings were weak in the poet's [Petrarch's] consciousness; and the place they left empty was filled by art. This weakening of the conscience, this cult for lovely form in the midst of the many discoveries of Graeco-Roman antiquity, are the two chief characteristics of the generation that followed the believing, virile, impassioned age of Dante.[147]

Over and over De Sanctis returned to this theme, illustrating it from the character and works of Alberti, Poliziano, Ariosto, and a host of other literati. These men had abandoned the world of the spirit for the world of nature, and that world was "empty and superficial, devoid

[145] B. Croce's preface to Eng. trans. of De Sanctis, *History of Italian Literature*, I, vi.

[146] De Sanctis, *Storia della letteratura italiana* (ed. B. Croce, Bari, 1925), I, 304 f; 333 f.

[147] *Ibid.*, I, 269 [I, 294].

of all the inner powers of the spirit, having no seriousness at all of means or of end." [148] Where Burckhardt and Symonds had seen an intense vitality, vigorous individualism, a positive attitude toward life, and keen curiosity regarding the world and man, De Sanctis saw only a spiritual void, indifference, negation, and a serene mocking spirit that took nothing seriously except art, which was "the one force that remained — the only virtue that was still intact." [149] De Sanctis could feel the charm of "the cult of lovely form," but his moral condemnation of the Renaissance writers was unsparing. His literati were hollow men, and the rest of Italy was like unto them. When Charles VIII rode into Italy, "he found a people who called him a barbarian; a people in the full vigour of its intellectual forces, but empty of soul and weak of fibre." [150]

But out of evil cometh good, and in the midst of this decadent society De Sanctis discerned in Machiavelli the prophet of a new age. The civilization of the Renaissance was "a reaction against mysticism and exaggerated spirituality, or, to be exact, it was a reaction against asceticism, symbolism, scholasticism — against everything that is known as the Middle Ages." [151] This reaction was implicit in the naturalistic, idyllic art and literature of the age. It became conscious with Machiavelli, and he gave it a new spiritual content. Italy had passed the point where it could be reformed by religion. A new and sound civilization could be constructed only on the basis of "effectual truth as shown by actual experience and by the intellect." Machiavelli met this need by establishing the science of man and society. He thus became "the Luther of Italy," "the consciousness and thought of the century." [152] De Sanctis is nowhere more Hegelian — or more obscure — than in his discussion of Machiavelli. His Machiavelli both expresses and rejects the spirit of his age. He is at once exclusively absorbed in practical experience and motivated by a rather incredible idealism. English-speaking readers in particular may well pause over

---

[148] *Ibid.*, I, 304 [I, 336].
[149] *Ibid.*, I, 390 [I, 433]. Cf. I, 414 [I, 462]: "Under the mantle of indifference was negation. In that immense void there was nothing left but art and culture, valued for themselves."
[150] *Ibid.*, I, 385 [I, 427].   [151] *Ibid.*, I, 416 [I, 464].
[152] *Ibid.*, I, 416 ff [I, 463 ff].

such sentences as: "To make this life on earth the important thing that it once had been, to give it a purpose, and to bring back health to the inner stream of character, to restore seriousness and activity to man — here is the vital motive that breathes in all the works of Machiavelli." [153] The key, of course, is to be found in Machiavelli's patriotism. He was unique in the Renaissance because "his conscious‑ ness was not empty: it contained the ideal of freedom, the independ‑ ence of his country." [154] But what has this to do with his basic belief that "things must be judged as they are and not as they ought to be"? [155] The *non sequitur* can be avoided only by conceiving Machia‑ velli as an Hegelian before Hegel and by accepting Hegel's doctrine of the state as the ultimate product of reason. The following summary of Machiavelli's significance may then become clearer — if not more credible.

> That "ought to be," that tendency of both the Middle Ages and the Renaissance alike, must give place to what is, or, as he puts it, to "effectual" truth. The basis of all his teaching is the principle that imagination, whether in religion or art, must be made subordinate to the real world as shown by experience and observation.
> Having entirely scrapped the superhuman and the supernatural, he sets up the fatherland as the basis of life. The first mission of man on earth and his first duty is patriotism — the duty of working for the glory, the greatness, the freedom, of his country.[156]

One may feel that this does not greatly clarify the history of the Renaissance, but it does undoubtedly help to clarify much recent Italian thought.

While the German philosophical spirit thus lived on in the Neapoli‑ tan De Sanctis, the two principal German histories of Italian literature written during this period showed little sign of it. As might be ex‑ pected from the editor whose solemn erudition strove to transform Burckhardt's *Civilization of the Renaissance in Italy* from a brilliant essay into a reference work, Ludwig Geiger's general conception of the Renaissance was Burckhardtian. But in his *Renaissance and Human‑ ism in Italy and Germany* (1882) [157] the general conception is buried

---

153 *Ibid.*, II, 64 [II, 545].   154 *Ibid.*, II, 59 [II, 538 f].
155 *Ibid.*, II, 64 [II, 545].   156 *Ibid.*
157 L. Geiger, *Renaissance und Humanismus in Italien und Deutschland* (Berlin, 1882).

under masses of factual information. To a slightly lesser extent this is also true of Adolf Gaspary's more readable *History of Italian Literature* (1885–88),[158] of which the second volume treats the age of the Renaissance. Gaspary was himself aware of his tendency to give more attention to individual personalities than to general development, judging the historian there to be on safer ground.[159] Where interpretative comment does appear, however, and in the unconscious bias of the entire work, the influence of Burckhardt and Voigt is clearly visible.

It was France which produced the best example of the cultural-historical approach to Italian literature in Philippe Monnier's delightful study, *The Quattrocento* (1900).[160] Though neither very original nor well thought out, it is pure *Kulturgeschichte,* enlivened by a Gallic verve and piquancy of phrase that leave a memorable impression of the character of the age. The first hundred-odd pages were devoted to the political and social conditions of Italy. The treatment here was nine-tenths Burckhardt, though with a tendency to heightened dramatic effect and an emphasis upon the Renaissance man's youthful and pagan enjoyment of life that is reminiscent of Symonds. The Burckhardtian conception of Renaissance society remained the basis of interpretation throughout the entire work, but in his treatment of humanism Monnier derived both material and opinions more directly from Voigt, with something of De Sanctis' conviction that the humanists were decadent aesthetes. His borrowings from Voigt, however, were always pointed up, phrased a little more strongly. Where Voigt had said of Petrarch: "Schreiben und Leben ist ihm eins," [161] Monnier wrote: "Il ne vit pas: il écrit." [162] And Voigt had never put his opinion of the paucity of content in humanist literature so forcefully as Monnier's "Having nothing to say, they said nothing interminably." [163]

It was France, too, which produced the most significant attempt at a cultural-historical interpretation of the art of the Italian Renaissance.

[158] A. Gaspary, *Geschichte der italienischen Literatur,* 2 vols. (Berlin, 1885–88).
[159] *Ibid.,* Preface to Vol. II.
[160] P. Monnier, *Le Quattrocento, Essai sur l'histoire littéraire du XVᵉ siècle italien,* 2 vols. (Paris, 1900; new ed. Paris, 1924).
[161] G. Voigt, *Die Wiederbelebung des classischen Alterthums* (Berlin, 1859), p. 21.
[162] Monnier, I, 136.   [163] *Ibid.,* I, 228.

At the moment when the Hegelian school of idealistic interpretation was losing popularity, Hippolyte Taine furnished a new generation nourished in awe of the natural sciences with a philosophy and method that lent a respectable air of detached scientific analysis to the current concepts and prejudices of art history. As a result, despite their manifold defects, Taine's lectures on the *Philosophy of Art in Italy* (1866) [164] probably had more widespread influence than had most of the contemporary histories of Renaissance art, devoted as the latter were primarily to the task of describing and classifying artistic production according to masters, schools, techniques and types, with the cultural background taken more or less for granted.

Taine's historical philosophy, already expounded and illustrated in his immensely successful *History of English Literature* (1863-64),[165] stemmed from two diverse sources: the positivist philosophy of Comte and the German Romantic theory of the creative force and unchanging character of the national spirit.[166] From Comte he borrowed the concept of the *milieu*, i.e., the idea that all the intellectual and aesthetic expressions of an age are determined by the environment which produced them, and that this environment must be studied with the objective observation used in the physical and biological sciences.

We come then [he wrote] to posing this rule, that to comprehend a work of art, an artist, a group of artists, it is necessary to represent with exactitude the general state of mind and of manners of the age to which they pertain. There the final explanation will be found; there is the original cause which determines everything else.[167]

And again:

Just as there is a physical temperature which by its variations determines the appearance of this or that species of plants, so there is a moral temperature which by its variations determines the appear-

---

[164] H. Taine, *Philosophie de l'art en Italie* (Paris, 1866). Eng. trans. (London, 1866). It was followed by *Philosophie de l'art dans les Pays Bas* (Paris, 1869).
[165] H. Taine, *Histoire de la littérature anglaise*, 5 vols. (Paris, 1863-64). Eng. trans., 2 vols. (Edinburgh, 1871).
[166] For his own exposition, see *ibid.* introd. Cf. E. Fueter, *Geschichte der neueren Historiographie* (Munich, 1936), pp. 582-90; H. Sée, "Taine, historien de littérature et de l'art," *La grande revue*, CXXVI (1928), 631-43.
[167] Taine, *Philosophie de l'art* (I use 20th ed., 2 vols., Paris, s.d.), I, 7.

ance of this or that species of art. . . . The products of the human
spirit, like those of living nature, can be explained only by their
milieu.[168]

In short, history should be "a kind of botany, applied not to plants, but
to the works of man." [169] But Taine also drew analogies from the
physical sciences and hoped by applying their method to achieve still
more significant results. He believed it possible to induce certain
general laws of history, comparable to those of physics or mechanics.
"He ended by conceiving history as a problem in psychological mechanics, a matter of forces, directions, and masses." [170] And these
forces he classified under the names of race, milieu, and moment. Race
supplied the innate, hereditary disposition. The moment was the
momentum of great historical movements. The milieu included the
workings of both of these, plus climate, institutions, and social
organization.

But however much Taine might borrow terminology and method
from the natural sciences, the content of his thought derived from
another intellectual world, and it remained fundamentally unaltered
by his tardily acquired positivism. Moreover he lacked the methodology of the social sciences which might have made his study of the
milieu more fruitful. One of the few Frenchmen of his generation to
have plunged deeply into German literature, Taine's thought was early
and permanently influenced by the dominant ideas of German Romanticism and Hegelian philosophy. He might revolt against the
mysticism of the Romantic *Volksgeist,* but only to adopt the scarcely
less mystical racial theory formulated by Mme. de Staël.[171] Belief in the
unalterable difference between the Latin and Germanic races, qualified
by subsidiary national divergences, remained a basic dogma in all his
thought. It was always the primary factor in determining the milieu.
He might revolt, too, against the idealistic basis of Hegel's construction
of history, but the tendency to construct from *a priori* ideas remained.
Finally, he inherited from the Romantic historians the habit of assuming that all literary products of an age or nation can be safely accepted

---

168 *Ibid.,* II, 9.   169 *Ibid.,* II, 13.
170 Sée, in *La grande revue,* CXXVI, 640.   171 See above, p. 125.

as reliable sources for the analysis of its spirit, since all are the unconscious expression of that spirit.

These tendencies robbed Taine's method, as he practiced it, of any real scientific validity. The racial factor on which so much of it rested was a dogmatic abstraction. Only where he showed it qualified by historical conditions in a given nation did it assume anything approaching a solid body. And then it was pretty much our old acquaintance, the organically developing *Volksgeist*. True, Taine aspired to prove the validity of these concepts by sound scientific method. But the inductive process on which he relied was actually vitiated in practice by his arbitrary selection of data to illustrate his preconceived ideas. Try as he might, Taine could not be an inductive thinker. Moreover, his conscientious support of all generalizations by the examination of individual phenomena was further rendered almost useless by a deplorable lack of historical criticism; by naïve acceptance at their face value of memoirs, novels, anecdotes, scandalous gossip, tendentious pamphlets, and facts of more than doubtful verity, as scientifically valid data. At the same time, his theory that the character of a work of art is determined by the moral atmosphere, that "the state of manners and mentality is the same for the public as for the artists," [172] while partly true, led him in practice to a strange reversal of the doctrine of the milieu. While aiming at explaining the work of the artist by the character of the milieu, he more often than not formed his conception of the milieu in accordance with the work of a few carefully selected artists or writers.

The art of the Italian Renaissance seemed to Taine to furnish an example peculiarly well designed to illustrate his method. As always, he started with a preconceived idea of the character of the age, in this case drawn largely from Burckhardt, whose work he greatly admired [173] and helped to naturalize in France much as Symonds had done in England. Apart from Taine's scientific bias, the two men had much in common. Both sought primarily to establish the spirit of national culture in a given period. They believed this spirit to be the determining factor in shaping intellectual and aesthetic production,

[172] Taine, *Philosophie de l'art*, I, 4.
[173] Cf. *Ibid.*, II, 51 n.

and they tended to select and interpret all individual phenomena in accordance with it. Both sought the typical rather than the exceptional, and were interested in sources that revealed the state of mind rather than those that established facts and events. Moreover, both conceived the spirit of a culture to be the product of stable forces, of which the two most important were the permanent national (or racial) genius and the temporary conjunction of historical circumstances. The unscientific Burckhardt, however, was much less given to romantic exaggeration and considerably less naïve in his handling of sources.

Having declared the character of Italian painting in the High Renaissance to be laic and pagan, devoted predominantly to the physical beauty of man, Taine proceeded to lay down the conditions that shaped the determining milieu.[174] The "primary condition" was, of course, the race. If the Italians took this direction in art "it was by virtue of national and permanent instincts. The imagination of the Italian is classic, that is to say, Latin."[175] Then followed the "secondary conditions" which account for the appearance of this form of art at this particular time. The first of these was the emergence of the Italians in the fifteenth century from barbarism to cultivation, from the feudal to the modern spirit, a development he ascribed to the finesse of the Italian character plus the rebirth of antique civilization.[176] But this condition must be accompanied by a second. The Italians of that age were cultivated, but not to the point where images had been stifled and mutilated by ideas and by political, religious, and moral preoccupations, as in modern Europe.[177] Their images, and hence their art, were spontaneous. Here again we have the fundamental tenet of Renaissancism: the Renaissance as the beginning of the modern age, but with a freshness and vigor since lost. "The Renaissance was a unique moment, intermediary between the Middle Ages and the modern age, between insufficient culture and too much culture, between the reign of instincts and the reign of mature ideas."[178] The third condition was that quality in the basic character of the Renaissance Italians that directed their attention to the human physique. To

---

[174] For brief summary of his thesis, see *ibid.*, I, 203.
[175] *Ibid.*, I, 119.   [176] *Ibid.*, I, 124.
[177] *Ibid.*, I, 151 ff.   [178] *Ibid.*, I, 165.

account for this Taine examined the milieu further and noted the
insecurity of the age, its violence, the untamed physical passions of the
people, the prevalent immorality and license, all combined with the
greatest refinement and delicacy of taste. "These men were lettered,
connoisseurs, fine conversationalists, polished, men of the world, at the
same time, men of arms, assassins, and murderers. They acted like
savages and reasoned like civilized people: they were intelligent
wolves." [179] This is a conception of Renaissance society that had been
arrived at before by less scientific means.

Taine's lectures were aptly entitled *The Philosophy of Art*. They
were less a history of Renaissance art than the philosophical program
for such a history. That program was filled out, at length and in
detail, by Eugène Muentz, whose massive, three-volume *History of
Art during the Renaissance* (1889-95) [180] remains the most imposing
monument of the cultural-historical genre of art history in the Burckhardtian tradition. The meaning of the word Renaissance was no
longer a problem for Muentz. It had been definitively established by
the works of Michelet, Burckhardt, and Taine.

> It signified that rejuvenation of the human spirit, that emancipation
> of thought, that *essor* of the sciences and that refinement of civiliza-
> tion, that pursuit of distinction and beauty, which men affirmed in
> Italy about the fifteenth century under the influence of the lessons of
> antiquity. The discovery of the world and of man, softer and more
> humane manners, return to religious tolerance and cosmopolitanism,
> a more methodical activity and, as a result, a constantly increasing
> prosperity, the exuberance of life in twenty sovereign courts . . . . the
> cult of form re-established in all its rights: such were some of the
> traits which characterized this admirable movement.[181]

As an admitted disciple of Burckhardt, Muentz related all of this
directly to the rise of individualism.[182] His task, then, was not to discover the spirit of Renaissance society, since that had already been
done, but to write the history of the art it produced. But, being also a
disciple of Taine, he felt it necessary first to describe the milieu in full
detail, demonstrating its effect upon the art that grew out of it. Be-

[179] *Ibid.*, I, 178.
[180] E. Muentz, *Histoire de l'art pendant la Renaissance*, 3 vols. (Paris, 1889-
95).
[181] *Ibid.*, I. 1.   [182] *Ibid.*, I, 28 f.

ginning with the patrons of art, he passed on to the influence of revived antiquity, to religious life, to technical and theoretical discoveries,
clothing, manners, the organization of teaching and of labor, and a
host of other factors in the social and intellectual environment of the
artist. This environment was so abundantly illustrated, indeed, that it
ended by absorbing the individual artist almost completely. That
art is the product of the artist's milieu was an exceedingly fruitful concept. But Muentz, like Taine, tended to forget that it is also the
product of individual men, each of whom is, within the limits set by
his age, *sui generis*.

Muentz's work remained unique in its comprehensive scope, but
there were a number of detailed studies in the same tradition, designed
to fill out in detail some particular aspect of the influence of Renaissance society or thought upon the art of the age. Hubert Janitschek's
essays on *The Society of the Renaissance in Italy and Art* (1879),[183]
for example, dealt with such problems as "Women and Art" and "Public and Private Patronage." The interpretation of art in accordance
with a general history of Renaissance civilization continued into the
twentieth century, and indeed still continues. But as the century progressed, newer tendencies of criticism approached the problem from
other directions and under the influence of altered standards of taste.
The study of art as pure form and attempts to relate it to contemporaneous psychological or intellectual conditions led to a variety of new
interpretations. Most of these tended to limit the Renaissance to a
style concept, confined within a chronologically narrowed period, or to
depreciate it in other ways, generally to the advantage of the Gothic
or the Baroque. They were thus either antagonistic to the Burckhardtian tradition or, as in the case of Heinrich Wölfflin's analysis of
Renaissance art on the basis of "pure visibility," were so exclusively
interested in form as to have little bearing upon interpretation of the
culture of the age.[184] In the history of art, however, as in other fields,
the newer tendencies in intellectual history or *Geistesgeschichte* also
led to significant variants upon the Burckhardtian theme that the

---

183 H. Janitschek, *Die Gesellschaft der Renaissance in Italien und die Kunst*
(Stuttgart, 1879).
184 For discussion of these interpretations, see below, pp. 359 ff.

Renaissance represented a new age in the history of the European mentality. These belong more properly to the present discussion.

The Viennese art historian, Max Dvořák, was one of the most effective exponents of the close relation between artistic form and contemporaneous intellectual conditions. His lectures on *The History of Italian Art in the Age of the Renaissance*,[185] published posthumously in 1927–28, were constantly concerned with an analysis of the changing mental attitudes of the period and thus furnished an interpretation of its culture that went far beyond the field of art. In an earlier study he had demonstrated that realism and naturalism, which were traditionally considered to be novelties introduced by the Renaissance, were in fact also characteristic of the Gothic age and harmonized with major trends in medieval thought.[186] Nevertheless, he was convinced that in very important ways, if not precisely those that Burckhardt had stressed, the Renaissance marked a break with the Middle Ages.

> For the art historian there can be no doubt that it signified not merely a carrying further of medieval achievements, but a decisive change; and if this cannot be clearly defined from the old points of view from which the Renaissance has been regarded, that means only that the old points of view were wrong, or at least not adequate.[187]

Dvořák's revision of the traditional interpretation, then, implied no denial of the originality of the Renaissance. Rather he reaffirmed it, but on the basis of new criteria.

> The great achievement of the founders of the Renaissance [he asserted] was not, as Burckhardt taught, the discovery of the world and of man, which had already been accomplished in the *Weltanschauung* of the Gothic, but the discovery of material accordance with law (Gesetzmässigkeit) and objective causality as the most important aim in the observation of bodies, their functions, and their relation to one another in space. To win a new mastery of representation, a new conquest of the world, by means of this discovery which was closely related to the antique view of the world was the sense and content of the following development.[188]

This new way of seeing nature, so different from the subjective Gothic view of individual phenomena, was expressed as early as Giotto in a

---

[185] M. Dvořák, *Geschichte der italienischen Kunst im Zeitalter der Renaissance*, 2 vols. (Munich, 1927–28).
[186] See below, p. 371 f.   [187] Dvořák, I, 4.   [188] *Ibid.*, I, 59 f.

new principle of composition, founded entirely on the laws of objective vision.[189] And what Giotto began, Masaccio and the other painters of the fifteenth century completed. It amounted to a revolutionary change in man's relation to the world.

This thesis, or a very similar one, was further elaborated in Dagobert Frey's brilliant essay, *Gothic and Renaissance as Foundations of the Modern World View* (1929).[190] Frey stated as his methodological premise the assumption that what is significant for *Geistesgeschichte* is not the evolution of ideas as such, but the changes in ways of thinking or of forming ideas (Vorstellungsweise). "What we designate as *Vorstellungsweise*," he explained, perhaps not unnecessarily, "is not determined by the content of ideas, but by the form of ideas, by the characteristic structure of ideas."[191] And the structure of ideas of the Renaissance, Frey thought to be fundamentally modern. We can find ourselves at home in the intellectual atmosphere of the Renaissance as we never can in that of the Gothic age. To demonstrate this assertion, Frey undertook an analysis of the changes in the perception of space (Raumvorstellung) illustrated by the transition from Gothic to Renaissance art, with special emphasis on the introduction of linear perspective. This, he thought, was more than a mere principle of formal style, more than a mere technical aid to artistic production. It reflected a new perception of the world, founded upon objective, scientific, and mathematically determined accuracy of vision, which was entirely modern. "The essential factor was not merely a widening of the sphere of expression, nor fuller development of means of expression, but a new way of seeing the world."[192]

[189] *Ibid.*, I, 20.
[190] D. Frey, *Gotik und Renaissance als Grundlagen der modernen Weltanschauung* (Augsburg, 1929).
[191] *Ibid.*, p. xxix.   [192] *Ibid.*, p. 6.

CHAPTER NINE

The Traditional Interpretation of the Renaissance in the North

THE NORTHERN RENAISSANCE had no Burckhardt. It is doubtful indeed if even his genius could have created as coherent a synthesis for the countries north of the Alps as he did for Italy. As a result the historical interpretation of the Renaissance in the northern countries is on the whole much less comprehensive and shows less uniformity than characterized that of Italy in the post-Burckhardtian era. Nevertheless, there were certain commonly accepted ideas which make it possible to speak of a traditional interpretation, at least as opposed to the views of recent revisionists. These ideas had remained fundamentally constant, despite variation in point of view, through a long series of interpretations — humanist, Protestant, rationalist, and liberal — and had finally received a new orientation from Burckhardt's synthesis of the Renaissance in Italy. Allowing for much variety of definition and value judgment, those works will here be classified as following the traditional interpretation which proceed from three basic ideas: that the Renaissance began in Italy and later spread across the Alps, altering its character somewhat in each country it entered; that the revival of antiquity was everywhere a dominant factor; and, finally, that it marked the end of medieval civilization and the dawn of the modern age.

PROBLEMS OF THE NORTHERN RENAISSANCE

Historians attempting to construct a coherent interpretation of the Northern Renaissance have been confronted by problems inherent in the intractable nature of their material, problems which did not exist for the historians of Italy or of which, at any rate, the latter were but vaguely aware. Nor do the problems become much less difficult when the effort at synthesis is restricted to the Renaissance in a particular country, as has been most generally the case. Each country presents its own peculiar problems while at the same time sharing those of the Northern Renaissance in general, and no northern country could be so easily disassociated from its neighbors and treated in isolation as could Italy. The Renaissance, therefore, has been a less satisfactory, as well as a less unified, concept in the history of the transalpine lands.

It has also been a less important concept. Even in its early and elementary form as a mere series of revivals of antique culture, of art, or of literature it played a larger part in the history of Italy than of any other country. Nineteenth century historians greatly expanded the content of the Renaissance, but they did so primarily in relation to Italy. The Romantic Renaissance of Stendhal, Byron, and Browning, with all its unholy charm, was exclusively Italian. Michelet, who first established the Renaissance as an historical epoch, did, it is true, conceive it as an era in European history with special application to France. But Burckhardt's much more decisive work restored it to Italy and bound it up with conditions that were peculiar to Italian history. The Renaissancism of the late nineteenth century undoubtedly influenced the interpretation of French, English, and German history, but its nostalgic enthusiasm was nourished almost entirely by Italy. Historians of Italy could no more ignore the Renaissance than could German historians the Reformation or English historians the constitutional struggle of the seventeenth century; yet an English historian could write: "It is difficult for the average Englishman to think of or even to remember the Renaissance as a great land mark or watershed in our history." [1] The conception of the Renaissance as a distinct historical era had in fact never been fully established in the history of any of the northern countries. Almost without exception the northern historians have remained closer to the original conception and have regarded it as one aspect of their history, as an intellectual or aesthetic

[1] A. E. Lovett in F. J. C. Hearnshaw, ed., *Social and Political Ideas of some great Thinkers of the Renaissance and Reformation* (London, 1925), p. 61.

movement or as a spiritual force inspiring much of the thought of the age but not including all facets of its civilization. Thus it has often been treated as something contemporary with but distinct from the Reformation or even, occasionally, from humanism.

From this tendency to identify the Renaissance with specific movements a chronological problem results, which in turn becomes one of the most formidable obstacles to the formation of a more general, epochal concept. Its chronological scope may be defined differently for the history of learning, literature, or the arts in any one country, and the confusion increases in arithmetical progression as the concept is expanded to include all the European nations. Even when Italy, with its exceptionally early development, is excluded the chronological problem of a Renaissance epoch for Western Europe is a baffling one. No single set of dates will be satisfactory everywhere; yet there is something very unsatisfactory about an historical period that differs in time from country to country or, still worse, from one discipline to another.

All of the foregoing problems are related more or less closely to the fundamental dogma that the Renaissance was not indigenous to the North. An importation in all the transalpine lands, it remained to some degree an alien element in their culture. Awareness of this, faint if present at all in the early tradition, has grown increasingly strong with the growth of national consciousness. Recent northern historians, especially those primarily interested in the history of ideas, have tended to stress as strongly as have the Italians the notion that the revival of Latin antiquity was the revival of Italy's own national past. Thus to the idea that the Renaissance originated in Italy has been added the idea that it there became a conscious revival of national culture in a sense impossible elsewhere. This was a major part of Konrad Burdach's thesis;[2] but it has been expressed also by Paul Joachimsen who was no friendly critic of Burdach's interpretation.

Petrarch [Joachimsen wrote] is the first humanist in so far as he is the first Italian patriot. For humanism in its origins and development is a national Italian phenomenon. Only here in Italy had its expression something of the happy charm of naturalness and youthful

[2] Cf. K. Burdach, *Deutsche Renaissance* (Berlin, 1918), pp. 17 ff. See below, pp. 306 ff.

energy which we first find among us in the period of *Sturm und Drang*. In the other countries, especially in Germany, it was mere mummery.[3]

On similar grounds Karl Brandi argued that one should term Renaissance only the Italian culture and that immediately derived from it. In the Northern countries "Italian culture was never taken over as a whole; that was impossible by its very nature. So we have to do only with individual cultural elements . . . ."[4] The idea that the Renaissance was everywhere in the North a derivative movement provides a certain basis for generalization regarding the Northern Renaissance as contrasted with the Italian. Its unifying effect for a general synthesis, however, is largely vitiated by the variety of time, manner, and extent of the northern absorption of the "individual cultural elements" imported from Italy. There is also inherent in it the perpetually troublesome problem of the conflict of native cultural traditions and tendencies with the foreign importation.

A further basis for generalization, also related to the idea of contrast with Italy, is to be found in the obviously religious character of much of northern humanism, welded as it was into something like a united movement by the dominant and international influence of Erasmus. The traditional interpretation of northern humanism as predominantly Christian and as helping to prepare the way for the Reformation is as old and well established as that of the pagan character of the Italian Renaissance. But the unifying effect here too is vitiated, partly by a tendency to regard Christian humanism as merely one rather eccentric aspect of the Renaissance, if not indeed a separate phenomenon, but still more by the general separation of Renaissance and Reformation into two separate and distinct movements. For many historians the Reformation has almost completely overshadowed the Renaissance. In any case, the separation of the two has greatly hindered a coherent in-

---

[3] P. Joachimsen, *Geschichtsauffassung und Geschichtschreibung in Deutschland unter dem Einfluss des Humanismus* (Leipzig and Berlin, 1910), p. 16. See also H. W. Eppelsheimer, *Petrarca* (Bonn, 1926), p. 183: "The Renaissance is Roman, that is to say, a national affair of the Italians. This explains its force and also its limitations. The Renaissance occurred fundamentally only in Italy and in a certain sense in the Romance lands; in all others there was at most Renaissancism and humanism."

[4] W. Goetz, ed., *Propyläen Weltgeschichte*, IV (Berlin, 1932), 258.

terpretation of the character of the age, while the question of the interrelations between them has proven one of the most controversial of historical problems.

Finally, among the obstacles to synthesis which have plagued the historians of the Renaissance in the northern countries, the prestige of Burckhardt's work should almost certainly be included. It is true that his example furnished a powerful stimulus to imitation, but it also made the creation of a similar synthesis more difficult. Dazzled by the brilliance and coherence of his interpretation of the Renaissance in Italy, northern scholars have tended to identify with the Renaissance only those characteristics that fitted into his picture. And Burckhardt himself made it abundantly clear that the civilization of the Renaissance was in large part the product of social and political conditions peculiar to Italy. Nowhere else could feudalism, scholasticism, and other remnants of medievalism be so confidently ignored, and nowhere else could one find a society so in harmony with the individualism, the perfection of the fully rounded personality, the worldliness, and the aesthetic ordering of social and political life which were the characteristic traits of his Renaissance. So long as Burckhardt's Renaissance remained the prototype, it could be applied to the northern countries only in part and was therefore almost necessarily reduced to the status of an influence or a movement. The Northern Renaissance has thus remained a confused, derivative concept. Its history has been written almost entirely as the history of literature, learning, or art in some particular country, though always against the background of an assumption that the particular national Renaissance was part of a more general European phenomenon.

THE RENAISSANCE IN FRANCE

France provided the most favorable soil for the transplantation of the Renaissance, whether it be considered as an actual cultural phenomenon or as an historiographical conception. French culture was in fact more directly influenced by Italian models than was that of either England or Germany. And the tradition of a *renaissance des lettres et des beaux arts* was early naturalized in France and was given a definite date of beginning: the reign of Francis I.[5] It was in French historiography, too, that Michelet had created his epoch-making Age of the Renaissance. Here, if anywhere, we might expect to find the Renaissance treated as an historical era of comprehensive significance. There is indeed one general history of sixteenth century France which bears the title, *The Century of the Renaissance*,[6] though as *Kulturgeschichte* it is a very disappointing work. But for the most part, here as elsewhere in the North, we will have to look for interpretations of the Renaissance in the histories of literature and art. Even where the term Renaissance occurs as a sectional subtitle in such comprehensive histories of France as that edited by Ernest Lavisse [7] its application is limited to chapters on the literary and artistic developments of the age.

The interpretation of the Renaissance has always been conditioned more or less by value judgments. Given the natural human tendency to find what one is looking for, historians have commonly stressed, if not exaggerated, those aspects of the civilization of the Renaissance that they approved, or abhorred. And there have been conflicting currents in French thought which have caused French historians to view the Renaissance with mixed emotions, and hence to portray it in varying colors. The potent element of classicism in French culture has made it difficult for French critics not to view the traditional Renaissance with veneration as the birth hour of their modern literature and art.[8] In much the same way, the strong currents of rationalism, anti-clericalism, liberalism, and individualism have tended to create a bias favorable to the Renaissance in its traditional form and occasionally also to the early Reformation. But all of these tendencies are seldom active, or if so not in the same degree, in the thought of individual historians. And on the other side are the currents, by no

5 See discussion of Amyot, Bayle, Voltaire, above, pp. 31; 72; 94. See also E. Renan in *Histoire littéraire de la France*, XXIV (Paris, 1862), 603; 683; 690.

6 L. Battifol, *Le siècle de la Renaissance* (Paris, 1916).

7 Cf. E. Lavisse, *Histoire de France illustrée depuis les origines jusqu'à la Révolution*, V (Paris, 1926).

8 French classicism also tended in one respect to minimize interest in the Renaissance by fixing academic attention almost exclusively on the seventeenth century literature. Toward the end of the nineteenth century, however, there was a great revival of interest in the sixteenth century, largely from a pro-classical point of view. See the historiographical introduction to H. Chamard, *Les origines de la poésie française de la Renaissance* (Paris, 1932), pp. 17–38.

means negligible, of Catholicism, Romantic medievalism, conservatism, and nationalism. In extreme cases these have led to a more or less complete negation of the traditional interpretation. Such instances will be treated in later chapters. More frequently they have merely altered the colors of the traditional picture or have added to the confusion of concepts by a tendency to create arbitrary distinctions.

Gustave Lanson's *History of French Literature* (1894)[9] may serve as a point of departure for the study of recent conceptions of the Renaissance in the history of French literature. It contains what is almost a classic expression of the traditional interpretation, embodied in a work familiar to innumerable students and still widely read. Lanson's view of the Renaissance in France proceeds from the conviction that the disintegration of medieval civilization during the fourteenth and fifteenth centuries had resulted eventually in complete cultural sterility. "The fifteenth century closed leaving the impression of a world that was ended, of an irremediable and disastrous abortion."[10] The new age opened with the "discovery of Italy" by the French invaders, and by 1525 the penetration of the French spirit by the Italian was an accomplished fact. What the French gained from Italy was primarily "the idea of art"; but they also learned from the Italian interpretation of antiquity and the example of Italian society a new attitude toward life and nature and a new confidence in man and reason. Lanson's Italian Renaissance is pure Burckhardt and for him "the French Renaissance is in fact a prolongation of the Italian Renaissance." But if the original came from Italy, the resulting product was French. "It is curious to see how, in this contact with a superior civilization, which dominated it so powerfully, France preserved, even developed, its literary originality; each element of the Italian Renaissance was adopted, transformed or eliminated by the French genius whose energy it had suddenly awakened."[11] French genius, like that of the other northern countries, Lanson thought more inclined to seek moral and scientific truth than pure art. Under its influence the elements of the Renaissance, which were intermingled and confused in the age of Francis I, gradually be-

[9] G. Lanson, *Histoire de la littérature française* (Paris, 1894; I use 7th ed. Paris, 1902).
[10] *Ibid.*, p. 112; cf. p. 221 f.   [11] *Ibid.*, p. 225.

came separated and developed along divergent and even antagonistic lines. Thus the Renaissance resulted finally in such varied products as Budé's philological humanism, Calvin's peculiarly moral Reformation, the naturalism of Rabelais, the practical morality of Montaigne, and the art of the Pléiade.

To the relative unity of this interpretation Emile Faguet's *The Sixteenth Century*,[12] published in the same year, opposed a tripartite conception, confused rather than clarified by arbitrary distinctions. Looking upon the sixteenth century with a less admiring eye, Faguet saw in it the origins of modern chaos and found its only common characteristics in revolt against the Middle Ages and return to the distant past. But it was not a unified return, nor a return to the same past. In place of a general intellectual phenomenon, later separating into clearly defined movements, Faguet saw three entirely separate currents: the Reformation, the Renaissance, and humanism.[13] To establish the distinction between these required a new definition of terms. The Renaissance he defined as "the emancipation of the human mind brought about by commerce with antique thought," but added that like most emancipations it was merely a change of servitude. Under its influence "men left the school of the Church to enter the school of the ancients" and in doing so lost the sense of the reality of God. The Reformation was also a break with medieval tradition, but of a different and contrary spirit. It was the rebirth not of antiquity but of primitive Christianity. It was at war with both the Middle Ages, which had perverted the early Christian spirit, and with the Renaissance, which had restored antique paganism. The Renaissance, on the other hand, was at war with both the Middle Ages and the Reformation, because both were Christian. Finally, humanism was a return to antiquity on still another level. "The Renaissance is the resurrection of antique ideas; humanism is the taste for antique art," and there was no necessary connection between them nor between humanism and the Reformation. In short, humanism is mere literary imitation of the classics, and as such had existed all through the Middle Ages. Faguet's humanists are timid traditionalists, neither for the Reformation nor

---

[12] E. Faguet, *Le seizième siècle, études littéraires* (Paris, 1894).
[13] *Ibid.*, p. v ff.

against it, lacking in depth, and taking from antiquity only its most innocuous elements. They were, he thought, the most common type of sixteenth century intellectual. By this definition, Rabelais must be considered a man of the Renaissance rather than a humanist. But Faguet is at some pains to deprive even Rabelais of significance as a thinker and he warns against taking too seriously the book that represented only the good doctor's "digestive hours." [14] Faguet's definitions force him into a number of odd contradictions, but his whole interpretation suffers still more from a basic lack of historical development. His three elements remain static ingredients in the civilization of France throughout the sixteenth century.

A more evolutionary interpretation with a different, if equally arbitrary, set of definitions appeared a decade later in the *History of Classic French Literature*[15] of that giant of French literary history, Ferdinand Brunetière. In his view the French Renaissance was the third in a series of closely related but chronologically successive movements. The first of these Renaissances was "properly and exclusively Italian," a return of Italian genius to its own past. Admiring references to Burckhardt, Symonds, and De Sanctis suggest the sources for his interpretation here. The Italian Renaissance had the positive force of free individualism, but the return to antiquity led to a completely pagan morality and ended in a ruinous indifference to content in literature.[16] The second Renaissance was European in scope. It lacked the naturalism, the sentiment of art, and the paganism of the Italian movement. Its characteristic was not individualism, as in Italy, but "its tendency to humanism." Like Faguet, Brunetière is here forced to an arbitrary definition of humanism. It is "man become the measure of all things . . . . it is everything brought back to the measure of man, conceived in relation to man, and expressed in terms of man." [17] Its greatest exponent was the cosmopolitan humanist, Erasmus. The third Renaissance, the French, began with the invasions of Italy, but it did not become effective in French literature until it had been naturalized at the court of Francis I and until Budé with the king's aid had found-

[14] *Ibid.*, p. 83.

[15] F. Brunetière, *Histoire de la littérature française classique* (Paris, 1904; I use 4th ed. Paris, 1921).

[16] *Ibid.*, pp. 12 ff.   [17] *Ibid.*, p. 30.

ed classical education in France. The French Renaissance necessarily followed the Italian and the European for it "could not triumph absolutely save by the intermediation of humanism." [18] Brunetière's conceptions of Renaissance and humanism, while not entirely identical, are thus closely related and in no way antagonistic. It was otherwise with the Renaissance and the Reformation, which he regarded as two distinct and opposed movements, having little in common except that they were contemporary. Indeed "the Reformation was the condemnation of the spirit of the Renaissance." [19] And that spirit was essentially pagan, being founded on faith in the goodness of nature. It was the spirit of Rabelais and, with variations, of Montaigne.[20]

The interrelation between humanism and the early reforming tendencies in France was, however, too close to be dismissed by the simple technique of defining humanism and the Reformation in mutually antagonistic senses. A searching analysis of this rather neglected field appeared in 1897 in an article on "Humanism and the Reform in France" [21] by the young Henri Hauser. Though necessarily less than a full treatment, it contained a number of pregnant observations and its influence is attested in innumerable footnotes. In opposition to Faguet, Hauser returned indignantly to the conventional definitions.[22] He refused to recognize as humanism occasional medieval imitations of the classics. "It did not appear until the time when antique art was understood and felt to its very depths, the time when from a simple model it became a principle of life and of *renaissance*." [23] This humanism, which first appeared with Petrarch, was an Italian phenomenon, later imported into France together with the Renaissance by the soldiers of Fornova. There it became a thoughtful humanism, even more than in Italy concerned with the ideas as well as the forms of antiquity and hence even more closely identical with the Renaissance. It was also for all practical purpose identical with the early reform movement in

18 *Ibid.*, p. 67.   19 *Ibid.*, p. 196.   20 Cf. *ibid.*, p. 610 f.
21 H. Hauser, "De l'humanisme et de la Réforme en France," *Revue historique,* LXIV (1897), 258–97.
22 Cf. *ibid.*, p. 259 f. After citing the usage of Burckhardt, Voigt, and De Nolhac, he adds: "It seems to me that, save in the case of absolute necessity, it is a grave matter to renew in the scientific domain the miracle of the confusion of tongues."
23 *Ibid.*, p. 261.

France. "The fact is, if all important reformers had passed through the school of humanism, almost all humanists had favored a religious revolution." [24]

As Hauser analyzed the two movements, he found a "profound affinity" between Renaissance and Reformation in the search for a more simple and rational dogma, shorn of many unessential intermediaries, mysteries, and ceremonies. Humanists and reformers had the same enemies in the scholastics. They both sought to purify religion by return to the Bible. The humanists supplied the reformers with the formidable weapon of philological criticism. Finally, humanism aided the Reformation, "because it substituted for authority the spirit of free examination." But the close union of the two movements could not be maintained beyond the time when, for France at least, the Reformation was no more than an undefined tendency toward evangelicism and the practical reform of the Church. As Protestantism became more dogmatic they drifted apart until in the forties two events effected an irreconcilable cleavage: the definition of Catholic faith by the Council of Trent and Calvin's definition of Protestantism. Together they made a semi-adhesion to the Reformation impossible. Calvin had realized the necessity of re-establishing dogma, authority, and a morality based on original sin and understood that this could be accomplished only by a definite rupture with the Renaissance. "He understood that the basis of the Renaissance was free thought, that is to say, the heresy *par excellence,* the sin against the Holy Ghost." [25] The humanists, on the other hand, could accept neither original sin nor the restitution of authority. Some returned to Catholicism in a spirit of resignation. Others, like Rabelais, under the cloak of a formal Catholicism developed the essentially anti-Catholic Renaissance doctrine of naturalism, i.e., "a morality founded entirely on the conformity of man with nature and on a free and happy adhesion to natural laws." [26]

The problem of the relation of humanism — or the Renaissance — to the Reformation naturally raises the complementary problem of the relation of the former to orthodox Catholicism. An answer to that problem is implied in Hauser's thesis. From a different point of view many dogmatic Catholics have reached a somewhat similar solution,

[24] *Ibid.,* p. 268.   [25] *Ibid.,* p. 290.   [26] *Ibid.,* p. 295; cf. p. 285 ff.

at least to the extent of regarding the Renaissance and humanism as antagonistic to the Catholic faith, but closely associated with the Reformation.[27] Writing in 1905, Mgr. Baudrillart, then rector of the Catholic institute of Paris, gave a semi-official status to this interpretation.[28] Renaissance and Reformation were in his opinion two great heretical movements which, despite apparent opposition, were closely united and had a common source in the principle of autonomy or absolute independence of the individual intellect. Baudrillart fully recognized the religious interests of northern humanism which distinguished it from the paganism of the Italian movement, but that very preoccupation with religious matters made it but the more prone to heresy.

Not all French historians of Catholic tendency, however, have regarded humanism as dangerous or opposed to the faith. In his monumental study of *The Origins of the Reform* (1905-35),[29] Pierre Imbart de la Tour boldly proclaimed the essential kinship of humanism and true Catholicism. Warmly devoted to his faith and his church, yet without the logical dogmatism of the professional theologian, he viewed the crucial problems of the early sixteenth century with a broad historical comprehension reminiscent of Ludwig von Pastor. His thesis was that Catholicism had passed through a great crisis in the generation before Luther, a crisis caused by the new national opposition to Rome, by abuses in the Church, and by the Renaissance. But it had already passed the crisis and was taking on new life when the Protestant Reformation broke the unity of the Catholic world. The crisis, in short, was followed by a rebirth of Catholic Christianity, and to this rebirth the humanists made an invaluable contribution.

Despite his somewhat unconventional conclusion, Imbart de la Tour's general conception of the Renaissance bore all the marks of tradition. He could write about it almost in the language of Michelet.

The century which was opening was not merely a new stage, but a dawn. Rarely has man entered on the scene with greater confidence

27 See, for example, M. de Wulf, *Histoire de la philosophie médiéval* (Louvain, 1905), p. 493.
28 A. Baudrillart, *L'Eglise catholique, la Renaissance, et Protestantisme* (Paris, 1905). Eng. trans. (London, 1908).
29 P. Imbart de la Tour, *Les origines de la Réforme*, 4 vols. (Paris, 1905-35).

in himself. He felt himself young and strong. He dared because he willed. And it seemed to him that before him nothing had been done, because he himself was a beginning. The Renaissance was the intellectual expression of this movement. . . . It was not a system, but a spirit.[30]

Though varying from person to person and country to country, this movement showed certain common traits which he analyzed at some length: return to antiquity with full comprehension; reaction against the whole intellectual system of the Middle Ages; a new conception of knowledge; a new conviction of the importance of man and of the goodness and beauty of life; and, finally, the formation of a new intellectual élite who were predominantly laic rather than clerical.[31]

But if the Renaissance was a return to the ideas as well as the forms of antiquity, what of its relation to Christianity? Imbart followed the tradition of the pagan Renaissance in regarding Valla and many of his Italian contemporaries as clearly opposed to Christian teaching. The reconciliation of Christianity with antiquity, however, was begun by the Florentine Platonists. It was completed by the thoughtful and deeply religious spirit of the German Renaissance. Italy had discovered classical antiquity; Germany (with Reuchlin and Erasmus) restored the Bible.[32] By the beginning of the sixteenth century the intellectual work of Italy was completed. "The Renaissance became a European fact. . . . But at the same time it became a Christian fact. Germany had baptized it, and the restoration of sacred letters became as general as that of [profane] letters." [33] The union of the two became the dominant idea of all the great French humanists. "It was thus that in France, as in Italy, as in Germany, the resurrection of antiquity led to a restoration of religious thought. This was to be achieved, from the end of the fifteenth century, with Lefèvre d'Etaples, who was to be the greatest French representative of Christian humanism." [34] As Imbart conceived it, Christian humanism was a reforming movement, but one which aimed to renew religion within the Church, while leaving dogma and cult unchanged. The humanists' conception of religion was primarily a union with God. It was not so

[30] Ibid., II (1909), 314.   [31] Ibid., II, 315–34.
[32] Ibid., II, 335 ff.   [33] Ibid., II, 345.   [34] Ibid., II, 382.

much a system as a way of life. It was not heretical, although it was a thorough attack, in many ways unjust, upon the whole system of scholasticism. Nevertheless, "it was no small service to have Christianized the Renaissance, to have awakened religious thought which had become too rigid, and, having united it with classical culture, to have turned it back to the Bible and the Fathers." [35] Imbart admitted, somewhat reluctantly, that the humanists had helped to prepare the way for the Reformation, though they abandoned it when its doctrines became precise. Again and again he insisted that humanism was itself essentially Catholic.

> Yes, [he conceded] one cannot deny that, by their critical work, the Humanists rendered more easy the revolution that was beginning. In that only. Their positive work was of another sort. And there is not even one of their ideas that had not, outside them, before them, its representatives or its precursors in Catholicism.[36]

And again:

> Between the fundamental principle of the Reformation and that of humanism there was an abyss. The latter not only wished to remain Catholic. It was Catholic, by its submision to external unity, by its doctrine of liberty, and by the spirit of equilibrium and measure so conformable to the habits of thought and of life of Catholicism.[37]

The twentieth century has been peculiarly fruitful in histories of the literature of the French Renaissance, but most of those that could be included in this chapter added little to the views already noted here. For English-speaking readers, J. E. Spingarn's masterly *History of Literary Criticism in the Renaissance* (1899) reaffirmed the traditional premise of the influence of Italian models in the field of French criticism and poetic theory. The standard English work on the history of French literature during the period, Arthur Tilley's *Literature of the French Renaissance* (1904) is scholarly but entirely conventional, as is also Jean Plattard's nicely written survey (1925).[38] A somewhat different note in the traditional theme of Italian influence, however, appeared in a monograph on *The Sources and Development of Ra-*

---

[35] *Ibid.*, II, 438 f.   [36] *Ibid.*, II, 439.   [37] *Ibid.*, II, 441.
[38] J. Plattard, *La Renaissance des lettres en France* (Paris, 1925).

tionalism in the French Literature of the Renaissance (1922) [39] by H. Busson. Here Busson ascribed the skeptical rationalism of the French Renaissance less to the influence of antiquity than to that of the Averroist doctrines of the University of Padua. This idea was later incorporated into Raoul Morçay's *The Renaissance* (1933),[40] along with almost all the other interpretations, contradictory though they might be in part, which we have met in this chapter. Morçay's work was, indeed, notably eclectic as well as comprehensive. Within the limits of a mild Catholicism, he seemed to have kept an open mind through which all winds of critical tendency might sweep freely. The result is a very satisfactory summation of the traditional interpretation with all its minor variants. A recent American critic has described it as the best general treatment existing today of French letters in the sixteenth century.[41]

In the history of French Renaissance art, recent trends of Romantic nationalism and medievalism have led to some decided reactions against the traditional interpretation, as will appear hereafter. The majority of French historians of art, however, have remained within the traditional pattern in a state of relative harmony. Controversies there have been, but mostly over matters of detail. Both the influence of the classical-Italian prototypes introduced into France during the Italian wars and the continuation of a gradually altering native art have seemed too obvious to merit much argument. That the former was decisive and marked a distinct departure from medieval forms has been generally admitted, though few twentieth century historians would accept Renan's dogmatic statement: "The Renaissance was not guilty of having stifled the art of the Middle Ages: the art of the Middle Ages was already dead." [42] Adequate summaries of the work of the specialists may be found in the fifth volume of Lavisse (1926) and in Arthur Tilley's *The Dawn of the French Renaissance* (1918). Much the best treatment of the whole subject at the time it was written was that contained in

---

[39] H. Busson, *Les sources et le développement du rationalisme dans la littérature française de la Renaissance* (Paris, 1922). This theme had been already developed by E. Renan in *Averroès et l'Averroisme* (Paris, 1852).

[40] R. Morçay, *La Renaissance*, 2 vols. (Paris, 1933).

[41] S. F. Will, "French Literature," *Modern Language Quarterly*, II (1941), 463 f.

[42] E. Renan in *Histoire littéraire de la France*, XXIV (Paris, 1862), 690.

the two volumes devoted to the Renaissance in the collaborative *History of Art* edited by André Michel (1912–13).[43] It still remains the most comprehensive history of French Renaissance art, and an almost classic statement of the traditional interpretation.

Michel's own "Conclusion on the Renaissance"[44] is of special interest, for there the editor ignored detail and dealt directly with the problem of interpretation. He defended the use of the term *Renaissance* on the ground that "it is useless if not dangerous to change a terminology consecrated by universal usage," and defined the term as applying to "the whole period which saw first the sporadic return, then the progressive conquests, and finally the universal triumph of forms of revived Greco-Roman art."[45] "One may," he added, "discuss the value, the effects, and the beneficence of this phenomenon; but one cannot deny it, nor its place of origin," which was, of course, the Italy of the *Quattrocento*. In conscious opposition to recent Romantic views, Michel insisted on the decisive importance of the revival of antique culture for the formation of Renaissance art. It was the humanists who created the milieu in which it grew and came to full fruition. It was they who brought the artists in contact with antiquity and taught them to see it clearly. Thanks to them, between the time of Giotto and that of Michelangelo, "eyes and minds were renewed, and in the order of ideas as in the order of forms a profound work had been accomplished." Many varied factors undoubtedly contributed to the great art of the Renaissance, "but all this was produced, combined, and conditioned in a milieu more and more penetrated by the taste, the curiosity, and the religion of antique beauty . . . . It was under the invocation of the gods brought back to life that the Renaissance was created."[46]

THE RENAISSANCE IN ENGLAND

The sixteenth century was a great age in the history of England, but it was seldom considered as primarily the age of the Renaissance. Rather it was the age that saw the establishment of the Church of

---

[43] A. Michel, ed., *Histoire de l'art,* IV–V (Paris, 1912–13).
[44] *Ibid.,* IV, Pt. 1, 483 ff.   [45] *Ibid.,* IV, Pt. 1, 486.   [46] *Ibid.,* IV, Pt. 1, 495.

England, the birth of British sea power, and England's first great economic expansion, the age when modern England began to take shape under the imperious eye of the Tudor dynasty. The Renaissance, limited by the tradition that conceived it as an intellectual or spiritual movement originating in Italy with the revival of antiquity, has been for most English historians merely one aspect of the Tudor age. As a symbol of emancipation from the thraldom of the Middle Ages, it might be accorded a paragraph or two in general histories. Full treatment has been confined almost entirely to histories of English literature.

The problems involved in the traditional interpretation seem much simpler here than in France. There was scarcely enough art in sixteenth century England to make it a complicating factor. Even the problem of the relation of Renaissance to Reformation has not greatly perturbed most English scholars. The strains of Protestant and liberal interpretation were here relatively little modified by Catholic fears of heresy and paganism or by Romantic nostalgia for the Middle Ages. Nor has the national sentiment here created the artificial difficulties encountered in France and Germany. Nineteenth century Englishmen loved Italy and were seldom disposed to question the regenerative potency of classical, particularly Greek, culture. Confident at the same time of the Englishman's capacity to absorb foreign influences and still remain English, they have seen little reason why they should not admit freely the debts of English literature to antiquity, to Italy, or to France. Finally, English historians have been less inclined to fabricate "constructions" of history or to treat concepts as historical realities than have the continental scholars.

But while freedom from the tyranny of concepts may be a cherished right of every free-born English scholar, it is also a right that may be abused. By generally refusing to think about the Renaissance as a concept, English-speaking scholars have, indeed, avoided many methodological pitfalls and much pointless controversy. But they have not thereby avoided the dangers that result from the unconscious interpretation of their cultural history in terms of concepts which they have not examined carefully and which, in any case, were founded upon the somewhat different experience of Italy or France. As Rosemond Tuve recently observed, in a shrewd analysis of the current trends in the study of the English Renaissance, a major weakness in that field has been "the lack of adequate generalizations about the period *in England*," with the result that "much scholarship in the field of English letters has operated and does still operate under the unrealized domination of the Michelet-Burckhardt conception of the Renaissance."[47] For England, then, rather more than for the other northern countries, the Renaissance has remained a derivative concept, never thoroughly naturalized by the acquisition of a specifically English character.

The one serious attempt to construct a cultural-historical Age of the Renaissance for England was of foreign origin. Hippolyte Taine's *History of English Literature* (1863–64)[48] was a unique event in English historiography. Never imitated, it has nevertheless left traces of its influence in the works of many later writers. Taine's historical philosophy and his pseudo-scientific method, as well as his somewhat exaggerated version of the Burckhardtian tradition, have been noted in the preceding chapter in relation to his lectures on the art of the Italian Renaissance. The history of English literature provided a larger, more varied, and more congenial field for the operation of his historical mechanics of race, milieu, and moment. And nowhere more so than in the period of the Renaissance.

Taine's Renaissance, like Burckhardt's, was a distinct period, clearly differentiated from the Middle Ages and inspired by a fundamentally constant spirit. The Middle Ages had ended in intellectual and literary sterility, its roots cut off by scholastic philosophy.[49] The European Renaissance was a new birth, conformable in each country to the national genius. In Italy the revival of classical antiquity combined with the genius of the Latin race and the peculiar social and political milieu to produce a Renaissance that was altogether pagan and that eventually became vicious.[50] In Germany "the great human renovation . . . . meeting with another race" produced the Christian Renaissance, that great renewal of conscience that was the Reforma-

---

[47] R. Tuve, "A Critical Survey of Scholarship in the Field of English Literature of the Renaissance," *Studies in Philology*, XL (1943), 219 f.

[48] H. Taine, *Histoire de la littérature anglaise*, 5 vols. (Paris, 1863–64). Eng. trans., 2 vols. (Edinburgh, 1871).

[49] *Ibid.*, I, 228 f.   [50] *Ibid.*, I, 269 ff; II, 282 ff.

tion.[51] The English Renaissance was the product of these two "moments," transplanted into the English milieu and wedded to the Anglo-Saxon genius with readily predictable results, which Taine confidently determined by the methods of empirical science.

The two moments, so disparate in character, produced in fact two Renaissances. Taine considered the pagan Renaissance first, and began with an analysis of the social milieu. Here he found sixteenth century English society enjoying the material benefits of a newly acquired security and prosperity, which brought the realization that life was good. The result was a laic, pagan spirit, reflected in free vigorous action, in the flamboyance of colorful costume, and in the prodigality of feast and pageant. "To vent the feelings, to satisfy the heart and eyes, to set free boldly on all roads of existence the pack of appetites and instincts, this was the craving which the manners of the time portrayed. It was 'merry England' as they called it then." [52] In this lusty society the men of the upper classes sought their teachers and their heroes in ancient Greece and Rome. And being gentlemen, they were able to comprehend not only the language but the thought "of the great and healthy minds who had freely handled ideas of all kinds fifteen centuries ago." "Across the train of hooded schoolmen and sordid cavillers the two adult and thinking ages were united, and the moderns, silencing the infantine or snuffling voices of the Middle Ages, condescended only to converse with the noble ancients." [53] But the revival of antiquity, Taine thought, could never produce in a northern Germanic nation the sheer paganism that it did in Italy. The moment was the same, the milieu favorable, but the race was different.

> Transplanted into different races and climates, this [Italian] paganism receives from each distinct features and a distinct character. In England it becomes English; the English Renaissance is the rebirth of the Saxon genius. Invention recommences; and to invent is to express one's genius. A Latin race can invent only by expressing Latin ideas; a Saxon race by expressing Saxon ideas . . . .[54]

It is under this formula of paganism, transmuted by the "energetic and gloomy" English character, that Taine elucidates English litera-

---

[51] *Ibid.*, II, 289 ff.
[53] *Ibid.*, I, 268 f [I, 152].
[52] *Ibid.*, I, 264 [I, 150].
[54] *Ibid.*, I, 277 [I, 156].

ture from Surrey to Bacon and Shakespeare, and finally through the decadent Caroline poets.

Having thus established the pagan character of English society in the Tudor Age, Taine turned to the Christian Renaissance, i.e. the Reformation, which "was also in fact a new birth, one in harmony with the genius of the Germanic peoples." [55] Seeking evidence of a milieu in which this moral rebirth could thrive, Taine discovered another England. This England was peopled by men of tortured conscience, grim and lofty purpose, desperate and stubborn courage. He drew his materials here largely from contemporary sermons and tracts, amply supplemented by Froude, Foxe's *Book of Martyrs*, Burnet, and Carlyle. The Romanticist in Taine, his ability to create an atmosphere, and his intuitive perception of much that was basically true despite exaggeration never showed to better advantage than in this portrayal of the varied types of English Protestantism. Here he found the Saxon genius at its most English, altogether admirable and, to a Frenchman, altogether strange and peculiar. His two Renaissances, his two Englands, overlap, though not in exact superimposition. The pagan Renaissance began earlier than the Christian. The former was more characteristic of the aristocracy, the latter of the middle and lower classes. Only in High Church Anglicanism did the two merge in harmonious combination. But whether the Renaissance was pagan or Christian, the men who represented it were vital, forceful figures. Turning their backs on the dead Middle Ages, they were modern men, but with a youthful energy which modern men have since lost. [56]

Echoes of Taine's interpretation of individual writers occur frequently enough in the literary histories of the following generations, but his method and his historical philosophy were alike alien to English historiography. That the changes to be found in the literary works of the sixteenth century reflected a changing spirit or changing interests, which had their origins in the Italian revival of antiquity, was more frequently left implicit than explicitly developed. In the volume entitled *Renascence and Reformation* in the *Cambridge History of English Literature* the Renaissance (or "Renascence," as the

[55] *Ibid.*, II, 289 [I, 356].
[56] Cf. *ibid.*, II, 7 ff.

English purists insist on calling it) was rarely mentioned and there was very little direct comment on the spirit of the age.

Nevertheless there were English historians who followed more closely the continental tradition which defined the Renaissance explicitly as a great revolutionary movement of the human spirit, the causative force behind the achievements of the age. Sidney Lee's *Great Englishmen of the Sixteenth Century* (1904) furnishes a characteristic example. His statement of the thesis was categorical:

> Englishmen of the sixteenth century breathed a new atmosphere intellectually and spiritually. They came under a new stimulus, compounded of many elements, each of them new and inspiring. To this stimulus may be attributed the sudden upward growth of distinctive achievement among them. . . . The stimulus under which Englishmen came in the sixteenth century may be summed up in the familiar word Renaissance. The main factor of the European Renaissance, of the New Birth of intellect, was a passion for extending the limits of human knowledge, and for employing man's capabilities to new and better advantage than of old. New curiosity was generated in regard to the dimensions of the material world. There was boundless enthusiasm for the newly discovered art and literature of ancient Greece. Men were fired by a new resolve to make the best and not the worst of life upon earth. They were ambitious to cultivate as the highest good the idea of beauty.[57]

Lee insisted repeatedly that this creative stimulus was a European, not a national, phenomenon, though it might develop somewhat differently in different countries. "It was the universal spirit of the Renaissance, and no purely national impulse, which produced in sixteenth century England that extended series of varied exploits . . . . the like of which had not been known before in the history of our race." [58] But despite the suggestion of new activity in all fields implied in the phrase "varied exploits," Lee's great Englishmen are all men of letters. And his Renaissance becomes in fact a literary movement, beginning with More's *Utopia* and culminating in the work of Bacon and Shakespeare.

This interpretation of the English Renaissance as a sixteenth century

[57] S. Lee, *Great Englishmen of the Sixteenth Century* (New York: Charles Scribner's Sons, 1904), p. 2 f.
[58] *Ibid.*, p. 3.

literary phenomenon, which resulted from the stimulus afforded by a general European movement, was reflected again in Emile Legouis' *History of English Literature* (1924).[59] It seems, indeed, to be the orthodox dogma, whether directly expressed or merely implied. As a result of this conception, English scholars have given a good deal of attention to the foreign influences that provided English literature with the requisite stimulus. The importation from Italy and the later domestic cultivation of the ancient Latin and Greek literatures naturally ranked foremost among these. To a classically trained scholar like T. M. Lindsay they seemed sufficient motive for every-thing that was new in sixteenth century literature.

> Thus, classical learning, at first the possession of a favored few, then, by means of translations, the property of all people fairly educated, gradually permeated England so thoroughly that, though Shakespeare was not far distant from Chaucer in time, when we pass from the one to the other it is as if we entered a new and entirely different world.[60]

This is, however, a peculiarly exclusive view. More commonly the classics have been forced to share their influential position with the contemporary cultures of Italy and France. Lewis Einstein's *The Italian Renaissance in England* (1902) was the most complete study of the influence of the former; Sidney Lee's *The French Renaissance in England* (1910) of the latter.

The close relation of the English literary Renaissance to the con-tinental was, of course, particularly evident in the early humanist period when English writers shared with their European contempo-raries a common language, a common reverence for antiquity, and a common desire for religious reform. And here English historians could enjoy the unaccustomed pleasure of reversing the stream of in-fluence by demonstrating the extent to which Erasmus, the molder of European Christian humanism, drew his most significant ideas from his English friends, John Colet and Sir Thomas More. This was in part the thesis of Frederic Seebohm's ever popular *Oxford Reformers,*

---

[59] E. Legouis, *Histoire de la littérature anglaise: le Moyen Age et la Renaissance* (Paris, 1924), p. 195 f. Eng. trans. (New York, 1927).

[60] T. M. Lindsay in *The Cambridge History of English Literature*, III (Cam-bridge, 1918), 24.

first published in 1867. It was in many respects a pioneering work, for Seebohm was the first scholar to make full use of the ample source material to be found in the correspondence of the humanists. He was also a pioneer in his attempt to understand the thought of the Christian humanists for its own sake, rather than as a mere preparation for the Lutheran Reformation. Viewing them independently, he found them working for a general religious reform inspired by an undogmatic, simple, and ethical Christianity that was neither Protestant nor Catholic. It was founded upon the original teaching of Christ and was to be developed through freedom of thought, tolerance, and education. It was also fundamentally opposed to the Augustinianism that was common to both Catholic and Protestant theology.[61] In his enthusiasm, Seebohm exaggerated the influence of Colet upon Erasmus, while ignoring or being unaware of that of the Brethren of the Common Life and other European mystics. He also tended to overstate the modernity of Sir Thomas More. The study ends with Colet's death in 1519, thus avoiding the controversial problems presented by More's later career.[62] But for all its weaknesses, Seebohm's work marked an important step in the progress of humanist, and espcially Erasmian, studies.

The English, indeed, or rather English-speaking scholars — to include the Americans — have done rather more than their share in contributing to the vast international literature on Erasmus, a literature so extensive that we cannot attempt to treat it here.[63] One English contribution, however, is of such fundamental importance that it must at least be mentioned. P. S. Allen's great edition of the *Correspondence of Erasmus* (1906–41)[64] has placed the whole study of Erasmus and the contemporary humanists on a firmer foundation and has furnished invaluable material for every work on the subject written during the past four decades.

[61] Cf. F. Seebohm, *The Oxford Reformers* (Everyman's Library), p. 308 ff.
[62] For discussion of recent interpretations of the More enigma, see F. S. Baumann, "Sir Thomas More," *Journal of Modern History*, IV (1932), 604–15.
[63] See E. W. Nelson, "Recent Literature concerning Erasmus," *Journal of Modern History*, I (1929), 88–102.
[64] P. S. Allen, ed., *Opus epistolarum Des. Erasmi Roterdami*, 10 vols. (Oxford, 1906–41).

THE RENAISSANCE IN GERMANY

The German Renaissance differed from the English and French in both character and chronological scope. It was almost entirely lacking in the vigorous vernacular literature that was the chief glory of the English Renaissance and one of the most brilliant features of the French. On the other hand, Germany had in this age a splendid art, whereas England had little or none. Conventional German histories of art have generally recognized a Renaissance period and, like the French, have related it to the current of intellectual ferment which spread from Italy, as well as to the influence of Italian models. But they have also tended to emphasize more strongly than the French the spontaneous and variegated quality of German art, in short, its independent native character.[65] And in much recent literature on the subject there has been a marked tendency to minimize the Renaissance in both duration and content to the advantage of the more typically Germanic art of the Late Gothic and Baroque.[66] Finally, humanism played a more preponderant rôle in the German than in the French or English Renaissance, and the Reformation was of much more decisive importance. Though the chronological limits assigned to the Renaissance vary here as elsewhere, there has been a fairly general agreement that it began about the middle of the fifteenth century and that it did not long survive the Protestant Reformation. It was thus both earlier and of shorter duration than the Renaissance in the neighboring northern lands. For most German historians, indeed, the Renaissance has been a subsidiary phenomenon in German intellectual history, an alien importation, mostly in the form of humanism, and overshadowed by the Reformation, for which it helped to prepare the way.

Yet, despite the relative unimportance of the Renaissance in German history, the problem it presents has been more consciously considered and more acrimoniously debated by German scholars than by those of any other country. Articles discussing the Renaissance problem or

[65] For a moderate statement of the traditional interpretation of the German artistic Renaissance, see G. Glück, *Propyläen Kunstgeschichte*, X: *Die Kunst der Renaissance in Deutschland, den Niederlanden, Frankreich* (Berlin, 1928), Einleitung.

[66] See below, pp. 362 ff.

attempting to define the Renaissance concept have been a constantly recurring feature of the German learned periodicals for the past half-century.[67] Unlike the English historians, the Germans cannot be accused of taking their Renaissance for granted. Nor have they avoided the temptation to construct arbitrary systems. In such a controversial atmosphere the winds of revisionism have blown strongly and from many directions, as will appear in subsequent chapters. Aside from the generally *Begriff*-stricken character of German scholarship, this tendency to redefine the traditional interpretation of the Renaissance is probably the result, in part, of a chauvinistic rejection of foreign influences in German culture and, in part, of certain changes in the trend of German thought since the end of the nineteenth century. Gerhard Ritter has explained what he described as "the great change in our inner relation to the Middle Ages and the Renaissance" by the decline of that liberalism which had furnished the intellectual background for the Burckhardtian Renaissance.[68]

Certainly much of what independent value was left to the German Renaissance by the Protestant tradition, which assigned to it the rôle of John the Baptist to the Reformation, came from nineteenth century liberalism, superimposed upon eighteenth century rationalism. Under these influences, the German humanists were portrayed as free, enlightened thinkers, as champions of reason and individual liberty, who broke the bondage of ecclesiastical authority and medieval superstition. Even before Burckhardt, this view was expressed with masterly persuasiveness in D. F. Strauss's *Ulrich von Hutten* (1858).[69] Later this independent evaluation of the Renaissance was strengthened by a tendency to find in Germany those traits of individualism that had made Burckhardt's Italian Renaissance so attractive to the liberal mind. In

[67] See bibliography, below, pp. 398 ff. For surveys of the literature on the German Renaissance, see F. Schnabel, *Deutschlands geschichtliche Quellen und Darstellungen in der Neuzeit,* I (Leipzig, 1931); H. Rupprich, "Deutsche Literatur im Zeitalter des Humanismus und der Reformation," *Deutsche Vierteljahrsschrift für Literaturwissenschaft und Geistesgeschichte,* XVII (1939), Referatenheft, pp. 83–133; J. C. Kunstmann, "German Literature," *Modern Language Quarterly,* II (1941), 421–38.

[68] G. Ritter, "Die geschichtliche Bedeutung des deutschen Humanismus," *Historische Zeitschrift,* CXXVII (1923), 397.

[69] Cf. Schnabel, pp. 314 ff.

his conclusion to *The History of Germany at the End of the Middle Ages* (1912), Kurt Kaser wrote:

> The picture that Jacob Burckhardt drew of the civilization of the Renaissance in Italy may be traced step by step in Germany. Among us, too, men discovered the world and man; strong personalities strove for fuller development, for the most comprehensive activity possible, and would live in the memory of posterity . . . . They found their expression in word and picture: biographies, memoirs, and diaries were the fashion in all circles of society. Maximilian . . . . is the truest type of this individualistic and universally directed age.[70]

Karl Lamprecht, too, made the Burckhardtian contrast between the medieval sense of type and the Renaissance feeling for individualism one of the basic concepts of his highly controversial *German History* (1891–1909).[71] Such comprehensive applications of the Burckhardtian concept to German history were, however, rather rare. The commoner tendency in the traditional interpretation was to limit the scope of the Renaissance more closely to humanism and, while recognizing the parenthood of the Italian movement, to emphasize the national peculiarity of the German.

In this respect, as in many others, Ludwig Geiger's *Renaissance and Humanism in Italy and Germany* (1882) [72] was typical of the Protestant-liberal tradition. It was also for decades the standard work on the subject. It is therefore worth special consideration, despite its monumental dullness and its plethora of biographical detail. As might be expected of the too conscientious editor of *The Civilization of the Renaissance in Italy,* Geiger's treatment of the Italian Renaissance echoes the Burckhardtian thesis. And he concludes that " in almost every respect 'barbaric Germany' became the heir to Italy." [73] Yet as his history of the German equivalent develops, it appears that Germany inherited only a portion of the Renaissance and that in an altered form. His German Renaissance is mostly humanism, and it is humanism of a very different kind from the Italian.

[70] K. Kaser, *Deutsche Geschichte am Ausgang des Mittelalters, 1438–1519* (Stuttgart, 1912), II, 526.

[71] K. Lamprecht, *Deutsche Geschichte,* 12 vols. (Berlin, 1891–1909).

[72] L. Geiger, *Renaissance und Humanismus in Italien und Deutschland* (Berlin, 1882).

[73] *Ibid.,* p. 320.

The new movement was tied to Italy . . . . but despite this close relation to, even dependence on, Italian culture what a difference between
Italian Renaissance and German humanism! In Italy it was a powerful spiritual current flowing uninterrupted for nearly two centuries;
. . . in Germany a movement which, lasting scarcely half a century,
arrested in its triumphant progress by equally powerful opponents,
was finally turned into other paths by a decisive event which swept
the whole nation. In Italy the foreign invasions and religious reaction
brought an end to the Renaissance; in Germany in place of humanism
came the Reformation.[74]

In short, as Geiger viewed the two national movements, the Italian
resulted in "a reform of the whole direction and attitude toward life"
affecting all classes, whereas the German was principally a change in
learned culture. As a result, the latter did not bring an awakening of
national literature, despite its close relation to popular religious feeling.[75]
The German movement was limited to a relatively small class of
humanists, and even they did not present a united front. Its four
most significant exponents, Mutianus Rufus, Reuchlin, Erasmus, and
Hutten, all had different aims, though sharing certain common characteristics.[76] All were enemies of "the barbarians," that is, the conservative heirs of scholastic education and theology; in varying degrees they
defied the authority of the medieval church; and all helped more or
less to prepare the way for Luther. At the same time, none of them
were true adherents of the Reformation, which in fact ended and partially destroyed their work. Of the four, Geiger seemed to have the
warmest feeling for Hutten, the patriot and champion of religious and
intellectual freedom, who possessed in a special degree the two traits
that were most notable in German humanism: cheerful optimism
and youthful energy.[77]

Since the early years of the twentieth century, the storm of revisionism has rendered the adherents of the traditional interpretation more
wary and has forced an extension of interest. Its essential characteristics, however, survived. A fairly typical example may be found in
Karl Hasse's semi-popular book, *The German Renaissance* (1920).[78]

[74] *Ibid.*, p. 323 f.   [75] Cf. *ibid.*, p. 324 f.
[76] Cf. *ibid.*, pp. 333 ff; 432 ff; 524 ff; 544 ff; 560 ff.   [77] *Ibid.*, p. 563.
[78] K. P. Hasse, *Die deutsche Renaissance*, 2 vols. (Meerane, 1920).

Freely paraphrased, his thesis runs something as follows. In the fifteenth century, when the Renaissance was reaching its peak in Italy, there was a kindred stirring in the German soul. This was apparent in the development of the rising burgher class and in the growth of industries, printing, learning, and art. The Renaissance came from Italy, but there it was chiefly a striving for beauty of form. This the Germans could not follow because of their "overpowerful inwardness." Art was pursued in Germany not for its own sake, but to express the religious life of the people. Hence the influence of antiquity was limited. But, though there was no reawakening of classical antiquity comparable to that of Italy, at least in art, there was a German Renaissance. It was not so much a rebirth of form as a rebirth of the spirit, which found its best expression in humanism. The chief aim of the humanists was the revival of classical antiquity, but they used their classical learning to recover the original meaning of the Bible, and thereby opened the door to the Reformation.[79]

A decade later the traditional interpretation was reanalyzed in a thoughtful article entitled "Humanism and the Development of the German Mind"[80] by Paul Joachimsen. Written in the last year of his life, this essay represented the mature consideration of one of the sanest and most learned of recent German historians. Joachimsen's point of view was essentially Protestant and liberal; he belonged to the school of *Geisteswissenschaften* founded by Dilthey, but he was fully aware of all the contrary trends. To avoid confusion with the numerous loose usages of the term, he defined humanism as "an intellectual movement which was rooted in an urge toward the rebirth of classical antiquity."[81] This rebirth the humanists desired in the sense of gaining therefrom both forms and standards or norms for their own culture. Thus defined, there was no humanism in the Middle Ages. It began with Petrarch's romantic nostalgia for antiquity. The first total civilization to be formed and normalized by antiquity was the Italian Renaissance, which Joachimsen defined as a

[79] Cf. *ibid.*, I, 86–90.
[80] P. Joachimsen, "Der Humanismus und die Entwicklung des deutschen Geistes," *Deutsche Vierteljahrsschrift für Literaturwissenschaft und Geistesgeschichte*, VIII (1930), 419–80.
[81] *Ibid.*, VIII, 419.

period in Italian history (c. 1250–1550) characterized by the rebirth of the antique *polis*. In these Italian city states there developed a new type of individualistic men, whose individualism consisted of an affirmation of their egoistic humanity and the making of it a standard by which they lived. This was fundamentally Burckhardt's thesis, and Joachimsen adds with a touch of bellicose spirit: "I hold this [Burckhardt's] formula against all modern misunderstandings as still fully justified and as the only significant characteristic of that which men call the spirit of the Renaissance, the Renaissance being taken as a cultural epoch." [82] Joachimsen made it clear that the revival of antiquity was not the original source of this Renaissance civilization. It sprang from the political and social development of the cities and from nascent capitalism. But after the first century, humanism furnished it in increasing degree with its forms and standards. One result of this was the destruction of the medieval antinomy of natural and supernatural; another the creation of the first modern society.

Having thus established the character of the Italian prototype as a basis for comparison, Joachimsen turned to consideration of Germany and found there conditions much less apt to harmonize with humanism than in the Italian city states. There, the effort to found a national culture upon the forms and standards of antiquity broke down. Even the humanists, devoted as they were to the forms of classical antiquity, could not base their life upon the antique norm. Many of the early German humanists were half scholastic and much too close to medieval religious thought and feeling, while the later "poets" were too deeply impregnated with their own national traditions. Joachimsen regarded the strain of "national romanticism" as one of the most significant features of the German humanist movement. This was a theme he had developed in earlier works and here summarized once more.[83] For humanists of this national romantic type, Germany had its own antiquity to be revived, its own social and ethical norms in the German *Urzeit* as rediscovered in Tacitus. They were resentful

[82] *Ibid.*, VIII, 426.
[83] *Ibid.*, VIII, 443 ff; cf. P. Joachimsen, *Geschichtsauffassung und Geschichtschreibung in Deutschland unter dem Einfluss des Humanismus* (Leipzig, 1910); and "Tacitus im deutschen Humanismus," *Neue Jahrbücher für das klassische Altertum, Geschichte und deutsche Literatur,* XIV (1911), 697–717.

of Italian claims to cultural superiority and were frequently opposed to the supremacy of the Roman pontiff. The latter tendency helped to identify national romanticism with another major current in German humanism, that of enlightened religious reform. In this movement the originator and leader was Erasmus, whose aim was to reform Western civilization as a whole by means of a new conception of the teaching of Christ, seen against the background of newly understood antiquity. By reconciling Christian and pagan antiquity, he furnished the intelligentsia of Germany with their nearest approach to full acceptance of both forms and norms of antiquity. All types of German humanists were able to unite for a time under his leadership and found in his program a rallying point for their antagonism to Rome or to the "barbarians" in school and church. "The Erasmian philosophy thus became the most dangerous enemy of the contemporary Church." [84] Joachimsen was convinced that humanism aided the Reformation, but also that the two movements were of essentially different character. Neither the romantic nationalism of Hutten nor the religious enlightenment of Erasmus harmonized with Luther's conviction of sin or his theocentric Augustinian philosophy. The Reformation brought the end of humanism in Germany.

It was obviously the Reformation rather than humanism which Joachimsen regarded as the decisive event for Germany at the beginning of the modern age. Though humanism brought "an extraordinary broadening of the intellectual horizons of the German people," it furnished them only with "a series of half-solutions." [85] The Reformation, on the other hand, was "the greatest spiritual revolution that any nation of the West had experienced." [86] It brought "a revaluing of all values," and all the old forces had to reorient themselves by it.

Much the same impression emerges from Willy Andreas's comprehensive study, *Germany before the Reformation* (1932).[87] This was an ambitious and frequently successful attempt, the first of its kind since Janssen, to weld the history of pre-Reformation Germany into a cultural-historical synthesis. Like Joachimsen, Andreas recognized the

[84] Joachimsen, "Der Humanismus," *Deutsche Vierteljahrsschrift*, VIII, 458.
[85] *Ibid.*, VIII, 477; 480.   [86] *Ibid.*, VIII, 467.
[87] W. Andreas, *Deutschland vor der Reformation, eine Zeitenwende* (Stuttgart, 1932).

Renaissance, in much the Burckhardtian sense, as an historical epoch, but only for Italy.[88] In his terminology as applied to Germany, the fifteenth century belongs to the late and disintegrating Middle Ages, while the sixteenth century is the century of the Reformation. The end of the former and beginning of the latter he defined as a *Zeitenwende,* an age of rapid and violent transition, a cataclysmic crisis in the history of German civilization preceding the decisive advent of the Reformation. But though he did not call this period of crisis the Renaissance he did use the term frequently. He evidently regarded it as one of the significant factors in shaping the transition from the Middle Ages to the Reformation. Most frequently the term appears in comments on "the Renaissance tone" of literature, science, or general attitude toward life.[89] Again, he referred to "Renaissance influences" in relation to humanism or art. Putting together all these undefined usages, it would appear that what Andreas meant by the term "Renaissance" was a movement or type of culture which characterized an historical period in Italy, but which was elsewhere merely one of the characteristics of a changing age. Or perhaps it would be more accurate to say that it was the evidence of certain characteristics held in common with the Italians of that age or taken over from them and half assimilated by the northern peoples. In any case, what was said at the beginning of this chapter may be here repeated. After three decades of twentieth century research, the Renaissance remained more than ever a confused and derivative concept for northern history.

Whatever his conception of the Renaissance, no German historian could altogether avoid the problem of its relation to the Reformation. In so far as the Renaissance in Germany was identified with humanism, the problem was relatively simple and could be solved by the Protestant-liberal interpretation. When it was regarded as merely one aspect of German culture in the pre-Reformation period, it could also be dismissed rather easily. But for those historians who thought of the Renaissance as a European phenomenon, or at any rate as a form of *Weltanschauung,* an intellectual movement including all aspects of

---

[88] Cf. *ibid.,* pp. 486; 527.

[89] See, for example, chapter entitled, "Renaissancestimmungen in Naturwissenschaft und Naturphilosophie"; cf. *ibid.,* pp. 492; 504; 530; 547; 619 f.

culture, the problem was more complex. For out of it grew the further problem, inherent in the traditional interpretations of both Renaissance and Reformation, of the manner and degree in which each had
contributed to the founding of modern civilization. One solution,
suggested by Michelet and Taine, was to assimilate the Reformation
into the Renaissance as simply the German form of the latter. German
historians were less likely than others to accept this subordination of
their own great intellectual revolution, but there were exceptions.
Writing in 1878, Wilhelm Windelband, the distinguished historian
of philosophy, stated a similar thesis with dogmatic clarity. "What one
is accustomed to designate as religious Reformation or simply as Reformation is a partial phenomenon of the general Renaissance, which
certainly occupied a large place therein, but which did not as has often
been stated, form its weightiest or most potent motive." [90] Still another solution, and one adopted more widely in recent years, was to
consider Renaissance and Reformation as national movements, running parallel to one another but of different character, each making its
peculiar contribution to the formation of modern civilization. This
interpretation has been summarized by Hajo Holborn in the introduction to his *Ulrich von Hutten and the German Reformation*
(1937).

> The Renaissance in Italy and the Reformation in Germany constitute
> the decisive emergence of the modern world. Along with these two a
> third must be mentioned which has likewise a crucial rôle, namely
> the idea of nationalism . . . . The German Reformation and the Ital-
> ian Renaissance are themselves in large measure the expression of a
> nascent nationalism to which in turn both contributed resilience and
> power.[91]

The whole problem has been most fully considered by two of
Germany's most distinguished practitioners of intellectual history, for
whom the solution became to such an extent the principal object of research that it has seemed advisable to treat them together as fellow
members of a somewhat distinct category. Wilhelm Dilthey and Ernst

90 W. Windelband, *Die Geschichte der neueren Philosophie* (1878; 8th ed.
Leipzig, 1922), I, 25.
91 H. Holborn, *Ulrich von Hutten and the German Reformation* (New Haven,
Yale University Press, 1937), p. 1.

Troeltsch both came to historiography from other disciplines, the former from philosophy, the latter from theology. And what attracted both to the history of the fifteenth and sixteenth centuries was the search for the spiritual origins of the modern world. Asking the same questions, they found radically different answers.

Something of Dilthey's philosophical interpretation of the Italian Renaissance has been noted in the preceding chapter.[92] It was in the work there reviewed that he undertook to analyze the intellectual development of Germany in the sixteenth century. Dilthey interpreted both Renaissance and Reformation as aspects of a general European struggle for intellectual freedom.[93] The origins of the two he found in the rise of cities, the burgher class, industry, commerce, and a new prosperity, and in the growth of strongly governed states in place of the old feudal anarchy.[94] This was true everywhere in Western Europe, but in Germany the protest against the formalism and authoritarianism of the Church was stronger than elsewhere and there was a more intense demand for reform and for a more inward religion. "So it happened that in the German-speaking lands the intellectual movement which was progressing from land to land in Europe took a religious expression." [95]

Dilthey found the contribution of German humanism to consist primarily of two ideas, both strongly influenced by antique Stoicism: a "religious-universal theism" and a new ideal of life. The former he defined as "the conviction that divinity has been and still is equally active in the various religions and philosophies." [96] With it went a pantheistic conception of the universal action of divinity in all nature and the resulting conception of a natural morality, in direct opposition to the monastic morality and formal discipline of the medieval church. Originating in Italian Stoicism and Platonism, this theism was a powerful factor in the thought of the Erfurt humanists as well as of Reuchlin and Erasmus. It was the principal source of the latter's new evangelical theology. The new ideal of life, which consisted of recog-

92 See above, p. 217 f.
93 Cf. W. Dilthey, "Auffassung und Analyse des Menschen im 15 und 16 Jahrhundert," *Gesammelte Schriften*, II (Leipzig, 1923), 16.
94 Cf. *ibid.*, II, 16; 39; 53.
95 *Ibid.*, II, 40.   96 *Ibid.*, II, 45.

nition of the independent worth of individual personality, was also closely connected with it.[97] This new ideal had already destroyed the Christian-ascetic ideal in Italy. Now in Germany, too, where humanism worked there appeared a stronger consciousness of self, founded upon reverence for the moral greatness of the ancients. It showed itself in unbounded enjoyment of activity in this world and in moral autonomy and independent belief as opposed to the domination of the Roman Church. Examples of such personality were to be found in Hutten and Pirckheimer. Indeed, "in all the literature before Luther's appearance the quiet and firm confidence of the ethically active man in himself and in his natural relation to God speaks out in opposition to church discipline and asceticism."[98]

Then came Luther. Dilthey's admiration for the great reformer was intense. He saw in him the hero who concentrated in himself all the motives of opposition to the old ecclesiastical system. "As the emancipator of personal religion from Roman priestly rule . . . he drew after him the best of his age."[99] Luther did not break entirely with the past, however. Much of his appeal depended upon his adherence to the continuity of religious tradition. His Augustinianism was merely an altered form of the dominant doctrine of the Middle Ages. Nevertheless, Dilthey felt that what was not medieval was the most significant part of Luther's thought. The reformer's perception of man's relation to the unseen was based on personal experience; it was an inner, autonomous conviction. Its result was "the royal freedom of a Christian man" and the priesthood of all believers. Moreover, "this freedom is not only external freedom from churchly discipline, but also inner freedom from the whole power of the world, in harmony with the Stoic concept of freedom."[100] In contrast to the ascetic ideal, Luther also turned the moral energy of men toward work in this world. In both these respects he was in harmony with the Renaissance ideal of life and directly opposed to the medieval. On the whole, then, Dilthey regarded Renaissance and Reformation as closely related movements. Both broke decisively with the currents of medieval thought, and the two together, as he demonstrated in later essays, led inevitably

---

[97] *Ibid.*, II, 48 ff.
[99] *Ibid.*, II, 55.
[98] *Ibid.*, II, 50.
[100] *Ibid.*, II, 60.

into the "natural" metaphysic, the rationalism, and intellectual autonomy of the seventeenth and eighteenth centuries.[101]

The effect of Dilthey's construction of history was to combine and
harmonize the two traditional interpretations which had ascribed the
origins of the modern world to the Renaissance and Reformation respectively. Ernst Troeltsch separated the two and while accepting the
former rejected the latter. A theologian who took an active part in
political controversy in an effort to democratize the contemporary
Lutheran church, Troeltsch approached the history of the Reformation
with strong prejudices.[102] He saw in Luther and the "Old Protestantism"
the origins of the modern authoritarian state and the state-controlled
church, both of which he detested. His view of the early Reformation,
therefore, was almost as jaundiced as that of Nietzsche or Janssen,
though for quite different reasons. Convinced that no good thing
could come out of that Galilee, he refused to admit that the Reformation had in any significant way contributed to the rise of modern civilization.

Troeltsch's thesis was first stated in two monographs, both published
in 1906: *Protestant Christianity and Churches in the Modern World,*
and *The Significance of Protestantism for the Rise of the Modern
World.*[103] Briefly summarized, it was that early Protestantism, as distinct from its greatly altered modern version, was essentially an authoritative church civilization like that of the Middle Ages. It was
in its most significant aspects more medieval than modern. "Despite
its universal priesthood and its primary inwardness of conviction, Old
Protestantism falls under the concept of a strictly ecclesiastical, super-
naturalistic culture, which rested upon an immediate and sharply defined authority, clearly distinguished from the secular."[104] Its preoccupation with the problem of salvation was based upon medieval
presuppositions, even though it offered a different solution. And its

---

[101] See the remaining articles in *ibid.,* II.
[102] Cf. Schnabel, pp. 340 ff; E. W. Lyman, "Ernst Troeltsch's Philosophy of
History," *Philosophical Review,* XLI (1932), 443–65.
[103] E. Troeltsch, *Protestantisches Christentum und Kirche in der Neuzeit,
Kultur der Gegenwart,* I, Teil IV (1906); *Die Bedeutung des Protestantismus für
die Entstehung der modernen Welt* (Munich, 1906, I use 3rd ed. Munich, 1924).
Eng. trans., *Protestantism and Progress* (New York, 1912).
[104] Troeltsch, *Bedeutung des Protestantismus,* p. 26.

asceticism and otherworldliness differed from the medieval only in being more comprehensive because taken out of the cloister into the world.

If one puts all this together [Troeltsch concluded], it becomes clear that Protestantism does not signify in any immediate way the preparation for the modern world. On the contrary, despite all its great new ideas, it seems primarily the renewing and strengthening of the ideal of ecclesiastical, authoritative civilization (kirchliche Zwangskultur), a complete return to medieval thought, which swallowed up those beginnings of a free and secular culture that had already been achieved. .... Furthermore, it inspired Catholicism to a revival of its idea, and, as a result, despite the contemporary diffusion of the ideas and patterns of life of the Renaissance, Europe lived through two more centuries of the medieval spirit .... Anyone who comes to the problem from the history of religion, ethics, or science will be unable to avoid the impression that it was only the great struggle for freedom of the late seventeenth and eighteenth centuries that in a fundamental way ended the Middle Ages.[105]

As was to be expected, Troeltsch soon found himself the center of a learned controversy, which he himself helped to keep alive by the reiteration of his ideas in major works on cognate subjects: *The Social Teaching of the Christian Churches and Groups* (1912), and *Historicism and its Problems* (1922).[106] Much of this controversy focused upon his conception of the nature of early Protestantism and upon his belief that the modern age did not begin until the Enlightenment. But inseparable from these was the question of the relation of the Reformation to the Renaissance. He had touched on this only incidentally or by implication in his early works. The exigencies of controversy, however, soon forced him to clarify his position. In an article entitled, "Renaissance and Reformation" (1913),[107] he restated his thesis in relation to the Renaissance and, incidentally, sowed the seed for a new crop of controversial literature.[108] Here he denied explicitly the idea that

105 *Ibid.*, p. 44 f.
106 E. Troeltsch, *Die Soziallehren der Christlichen Kirchen und Gruppen* (Tübingen, 1912). Eng. trans., 2 vols. (London, 1931); *Der Historismus und seine Probleme* (Tübingen, 1922).
107 E. Troeltsch, "Renaissance und Reformation," *Historische Zeitschrift,* CX (1913), 519–55.
108 See the heated reply by F. Strich, "Renaissance und Reformation," *Deutsche Vierteljahrsschrift für Literaturwissenschaft und Geistesgeschichte,* I (1923), 582–612.

Renaissance and Reformation were kindred movements which together led out of the Middle Ages into the modern spirit. While granting some validity to the argument of Dilthey, Wernle,[109] and others that there were points of resemblance or interrelation between the two, he queried "whether it is on this side that the character and universal-historical position of the two movements is to be seized or whether their significance is not to be found rather in the differences and antitheses." [110]

Troeltsch defined the Renaissance, with no great originality, as a cultural phenomenon of Italian origin which arose from the peculiar social and political conditions of Italy in conjunction with the revival of antique culture. Its characteristic traits were unbridled individualism and, more important, a change in the direction of interest, a turning away from otherworldliness, the Church, and the ascetic ideal. Though embodying no new philosophy, this emancipation from the otherworldly led in fact to the autonomy of thought of such independent thinkers as Bruno and Galileo. "It was, in a word, reaction against Christian asceticism." [111] Thus defined, the contrast between the Renaissance and Troeltsch's conception of the Reformation was obvious. They were fundamentally antagonistic. Even the Catholicism of the Counter-Reformation, he thought, had more in common with the Renaissance than had early Protestantism. Troeltsch saw in the Renaissance the seeds of "a new, comprehensive, modern principle of life," but its culture was aristocratic and parasitical, dependent upon patronage by church and state. Hence the Reformation was for two centuries the stronger form of civilization and the modern principle did not triumph until the eighteenth century.

[109] Cf. P. Wernle, *Die Renaissance des Christentums im 16. Jahrhundert* (Tübingen, 1904).
[110] Troeltsch, "Renaissance und Reformation," *Historische Zeitschrift*, CX, 523 f.
[111] *Ibid.,* CX, 529.

CHAPTER TEN

Reaction Against the Burckhardtian Tradition: The Origins of the Renaissance Thrust Back into the Middle Ages

THE BURCKHARDTIAN CONCEPTION of the Italian Renaissance and the closely related traditional interpretation of the Renaissance in the North encountered but little opposition on fundamental grounds during the last forty years of the nineteenth century. Minor deviations there were in plenty, but these left the heart of the tradition untouched. Toward the end of the century, however, there were several essays in the direction of more basic reinterpretation, but they were isolated voices crying in the wilderness and remained long unheard. Through the first decade of the twentieth century the voices of dissent became more numerous and more audible. They rose during the three following decades to a strident if confused and inharmonious chorus. Then, with the problem still unsolved, the sounds of scholarly controversy were blanketed by the tumult of a world at war.

THE GENERAL PROBLEM AND THE MOTIVES OF REACTION

During the period of revisionism, as during the preceding era of unchallenged tradition, Jacob Burckhardt's essay, *The Civilization of the Renaissance in Italy,* retained its place of decisive importance for Renaissance historiography. There can be no conscious heresy without an established orthodoxy, and for traditionalists and revisionists alike Burckhardt's work still served as the canon of orthodox interpretation.

290

The problem of assessing the motive forces that inspired revision or rejection of the traditional interpretation must, therefore, be focused primarily upon his work. What were the qualities in it that provoked revision? And what changing currents of thought made it seem less attractive or less convincing than it had been? The answers to these questions are very diverse and some of them by no means clear.

Perhaps an increasing tendency toward modification of Burckhardt's synthesis was in course of time inevitable. The very qualities that had made it so effective invited attack once its charm had begun to be dimmed by time and staled by endless repetition. That beautifully co-ordinated picture of a unique civilization was too perfect. The sober historian is tempted to suspect that such perfection could be achieved only by art and at the cost of distorting reality. And in fact there were weaknesses in Burckhardt's method which partially vitiated the product of his intuitive genius. His aim to discover and define the peculiar spirit of a nation in a given period, together with his use of the topical method to the practical exclusion of the chronological, tended to minimize the sense of historical development within the period while exaggerating the contrast with the preceding age or with the contemporary civilization of other countries. His Italian Renaissance thus remained in some degree a static phenomenon, isolated in time and space, and to that degree unhistorical. At the same time, his selection of sources for their ability to illustrate what he regarded as typical, while making his synthesis more coherent, tended to leave unnoted much contrary evidence. Finally, his basic premise that there exists in a whole nation during a given period a typical psychological character or mentality was in itself a hazardous assumption.

Even during the period of Burckhardt's unchallenged ascendancy, the detailed research of innumerable historians was piling up the materials for revision. Articles, monographs, and biographies, though mostly conceived within the framework of his synthesis, frequently pointed to neglected features of the civilization of the age. Greatly intensified research into the history of the Middle Ages, and of the northern countries during the fourteenth and fifteenth centuries, was at the same time lighting up that dark area which had formed the contrasting background for his Renaissance. As a result, the clear outlines of Burckhardt's picture became increasingly blurred.

This process was further accelerated after the turn of the century by the growth of the school of intellectual history or of the history of ideas, of which Wilhelm Dilthey was one of the pioneers. Burckhardt had certainly not ignored the ideas or the *Weltanschauung* of the Renaissance, but he had treated them in rather general terms in relation to the mentality of the Renaissance man. Historians of the new school examined specific ideas more closely and became more fully aware of both the variety and the continuity of ideological traditions. Though many of them continued to maintain the essential validity of Burckhardt's view, the cumulative effect of their work was to crowd the canvas and leave the picture more confused. Meanwhile, a significant by-product of the history of ideas was a new interest in the development of the concept of the Renaissance itself in modern historiography. An ever increasing volume of articles on "the Renaissance problem," beginning with Karl Brandi's pioneer essay of 1908,[1] reminded historians that their conception of the Renaissance was the product of a long historical evolution and that each generation had viewed the Renaissance somewhat differently in the light reflected partly by tradition and partly by their own interests and prejudices. The authors of these articles themselves expressed varying points of view, but whatever their own opinion the effect of their work was to summon historians to a re-examination of accepted beliefs.

It is possible, too, that tendencies to revision were at times reinforced by motives arising from the very nature of the historical profession. The number of professionally trained historians and the amount of published research have both increased tremendously in the past half-century or so. Thus a mounting pressure of academic competition has been accompanied by a growing scarcity of subjects of research suitable for publication. It may not be unjust to suggest that these factors have presented the temptation to find an original and publishable thesis in the modification of long established traditions. To this may also be added the natural desire of historians of the Middle Ages to redress the balance between their own chosen field and the popularly favored Renaissance.

---

[1] K. Brandi, *Das Werden der Renaissance* (Göttingen, 1908). For bibliography of works on the Renaissance problem, see below, pp. 398 ff.

But aside from these purely scholarly inclinations, there were motives for reaction against the traditional interpretation in nationalist, religious, anti-rational, and other currents of thought, as well as in changes in artistic taste, which were more or less fundamentally antagonistic to it. It was from these that the most sweeping revisions sprang. The Burckhardtian Renaissance had grown out of the long established tradition of classical humanism and of classical standards in art, qualified successively by Protestantism, eighteenth century rationalism, and, finally, by the positivism and rational liberalism of the nineteenth century. Toward the end of the nineteenth century, however, these currents of thought, which had so largely dominated the intellectual atmosphere of Europe since the decline of the Romantic movement, were beginning to lose their force. Reaction against any one or more of them might well make Burckhardt's conception of the Renaissance seem less attractive and also less convincing, for, inasmuch as the Renaissance was traditionally regarded as the birth hour of the modern world, its interpretation was inseparably bound up with attitudes toward contemporary civilization and hopes for the future. That there was widespread reaction about the turn of the century is clear, though its motive forces may not be. We are still too close to the early decades of this century to have charted all their numerous and conflicting currents of opinion. And this is not the place for an intellectual history of the past half-century. But, since the changes in the interpretation of the Renaissance were so closely related to the contemporary changes in the climate of opinion, we can scarcely avoid the obligation to note, if only in the way of generalized and unsupported statement, those aspects of the latter which seem to bear directly upon our theme.

The positivism, rationalism, and liberalism of the nineteenth century had been products of an era of security, of great material progress, of peace and a fairly general prosperity. As the twentieth century progressed, however, growing economic insecurity and the chaos of the first World War did much to mar the complacency with which men of the preceding century had regarded the progress achieved by reason and science. The same factors and other less obvious ones were at the same time shaking the faith of many of Europe's intelligentsia in the individualistic doctrines of political and economic liberalism. These tendencies assumed in many respects the characteristic traits of Romanticism.[2] Even before the end of the nineteenth century there were signs of a growing Neo-Romantic movement, reminiscent of that with which the century had opened. The ingredients of the new Romanticism were indeed very similar to the old. It began in an analogous revolt against classicism and the rigidity of rules in art and against the spiritual inadequacy of positivism and materialism in thought. And it became, in much the same way, more profoundly irrational as a bewildered generation, shaken by a great war, began to turn its back upon reason and individual autonomy to seek assurance in religious, nationalist, or class mysticism. The irrationalism of the twentieth century also found support in certain ideas of varied origin, which had been lacking in the first Romantic movement. Freudian psychology and the social sciences had furnished this age with a greater awareness of unconscious motives and of the irrational aspects of social behavior. Belief in the creative activity of the national folk soul was both strengthened and distorted by racial doctrines, to which a jargon borrowed from anthropology lent a semblance of scientific dignity. Hegelian philosophy, eclipsed during the second half of the nineteenth century but never wholly abandoned, still lent support to all the antiliberal tendencies of nationalism, racism, and statism, while the inverted Hegelianism of Karl Marx furnished the twentieth century with a new ideal community and a new social dogma within which reason and individual rights were submerged. These characteristics of twentieth century thought were, of course, by no means universal, and they were seldom all present in any one person. But in varying combination and proportion they appeared ever more frequently as part of an ideological *Gestalt* which was radically different from that most typical of the generation that had witnessed the high tide of Renaissancism.

2 The existence of a Neo-Romantic movement in the late nineteenth and twentieth centuries has been recognized more frequently by European than by American scholars. See, for example, the innumerable works on the subject by Ernest Seillière, particularly *La religion romantique et ses conquêtes (1890–1930)* (Paris, 1930); *Le romantisme et la politique: essais sur le mysticisme racial et le mysticisme social* (Paris, 1932); *Le néromantisme en Allemagne* (Paris, 1928–30). See also I. A. Thomése, *Romantik und Neuromantik* (Hague, 1923); K. Hilzheimer, *Das Drama der deutschen Neuromantik* (Halle, 1938).

Burckhardt's own conception of the Renaissance, it is true, owed something to the Romantic movement, notably the rôle he attributed to the Italian *Volksgeist*. The aesthetic immoralism characteristic of some of the extremists of Renaissancism from Stendhal to Nietzsche had also taken its coloring from one of the facets of Romanticism. But in general Romantic or irrational trends of thought were hostile to the Renaissance as conceived by humanist, rationalist, or liberal traditions. This was evident in the Romantic reaction against the Renaissance in the early nineteenth century. That produced by the new Romanticism was very similar. Its most obvious result for historiography was the return to a more sympathetic appreciation of medieval civilization. This might appear as a tendency to find the origins of the Renaissance, and hence of the modern civilization to which it gave birth, in the Christian-Germanic culture of the Middle Ages. Or it might take the form of greater emphasis upon the medieval elements within the Renaissance itself. Or again, it might be simply a glorification of the Middle Ages at the expense of the classical, pagan, and calculating Renaissance. In any case, the new Romanticism, like the old, was inclined to favor the Christian and Germanic, the mystical and irrational elements in the evolution of European civilization, while deprecating the pagan or secular, the classical, the rational, and individualistic.[3]

Almost without exception, save perhaps in the history of art, where the relation of Renaissance style to Baroque had been a controversial subject, the new interpretation of the Renaissance focussed attention upon the relation of the Renaissance to the Middle Ages. That problem solved, the relation of the Renaissance to modern civilization might almost be taken for granted, since the degree to which the Renaissance was conceived as differing from the Middle Ages largely determined the degree to which it might be considered the dawn of the modern age. And in general the effect of revisionism was to break down the contrast between medieval and Renaissance civilization either by finding the roots of the Renaissance in medieval culture or by demonstrating the continuation of medieval elements through the Renaissance.

[3] Cf. H. W. Eppelsheimer, "Das Renaissance-Problem," *Deutsche Vierteljahrsschrift für Literaturwissenschaft und Geistesgeschichte*, XI (1933), 484 ff.

ROMANTIC-RELIGIOUS REACTION:
THE ORIGINS OF THE RENAISSANCE IN MEDIEVAL MYSTICISM

The two tendencies noted above resulted in many instances from very similar bias, but with the distinction that those historians who followed the former were more inclined than those who followed the latter to admire the Renaissance and to consider it the birth hour of the modern world, though they would attribute to it a different character and different and earlier origins than had Burckhardt, Voigt, and the traditional school. And while finding the beginnings of the Renaissance in certain elements of medieval culture they frequently implied that these were not characteristic of the Middle Ages as a whole, that they were late developments or symptoms of revolt against the general pattern of medieval civilization.

The mere discovery of occasional Renaissance characteristics in the Middle Ages does not, however, imply a revision of the traditional interpretation. From early times historians had claimed as forerunners of the Renaissance those free, rational, or rebellious spirits who did not seem to fit into the prevailing picture of the Middle Ages. But this was no more than a by-product of the traditional idea that the Middle Ages were a period of cultural darkness and spiritual bondage, with here and there isolated rays of light shining through the general gloom. Thus early Protestant historians had recognized in the medieval heretics predecessors of the later humanists and reformers, an idea still current in more recent times.[4] Burckhardt himself had noted traits of the Renaissance spirit in the "Clerici vagantes" of the twelfth century, a suggestion frequently repeated and elaborated.[5] And Michelet had hailed as apostles of the Renaissance emancipation of the human spirit the medieval figures of Peter Abelard, Roger Bacon, and Joachim of Flora. Reading into Joachim's prophecy of a coming "reign of the free spirit and age of science" a quite anachro-

---

[4] See, for example, R. Wolkan, "Über den Ursprung des Humanismus," *Zeitschrift für die österreich. Gymnasien*, LXVII (1916), 241–68.

[5] J. Burckhardt, *Die Cultur der Renaissance in Italien* (Basel, 1860), pp. 173 ff. For fuller development of this idea, see A. Bartoli, *I precursori del Rinascimento* (Florence, 1876); H. Süssmilch, *Die lateinische Vagantenpoesie des 12 und 13 Jahrhunderts* (Leipzig, 1917); E. Müntz, *Les précurseurs de la Renaissance* (Paris, 1882).

nistic sense, Michelet proclaimed the *Eternal Evangel* "the alpha of the Renaissance." "The first word of the Renaissance had been spoken, and that most strongly." [6]

Michelet's enthusiastic discovery of the prophet of Flora served to call particular attention to the Italian mystics as pioneers of the spiritual freedom of the Renaissance. Ernest Renan devoted a long essay to Joachim of Flora in the *Revue des Deux Mondes* of 1866,[7] but his warmest appreciation was reserved for St. Francis of Assisi.[8] In him he perceived a subjective individuality in sharp contrast to the general character of medieval society and religion. What was peculiar to St. Francis, Renan thought, was his way of feeling,[9] a combination of naïve faith and boundless love that made him "since Jesus . . . the only perfect Christian." [10] He was, moreover, "almost the only man of the Middle Ages who was completely free from the leprosy [of scholasticism]." [11] And in one particular Renan hailed him specifically as having prepared the way for the Renaissance: he was "the father of Italian art." [12]

Renan did little to develop this idea. It was thrown out casually, one of those brief flashes of intuition that so frequently illuminated his essays. It did not apparently change his own general conception of the Renaissance, which was in the true classical rational tradition.[13] But it did give a specific direction to the interest in St. Francis, which his warm appreciation helped to arouse, and which grew toward the end of the century into something like a new Franciscan cult. The Romantic historians had been the first to discover the poet in the saint of Assisi,[14] and much of the later enthusiasm for him was of purely ro-

---

[6] J. Michelet, *Histoire de France*, VII (Paris, 1855), p. lxv.

[7] Republished in E. Renan, *Nouvelles études d'histoire religieuse* (Paris, 1884), pp. 217–322.

[8] See the essay entitled "St. François d'Assise," *ibid.*, pp. 323–51.

[9] "Ce qui n'appartient qu' à lui, c'est la manière de sentir." *Ibid.*, p. 329 f.

[10] *Ibid.*, p. 334; cf. p. 325.

[11] *Ibid.*, p. 341.   [12] *Ibid.*, p. 337.

[13] Cf. Renan's preface to his *Averroès et l'averroïsme* (Paris, 1852), and his contribution to the *Histoire littéraire de la France*, XXIV (Paris, 1862), 604 ff.

[14] Cf. J. Görres, *Der heilige Franz von Assisi: ein Troubadour* (Strassburg, 1828). For discussion of the historical interpretation of St. Francis, see H. Tilemann, *Studien zur Individualität des Franziskus von Assisi* (Leipzig, 1914), pp. 1 ff.

mantic or mystical inspiration. This was understandable; but the wider appeal of St. Francis to skeptical souls like Renan seems to require more explanation. Much of it rested on the conception of Francis as a free, natural individual, who had broken through the dogmatic and corporate limitations of medieval society and had rebelled against the *contemptus mundi* of medieval asceticism. But there may also be a good deal of truth in Gabriel Monod's analysis of Renan's feeling for Francis. Monod pictured his friend and master as the faithful interpreter of his age, who represented its "scientific positivism, united to regret for lost faith," and added:

> Our age has lost faith and admits no other source of certainty than science, but at the same time it has not been able to resolve, as positivism would wish, not to reflect and to remain silent about what it ignores . . . . It has the feeling that, without faith or hope in invisible realities, life loses its nobility, and it demonstrates for the heroes of religious life, for the mystical souls of the past an attraction and a tenderness composed of futile regrets and of vague aspirations.[15]

Renan's view of the originality of St. Francis, like the other discoveries of various isolated forerunners of the Renaissance, left the traditional interpretation fundamentally unchanged. It did, however, point the way toward the essentially new interpretation of the Renaissance, which first appeared in Henry Thode's *Francis of Assisi and the Beginning of the Art of the Renaissance in Italy* (1885).[16] Here St. Francis was declared in no uncertain terms to be not merely a forerunner of the Renaissance but the originator of the entire movement. The result was to thrust back the whole lower boundary of the Renaissance and, still more important, to alter the conception of its essential character. It was the first major break with the Burckhardtian tradition, the substitution of an irrational, Romantic picture for the rational, classical view of the Renaissance in Italy.

Henry Thode was an art historian of considerable note, an intimate of Wagner's circle, and deeply impregnated with the Christian-Germanic Romanticism that was endemic at Bayreuth. In strongly emo-

15 G. Monod, *Les maîtres de l'histoire, Renan, Taine, Michelet* (Paris, 1895), p. 43.
16 H. Thode, *Franz von Assisi und die Anfänge der Kunst der Renaissance in Italien* (Berlin, 1885; I use ed. Vienna, 1934).

tional reaction against the positivism and materialism of his century, Thode proclaimed the inseparable kinship of art, religion, and civilization, and reiterated a mystical faith that all three could flourish only when rooted in a deeply subjective *Innerlichkeit.* "In die Tiefe und aus ihr die Kultur!" [17] This faith in the creative power of unhampered subjective feeling was one of the persistent strains in the complex of Romanticism. Thode felt that it applied to Germany of his own day as much as to Italy of the Renaissance. His interpretation of the origins and nature of the Renaissance, indeed, served a propagandist purpose, demonstrating the way in which contemporary German culture might achieve a new birth.

Two aspects of the Burckhardtian Renaissance appealed strongly to Thode: individualism, which he interpreted largely as subjectivism, and that keen awareness of both internal and external nature that Michelet had called "the discovery of the world and of man." But he could not accept the tradition that, even as modified by Burckhardt, attributed to the revival of classical antiquity a decisive influence in the shaping of Renaissance culture. Such an idea would have offended both sides of his Christian-Germanic sentiment. Moreover, his belief that art can grow only out of religion and that the sources of culture in general are pre-eminently irrational prevented him from accepting an interpretation that made the Renaissance predominantly secular, if not pagan, and at the same time made it the product of conscious reason, freed from all irrational or mystical qualities. From the dilemma presented by this mixture of attractive and repellent elements in the Burckhardtian tradition, Thode escaped by discovering a different original source and by remolding the whole movement of culture nearer to his heart's desire.

In a lengthy introduction to his *Francis of Assisi,* Thode expounded his thesis concerning the origins of Renaissance art and, indeed, of all modern culture. Born at a crucial time, St. Francis was the decisive figure in the evolution of European civilization.

In Francis of Assisi a great movement of the Western Christian world reached its highest point, a movement not limited to the religious

[17] H. Thode, *Kunst, Religion, und Kultur* (Heidelberg, 1901), p. 11. This address to the students of Heidelberg is one of the most revealing expressions of the tone of Thode's thought.

sphere but universal in the truest sense, a movement which is the
predisposing and driving force of modern civilization. To designate
it in a word, I might call it the movement of humanity . . . . Its content was the freeing of the individual, which, in a subjective, harmonious, emotional conception (Gefühlsauffassung) of nature and
religion . . . . proclaimed its rights against the community.[18]

Thode found the origins of this movement in the rise of the burgher
class. With considerable historical insight he depicted the burghers
as a new element in medieval society, whose interests were necessarily
antagonistic to the twin systems of feudalism and ecclesiastical hierarchy. Revolt against the emperor, the personification of feudalism,
won for the Italian communes political and social freedom. Revolt
against the Church led to the growth of heretical sects. Like many
other Protestant historians, Thode saw in the Albigenses, Waldenses,
and other heretical groups champions of religious freedom.[19] He
was more original, however, in his indentification of the heresies with
the struggle of the burgher class for "the free rights of the individual"
against the "schematic generalizing division of mankind into free
and unfree," which was common to both feudalism and the hierarchical church.[20] The rise of the bourgeoisie was thus a movement inherently dangerous to the church. It was saved for the Church and
the Church was reformed to meet its demands by St. Francis and the
work of his order.

Thode's portrayal of the character of St. Francis, founded on the
legends, was very much like Renan's. Francis was completely a man
of the heart, unhampered by intellectual criticism. "His religion was
feeling; the preaching in which he revealed it worked through feeling;
his relation to men and nature was conditioned by feeling. His life
was a great *Dithyrambus* on feeling. Therein lay the explanation of
his powerful influence." [21] Love of God and man was the meaning of
his life, and he extended the love of God to include all His creatures,
the whole of nature. It was this love of nature, combined with his
liberation of individual feeling, that inspired the new Christian-burgh-
er art and poetry of the Renaissance. Francis had reconciled religion

---

18 Thode, *Franz von Assisi*, p. 14.
19 *Ibid.*, p. 18 ff; cf. pp. 41 ff for comparison of Peter Waldo with St. Francis.
20 *Ibid.*, p. 21; cf. p. 44 f.   21 *Ibid.*, p. 68.

with nature and had established the unity of the two. By recognizing the human in Christ and the divine in man, he made it possible for art to portray the divine by the idealization of the human.[22] At the same time, his human conception of the life of Christ, together with his own legend, gave Christian art a new material suitable for natural treatment. The art that resulted, from Giotto to Raphael, was "a unified development, founded upon a unified view of the world and conception of religion." Its living force lay in a strong individual feeling for nature. "What the antique contributed to the movement was no more than formal instruction and practical teaching."[23]

The remainder of Thode's study was a detailed expansion of this thesis. Later, he developed it still further in a monograph on Giotto (1899)[24] and in 1903 he recapitulated and clarified his interpretation of the whole of Renaissance culture in a second lengthy introduction, this time to the second volume of his *Michelangelo and the End of the Renaissance*.[25] Here he maintained that pictorial art was the most perfect expression of the spirit of the Italian people in this age, the only one with an unbroken tradition. For only in art could the Franciscan ideal of the close interrelation of the human and the divine find fulfillment. It furnished the ideal of beauty toward which artists strove until final perfection was attained in the generation of Leonardo, Raphael, and Michelangelo. Until that point had been reached, not even the new discovery of antiquity could turn the Italian people from the road they had entered. "Only when the work of centuries was ended and the dream picture of perfect harmony of form and color had become reality, when there was nothing more to strive for, only then did the world of the antique gods enter the artistic workshops which Christian genius had abandoned."[26]

Thode was prepared to admit a larger, though ruinous, antique influence on Italian poetry. The great poetry of Dante's age sprang, like pictorial art, from the religious-social movement. But the Christian material could not give poets the possibility of achieving perfect

---

[22] *Ibid.*, p. 79. [23] *Ibid.*, p. 81.
[24] H. Thode, *Giotto* (Bielefeld and Leipzig, 1899).
[25] H. Thode, *Michelangelo und das Ende der Renaissance* (Berlin, 1903), II, 1–96.
[26] *Ibid.*, II, 16; cf. II, 19.

form. Unsatisfied, they turned to antiquity for inspiration — with disastrous results.[27] Imitation of an alien, already perfected literature and the superficial adoption of pagan ideas sapped the vitality of poetry and broke its connection with the folk soul. Inspiration survived only in the naïve popular folk poetry. Having thus damned at some length almost all Italian poetry after Petrarch, Thode concluded rather surprisingly:

> There can be no talk of anything originally new having entered with humanism. Everything artistically significant in the poetry of the Quattrocento and Cinquecento was rooted in the ideas and forms of the foregoing centuries. The poetic art of the Renaissance demonstrates the unity of civilization from the twelfth to the sixteenth centuries no less, if also less significantly, than does the pictorial art.[28]

Even in the more learned fields Thode found Franciscan mysticism to be the sole fruitful source of inspiration.[29] What was best in humanism itself was "a result of that humanity, of the free *Menschlichkeit* which the reform of Francis had given Italy."[30] The humanist historians were original because they found their material in the social and political development of the preceding age. And, finally, Ficino's Platonism was the completion of the Franciscan idea of love, just as Raphael's Madonnas fulfilled the development of the ideal of beauty awakened by the religious revolution of the thirteenth century.[31] To the end, Thode's logic remains consistent. Everything significant in the Renaissance is part of the great unified movement, which began in the age of St. Francis. Otherwise it would not be significant.

The immediate reception of Thode's *Francis of Assisi* was disappointing. His thesis received a satisfactory hearing only after the originality and modernity of the Franciscan movement had been further popularized by Emile Gebhart and Paul Sabatier.

Emile Gebhart followed closely in the footsteps of Renan, but with a noticeable drift toward Romantic mysticism in his later years. Historian and man of letters, a classicist by early training, he had the literary charm necessary to gain a wide reading public for his imagin-

27 *Ibid.*, II, 32 ff.   28 *Ibid.*, II, 46.   29 *Ibid.*, II, 53 ff.
30 *Ibid.*, II, 56.   31 *Ibid.*, II, 68.

ative if not very profound historical studies. In his first two works on the Renaissance, *The Origins of the Renaissance in Italy* (1879) [32] and a long critical review of Burckhardt's *Civilization of the Renaissance in Italy*, published in 1885,[33] Gebhart modified the traditional interpretation by insisting that the origins of the Renaissance were to be found much earlier in the history of Italy.

> The Italian Renaissance [he wrote] began in reality before Petrarch, for already in the works of the Pisan sculptors and Giotto, as well as in the architecture of the twelfth and thirteenth centuries, the arts were renewed . . . . The origins of the Renaissance were very distant and preceded by a great deal the learned education which the literati of the fifteenth century diffused about them.[34]

Among the medieval sources of the Renaissance, Gebhart noted particularly the undogmatic attitude of the Italian people toward religion, an attitude typified and reinforced by St. Francis and his followers, the rise of the free communes, and the unbroken classical tradition in Italian culture. Thanks to these the Italians won spiritual freedom at a time when culture was being frozen into sterility north of the Alps. In short: "The whole moral history of the Italians in the Middle Ages prepared a reawakening of the human spirit such as had not been known since the Greeks." [35]

Thus far, Gebhart had noted the Franciscan movement as but one of the factors in the history of medieval Italy which helped to prepare the way for the Renaissance. Then, in his most popular work, *Mystic Italy, a History of the Religious Renaissance in the Middle Ages* (1890),[36] he concentrated his whole attention upon it. Here he presented a series of warmly sympathetic studies of Joachim of Flora, St. Francis, the later Franciscan mystics, and finally Dante. There was still more of Renan than of Thode in Gebhart's interpretation. And, indeed, there is no direct evidence that he had read the latter,

---

[32] E. Gebhart, *Les origines de la Renaissance en Italie* (Paris, 1879).

[33] E. Gebhart, "La Renaissance italienne et la philosophie de l'histoire," *Revue des Deux Mondes,* LXXI (1885), 342–79.

[34] E. Gebhart, *Les origines,* p. vii.   [35] *Ibid.,* p. 227.

[36] E. Gebhart, *L'Italie mystique, histoire de la Renaissance religieuse au Moyen Age* (Paris, 1890; I use 2nd ed. Paris, 1893). Eng. trans. *Mystics and Heretics in Italy* (New York, 1922).

though it seems likely. He still emphasized "the rationalistic spirit" of Italy and was much less schematic than the German historian in his construction of history. Yet the effect of his charming book was certainly to give persuasive, if unconscious, support to Thode's thesis, particularly as it applied to art. On this point Gebhart was explicit: "The religious revival of Assisi gave new life to Italian art at the same time that it raised men's conscience."[37]

Renan, Thode, and Gebhart had all contributed to the growing cult of St. Francis. Paul Sabatier completed the modern apotheosis of the saint with his memorable *Life of St. Francis of Assisi* (1894).[38] Few biographies have enjoyed such resounding success. It was read and enjoyed by men of all faiths or none. Sabatier was himself a Protestant pastor and he had studied under Renan, who had first suggested to him the task of writing a life of St. Francis.[39] The conception of St. Francis presented by the skeptical Renan and the Protestants, Thode and Sabatier, seemed in fact to present a particular appeal to non-Catholics. It emphasized the undogmatic, unsacerdotal character of his religion and portrayed him as an unconscious rebel against the rigid, authoritarian, mechanical, and world-denying medieval church.[40] Both Renan and Sabatier proclaimed St. Francis the most perfect Christian since Christ. And to the skeptical anticlerical or the Protestant, however tolerant, that could have but one meaning. In any case the very conception of the originality of St. Francis implied that he had introduced something new into the medieval church, something, therefore, not characteristic of it. Sabatier made little attempt to connect St. Francis directly with the Renaissance,[41] but the whole tenor of his work presented the saint as the originator of a new spirit, as an essentially modern man.

[37] *Ibid.*, p. 282 [p. 234].
[38] P. Sabatier, *Vie de St. François d'Assise* (Paris, 1894; I use 40th ed., Paris, s. d.). Eng. trans. (London, 1894).
[39] P. Sabatier *et al.*, *L'Influence de Saint François sur la civilization italienne* (Paris, 1926), p. 9.
[40] Cf. Sabatier, *Vie de St. François*, pp. v ff; 17 ff; 31 ff. Cf. Sabatier, "L'originalité de Saint François d'Assise," *Franciscan Essays*, I (Aberdeen, 1912), 9, where he admitted that he had been accused of making St. Francis a precursor of the Protestant Reformation.
[41] Sabatier did, however, regard St. Francis as the initiator of the artistic movement which preceded the Renaissance. Cf. Sabatier, *Vie de St. François*, pp. 203 ff.

Few historians adopted Thode's thesis of the Franciscan origins of the Renaissance in its exclusive form.[42] Nevertheless, his work, after being reinforced by the charm of Gebhart's studies and Sabatier's matchless *Life,* made a profound impression. During the early decades of the twentieth century the Franciscan movement was frequently placed beside the other, more traditional sources of Renaissance art and civilization. Over-stated though it was, his theory helped to illuminate one of the many facets of the Renaissance and to call attention to the religious element in what had too long been considered a pagan or purely secular culture. At the same time, it did not go unchallenged. Robert Davidsohn, the scholarly historian of Florence, rejected it decisively.[43] Heinrich Tilemann struck at the heart of the Thode-Sabatier interpretation by denying the originality, the independence, and the individualism of St. Francis. He concluded that "the piety of St. Francis represents the type of medieval religiosity in its most complete form."[44] Hubert Schrade minimized the influence of Francis upon early Renaissance art in his study of Giotto.[45] Finally, Walter Goetz threw the weight of his magisterial authority against the whole conception. In two thoughtful articles he argued, first, that the influence of antiquity which Thode had rejected was indispensable to the growth of Renaissance culture, and, second, that St. Francis was fundamentally opposed to the secular materialism of the urban society out of which the Renaissance grew.[46]

We have gained much from Thode and Sabatier [Goetz wrote in 1927], but the ultimate result is nevertheless the final and complete rejection of their theories. Francis of Assisi was neither the pioneer of the Renaissance nor the protagonist of a modern religious individualism — he was purely medieval; and what he wished for and what

---

[42] As one of the few, see C. de Mondach, *St. Antoine de Padoue et l'art italien* (Paris, 1899).

[43] R. Davidsohn, *Geschichte von Florenz,* II (Berlin, 1908), 1, 122.

[44] H. Tilemann, *Studien zur Individualität des Franziskus von Assisi* (Leipzig, 1914), p. 213.

[45] H. Schrade, "Franz von Assisi und Giotto," *Archiv für Kulturgeschichte,* XVII (1927), 150–93. His conclusion is that the Franciscan movement was "nur Teilerscheinung grösserer kultureller Ereignisse." *Ibid.,* p. 193.

[46] W. Goetz, "Renaissance und Antike," *Historische Zeitschrift,* CXIII (1914), 237–59; "Franz von Assisi und die Entwicklung der mittelalterlichen Religiosität," *Archiv für Kulturgeschichte,* XVII (1927), 129–49.

he realized in his own person stood in deepest opposition to the new
Italian culture of the thirteenth century and to the coming Renaissance.[47]

It may be worth noting in this connection, however, that although
Goetz rejected Thode's thesis and adhered in general to a modified
Burckhardtian interpretation, he too was inclined to seek the origins
of the Renaissance in certain aspects of medieval culture and so to
stretch its roots further into the past than was customary. Goetz was
always deeply impressed with the continuous, evolutionary nature of
history, and it seemed natural to him that the Renaissance should have
had its beginnings in social and intellectual movements that had
evolved within the civilization of the preceding period. This theory, suggested in the articles cited above, was more clearly stated in a later
article on "The Development of a Sense of Reality from the Twelfth
to the Fourteenth Century" (1937).[48] Here he posited as one of the
criteria by which the Renaissance was to be distinguished from the
Middle Ages a direct, objective apprehension of reality. And he found
the origins of this unmedieval quality of thought in two movements
which began in the twelfth century and grew much stronger in the
thirteenth: the development within scholasticism of an interest in natural science as a result of the recovery of ancient learning and, of
more widespread importance, the growth of a lay, secular culture,
first in the northern courts and then in more revolutionary form in
the Italian cities.

Meanwhile, an interpretation of the origins and character of the
Renaissance somewhat similar in effect to Thode's, though based on
other grounds and on a different methodology, had been enunciated
by Konrad Burdach. With his peculiar combination of philological
method and mystical intuitions stemming from religious-national Romanticism, Burdach is one of the most puzzling phenomena of recent
German scholarship. A foreigner not attuned to his mental processes
may find it difficult to understand either the meaning of his work
or its undoubted vogue among younger German historians, a vogue

[47] *Ibid.*, XVII, 129.
[48] W. Goetz, "Die Entwicklung des Wirklichkeitssinnes vom 12. zum 14.
Jahrhundert," *Archiv für Kulturgeschichte*, XXVII (1937), 33–73. For fuller
discussion of Goetz, see above, p. 226 f.

amply attested by articles in the *Deutsche Vierteljahrsschrift für Literaturwissenschaft und Geistesgeschichte* and other publications.[49] If I understand Burdach aright — a phrase to which even his German contemporaries frequently resort — his thesis proceeds from two premises. The first concerns the science of linguistics, his original field of study. It is that the development of language and style can be explained only as a reflection of the evolution of higher culture, and that this in turn can be understood only through more fundamental changes in civilization. The second premise is the dogmatically stated belief that the mainspring of Renaissance culture was a renewal of the human soul, which resulted from a new consciousness of religious, personal, and national rebirth. This causative consciousness of rebirth arose in Italy during the thirteenth century under the influence of Franciscan mysticism, qualified by classical traditions of national rebirth inherited from ancient Rome, and was carried to the German court of Bohemia by Cola di Rienzi. From this resulted the German Renaissance, which began in the court of Charles IV and was reflected in the changing style and vocabulary of the Bohemian chancellory and of such writers as Johann von Neumarkt and the Ackermann aus Böhmen.[50]

Burdach's life work was the editorship of a great co-operative linguistic study of German literature of the fourteenth and fifteenth centuries, in the form of monographs and critical editions, which would interpret the transition from the Middle Ages to the Reformation on the basis of these two premises.[51] Following the linguistic theory suggested in the first premise, it was apparently intended to clarify the evolution of German language by relating it to the spiritual changes stated in the second. It tended, however, particularly in Burdach's own contri-

---

[49] The degree to which the more sober aspects of Burdach's theory of the origins of the Renaissance have become commonplace in German scholarship is attested by its inclusion in such generally conventional histories of literature as W. Stammler, *Von der Mystik zum Barock, 1400–1600* (Stuttgart, 1927).

[50] For statement of this thesis, see K. Burdach, *Vom Mittelalter zur Reformation* (Halle, 1893); also *Deutsche Renaissance: Betrachtung über unsere künftige Bildung* (1916; enlarged ed., Berlin, 1920), and the works by Burdach cited below.

[51] K. Burdach, ed., *Vom Mittelalter zur Reformation, Forschungen zur Geschichte der deutschen Bildung,* 6 vols. (Berlin, 1912–39).

butions, to be rather a philological demonstration of the second premise by calling attention to every possible instance of the use of words or symbols signifying rebirth or reformation. In the monograph on *Rienzo and the Spiritual Changes of his Age* (1913–1928),[52] which he contributed to this work, and in the separately published study of the *Sense and Origin of the Words Renaissance and Reformation* (1910),[53] what emerges is a history of the Renaissance treated as a history of words.

By tracing, with immense erudition, the historical evolution, and by demonstrating the originally identical meaning, of the words "reform" and "rebirth," Burdach undoubtedly made a material contribution to our knowledge of the history and meaning of the words reform and rebirth. In this respect his work is comprehensible. It is his assumption that he has thereby explained the origins and nature of Renaissance civilization in Italy and Germany that is baffling to the uninitiated.[54] His Renaissance was a purely spiritual phenomenon, "a truly inner movement," which "grew out of the innermost life-kernel of the Italian people."[55]

> What may bear the name Renaissance was a spiritual movement
> . . . . It comprehended the inner life of men and their ideal aims.
> It fulfilled itself in the sphere of the aesthetic and the moral . . . . But
> it worked chiefly outside the world of commerce and it had from
> its very nature nothing in common with the economic forces or the
> changes in the external life of Europe. At any rate, it was not called
> forth by them.[56]

On the contrary, it was called forth exclusively by the idea of rebirth. The mystical idea of personal rebirth in a religious sense was common to all Christian teaching, but it was powerfully revived by St. Francis and it was carried further to include the rebirth or reform of the

[52] K. Burdach, *Rienzo und die geistige Wandlung seiner Zeit,* in *Vom Mittelalter zur Reformation,* II, Teil 1, Heft 1–2, (1913–28).

[53] K. Burdach, "Sinn und Ursprung der Worte Renaissance und Reformation," *Sitzungsberichte der preussischen Akademie der Wissenschaften,* XXXII (1910), 594–646.

[54] Cf. G. Toffanin, "Orientamenti bibliografici sull'umanesimo," *La Rinascita,* I, 4 (1938), 56 f.

[55] Cf. Burdach, *Deutsche Renaissance,* p. 31; *Sitzungsberichte der preussischen Akademie,* XXXII, 645.

[56] Burdach, *Deutsche Renaissance,* p. 19 f.

Church in the chiliastic prophecies of Joachim of Flora. Parallel with this ran the antique idea of the rebirth of the Roman state.[57] The Renaissance resulted when these two traditions were united in the work of Dante, Petrarch, and, most important of all, Cola di Rienzi. Of these three, whom he calls "the three great renewers of world culture," "the three great pioneers of humanism," "the great preparers of the way for the coming Renaissance," it was Cola di Rienzi who in Burdach's view was by far the most important.

> As the Roman Empire sank into death, Rienzi proclaimed, as a student of Dante and under the encouragement of Petrarch, the reformation and regeneration of the city of Rome, and therewith a new Roman Empire. That is the Renaissance, which created a new concept of man, of art, of literary and scientific life, which founded a new world dominion: the world dominion of a spiritual ideal over formulas of a frozen dogma, not in opposition to the Christian religion, but out of the full force of a religious resurgence.[58]

Burdach proved beyond doubt by innumerable citations that Dante, Petrarch, Reinzi, and other later Renaissance men frequently used words or metaphors signifying rebirth, though it is doubtful if these examples, taken in context, always meant as much as he suggests. But that the consciousness of personal, religious, and national rebirth, later secularized in the Italian Renaissance but retaining its religious character in the German Reformation, was the primary motive of European civilization during a period of more than two hundred years has seemed unconvincing to many scholars.[59] And the overwhelming importance he attributed to Cola di Rienzi was greeted in more than

---

[57] Cf. K. Borinski, "Die Weltwiedergeburtsidee in den neueren Zeiten," *Sitzungsberichte der bayerischen Akademie der Wissenschaften* (1919), Abh. 1, for fuller investigation of this concept of rebirth. Borinski regarded Burdach's emphasis on the religious origins of the concept of rebirth as exaggerated. See his criticism in *Zeitschrift für deutsche Philologie*, XLVIII (1920), XLIX (1923). For the history of the classical conception of rebirth in the Middle Ages, see also P. Schramm, *Kaiser, Rom, und Renovatio* (Leipzig, 1929).

[58] *Sitzungsberichte der preussischen Akademie*, XXXII, 645.

[59] See the criticism of Burdach's thesis in P. Joachimsen, "Vom Mittelalter zur Reformation," *Historische Vierteljahrsschrift*, XX (1920–21), 426–70. For Burdach's own review of the reception of his work, see his "Die seelischen und geistigen Quellen der Renaissancebewegung," *Historische Zeitschrift*, CXLIX (1933–34), 477–520.

one quarter with frank incredulity.[60] The enthusiasm with which his work was acclaimed by others was probably due less to his method or his particular thesis than to the general conception of the nature of the Renaissance to which he lent the support of an imposing, if not always relevant, erudition.

Burdach's interpretation, in fact, combined elements well calculated to appeal to those who, for various reasons, were repelled by the calculating rationalism of the Renaissance as Burckhardt had conceived it, by the exclusive classical tradition, or by the general idea of a sharp break with the Middle Ages. His Renaissance was in origin and spirit fundamentally irrational and divorced from all material forces. Like Thode, Burdach emphasized the religious, mystical sources of the Renaissance and retained the central theme of individualism, though understood in the sense of subjective feeling, deeply rooted in the folk soul. However, he also left a place for the influence of a continuous classical tradition, and he further broadened Thode's interpretation by introducing the element of national consciousness and by identifying the feeling of religious and personal with that of national rebirth.[61] The idea that the Italian Renaissance was a peculiarly national movement, the conscious revival of Italy's own national past, made a strong appeal to an age accustomed to interpret everything in terms of national sentiment. It had, indeed, been suggested in passing by Burckhardt,[62] and was adopted by many twentieth century historians who rejected the remainder of Burdach's thesis.[63] It was in all probability the feature of Burdach's interpretation most largely responsible for its favorable reception by many Italian scholars, including the distinguished literary historian, Vittorio Rossi, and the historian of Italian philosophy, Guido de Ruggiero.[64] But, while emphasizing

60 Cf. in addition to the article by Joachimsen cited above, K. Brandi, "Cola di Rienzo und seine Verhältnis zu Renaissance und Humanismus," *Deutsche Vierteljahrsschrift für Literaturwissenschaft und Geistesgeschichte,* IV (1926), 595–614; and "Renaissance und Reformation, Wertung und Umwertung," *Preussische Jahrbücher,* CC (1925), 120–35.

61 Cf. Burdach, *Deutsche Renaissance,* pp. 17; 21; 31.

62 Burckhardt, *Cultur der Renaissance,* p. 173.

63 See above, p. 255 f.

64 V. Rossi, *Il Quattrocento* (revised ed., Milan, 1933), pp. 1 ff; and "Il Rinascimento," *Nuova antologia,* CCLXVIII (1929), 137–50; G. de Ruggiero, *Rinascimento, Riforma e Controriforma* (2nd ed., Bari, 1937), I, 51; 61 ff.

the national character of the Renaissance, Burdach also insisted that it was a European phenomenon. Though most perfectly fulfilled in Italy, it operated in Germany and elsewhere, and everywhere it inspired a renewal of national consciousness. It thus furnished a model upon which a new German Renaissance in the future might be based.[65]

The theory that medieval religious mysticism was the source from which flowed the cultural current of the Renaissance was developed first in relation to Italy. But, as always, the new interpretation of the Italian Renaissance influenced the attitude of historians toward its northern counterpart. While some, like Burdach, founded a similar interpretation of the Renaissance in the North on the theory of diffusion from the Italian source, others discovered a parallel but independent current of exclusively northern character. Heinrich Hermelink made the first notable effort in the latter direction in a much discussed monograph on *The Religious Reform Effort of German Humanism* (1907).[66] Hermelink accepted fully Thode's thesis regarding the Renaissance in Italy. It was, he repeated, a reform movement, stemming from medieval religious sources and beginning with St. Francis and Dante. The "antiquizing paganism" of a Valla or a Machiavelli was no more than an unfruitful offshoot. And so it was with the Renaissance in the North.[67] But Hermelink also asserted that northern humanism — like most German scholars, he tended to identify the Renaissance in Germany with humanism — was an essentially independent native product, the sources of which must be found north of the Alps. Of these the most important was the rising wave of lay piety in the northern towns during the fourteenth and fifteenth centuries. This was a reform movement within the Church, inspired by the need of the growing burgher class for a more personal religion and for emancipation from the Church's institutionalized apparatus of salvation. It drew its religious ideas chiefly from the German and

---

[65] Cf. Burdach, *Deutsche Renaissance, passim.*

[66] H. Hermelink, *Die religiösen Reformbestrebungen des deutschen Humanismus* (Tübingen, 1907). See also his *Die theologische Fakultät in Tübingen vor der Reformation* (Tübingen, 1906). For critical discussion of Hermelink, Mestwerdt, and Hyma, see H. Baron, "Zur Frage des Ursprungs des deutschen Humanismus und seine religiösen Reformbestrebungen," *Historische Zeitschrift,* CXXXII (1925), 413–16.

[67] Hermelink, *Die religiösen Reformbestrebungen,* p. 5 f.

Dutch mystics, most especially from the Brethren of the Common Life in whose schools the new lay piety was combined with an interest in the ancient classics. But the reforming humanism which resulted from this current of mystical lay piety finally triumphed in the North only through alliance with another reform movement of the later Middle Ages, one which had developed within the scholastic circle of the universities. The pious humanists had, according to Hermelink, much in common with the scholastic champions of the *via antiqua* (the return to Thomism) against the dominant school of Occamist Terminism.[68] Like the humanists, these Neo-Thomists were returning to the sources, if not quite the same sources. Moreover they, too, were reviving interest in both literary and factual science which had been killed by Terminism. The growth of the natural sciences in the humanist age, Hermelink insisted, could not be attributed to Italian influence. It rose directly from the return to "reality" which was the watchword of the *via antiqua*.

Hermelink's argument for the scholastic origins of northern humanism, based as it was on an odd misconception of the meaning of Thomist "realism," was soon proven untenable by Gerhard Ritter and others.[69] His major thesis, which attributed the primary influence to mystical lay piety, had more success. During the second and third decades of the present century, there was a growing tendency to emphasize the rôle of the mystics in shaping the Northern Renaissance. Paul Mestwerdt's brilliant monograph, *The Beginnings of Erasmus: Humanism and "Devotio Moderna"* (1917),[70] demonstrated the preponderant influence of the Brethren of the Common Life upon the religious thought of Erasmus and his circle. And at about the same time Augustin Renaudet, in his monumental study of *Pre-reform and Humanism at Paris during the first Italian Wars (1494–1517)* (1916),[71] traced the reforming activity of the French humanists to the combined

[68] *Ibid.*, pp. 10 ff.

[69] Cf. G. Ritter, *Studien zur Spätscholastik*, 2 vols. (Heidelberg, 1921–22). That the natural sciences owed more to the Occamists than the Thomists was demonstrated by Pierre Duhem. See below, p. 337 f.

[70] P. Mestwerdt, *Die Anfänge des Erasmus; Humanismus und "Devotio Moderna"* (Leipzig, 1917).

[71] A. Renaudet, *Préréforme et humanisme à Paris pendant les premières guerres d'Italie (1494–1517)* (Paris, 1916).

influence of Italian humanism and Dutch mysticism. Neither Mestwerdt nor Renaudet denied the general dependence of northern humanism upon the Italian movement nor, in particular, did they ignore the long recognized influence of Florentine Platonism upon the reforming Christian humanists.[72] Other historians of more strongly national sentiment, however, adhered more closely to Hermelink's thesis that northern humanism was an autonomous movement growing in each country out of its own native past.

The Dutch-American scholar, Albert Hyma, proclaimed the originality and wide influence of the Dutch mystics in a study entitled, *The Christian Renaissance, a History of The "Devotio Moderna"* (1924). They owed nothing, he asserted, to Eckhart or the other German mystics, and very little to the Italians, but their influence was decisive for the thought of the northern humanists and of such varied religious reformers as Luther, Zwingli, Calvin, and Loyola.[73] Meanwhile, the German philosopher Heinz Heimsoeth had made even more sweeping claims for the mystics of his own country. Like Dilthey, Heimsoeth sought the origins of the modern world of ideas through a study of the evolution of European metaphysical thought. But the conclusions he reached in his much acclaimed work on *The Six Great Themes of Western Metaphysic and the End of the Middle Ages* (1922) [74] were very different from Dilthey's. The traditional view which ascribed the beginnings of modern thought to the Italian Renaissance seemed to him inherently improbable. "Is it not remarkable that German thought should have brought so little to our philosophical modern age, the Italian almost everything? Are the gifts of nations not strikingly similar in all ages? Where was in those centuries the speculative energy of the German mind, which later was un-

---

[72] See, for example, P. Wernle, *Die Renaissance des Christentums im 16. Jahrhundert* (Tübingen, 1904); P. Chiminelli, *Il contributo italiano alla riforma religiosa in Europa* (Rome, 1924); and W. Dilthey as cited above, p. 285 f.

[73] A. Hyma, *The Christian Renaissance, a History of the "Devotio Moderna"* (New York, 1924), pp. 300 ff.

[74] H. Heimsoeth, *Die sechs grossen Themen der abendländischen Metaphysic und der Ausgang des Mittelalters* (Berlin, 1922). For evidence of the esteem in which Heimsoeth's work was held in Germany, see J. Bernhart, "Vom Geistesleben des Mittelalters. Ein Literaturbericht," *Deutsche Vierteljahrsschrift für Literaturwissenschaft und Geistesgeschichte,* V (1927), 208 f.

paralleled by any other nation?"[75] To anyone capable of posing the question thus, the answer was already given. The Italian Renaissance, Heimsoeth insisted, contributed almost nothing to modern philosophy. It was disjointed and uncertain in its thought, derivative, yet undiscriminating even in its use of the antique heritage. German speculation, even in those apparently barren centuries before Leibnitz, was incomparably more profound. And it was rooted in the German mysticism of the fourteenth and fifteenth centuries. "Indeed mysticism was at that time the German philosophy."[76] Heimsoeth then proceeded to trace all that is most characteristic of modern thought to the inspiration furnished by Eckhart and his disciples. His exposition was limited to philosophy, but he added, in passing, the assertion that the same was true of every other intellectual field.[77]

ROMANTIC-NATIONALIST REACTION:
THE ORIGINS OF THE RENAISSANCE IN MEDIEVAL NATIONAL CULTURES

The Neo-Romantic reaction against the traditional interpretation of the Renaissance followed two main lines — religious and national — the two frequently running parallel to one another, as we have seen in the case of Heinz Heimsoeth and, *mutatis mutandis,* of Emile Gebhart and Konrad Burdach. We have now to consider those historians in whom national sentiment clearly outweighed, though it did not necessarily exclude, the Romantic feeling for medieval mysticism.

Of all the European scholars who were influenced by strongly national bias, the Italians were least likely to find grounds for objection in the traditional interpretation. Burckhardt and his successors had recognized in the most satisfactory way the priority of the Italian Renaissance; and the master himself had placed the genius of the Italian people on an equal footing with the revival of antiquity as a creative force in the making of Renaissance civilization. Most Italian historians were content to accept classicism as a national tradition, and the revival of antiquity as a return to their own national past. Yet even in Italy there were some who felt that to attribute creative power to the antique models was to do insufficient justice to the autonymous originality of the folk soul.

[75] Heimsoeth, p. 8 f.   [76] *Ibid.,* p. 11.   [77] *Ibid.,* p. 15 f.

A provocative article on "The Nature of the 'Rinascimento'" (1892)[78] by the distinguished art historian, Adolfo Venturi, furnishes an early and unusually clear example of the latter tendency. Italian art, Venturi argued, was the product of an indigenous popular development, similar in its evolution to that of the linguistic *volgare*. It had originated in ancient times in the provinces and among the lower classes and had been augmented by "the simple and most modest forms" of Christian art. "Thus, under the stratifications of Greek art in imperial Rome there lived already the popular forms, evidences of the artistic potentialities of the Latin race, which became, little by little, after long and progressive transformations, the living expression of the new social organism."[79] If this popular national art owed little to classical influence, Venturi thought it owed still less to the invading Germans or to medieval France.[80] It developed independently by a kind of Darwinian process in the Italian communes and city-states of the Middle Ages and the Renaissance. Except in Rome the antique had little effect upon Renaissance art, and even there it did not become predominant until the sixteenth century, when "servile imitation of the antique" inaugurated the period of decadence. Venturi is here in full accord with the Romantic dogma of the pernicious effect upon national culture of any alien, and particularly unchristian, influence.

> The pagan world that art recalled to life signified the submission, the oppression, not the evolution of the artistic *Rinascimento,* and inaugurated the decadence. But meanwhile, in Venice and in Emilia, the artistic tradition continued in accordance with its internal impulses and the laws of progress; and Romance art found in Titian and Correggio, as it had found in Leonardo, Michelangelo, and Raphael, the eternal forms of national beauty.[81]

This is an interpretation that, with possibly a little more emphasis on the Christian factor, might have appealed to the brothers Schlegel. Even as it stood it carried conviction to the Romantic Catholic heart of Franz Xaver Kraus, who found in Venturi a view even more to his liking than that presented by Gebhart.[82]

[78] A. Venturi, "La natura del 'Rinascimento,'" *Nuova antologia,* CXXIV (1892), 440–59.   [79] *Ibid.,* CXXIV, 442.
[80] *Ibid.,* CXXIV, 451 f.   [81] *Ibid.,* CXXIV, 457.
[82] Cf. F. X. Kraus, *Geschichte der christlichen Kunst* (Freiburg, 1896–1908), II, 3 f.

The Italian nationalist reaction, which was also shared by some northern scholars who felt Italy to be their second home, struck at only one side of the traditional interpretation. In the northern lands, the Romantic national reaction was not only more common, it might also be more comprehensive in its rejection of both sides of Burckhardt's formula: the originality of the Italian genius as well as the creative influence of the antique. Above all, it led to rejection of the traditional interpretation of the Renaissance in the North, an interpretation which, as already noted,[83] included among its essential ingredients the belief that the Renaissance began in Italy and later spread across the Alps, and that the revival of antiquity was everywhere a determinant factor.

The attack upon the classical-Italian origin of the Renaissance was led with great verve in the last years of the nineteenth century by the French art historian, Louis Courajod. His lectures at the Ecole du Louvre during the years 1887–1896 [84] were evidently a memorable experience for those who heard him and received the full force of his bellicose personality at first hand. Years later, André Michel described them with affectionate awareness of the master's temperamental peculiarities.

> Passionate and vibrant as he was [Michel wrote], he could dramatize his archeological conquests in retrospect; attribute to the actors of the historical drama, which his imagination and heart evoked, intentions, biases, ulterior motives, and hatreds which they had not always possessed; exaggerate one after another, and sometimes contradictorily, the conflicts or the reactions of elements whose strife was in his eyes the vital and poignant interest in the history of art. It was never resolved for him in pacific exchanges, in ingenious combinations; he saw only conquerors and conquered, oppressors and victims; and as certain profound instincts of the French soul, the better part of the artistic heritage of his country, seemed to him to have been oppressed, rejected, and thwarted since the ultramontaine invasion, he thought less of explaining than of avenging this tragedy. His filial piety and his bellicosity united to unmask, to flay, and to eject, if that were possible, the insolent usurper.[85]

[83] See above, p. 253.
[84] L. C. L. Courajod, *Leçons professées à l'Ecole du Louvre (1887–96)*, 3 vols. (Published posthumously with an introduction by André Michel, Paris, 1899–1903).   [85] *Ibid.*, II, viii f.

Courajod announced his major thesis in the opening lecture on "The origins of the Renaissance in France in the fourteenth and fifteenth centuries." [86] It may be summarized briefly as follows: Gothic art, the chief characteristic of which was pure idealism, declined at the end of the thirteenth century. It was the art of feudalism, the French art *par excellence*. And it died with chivalry. "It did not return from the Crusades." Under the Valois kings of the fourteenth century, a new society developed, with a strong monarchy supported by the bourgeoisie and a new aristocracy composed of varied elements. This society demanded a different, less idealistic, more practical art. "The hour of general renewal had come, and this need for a new state of things was the beginning of a vast movement, of which only the last period has been studied hitherto; it was the dawn of the sunny day that has been recognized only in its full noon and which is called the Renaissance." [87] The dominant notes of this fourteenth century French art were individualism and naturalism *à l'outrance*. Here lay the seeds of all the later developments of the European Renaissance. But this school of Northern French art, partly of Flemish origin, declined during the wars of the fifteenth century. The tradition was carried on in the Burgundian lands during that century and at the same time spread to Italy. Finally, the movement in its Italian form was brought back again to France at the turn of the century by the French invaders of Italy. The style of the mature French Renaissance resulted from the admixture of this imported style with the Burgundian, an admixture achieved by "the eclecticism, the reasoning and moderately emotional simplicity of the French genius." [88]

For Courajod, naturalism or realism was the essence of Renaissance art in all countries. And it arose first, as a spontaneous development, in France. These are his two major points. "Do not forget," he insisted, "that it was the Flemish school adopted by Northern France about the middle of the fourteenth century . . . . to which was due, I cannot repeat it too often, the general movement from which emerged the definitive style of the Renaissance, including the style of the Italian Renaissance." [89] This movement owed nothing, at least in its

[86] *Ibid.*, II, 1 ff.
[88] *Ibid.*, II, 19.
[87] *Ibid.*, II, 9.
[89] *Ibid.*, II, 12.

early stages, to the imitation of antique art. The latter was, indeed, of great service to the Italians as a counterbalance to unbridled realism, but it had in itself no generative power. It remained a dead letter until "the Italian consciousness was enlightened by the emancipating counsels of naturalism." Italian art remained "brutally Gothic," and lagged behind the French until the fifteenth century when "Italy at last entered the current of ideas which France and Flanders had brought to birth." It was only then that the authority of the classical aesthetic, moderating the naturalism imported from France, enabled the Italians, "the last-born sons of the Renaissance," to outdistance their elders.[90]

In this introductory lecture, Courajod was still relatively moderate and even generous in his treatment of the classical-Italian element in the Renaissance. But as the storms of controversy roused his fighting spirit, he lashed out in bitter invective against the savants, whom he held responsible for having invented the traditional view. His pamphlet on *The Part of Northern France in the Work of the Renaissance* (1890) [91] was a call to battle against the pedants who ascribed the beginnings of modern art entirely to the revival of antiquity and who refused to look for its origins anywhere but in Italy. Here he proclaimed once more, but with greater eloquence, that the art of the Renaissance was already born before the classicists seized it from its cradle and adopted it as their own. "It was thus," he concluded "that having been in some way stolen from its natural and legitimate family, the daughter of the Middle Ages and of the North of Europe was baptized Italian and dedicated, without having been consulted, to a more and more exclusive cult of antiquity." [92]

Traces of Courajod's influence are common in the work of French historians of art after the beginning of the twentieth century. His most consistent disciple, however, was a Belgian, Hippolyte Fierens-Gevaert, whose *Northern Renaissance* (1905) [93] was in almost all respects a reiteration and expansion of Courajod's thesis. What evidently

90 *Ibid.*, II, 22 f.
91 L. C. L. Courajod, *La part de la France du Nord dans l'oeuvre de la Renaissance* (Paris, 1890).   92 *Ibid.*, p. 33.
93 H. Fierens-Gevaert, *La Renaissance septentrionale et les premiers maîtres de Flandres* (Brussels, 1905).

appealed to the patriotic Belgian historian was the priority Courajod had assigned to the Flemish artists who worked in Paris in the fourteenth century and the importance he had also attached to the later Burgundian school. It was, at any rate this side of Courajod's argument that Fierens-Gevaert developed most fully, reinforcing it with a greater attention to painting than Courajod, the lover of sculpture, had been willing to offer. For the rest, the elements of his interpretation are the same. The art of the Renaissance was primarily naturalistic and individualistic. It was a spontaneous growth in the North, the product of northern genius, and it exerted a profound influence upon the artists of the Italian *Quattrocento,* including, among others, Jacopo della Quercia, Ghiberti, and Donatello.[94]

Reaction against the traditional interpretation of the French-Flemish Renaissance appeared most strenuously in the field of art history. The French historians of literature were more willing to grant the priority of Italy in the sphere of classical humanism, while, on the other hand, the growth of French vernacular literature had commonly been recognized, more or less, as a national evolution, influenced indeed by Italy and antiquity, but by its very nature a native product. It was for similar reasons, probably, that the English, whose Renaissance was so largely a literary phenomenon, took little part in the war against the classical-Italian tradition. Still, even in the field of literary history, there was room for revision in the direction of greater emphasis upon the continuity of national tradition from the Middle Ages to the Renaissance.

An early example of the search for medieval national origins of French Renaissance literature is furnished by the lectures on *The Origins of the French Poetry of the Renaissance,*[95] delivered at the Sorbonne in 1913–14 by Henri Chamard. Chamard's revisionism was of the mildest sort. His general conception of the French Renaissance would have satisfied his old teacher, Brunetière. He was quite prepared to admit the indispensable contribution made by Italy and antiquity. "If the Renaissance is an intellectual and moral renovation

---

[94] *Ibid.,* pp. 14 f; 83.
[95] H. Chamard, *Les origines de la poésie française de la Renaissance* (Paris, 1932).

due to the influence of antiquity better known and better comprehended, it is a fact universally admitted that this renovation was not
produced save through the action of Italy. It is from Italy that the
movement came which transformed the whole of Europe." [96] But,
while granting so much, Chamard insisted with some vehemence that
the French Renaissance had other roots as well, roots firmly planted
in native medieval culture. Among the origins of the Renaissance in
medieval France, two seemed to him most important: *l'esprit gaulois*
and *l'esprit courtois*.[97] From these sprang much of the spirit of the
French Renaissance as well as its literary forms, the latter evolving
continuously through the intermediation of the fourteenth and fifteenth century vernacular literature, in particular the *Roman de la
Rose* and the work of the *Rhétoriqueurs*.[98] Thanks to the decisive influence of these two qualities of the medieval French spirit, there was
no real break with the Middle Ages.[99] Chamard's conclusion is a
masterly statement of moderate Romanticism.

> I will be satisfied if this conclusion emerges for the reader, that the
> Renaissance, while bringing a new spirit, was not a brusque rupture
> with the Middle Ages; that the change was prepared from a distant
> time; .... that between the old France and modern France there was
> not, whatever people say, a breach of continuity; that in the incessant
> transformation which characterizes the literature of our country ....
> something continues to exist across the centuries: the vigor of the na-
> tional genius.[100]

Since the time when Chamard wrote, on the eve of the First World
War, the currents of nationalism have grown stronger. At the same
time, reverence for the classics and faith in their regenerative power
have somewhat declined, while a great expansion of medieval studies
has led to new realization of the originality and lasting influence of
medieval literature. All these factors combined have tended to re-en-
force the emphasis upon the national and medieval as opposed to the
foreign and classical sources of the French Renaissance. Of recent
years the tendency in this direction has been apparent even in the
work of American scholars who might be expected to enjoy a certain

---

[96] *Ibid.*, p. 194; cf. pp. 178 ff.   [97] *Ibid.*, pp. 41 ff; 64 ff.
[98] *Ibid.*, pp. 95 ff; 129 ff.   [99] Cf. *ibid.*, p. 85.   [100] *Ibid.*, p. 307.

immunity from the influence of French nationalism. W. F. Patterson, for example, in his huge study of *Three Centuries of French Poetic Theory* (1935), declared it his purpose "to stress constantly, as the *leit-motif* of the work, the continuity and originality of French poetic tradition throughout its history." [101]

A somewhat similar, though generally more positive, Romantic-national revisionism characterized the work of a number of German historians of literature since the beginning of the century. Here, too, there was no denial of the priority of Italy in the revival of the classics nor of the influence of Italian scholarship upon northern humanism, though its results might be deplored. But here, too, this admission was accompanied by insistence upon the continuity of national tradition and upon the medieval national origins of the spirit and forms of Renaissance literature. The latter tendency was clearly stated in Kuno Franke's studies of *Personality in German Literature before Luther* (1916), which, though written in English by a Harvard professor, was typical of much contemporary German thought. While proclaiming the dominance in modern civilization, as opposed to medieval, of "individual consciousness," Franke's whole philosophy of history was opposed to the characteristic doctrines of nineteenth century liberalism. It was founded explicit upon the Romantic theory of the *Volksgeist,* with Hegelian overtones.

> Personality and nationality [he stated in his opening remarks] are closely interrelated terms. To think of a nation as a conglomeration of isolated individuals pursuing only their private aims and their private happiness is as impossible as it is to think of an individual devoid of a share in the traditions of his folk. National life implies a kinship of aspiration in all fields of human activity . . . . National character, therefore, is both the source and the product of a great variety of individual characters, moved and directed by a common controlling spirit.[102]

On the basis of this theory, Franke sought to discover in the develop-

---

[101] W. F. Patterson, *Three Centuries of French Poetic Theory* (Ann Arbor, 1935), p. xiv. For review of this tendency, see W. L. Wiley, "The French Renaissance Gallicized: an Emphasis on National Tradition," *Studies in Philology,* XXXIV (1937), 248–59.

[102] Kuno Franke, *Personality in German Literature before Luther* (Cambridge, Mass.: Harvard University Press, 1916), p. 3.

ment of the German national character during the later Middle Ages
the source of those qualities of conscious personality or individuality
which, in common with Burckhardt, he regarded as typifying the
Renaissance. But, though his conception of the nature of the Renaissance was thus in agreement with the Burckhardtian tradition, his
whole thesis implied, as he himself noted, a rejection of Burckhardt's
theory "that in the intellectual history of the modern world, it was
the Italian Renaissance that first led to the 'discovery of man.'"[103]
Franke found the first evidence of this modern, or Renaissance, characteristic in the chivalrous poetry of the late twelfth and thirteenth century, in Walther von der Vogelweide, Hartmann von Aue, Wolfram
von Eschenbach, and Gottfried von Strassburg. These men shared
the corporate consciousness of their age and its spirit of caste, yet their
poetry also demonstrated an awareness of personal dignity and individuality, a heightening and intensifying of personal life. With the
rise of the bourgeoisie and peasantry during the two following centuries, the chivalric concept of a refined personality was democratized.
"These centuries then — the thirteenth to the sixteenth — are the true
incubation period of modern thought and feeling."[104] Franke gave
especial credit here to the German mystics, to Eckhart, Suso, and Tauler,
in the last of whom, indeed, "the conception of personality has
been heightened and deepened to such an extent that it seems impossible to heighten and deepen it further."[105] Compared with these,
Franke thought the humanists overrated, mere cold imitators of antiquity, who turned from the life and language of their own people
and split Germany into two classes of "the so-called educated and
the so-called uneducated."[106] He would except from this blanket
condemnation, however, the two heroes of German humanism, Erasmus and Ulrich von Hutten.

As the examples cited above suggest, much of the opposition to the
classical-Italian tradition sprang from Romantic national sentiment.
At the same time, however, nationalism was complicated by the racial
theories which, since the turn of the century, have increasingly influenced German thought. The historians who accepted these theories

103 *Ibid.*, p. 4.   104 *Ibid.*, p. 45.
105 *Ibid.*, p. 77.   106 *Ibid.*, p. 151 f.

tended to state the relation between the Northern and the Italian Renaissance primarily in terms of Germanic and Latin — or Aryan and Mediterranean — race. In milder form this racial distinction had been more or less commonplace in nineteenth century historiography since the time of Mme. de Staël.[107] Taine had made it one of the fundamental factors in his "scientific" analysis of the Renaissance in Italy, the Netherlands, and England.[108] But the French racialist had been content to let the peculiar genius of Latin or Teutonic race explain the form taken by the civilization of each country. He had not felt it necessary to defend the superiority of one or the other. Moreover, for both Mme. de Staël and Taine, whether they realized it or not, race was in fact a matter of language and inherited tradition rather than of biological inheritance. The newer racial doctrine, originated principally by Gobineau and Houston Stewart Chamberlain, went much further. It began and ended with the dogma of the absolute superiority of Germanic or Aryan stock, and would interpret the whole evolution of Western civilization in accordance with this biologically inherited factor.

This interpretation of history was most fully stated in Chamberlain's *Foundations of the Nineteenth Century* (1899),[109] the work that was chiefly responsible for introducing the racial theory into Germany. Organizing history on the basis of a new criterion, Chamberlain rejected the periodic divisions of Middle Ages and Renaissance, "those two absurdities . . . . by which more than anything else an understanding of our present age is not only obscured, but rendered directly impossible."[110] He would instead make a decisive turning point or beginning of a new era about the year 1200, the period that marked "the awakening of the Teutonic peoples to the consciousness of their all-important vocation as the founders of a completely new civilization and culture."[111] He thus freed the Germanic barbarians from responsibility for the darkness of the earlier Middle Ages — it was caused "by the intellectual and moral bankruptcy of the raceless chaos of human-

---

[107] See above, p. 125 f.   [108] See above, pp. 245 ff; 270 ff.
[109] H. S. Chamberlain, *Die Grundlagen des neunzehnten Jahrhunderts,* 2 vols. (Munich, 1899; I use 12th ed., Munich, 1918). Eng. trans., 2 vols. (New York, 1914).
[110] *Ibid.,* I, 8 [I, lxvii].   [111] *Ibid.,* I, 6 [I, lxv].

ity" [112] — and made the awakened Teuton the originator of all that was admirable in the following centuries. In this latter category he would include the culture of the Renaissance, but with reservations in regard to both the generative power and the cultural value of the antique element.

> It is untrue that our culture is a renaissance of the Hellenistic and the Roman: it was only after the birth of the Teutonic peoples that the renaissance of past achievements was possible and not vice versa; and this *rinascimento,* to which we are beyond doubt eternally indebted for the enriching of our life, retarded nevertheless just as much as it promoted, and threw us for a long time out of our safe course.[113]

The Renaissance, then, for what it was worth, grew out of the cultural awakening of the Teutonic race in the great thirteenth century. The concentration of genius in Italy was an awkward fact, but Chamberlain could dispose of it without difficulty — or proof. "The great Italians of the *rinascimento* were all born either in the north, saturated with Lombardic, Gothic, and Frankish blood, or in the extreme Germano-Hellenic south."[114]

The missing proofs in Chamberlain's theory of Renaissance genius were soon supplied. The master himself, while using anthropological data when it suited his purpose to do so, had at times a high disdain for the trifling exactitudes of the scientific method. "The hieroglyphics of nature's language," he objected, "are in fact not so logically mathematical, so mechanically explicable as many an investigator likes to fancy." [115] Skull measurements and such scientific minutiae were, he thought, often misleading and led only to confusion. He had rather more faith in the less exact science of physiognomy. (Dante furnished one example of "a characteristically Germanic countenance.") [116] But his ultimate appeal was to a higher authority than science. "Nothing," he declared, "is so convincing as the consciousness of the possession of race." [117] In a generation reared in reverence for science, however, it was inevitable that some of his disciples should seek to establish his theories upon more demonstrable scientific data. One of the most

112 *Ibid.,* I, 8 [I, lxvii].
114 *Ibid.,* I, 7 [I, lxvi].
116 *Ibid.,* I, 592 f [I, 538 f].

113 *Ibid.,* I, 9 [I, lxviii].
115 *Ibid.,* I, 591 [I, 537].
117 *Ibid.,* I, 320 [I, 269]; cf. I, 309 ff.

REACTION AGAINST THE TRADITION

active of these was the anthropologist Ludwig Woltmann. His monograph on *The Germans and the Italian Renaissance* (1905) [118] is of particular interest here, for in it he presented the most elaborate evidence to support Chamberlain's theory of the origin of Italian genius. Philological derivation of family and Christian names, together with studies of skull formations and physiognomy, all somewhat unconvincing to the skeptical mind, led him to the satisfactory conclusion that, on the basis of two hundred cases examined, "at least 85–90 percent of Italian geniuses must be ascribed altogether or in overwhelming degree to the Nordic race." [119]

The influence of the racial theory, usually in the form of a more diffused, less consciously dogmatic racial mysticism, is evident in the work of a considerable number of twentieth century historians. Most frequently it inspired a kind of medievalism, antagonistic to or tending to deny the originality of the Renaissance. But it might also lead to a substitution of the medieval-Germanic for the classical-Italian origins of the Renaissance in all countries, tracing its sources to the northern culture of the Middle Ages, to Gothic art, chivalrous literature, or simply to the creative energy inherent in Teutonic blood.

This form of Pan-Germanic Romanticism seems most common among historians of art. One of its most influential proponents, at any rate, was the German art historian, Carl Neumann. A thorough nationalist of the Romantic type, much given to talking in terms of "our art" and of "foreign art," Neumann believed that it was the duty of art critics to make the people more conscious of the national character of their culture, in fact to utilize the history of art for "political" ends.[120] In his youth he had imbibed at the source the Burckhardtian tradition of the Renaissance with all its connotations of classical and internationalism, but from these he turned later with decided revulsion. "Gradually," he wrote, "I freed myself from my teacher Jacob Burckhardt and his cult of the Renaissance, in proportion as I learned to

---

[118] L. Woltmann, *Die Germanen und die Renaissance in Italien* (Leipzig, 1905); republished in L. Woltmann, *Werke,* II (Leipzig, 1936).

[119] *Ibid.,* II, 182.

[120] See Neumann's very revealing autobiography in J. Jahn, ed., *Die Kunstwissenschaft der Gegenwart in Selbstdarstellungen* (Leipzig, 1924), pp. 33–75; cf. especially pp. 66 ff.

understand the distinctive character of *our* nordic world and of the
German soul and the mother force of the Middle Ages." [121] In this
later phase he resented, in common with many German Romanticists,
the idea that the culture of his country owed anything essential to foreign influence, whether classical or Italian. It was from the beginning
purely German in all its living forces. But to maintain this thesis, it
seemed necessary to deny to classical antiquity any regenerative or
creative power whatsoever. Neumann therefore proceeded, like Thode
and Courajod, to argue that the Renaissance even in Italy owed little
or nothing of its true glory to the influence of antiquity. Neumann's
approach to this problem, however, was in one respect original. In a
widely discussed article on "Byzantine Culture and Renaissance Culture" (1903),[122] he set up the following proposition: Byzantine culture
contained all through the Middle Ages those antique elements the
revival of which was supposed to have caused a Renaissance in Italy.
But Byzantium had no Renaissance. Therefore, the Renaissance in
Italy must have been caused by something else.

Neumann's argument may be summarized as follows. In the Byzantine Empire the Church was enslaved by the Roman state and the
true spirit of Christianity was sterilized by a half-antique rationalism.
But what was still more decisive, the Byzantine Empire never became
a barbarian state, and its culture, dominated by an exclusive aristocratic ruling class, was untouched by the invigorating barbarian influence. Byzantium experienced a revival of antiquity every century
or so, but no new culture resulted. In the West, on the contrary,
Christianity and barbarism operated freely and became the dominant
forces in medieval civilization. Through the combination of these two
immense forces, the Middle Ages created a new psyche. There is in
Dante a quality lacking in Homer, namely soul. In the fourteenth
century a new kind of man saw with new eyes, the eyes of the soul.[123]
Hence a new realism, which came not from antiquity but from the
ripening of medieval culture. The Christian tradition and the so-
called barbarism of the Middle Ages were the living forces of the

[121] *Ibid.*, p. 35.
[122] C. Neumann, "Byzantinische Kultur und Renaissancekultur," *Historische Zeitschrift*, XCI (1903), 215–32.
[123] *Ibid.*, XCI, 229.

Renaissance from Francis and Giotto through the realists of the fifteenth century. The revival of antiquity worked beneficially only so long as it was a mere pedagogical ingredient in the culture of the age. When it began to dominate, it became a danger to all modern civilization. The anarchical individualism inspired by pagan models was opposed in sharp antithesis to the true modern individualism introduced by the German Reformation. "The misguided Renaissance," so Neumann concluded, "and its false freedom ran counter to the true freedom which was born of the highest demands of conscience, and there can be no doubt whence this truly modern individualism drew its roots: from barbaric energy, from barbaric realism, and from the Christian Middle Ages." [124]

Despite continuous rebuttal by less chauvinistic German scholars,[125] this thesis enjoyed a considerable and lasting vogue. And that not only in Germany. Italian scholars, at any rate, whose patriotic sensibilities were wounded by the suggestion that their national Renaissance originated in "German barbarism," still felt it necessary to attack it acrimoniously and at some length two and three decades later.[126]

One further example of the Pan-Germanic or Nordic interpretation in art history may be cited in Berthold Haendecke's monograph, *The French-German-Netherlandish Influence on Italian Art from about 1200 to about 1650* (1925) [127] where it can be studied in isolated concentration. In a thoroughgoing attack upon the traditional interpretation, for which he held Burckhardt exclusively responsible, Haendecke denied the significant influence of Italy upon the art of other countries, and proclaimed in its place the unqualified dogma that all that was new and vigorous in the art of the Italian Renaissance came from beyond the

---

[124] *Ibid.*, XCI, 232.

[125] See, for example, K. Brandi, *Das Werden der Renaissance* (Göttingen, 1908), p. 27; A. Heisenberg, "Das Problem der Renaissance in Byzanz," *Historische Zeitschrift*, CXXX (1926), 339–412.

[126] Cf. G. Volpe, "La Rinascenza in Italia e le sue origini," in his *Momenti di storia italiana* (Florence, 1925), pp. 99 ff; E. Anagnine, "Il problema del Rinascimento," *Nuova rivista storica*, XVIII (1934), 556; I Siciliano, *Medio Evo e Rinascimento* (Milan, 1936), pp. 21 ff.

[127] B. Haendecke, *Der französisch-deutsch-niederländische Einfluss auf die italienische Kunst von etwa 1200 bis etwa 1650: eine entwicklungsgeschichtliche Studie* (Strassburg, 1925).

Alps. The North gave Italy Gothic art in the twelfth and thirteenth centuries with all its superior moral sense and its more intense innerness. "Law, life, personality, pure, strong humanity — these lay hidden in the Gothic of that age. And these greatest forces of art were given by the lands on this side of the Alps, by France and Germany, to an Italy oppressed by dessicated tradition." [128] The spiritual and religious evolution of Italy in the following centuries sprang directly from the Gothic spirit. "Gothic signified for Italy the renewal of life and the affirmation of life." [129] France set the standard of literature and social manners for Italy in the fourteenth century, but it was in art that the influence of the northern masters was clearest. "Northlandish sense of reality, nature, and a little 'antique' show themselves in the work of Brunelleschi, Ghiberti, and Donatello." [130] Even Michelangelo may be considered "the last continuer of this Northlandish-Gothic tendency." [131] This all-embracing northern influence was also evident in painting, as well as in architecture and sculpture.

For Haendecke, all northern art, from whatever country it came, was Germanic. And that it could take root and grow in the alien soil of Italy was made possible, he thought, by the fact that the upper classes of Italy were descended from Germanic stock. "This inner understanding of the spirit from which the northlandish art was drawn must have aided extraordinarily the reception of the French-Netherlandish-Rhenish painting." [132] In his conclusion, a magnificent example of dogmatic statement, but too long for full quotation here, Haendecke returned again to the theme of racial kinship.

As the general result of our research we may establish: the Northlandish art had awakened the figurative art of Italy, which was, on the one hand, frozen into an essential sterility and, on the other, strongly orientalized, to new life, to the life-loving, forceful Gothic, filled with inner energy. Thereby there grew anew the close connection with the northern culture-folk with whom the Italians, as, Aryans, were blood related.[133]

Haendecke does not make the point, but apparently the supply of Germanic blood in Italy was insufficient in quantity to have furnished the Italians themselves with the creative force of originality.

[128] *Ibid.*, p. 2.   [129] *Ibid.*, p. 9.   [130] *Ibid.*, p. 20.
[131] *Ibid.*, p. 22.   [132] *Ibid.*, p. 25.   [133] *Ibid.*, p. 66 f.

CHAPTER ELEVEN

The Revolt of the Medievalists. The Renaissance
Interpreted as Continuation
of the Middle Ages

OF THE TWO COMPLEMENTARY CURRENTS of reaction against the Burckhardtian tradition, both tending to obliterate the line of demarcation between the Middle Ages and the Renaissance, that which tended to shift the center of interest to the Middle Ages and to view the Renaissance as largely a continuation, or even decline, of medieval culture has of late been much the stronger and more scholarly.[1] The most potent solvent of Burckhardt's synthesis has been the immense increase in detailed research into the cultural history of both periods, but particularly of the Middle Ages. Discovery of new evidence has led many scholars to redress the balance between the two ages by demonstrating the existence in the medieval period of elements of culture traditionally regarded as having originated in the Renaissance or, conversely, by emphasizing those medieval features of Renaissance civilization that were slighted or glossed over in Burckhardt's picture. Despite the generally scholarly character of this tendency, however, it too has been inspired at times by motives of religious or national sentiment or by aesthetic or intellectual predilection.

[1] For discussion of the recent interpretations of the Renaissance in relation to the Middle Ages, see especially I. Siciliano, *Medio Evo e Rinascimento* (Milan, 1936).

The Revolt of the Medievalists

Few aspects of twentieth century historical research are more striking than the renewed interest in the Middle Ages. Many factors undoubtedly played their part in arousing this new enthusiasm for medieval studies. But in the main it was probably no more than the natural
result of the recent development of cultural and intellectual history, together with the intensive methods of research and the improved facili-
ties characteristic of this age. The trained academic historian needed
no Romantic nostalgia to turn his attention to the Middle Ages. For,
even after a century of learned study and documentary research devoted to the political and institutional side of medieval history, the
cultural and intellectual history of the Middle Ages was still almost a
virgin field. Certainly there were few other periods which presented
so many tempting opportunities to bring new material to light or to
disprove commonly accepted notions. The new medievalists were almost all conscious revisionists. This growth of interest in medieval
history has been particularly marked in the United States, where, with
little incentive from either religious or national romanticism, medieval
studies have flourished with a luxuriance that seems at times to scholars in other fields almost excessive. This is rather difficult to explain
except by the fact that America's great age of academic scholarship
coincided with the rising tide of scholarly medievalism and reaction
against the Renaissance. It may be, too, that Americans have their
own peculiar form of romanticism: the reverence of a young nation
for anything that is old.

The result of the new tendency, at any rate, has been a "rehabilitation of the Middle Ages," comparable in enthusiasm to that achieved
by the Romantic historians of the early nineteenth century, though
very different in spirit and effect. The Romanticists did nothing to
break down the contrast between the Middle Ages and the Renaissance. On the contrary, they made it sharper than ever. Their Middle
Ages were the antithesis of the Renaissance, pious and otherworldly,
corporate rather than individualistic, irrational in thought and unclassical in forms of expression, idyllic and chivalrous in emotion.
Their unilateral view had, in fact, warped the generally accepted pic-

ture of the Middle Ages as much as had the exclusive classicism of the humanists that of the Renaissance. Still persisting today, their conception of medieval culture goes far to explain the appeal of the Middle Ages to some twentieth century romanticists. The major tendency of the new school of medieval scholars, however, was on the contrary to rectify the Romantic picture of the Middle Ages in ways that lessened or obliterated the contrast with the Renaissance. At the same time, they were more consciously concerned with defending the Middle Ages against the unjust charges brought against it for centuries by the long series of humanist, Protestant, and rationalist historians, most of whom had laid themselves open to attack by their obvious bias or by equally obvious ignorance. The result has been a constant stream of books, monographs, and articles designed to show that there was more of this or that "unmedieval" characteristic to be found in medieval civilization than had commonly been supposed. Scholarly medievalists have also protested strongly against the forcing of all medieval civilization into one inclusive category, as both the Romanticists and their opponents had too often done.[2]

It is clearly impossible to attempt here an adequate treatment of the great mass of recent literature on the Middle Ages. We shall have to be satisfied with noting a few typical examples which demonstrate the various trends of revision.

One of the oldest and most firmly rooted opinions regarding the Middle Ages was that medieval men produced neither secular learning nor good Latin literature and that they had little or no real knowledge of or feeling for the classics. Charles Homer Haskins decisively rejected this judgment in one of the most influential works of recent medieval historiography, *The Renaissance of the Twelfth Century* (1927), which he later reinforced with his learned *Studies in Medieval Culture* (1929). A great teacher as well as a profound scholar, Haskins was personally responsible for a good deal of the remarkable popularity of medieval studies in the United States during the past generation. His *Renaissance of the Twelfth Century,* limited though it was to Latin

---

[2] See, for example, W. Stammler, "Ideenwandel in der Sprache und Literatur des deutschen Mittelalters," *Deutsche Vierteljahrsschrift für Literaturwissenschaft und Geistesgeschichte,* II (1924), 753 f.

literature and learning, was the nearest approach to a general intellectual history of the High Middle Ages written during this age of monographic study. It was one of the most widely read works in the field — at least every scholar had read the title — and its impact upon historical thought was proportionately great.

The idea of a medieval Renaissance, or of several such,[3] was by no means new. Most often, however, the phenomenon had been treated as something exceptional, as one or more isolated rays of light in the medieval gloom, foreshadowing the true Renaissance. Or it had been studied in only one limited aspect. It was significant that Haskins treated his subject as a broad cultural movement; that he related it to contemporary economic and political developments, as well as to those in the allied fields of vernacular literature and art; and, above all, that he regarded the Renaissance of the Twelfth Century as something characteristically medieval. Even the Goliardic verses, "so 'unmedieval,' so contrary to the conventional view of the Middle Ages which long prevailed," were for him true products of their age rather than of "some isolated genius, some sport of nature born out of due time into an age not his own."[4]

On the sensitive subject of the relation of the medieval to the Italian Renaissance, Haskins was soberly judicious. He made no excessive claims for his favorite period, and apparently he felt no urge to depreciate unduly the achievement of the later age. "There was," he granted, "an Italian Renaissance, whatever we choose to call it."[5] He thought of the two Renaissances as analogous movements, each "a revival of ancient learning and of ancient art, but still more an age of new life and new knowledge which carry us well beyond the ancients."[6] Nevertheless, the whole work was clearly inspired by a conscious, if moderate, revisionism. The Preface states his thesis:

> The title of this book will appear to many to contain a flagrant contradiction. A renaissance in the twelfth century! Do not the Middle

---

[3] See, for example, E. Patzelt, *Die karolingische Renaissance: Beiträge zur Geschichte der Kultur des frühen Mittelalters* (Vienna, 1924) and H. Naumann, *Karolingische und Ottonische Renaissance* (Frankfurt, 1926).

[4] C. H. Haskins, *The Renaissance of the Twelfth Century*. Cambridge, Mass.: Harvard University Press, 1927, p. 178.

[5] *Ibid.*, p. 5.   [6] *Ibid.*, p. 190.

Ages, that epoch of ignorance, stagnation, and gloom, stand in the sharpest contrast to the light and progress and freedom of the Italian Renaissance which followed? How could there be a renaissance in the Middle Ages . . . .? The answer is that the continuity of history rejects such sharp and violent contrasts between successive periods, and that modern research shows us the Middle Ages less dark and less static, the Renaissance less bright and less sudden, than was once supposed.

A statement with which few Renaissance historians would now disagree. Or again:

But — this much we grant — the great Renaissance was not so unique or so decisive as has been supposed. The contrast of culture was not nearly so sharp as it seemed to the humanists and their modern followers, while within the Middle Ages there were intellectual revivals whose influence was not lost to succeeding times, and which partook of the same character as the better known movement of the fifteenth century.[7]

At about the same time that Haskins was writing, two German scholars, Friedrich von Bezold in a study of *The Continued Life of the Antique Gods in Medieval Humanism* (1922) [8] and Fedor Schneider in his *Rome and the Idea of Rome in the Middle Ages* (1926),[9] presented impressive evidence of the continuity of classical tradition through the medieval period. Both works were concerned with very specialized aspects of medieval culture, but in treating the great revival of the eleventh and twelfth centuries, Bezold at least went beyond the confines of his subject to make a general analysis of the *Weltanschauung* of medieval humanism. It was a purely clerical humanism, yet in strong opposition to the contemporary growth of aescetic idealism. Bezold saw in it a new awareness of the world. It was the struggle for "the right to beauty" against the claims of extreme spiritualism, and it led naturally to a deeper understanding of the classical tradition. "As man began to see the nature about him and the world of man differently, so at the same time his ear for the tone of the past was sharpened, and

---

[7] *Ibid.*, p. 5 f.

[8] F. von Bezold, *Das Fortleben der antiken Götter im mittelalterlichen Humanismus* (Bonn, 1922).

[9] F. Schneider, *Rom und Romgedanke im Mittelalter* (Munich, 1926).

he hoped to find more in it than hitherto."[10] Some of the eleventh
century Latin verse, he thought, showed a "truly Renaissance spirit."[11]
Nevertheless, Bezold, like Haskins, considered this clerical humanism
a purely medieval phenomenon, which declined in the thirteenth century and had no direct connection with the Italian humanism of the
two following centuries.[12] The latter was the product of the cities and
the bourgeoisie. Bezold's assertion of the extent of medieval humanism
was carefully qualified. He still regarded the Renaissance as an important new development in European culture. But his research had
obviously modified his ideas so that he would no longer characterize
the Renaissance, as he had done some thirty odd years earlier, as "that
new, brilliant culture, whose essential core was the emancipation of
mankind from the weight of strictly ecclesiastical *Weltanschauung.*"[13]

There was somewhat less moderation in the claims made for medieval humanism by scholars whose predilection for the Middle Ages
was reinforced by religious or national interest. Catholic historians, in
particular, were pleased to discover that the Age of Faith had also
been an age of classical scholarship and secular enlightenment. In a
work more conspicuous for pious zeal than for objective scholarship,
James J. Walsh claimed these, as well as much else that had been more
commonly attributed to the modern age, for "the thirteenth the greatest
of centuries."[14] One need scarcely note the exaggerated assertions of
such forthright apologists as Belloc and Chesterton, whom one recent
Catholic scholar has accused of "using the Middle Ages as a stalking
horse behind which they are shooting the arrows of their wit at modern society."[15] But even the recent neo-Thomists, learned and
thoughtful though they are, frequently make claims for medieval humanism that may seem to the non-Catholic immoderate. Jacques
Maritain's identification of "true humanism" with the scholastic age
can be justified only by his special usage of the term.[16] And there is

10 Bezold, p. 20.   11 *Ibid.,* p. 39.
12 *Ibid.,* p. 88; cf. Haskins, p. 98 f.
13 F. von Bezold, *Geschichte der deutschen Reformation* (Berlin, 1890), p. 16.
14 J. J. Walsh, *The Thirteenth the Greatest of Centuries* (New York, 1907).
15 W. J. Grace, "Jacques Maritain and Modern Catholic Historical Scholarship,"
Journal of the History of Ideas, V (1944), 435.
16 J. Maritain, *True Humanism* (revised translation from the Spanish, New York,
1938). Cf. criticism by G. G. Coulton, "The Historical Background of Maritain's
Humanism," *Journal of the History of Ideas,* V (1944), 415–33.

at least a shift from the customary focus implied in Etienne Gilson's assertion that the scholastics were closer to the living tradition of antique thought than were the men of the Renaissance;[17] that, in short, the dissemination of Aristotle's philosophy was "a greater contribution to the spread of the ideas of antiquity than the imitation of a few verses of Homer or Sophocles."[18] Other Catholic scholars have found a more truly classical humanism in the earlier, less scholastic period. Dom David Knowles saw in the period between 1050 and 1150 a "deep and sympathetic humanism, which anticipated to an extraordinary degree much that is considered typical of the age of the Medici and of Erasmus;" but he also felt that there was thereafter "a very real change and declension . . . . which helped to make the culture of the thirteenth century, for all its intense speculative force and abiding power, less universal, less appealing, and, in a word, less humane than what had gone before."[19] In either case the Church's great age was rescued from the charge of being unclassical.

Like the Catholic scholars of all countries, northern Europeans of strongly national bias have frequently tended to overstate the achievements of their own medieval culture in relation to the Italian Renaissance. The motivation and emphasis may be different, but the results are much the same. The indefatigable Edmond Faral devoted volume after volume to the general thesis that Latin humanism sprang from the soil of France, that it inspired all medieval French literature — an opinion which would have shocked the Romantic critics — and finally, that it not only preceded but was little surpassed by the later humanism which spread from Italy. Of the twelfth century he wrote: "Rarely have the Latin classics found more passionate admirers, more zealous commentators, more enthusiastic disciples."[20] And again: "Everything that the sixteenth century possessed of Latin antiquity, except for two or three texts, the twelfth century had possessed, had medi-

---

[17] Cf. E. Gilson, "Le Moyen Age et le naturalisme antique," *Archives d'histoire doctrinale et littéraire du Moyen Age,* VII (1932), 5–37.
[18] E. Gilson, "Humanisme médiévale et Renaissance," in his *Les idées et les lettres* (Paris, 1932), p. 190.
[19] D. Knowles, "The Humanism of the Twelfth Century," *Studies: An Irish Quarterly Review,* XXX (1941), 44.
[20] E. Faral, *Recherches sur les sources latines des contes et romans courtois du Moyen Age* (Paris, 1913), p. 398.

tated." [21] "So that," he concluded elsewhere, "one of the most important factors of the Italian Renaissance, the antique influence, appeared as a gift from the people of the North, and the erudite and literary tradition . . . . resulted in making Italy the debtor of French culture for its first contact with Roman letters." [22]

The discovery of medieval humanism carried with it a necessary revision of the traditional belief that the medieval *Weltanschauung,* at least as reflected in clerical literature, was entirely otherworldly and ascetic.[23] Both Haskins and Bezold noted the existence of strong secular interests in the clerical writers of the twelfth century, as Gilson did in the schoolmen of the thirteenth, and Helen Waddell furnished examples, infinite in number and variety, of lyric worldliness in medieval Latin literature in her charming study of *The Wandering Scholars* (1927). They made it clear that the world and man had been discovered long before the Italian Renaissance. This current in medieval humanism has also received special study in several articles and monographs, notably Wilhelm Ganzenmüller's studies of the sentimental feeling for nature in medieval literature,[24] and Hennig Brinkmann's broadly conceived article on "The Secular Tone in the Middle Ages." [25] A disciple of Dilthey's school of *Geistes-*

---

21 E. Faral, *L'orientation actuelle des études relatives au latin médiéval* (Paris, 1923), p. 15.

22 E. Faral, *La littérature latine du Moyen Age* (Paris, 1925), p. 35.

23 This conception of medieval culture, long generally accepted, was most fully worked out in H. von Eicken, *Geschichte und System der mittelalterlichen Weltanschauung* (Stuttgart, 1887).

24 W. Ganzenmüller, *Das Naturgefühl im Mittelalter* (Leipzig, 1914); "Die empfindsame Naturbetrachtung im Mittelalter," *Archiv für Kulturgeschichte,* XII (1916), 195–228. In the latter he concludes: "What is already becoming ever clearer in other spheres appears here also: that the heritage of antiquity taken over by the Middle Ages was richer than was originally believed, and that in general where new and peculiar experience sought expression, it was forced to utilize the antique forms. That was true not only for the Church Fathers and the Carolingian court poets, but also for the Vaganti and the troubadours" (p. 227). For similar emphasis on the Latin inspiration of medieval courtly literature see Faral, *passim* and H. Brinkmann, *Entstehungsgeschichte des Minnesangs* (Halle, 1926).

25 H. Brinkmann, "Diesseitsstimmung im Mittelalter," *Deutsche Vierteljahrsschrift für Literaturwissenschaft und Geistesgeschichte,* II (1924), 721–52; see also his *Geschichte der lateinischen Liebesdichtung* (Halle, 1925); and K. Hampe, "Der Kulturwandel um die Mitte des zwölften Jahrhunderts," *Archiv für Kulturgeschichte,* XXI (1930–31), 129–50.

geschichte Brinkmann was concerned with men's subjective attitude toward the world rather than with the external forms of culture. And, like Dilthey, he sought to establish types of *Weltanschauung*. But, he insisted, the historian must also note those types of mind that are in the minority and that are too frequently overlooked in the illusory search for a common ground-tone in the culture of an age.[26] He would grant that the transcendental, the ascetic, and idealist element was preponderant in the twelfth century, but there was also a strongly opposing tendency, growing in force since the beginning of the eleventh century, of worldliness and immanence. The latter, for which he found evidence for the most part in clerical Latin poetry, had all the commonly recognized traits of Renaissance humanism: consciousness of freedom and independence, individualism, rebellion against authority, a sharp sense of actuality and leaning toward satire, cultivation of sensual pleasure, a rising cult of beauty, new appreciation of nature, and, finally, a closer and more understanding relation to antiquity.

> The tendency in the attitude of the new type of man is clear. He reacts against the spiritualizing of man since late antiquity. The sense of being lies for him not behind things; he seeks it in life itself. He rejects all transcendence in favor of immanence of values. This revaluation brings him back closer to the antique. The ground for the influence of antiquity is prepared.[27]

Meanwhile, the historians of science were discovering in the works of the schoolmen similar indications of an interest in the present world as well as in antique secular knowledge. Pierre Duhem was here the great pioneer. His massive study of classical and medieval cosmology, *The System of the World from Plato to Copernicus* (1913–17) [28] was never completed, but the five volumes published remain an impressive monument to the scientific investigation and speculation of medieval thinkers. There is a distinct note of patriotic as well as sectarian pride in Duhem's account of the scientific achievements of the Parisian school, both here and in his earlier *Studies on Leonardo da Vinci*

---

[26] Brinkmann, "Diesseitsstimmung," *Deutsche Vierteljahrsschrift*, II, 727.
[27] *Ibid.*, II, 744.
[28] P. Duhem, *Le système du monde. Histoire des doctrines cosmologiques de Platon à Copernic*, 5 vols. (Paris, 1913–17).

(1906–13),[29] where he asserted that the work of Leonardo and Galileo was simply a continuation of the Parisian Occamism of the fourteenth century. Since Duhem the history of medieval science owes most to American scholarship. Haskins made important contributions, though fragmentary and limited to the twelfth century, in his *Studies in the History of Medieval Science* (1924). By far the most important works in the field, however, are the two monumental general histories of medieval science by Lynn Thorndike [30] and George Sarton.[31] Both of these, like Duhem, tended to see no solution of continuity between scholastic science and that of the Renaissance. Both, in fact, regarded the Renaissance as a period of decline, at least in the field of their special interest. Further comment on their ideas may, therefore, be reserved for the concluding section of this chapter.

An altogether new emphasis on the rational character of scholastic philosophy accompanied this rediscovery of the scholastic interest in nature and in antique naturalism. Here there is a notable departure indeed from a venerable tradition. Protestants from Melanchthon to Hegel, eighteenth century rationalists, and nineteenth century liberals like Michelet were all in agreement on one point: that scholasticism was synonymous with ignorance, superstition, and profound irrationality. Even the Romanticists, in their wistful rediscovery of the Middle Ages, generally ignored scholastic philosophy while restating in different terms the traditional conception of the irrational quality of medieval thought. For all their aesthetic leaning toward Catholicism, the Romanticists were in fact not Catholic in the philosophical sense.[32] The prevailing view thus remained, as Etienne Gilson has summarized it, that "medieval philosophy signified, as though by definition, rou-

29 P. Duhem, *Etudes sur Leonard de Vinci: ceux qu'il a lus et ceux qui l'ont lu,* 3 séries (Paris, 1906–13). See especially the preface to Série III. For critical discussion of Duhem's thesis and the general question of the relation of Renaissance to medieval science, see D. B. Durand and H. Baron, "Tradition and Innovation in the Fifteenth Century," *Journal of the History of Ideas,* IV (1943), 1–49.

30 L. Thorndike, *A History of Magic and Experimental Science,* 6 vols. (New York, 1923–41).

31 G. Sarton, *Introduction to the History of Science,* 2 vols. (Washington, 1927–31).

32 Cf. A. von Martin, "Das Wesen der romantischen Religiosität," *Deutsche Vierteljahrsschrift für Literaturwissenschaft und Geistesgeschichte,* II (1924), 367–417.

tine, prejudice, abstract dialectic, and sterile religious obscurantism." [33] Rectification of this prejudiced interpretation first grew out of the neo-Thomist revival in the late nineteenth century. As that movement gained momentum in the present century the labors of a group of distinguished historians of philosophy have presented the thought of the Middle Ages in a light very different from that cast by the Romantic yearning for a simple, poetic, and unquestioning faith. In the neo-Thomist feeling for the Middle Ages there is, indeed, a distinct inversion of the Romantic medievalism. The nostalgia is there and also the search for spiritual values and the revulsion against the materialistic trends in contemporaneous civilization. But what offends twentieth century Catholic philosophers in the culture of their own day is not dependence on reason, but rather the irrationality of modern mass movements, the moral and spiritual uncertainty resulting from the bankruptcy of modern philosophy and the declining force of religious authority. What they seek in the Middle Ages is reason and order and a rational scheme of human behavior, which is not at all what early nineteenth century Romanticists were looking for in their flight from the complacent rationalism of the preceding generation. By emphasizing the schoolmen's interest in the rationalization of the physical universe and of life in this world, the neo-Thomists have claimed for medieval thought the rational attitude toward the physical and social sciences, which has been regarded as the outstanding achievement of the modern age, with the added advantage of a moral and spiritual authority founded upon revelation. For the neo-Thomist the scholastic age has thus become the age of "true humanism," the real age of reason.

Full acceptance of the neo-Thomist thesis, as presented by Jacques Maritain and others, is difficult if not impossible for non-Catholics, but the interpretation of scholastic philosophy as a closely reasoned, rational system has gained almost universal recognition among scholars of every faith. Of the recent Catholic historians who have helped to achieve this result, Etienne Gilson has been the most widely influential. Combining historical research with philosophical analysis in volume after volume, he has argued that medieval philosophy, as it reached its

[33] E. Gilson, *La philosophie au Moyen Age* (Paris, 1922), p. 6.

highest development in Thomism, was a reasoned philosophy which continued and added to the natural philosophy of the Greeks while harmonizing it with Christian revelation, and that in doing so it made an original and important contribution to philosophical thought. The historian who does not share Gilson's Catholic faith nor his predilection for scholastic speculation may suspect that some special pleading lies concealed beneath his persuasive dialectic and vast erudition, but he could find little to quarrel with in Gilson's thesis as thus stated, and he would be forced to go at least part way with him in the remarks with which he concluded his *Philosophy in the Middle Ages* (1922):

> Nothing is more false than to consider the medieval philosophy as an episode, which found in itself its own conclusion and which one may pass over in silence when one retraces the history of ideas . . . . It is necessary, then, to relegate to the domain of legend the history of a Renaissance of thought succeeding to centuries of sleep, of obscurity, and error. Modern philosophy did not have to undertake the struggle to establish the rights of reason against the Middle Ages; it was, on the contrary, the Middle Ages that established them for it, and the very manner in which the seventeenth century imagined that it was abolishing the work of preceding centuries did nothing more than continue it.[34]

One might add here that even the Renaissance Platonists' claims to philosophical originality have been attacked by Clemens Bäumker, who maintained that practically all their ideas are to be found in their scholastic predecessors.[35]

As one after another of the traditional elements of the Renaissance were claimed for the Middle Ages, there seemed little left that the latter could call its own. But in as much as medieval Latin culture was admittedly clerical, could not the Renaissance at least maintain its claim to something new in the rise of lay learning? To this James Westfall Thompson answered in a detailed study of *The Literacy of the Laity in the Middle Ages* (1939). While modifying his conclusions

---

[34] *Ibid.*, p. 311 f. For further development of his thesis, see E. Gilson, *The Spirit of Medieval Philosophy* (New York, 1936); and *Reason and Revelation in the Middle Ages* (New York, 1938).

[35] C. Bäumker, *Der Platonismus im Mittelalter* (Munich, 1916); and *Mittelalter und Renaissance. Platonismus* (Munich, 1917).

with careful qualifications, Thompson felt that he had accumulated sufficient evidence to demonstrate the thesis that "the common and widely accepted belief that in the Middle Ages no one not a cleric could read or write Latin is a gross exaggeration."[36]

Finally, even that quality of individualism which formed the central core of Burckhardt's conception of the Renaissance has been included in the medieval *Anschluss*. However, as Norman Nelson has pointed out in an acutely discriminating article,[37] most of the discoveries of individualism in the Middle Ages have resulted from the isolation of one or another of the elements of the concept which Burckhardt had united in a coherent synthesis, or simply from using the term in a sense quite different. As an example of the latter tendency, Nelson cites the argument of some Catholic medievalists that scholastic philosophy recognized the ultimate value of the individual soul, since it is the individual soul that is to be saved, and each soul is different from all others, and he adds: "That is what M. de Wulf means by individualism in the Middle Ages, but we can see how little that implies of Burckhardt's Renaissance individualism."[38] We have already noted examples of the tendency to isolate one aspect of individualism in Thode's identification of Franciscan subjectivism with individualism and in Kuno Franke's application of the term to the consciousness of personality which he found in the Minnesingers and the German mystics.[39] We might add one further example. In his *World History of the Modern Age* (1901), Dietrich Schäfer protested strongly against the idea, which he said had become commonplace since Burckhardt, that "the spiritual movement with the French name which spread from Italy signified the birth hour of individuality."[40] On the contrary, he insisted, in words that ring rather strangely in the ears of this post-Nazi generation, "the characteristic trait of medieval spiritual tendency is the pure German principle of individual worth, of the rights of the individual and the minority against the community and the majority."[41]

[36] J. W. Thompson, *The Literacy of the Laity in the Middle Ages* (Berkeley, 1939), p. 1.

[37] N. Nelson, "Individualism as a Criterion of the Renaissance," *The Journal of English and Germanic Philology*, XXXII (1933), 316–34.

[38] *Ibid.*, XXXII, 319.   [39] See above, pp. 299; 322.

[40] D. Schäfer, *Weltgeschichte der Neuzeit* (2nd ed. Berlin, 1907), I, 13.

[41] *Ibid.*, I, 15.

MEDIEVAL ELEMENTS IN THE LITERATURE AND *Weltanschauung*
OF THE RENAISSANCE

After those historians whom Huizinga called "the root-stretchers of
the Renaissance" [42] had thrust the origins of the Renaissance back into
the thirteenth century, and after the medievalists in their zeal to revise
the balance between the two ages had claimed the salient traits of the
Renaissance for the Middle Ages proper, the next step in the process
of destroying the antithetical conception of the two periods was to discover medieval characteristics in the Renaissance. This progression
was, however, more logical than chronological, as all three stages in
the process took place more or less simultaneously and with interacting
effect. What we have to consider here is essentially the reverse of the
tendency discussed in the preceding chapter; it is therefore more closely
related to it than to the rehabilitation of the Middle Ages, which was
an independent phenomenon related to the interpretation of the
Renaissance only by implication.

Both those historians who would have the Renaissance begin earlier
and those who would have the Middle Ages end later tended to emphasize particularly the religious tone of the traditionally "pagan"
Renaissance and to minimize the revolutionary effect of the revival
of classical antiquity upon life, letters, and art. Just at the time when
Henry Thode was tracing the origins of Renaissance culture to the
religious mysticism of the thirteenth century, Ludwig von Pastor asserted the partial continuation of medieval religious feeling through
the age of humanism in the Introduction to the first volume of his
immense *History of the Popes from the Close of the Middle Ages*
(1886–1933).[43] Pastor's view of the Renaissance in general and of
humanism in particular was founded largely upon Burckhardt and
Voigt. He could not reject entirely the prevailing opinion of his day
that the Italian humanists were, on the whole, more pagan than Christian. Yet, at the same time, he was not prepared to admit that classical
humanism, which he valued highly, was essentially antagonistic to his

---

[42] J. Huizinga, *Wege der Kulturgeschichte* (Munich, 1930), p. 109.
[43] L. von Pastor, *Geschichte der Päpste seit dem Ausgang des Mittelalters*,
16 vols. (Freiburg i/B, 1886–1933). Eng. trans. (London, 1899–1928).

faith, nor that the Church, which had also valued it, had erred in doing so. He therefore made a distinction between "two conflicting currents" in the stream of Renaissance culture, which were "discernible more or less in its gifted founders, Petrarch and Boccaccio." [44] One current, which he called the true Renaissance, was entirely in harmony with the Church and its teaching. He defined it as "the study of the past in a thoroughly Christian spirit." It "was in itself a legitimate intellectual movement, fruitful in fresh results alike for secular and spiritual science." [45] As such it could not but be approved from the ecclesiastical point of view. In short, "so long as the absolute truth of Christianity was the ground from which antiquity was apprehended, the Renaissance could only be of service to the Church." [46] This had been the attitude of the Church in general since the early Fathers. The promotion of classical studies by the Church of the Renaissance, therefore, "involved no breach with the Middle Ages as a whole and far less with Christian antiquity." [47]

At the same time Pastor admitted regretfully that the age of the Renaissance was "a melancholy period of universal corruption and torpor in the life of the Church," marked by a weakening of papal authority, by worldliness of the clergy, and by decline of scholastic theology and philosophy. Hence, "the dangerous elements in ancient literature were presented to an unhealthy generation." [48] And the result was a false or heathen Renaissance which ran contemporaneously with, but also in opposition to, the true or Christian Renaissance. Calling the roll of the leading humanists, Pastor carefully sorted out the sheep from the goats. Among the latter, Valla held the first rank, followed by Beccadelli, Poggio, Filelfo, Aeneas Sylvius, Carlo Marsuppini, and others.[49] On the other side were, among others, Manetti, Traversari, Leonardo Bruni, Francesco Barbaro, Matteo Vegio, Vittorino, and Nicholas V.[50] Outside the humanist circle there were also alarming symptoms of moral and religious decay, but there were as well heartening evidences of the continued vitality of religious feeling. Italy in this age had its saints and *beati* as well as its pagan devotees of the false Renaissance.

[44] *Ibid.*, I (2nd ed. Freiburg i/B.), 1 [I, 1]; cf. I, 12.
[45] *Ibid.*, I, 6 [I, 6].   [46] *Ibid.*, I, 7 [I, 7].   [47] *Ibid.*, I, 11 [I, 12].
[48] *Ibid.*, I, 12 [I, 12].   [49] *Ibid.*, I, 12 ff.   [50] *Ibid.*, I, 36 ff.

Recognition of the existence of a strong religious element in the culture of Renaissance Italy became more common with the growing tendency to revise the Burckhardtian tradition. Yet, two decades after the publication of Pastor's first volume, Charles Dejob found it still the prevailing opinion among historians that Italian society of that age was generally skeptical or irreligious. In a vigorously stated and well documented study of *Religious Faith in Italy in the Fourteenth Century* (1906),[51] he argued against this misconception, asserting that medieval religion continued without diminution in Italy through the fourteenth century and well into the fifteenth. During this whole period, which was commonly included in the Renaissance, religious faith, he insisted, was both widespread and profound, "its action on conduct, on the way of thinking of individuals, of society, and of governments was very strong."[52] Why then, he asked, was this obvious fact so generally denied? His answer to that historiographical problem, though somewhat unilateral, is sufficiently astute to deserve quotation in full.

No matter how hard we try, we can never arrive at absolute impartiality. We may do justice to the opponents of our beliefs because we feel that this courteous concession is not compromising; it hurts us nevertheless to recognize that a principle which we do not like has reigned for a long period without serious opposition and especially that it has reigned over superior men. A Protestant, a free thinker, a lover of natural law finds it indeed diffiicult not to antedate the appearance of skepticism in the modern world . . . . He will abandon to Catholicism the centuries of ignorance and even appreciate the faith which bears its excuse in its lack of enlightenment; but he will have it that the dawn of the Renaissance opened all eyes that were not myopic. It is curious to see how Burckhardt, who refused all faith to the Italian Renaissance, but who knew many facts from which, less biased, he might have drawn a different result, so often exercises ingenuity to ecape the true conclusion, so often contradicts himself.[53]

---

[51] C. Dejob, *La foi religieuse en Italie au quatorzième siècle* (Paris, 1906).
[52] *Ibid.*, p. 1; cf. pp. 11; 393.
[53] *Ibid.*, p. 14 f. As a concrete example of the tendency he was discussing, Dejob added that when Voigt found Petrarch talking like a Christian he put it down to hypocrisy, thus defending Petrarch's intelligence at the expense of his character.

On the whole a penetrating analysis of historiographical motives, but one that, applied to a devout Catholic, might well work in the opposite direction in relation to the Renaissance.

Consciously revisionist though Dejob's interpretation of the Renaissance was, it was so only in respect to the traditional chronology. Like Pastor, he made a distinction, though his line of demarcation was horizontal rather than vertical. He thought Burckhardt's error lay in applying to three centuries what became true only toward 1500, with the result that anything in the whole period that did not fit into his picture Burckhardt dismissed as mere individual singularity. Admitting the irreligious character of the Renaissance proper, Dejob would thus have the Middle Ages continue far into the *Quattrocento*. His reasoning was, for a professor at the Sorbonne, in one respect rather curious. He devoted a considerable section of the book (pages 32 to 108) to the argument that fourteenth century Italian society was still too generally "naïve," not yet intellectually mature enough for skepticism.[54] True of Dante, Petrarch, and Boccaccio, this was still more true of lesser writers like the Villani, who, despite the practical experience with affairs which might have matured them, "remained by the turn of their thought men of the Middle Ages."[55] Certainly not an argument that would appeal to many Catholic philosophers, much as they might welcome Dejob's conclusions.

That Renaissance Italy was deeply religious has remained a favorite theme among recent Catholic writers, though by no means limited to them. An outstanding example of this tendency may be found in Vladimiro Zabughin's fervently Catholic *History of the Christian Renaissance in Italy* (1924).[56] Most of the historians who have stressed the Christian piety of the age have regarded it as evidence of the continuation of medieval culture, in short as sufficient reason for annexing the Italian Renaissance in whole or in part to the Middle Ages. And certainly the depiction of the Renaissance as a religious age does lessen

---

[54] Cf. *ibid.*, p. 108: "Donc l'Italie au quatorzième siècle, malgré toute sa supériorité dans les arts et les lettres, tranche au fond beaucoup moins qu'on ne croit sur le reste de l'Europe et demeure naïve; elle n'est nullement arrivée à ce point de maturité où il est plus difficile de conserver la foi."

[55] *Ibid.*, p. 50.

[56] V. Zabughin, *Storia del rinascimento cristiano in Italia* (Milan, 1924).

the contrast between it and the preceding period. Yet it does not necessarily follow that a Christian civilization, or even one inspired by a specifically Catholic faith, must be essentially medieval. There has been a good deal of Catholic as well as other forms of Christian piety in the modern world, and one would hesitate to describe the early Church Fathers as medieval. It should be possible then, *a priori,* to admit the existence of a strong current of Christian faith in the Renaissance and still maintain a distinction between it and the Middle Ages. Such, indeed, has been the traditional practice in the interpretation of the Renaissance in the North, where the deeply religious feeling of the humanists has always been fully recognized. Northern humanism, it is true, was a reforming movement, highly critical of the Church, and so might easily be represented as marking a breach with medieval tradition, despite its religious content. The tendency to regard religious feeling in Renaissance Italy as evidence of the continuation of medieval civilization may thus be justified in part by the fact that the piety of the Italian humanists was more complacent in its attitude toward the traditional church. To a greater extent, however, it is probably no more than the reverse side of the traditional conception of the pagan Renaissance, which for so long maintained the dogma that what was not unchristian was not Renaissance.

If we grant, then, that the existence of religious faith or emotion is not in itself enough to stamp the age of the Renaissance as medieval, we may regard those historians as closer to the heart of the problem who have extended their research for evidences of medievalism in the Renaissance to include that vague but important factor in the history of ideas, which is known even to English-speaking scholars as *Weltanschauung.* Here the problem is to determine to what extent the attitude of the men of the Renaissance, or of the humanists as the articulate representatives of their age, toward God, the universe, and life in this world was founded upon medieval preconceptions and specifically medieval religious ideas. Two early works of that indefatigable analyst of historical concepts, Alfred von Martin, are of epoch-making importance in this field. Both studies concentrated attention on the thought of one of the most typical figures in the early period of Italian humanism. In the first of these, *Medieval Attitudes toward the*

World and Life as Reflected in the Writings of Coluccio Salutati (1913),[57] Martin isolated for exclusive study only those aspects of Salutati's thought that seemed to him characteristically medieval. And they were many. Taking as his criterion, Heinrich von Eicken's famous analysis of the medieval *Weltanschauung*,[58] Martin found in Salutati's works every evidence of that combination and interaction of ascetic flight from the world with faith in the domination of the world by a hierarchical Church founded upon external authority, which was for him the essence of medieval thought. "So," Martin declared, "I believe that I have found here a classic example of medieval *Weltanschauung*, that is, of conscious medieval Catholicism." [59]

Martin then strove to present a more rounded picture of Salutati and his fellow-humanists in his second study, *Coluccio Salutati and the Humanist Ideal of Life; a Chapter from the Genesis of the Renaissance* (1916).[60] He still found Salutati's thought filled with the old "ascetic-hierarchial ideal of the Christian Middle Ages." [61]   But he now balanced the medieval elements with evidence of new, typically Renaissance attitudes. For these he drew his criteria almost entirely from Burckhardt. Martin's basic conception of the Renaissance was in fact very close to the Burckhardtian tradition, which also fitted perfectly with Eicken's portrayal of the spirit of the Middle Ages. He himself admitted his general adherence to Burckhardt's interpretation in the interesting historiographical essay that served as an introduction to this volume. His chief objection to Burckhardt was that his Renaissance was too static. "It had no history, no rise or development." [62] What Martin was attempting to show in his analysis of Salutati was the gradual transition from medieval to Renaissance culture. On the whole, he thought that in Salutati the former still predominated, while symptoms of the latter appeared in him only half-consciously. Yet there was enough of the new to create conflict within him and to make him "the characteristic phenomenon of a transitional age." [63]

[57] A. von Martin, *Mittelalterliche Welt-und Lebensanschauung im Spiegel der Schriften Coluccio Salutatis* (Munich, 1913).

[58] H. von Eicken, *Geschichte und System der mittelalterlichen Weltanschauung* (Stuttgart, 1887).   [59] Martin, p. viii.

[60] A. von Martin, *Coluccio Salutati und das humanistiche Lebensideal: ein Kapitel aus der Genesis der Renaissance* (Leipzig, 1916).

[61] *Ibid.*, p. 74.   [62] *Ibid.*, p. 14 f.   [63] *Ibid.*, p. 261.

In his later work Martin returned more and more to the traditional
conception of the Renaissance as a clearly distinguishable age beginning with Petrarch, though his analysis was always colored by
sociological and psychological methodologies of which Burckhardt had
been happily innocent.[64] The search for medieval elements in the
Weltanschauung of the Renaissance was, however, continued through
the two following decades by Ernst Walser and others.[65] Walser's
fundamental feeling for what was new in the Renaissance was derived
from Burckhardt, who had been his teacher at Basel.[66] But he had also
studied in Paris under Charles Dejob and had learned from him to
see the strong evidences of religious faith in Renaissance Italy. Moreover, he had inherited "a mild and liberal Catholicism," [67] which
may have made him more willing than Burckhardt had been to admit
a true Catholic piety in the men of his chosen period. Whatever the
cause, he reacted with considerable emotion against the commonly
accepted notion that the Renaissance was an internally unified age,
markedly different from the preceding period. He therefore devoted
the greater part of his scholarly life to counteracting this idea in a
series of studies designed to show the continuation of specifically
medieval preconceptions in the *Weltanschauung* of the Italian humanists.

Walser's work consisted principally of detailed studies of humanist
writings, wherein he collected empirical evidence with which to ex-
plode the traditional Renaissance myth and to show that Petrarch,
Boccaccio, Salutati, Poggio, and even Valla and Luigi Pulci were much
closer to the Middle Ages than had commonly been supposed.[68] The

---

[64] See above, pp. 229 ff.

[65] See, for example, E. Mehl, *Die Weltanschauung des Giovanni Villani. Ein
Beitrag zur Geistesgeschichte Italiens im Zeitalter Dantes* (Leipzig, 1927). Mehl
regarded Middle Ages and Renaissance as characterizd by contrasting *Weltanschauung* (cf. p. 180 f), but thought Villani belonged in essence to the earlier
period.

[66] Cf. E. Walser, "Der Sinn des Lebens im Zeitalter der Renaissance," *Archiv
für Kulturgeschichte*, XVI (1925), 300–316. Here Walser abandoned his customary unilateral stress on the medieval elements in the Renaissance for a more
balanced portrayal in a generally Burckhardtian tone.

[67] Cf. H. Rupprich, "Deutsche Literatur des Humanismus und der Reformation:
ein Bericht," *Deutsche Vierteljahrsschrift für Literaturwissenschaft und Geistesgeschichte*, XVII (1939), Referatenheft, p. 96.

[68] See especially E. Walser, *Poggius Florentinus, Leben und Werke* (Leipzig,
1914); *Lebens-und Glaubensprobleme aus dem Zeitalter der Renaissance: die*

general results of his findings were best presented in a brief but illuminating monograph, entitled *Studies of the Weltanschauung of the Renaissance* (1920).[69] After a finely phrased, if somewhat malicious, summary of Burckhardt's interpretation of the Renaissance, Walser asserted flatly that it is not borne out by direct observation of the life and works of the leading personalities of the age. He then proceeded to attack in systematic fashion what seemed to him the most significant error in the works of Burckhardt, Voigt, Monnier, and others, the idea that the Christian faith of the humanists and their devotion to the Church had been shaken, or at least altered, by the revival of antiquity. Walser found but one basically new element in the classical humanism of the Renaissance: a new artistic perception of the formal beauty of antique letters and art. This was the one trait that had not been common to medieval learning. Hence he maintained that the content of humanism remained largely medieval, while "the paganism of the Renaissance in all its thousand-fold forms, in literature, art, and popular festivals, etc., was a purely external, fashionable, formal element."[70] The humanists did, indeed, develop new methods of criticism, but these were applied chiefly to classical philology. If they were turned against Christian teaching at all, it was only against scholasticism, which the Church itself did not regard as above criticism. Walser admitted that there was much anticlerical literature in the Renaissance, but there had been also in the Middle Ages. It was no proof of either infidelity or antagonism toward the Church. Walser's conclusion has almost the ring of a confession of faith. "It concerns me above all to insist that there can be no talk of a common humanist religion composed of skepticism and intellectual aestheticism, nor of a common Renaissance-indifference and Renaissance-skepticism."[71]

Compared with the moderate revisionism of Martin and Walser, the thesis presented by Giuseppe Toffanin was a dramatic reversal of con-

---

Religion des Luigi Pulci, ihre Quellen und ihre Bedeutung (Marburg, 1926); *Gesammelte Studien zur Geistesgeschichte der Renaissance* (Basel, 1932), edited with biographical introduction by Werner Kaegi.

[69] E. Walser, *Studien zur Weltanschauung der Renaissance* (Basel, 1920). Repub. in *Gesammelte Studien*, pp. 96–128.

[70] *Ibid.*, p. 117. [71] *Ibid.*, p. 126.

cepts, an historical *tour de force*. In a series of works, of which the most widely noted was the challenging *What Humanism Was* (1919),[72] Toffanin depicted the classical humanism of Italy as an entirely ortho-dox Catholic movement, which indeed served as a temporary defence of the Church against the heretical individualism which came before it and followed after. Toffanin's thesis did not go unchallenged;[73] but it gave support to a growing tendency in the interpretation of the Renaissance, and, despite its paradoxical excesses, it has been given sober consideration and qualified approval by a number of scholars who shared neither Toffanin's Catholicism nor, certainly, his Italian national sentiment.[74]

Toffanin's argument is sometimes rather difficult to follow, a difficulty occasionally made more pronounced by an obscurity of style so marked that it could scarcely be unintentional. The key to much that is at first glance puzzling lies in his equation of the *volgare* with individualism and heresy, and of classical Latin with universality and Catholic orthodoxy. The Church was universal; it was also *Romana ab antiquo*.[75] Humanism, though an essentially Italian thing, was characterized by a passion for the antique world and by a deep faith in the universality of culture embodied in the Roman Empire and the Roman Church under the auspices of classicism.[76] Humanism and the Church, then, were in perfect harmony. On the other hand, the litera-

[72] G. Toffanin, *Che cosa fu l'umanesimo. Il risorgimento dell' antichità classica nella coscienza degli italiani fra i tempi di Dante e la riforma* (1919; I use 2nd ed., Florence, 1929). See also his *La fine dell'umanesimo* (Milan, 1920); *Storia dell'umanesimo dal XIII al XVI secolo* (Naples, 1933); *Il Cinquecento* (Milan, 1928).

[73] See especially L. Arezio, "Rinascimento, umanesimo e spirito moderno," *Nuova antologia*, 272 (1930), 15–38, in which there is a valuable summary of Toffanin's thesis as well as a vigorous rebuttal. Croce may well have had Toffanin, among others, in mind when he wrote: "Certain contemporary artificial theories, constructed by Catholic or Catholicizing writers and by paradox-mongers who try to represent humanism as though it had been born in the service of Catholicism and of the Roman Church, a sort of rebirth of the thought of the Early Fathers, are so riddled with sophistries as to forget the meaning of the very words they use." B. Croce, *History as the Story of Liberty* (London, 1941), p. 318.

[74] See for example E. F. Jacob, "Changing Views of the Renaissance," *History*, N. S. XVI (1931–1932), 214–29, in which Toffanin's work is described as "stimulating if a trifle overimaginative" (p. 224); D. Bush, *The Renaissance and English Humanism* (Toronto, 1939), p. 24; R. Bainton, "Changing Ideas and Ideals in the Sixteenth Century," *Journal of Modern History*, VIII (1936), 421 f.

[75] Toffanin, *Storia*, p. 314.   [76] Cf. Toffanin, *Che cosa*, 3 ff; 123.

ture in the *volgare*, issuing from the democratic particularism of the thirteenth century communes, was the expression of a society fermenting with heresy.[77] Dante's "love of the plebean language germinated in a communal and virtually heretical state of mind," though he later "turned to Virgil in order to approach, outside of heresy, closer to Christian Rome."[78] It was this democratic civilization of the communes to which individualism may be ascribed more properly than to humanism, with its passion for universality.[79] The Church favored the return to pure Latin, which constituted a separation of culture from the people, because it regarded it as a healthy reaction against undisciplined mysticism.[80] The humanists, for their part, saw in classicism a support for orthodox religion and morality.[81] Staunch defenders of the Roman faith, they were rebelling against the unclassical and skeptical philosophy of the Averroists, the true pagans of the age, as well as against the heretical individualism of the *volgare*. For a time humanism held both heresy and skeptical philosophy in check. But only for a time. With the Reformation heresy burst forth again, accompanied, as in the communes, by opposition of individualism and the popular tongue to Latin universality.[82] And this, in turn, was soon followed by the renewal of "that higher heresy called philosophy."[83] Here Toffanin set up an interesting pair of antitheses and equations: humanism *vs.* individualism, which is equal to the antithesis of culture or classicism *vs.* philosophy or Romanticism. Philosophy and humanism are thus antithetical. When one is born the other ends.[84] Summing up his argument, Toffanin concluded:

> That particular state of mind and culture to which in Italy, from the fourteenth to the sixteenth century, we give the name of humanism was a rebellion and acted for at least two centuries as a barrier against certain heterodox and romantic inquietudes, which were present in germ in the communal state and afterwards triumphed in the Reformation.[85]

[77] Cf. *ibid.*, pp. 6 ff.
[78] *Ibid.*, pp. 20; 111.
[79] *Ibid.*, p. 23 ff; cf. p. 130.
[80] *Ibid.*, 31.
[81] Cf. *Storia*, p. 310 f.
[82] Toffanin, *Che cosa*, p. 131 f.
[83] Cf. *ibid.*, p. 124.
[84] *Ibid.*, p. 132: "Se la parola individualismo ha un significato concreto, le fa riscontro nell' altra, umanesimo, quella stessa antitesi ch' è tra cultura, la quale è un po'sempre classicismo, e filosofia, la quale è un po'sempre romanticismo. Nasce la filosofia e l'umanesimo finisce."
[85] *Ibid.*, p. 134 f.

A similar tendency to stress the persistence of medieval elements has also been evident of late in many studies of the various national Renaissances in the lands north of the Alps. But, as has generally been the case, the treatment of the Renaissance in the North has lacked the precision, the consciousness of conception that has marked the interpretation of the Renaissance in Italy. Having no Burckhardt of their own against whom to react, northern scholars have on the whole reacted less consciously against the traditional interpretation of their native Renaissance. Considerable heat, it is true, if not always an equal amount of light, was generated by those historians of strongly national bias, discussed in the preceding chapter, who would find the origins of their country's Renaissance exclusively in late medieval national culture rather than in the Italian revival of antiquity. The complementary tendency to find in the Renaissance elements of purely medieval tradition has been rather more general, but usually less strident in tone. The continued influence of medieval national tradition in Renaissance literature and art was never wholly denied by the traditional interpretation. And the religious character of northern humanism had long been recognized, so that it was less necessary than in Italy to combat the notion of a pagan Renaissance. Historians, then, have been less apt to regard all signs of active religion in the North as evidence of continued medievalism, though that has been done.

French historians have, on the whole, remained fairly well satisfied with the essentially modern character of their national Renaissance, by which they have normally meant the sixteenth century. As recently as 1930, the authoritative hand of Henri Hauser placed the seal of modernity upon the whole cultural, social, and political life of sixteenth century France.[86] There is evidence, however, of a growing awareness of the continuity of medieval tradition in French literature and humanism. Pierre Villey's study of *Marot and Rabelais* (1923) [87] is a characteristic example of moderate revisionism, which Villey himself did much to make popular. An erudite and prolific scholar, Villey was constantly preoccupied with the problem of the sources of Renaissance

---

[86] H. Hauser, *La modernité du XVIᵉ siècle* (Paris, 1930).

[87] P. Villey, *Les grands écrivains du XVIᵉ siècle: I. Marot et Rabelais* (Paris, 1923).

literature.[88] He regarded it as an essentially new phenomenon,[89] but his attention to sources had made him very much aware of the medieval traditions still active in the sixteenth century. For example, he noted that even after humanism was well established in France, Marot and his generation were still deeply attached to the popular poetry of the late Middle Ages.[90] And, while proclaiming Rabelais one "of the race of great humanists for whom antique thought served as a lever to change the face of Europe," [91] he also described the author of *Pantagruel* as "penetrated with the clerical tradition of the Middle Ages and the *Roman de la Rose* which remained the breviary of clercs." [92] Finally, Villey rejected entirely Michelet's formula of the "discovery of the world and of man." The modern idea of science, he asserted, was still foreign to the sixteenth century.[93] The humanists merely substituted one authority for another; their science was philology and erudition. "In summation, the sixteenth century did not bring a new vision of the universe, of man, and of nature; it merely rediscovered in books the visions which the ancients had had and which imposed themselves upon it by the prestige of antiquity." [94]

Scholars of a more obviously Catholic point of view have added a more emphatic denial of the originality and modernity of the French Renaissance. Henri Bremond, in his *Literary History of Religious Sentiment in France* (1916),[95] argued that there was nothing really new about the sixteenth century humanists. They were inferior in character, more infantile in their affectations and enthusiasms, more assertive in their glorification of man, but otherwise very little different from the humanists of the Middle Ages. Danger to the Church came not from the humanists, who were entirely orthodox and rather timid, but from the tradition of Occamism. The Jesuits were champions of humanism against the latter.[96] On much more precise grounds,

---

[88] See P. Villey, *Sources italiennes de la "Deffense et illustration de la langue françoise"* (Paris, 1908); *Sources et l'évolution des Essais de Montaigne,* 2 vols. (Paris, 1908); *Sources d'idées au XVIe siècle* (Paris, 1912).

[89] "C'est tout une flore nouvelle qui jaillit sur les ruines du passé," Villey, *Marot et Rabelais,* p. x.

[90] *Ibid.,* p. 120 ff.   [91] *Ibid.,* p. 162.   [92] *Ibid.,* p. 176.

[93] *Ibid.,* p. xiii.   [94] *Ibid.,* p. xiv.

[95] H. Bremond, *Histoire littéraire du sentiment religieux en France* (Paris, 1916), I, 3 ff.   [96] *Ibid.,* I, 13 ff.

Etienne Gilson also denied to humanism credit for originality. We have already noted his conviction that the medieval schoolmen had revived all that was most important in ancient thought.[97] Turning to the sixteenth century he presented the corollary argument that the humanists, as represented by Rabelais, were deeply indebted to scholasticism.[98]

In the study of English letters — and for England the Renaissance has been almost exclusively a literary phenomenon — the tendency under discussion has been rather more general than in French literary history, but not, as a rule, more conscious. We have already commented upon the notable lack in English scholarship of conceptual generalizations about the Renaissance in England and the resulting unconscious traditionalism which has dominated so much work in that field.[99] Of recent years, however, a tendency toward revisionism, if only of a half-conscious sort, has been increasingly evident. Detailed studies have accumulated contrary instances tending to modify the over-simplified conception of the Renaissance as presented by the traditional interpretation. To quote Rosamond Tuve again: "English studies have been more generally characterized by attempts to gather facts indicating medieval survivals; calling the phenomenon itself in question, the next step, is not generally taken."[100] Miss Tuve's bibliography of works illustrating the search for medieval characteristics in the English Renaissance[101] is so complete that little need be added here. E. M. Tillyard's *The Elizabethan World Picture* (1944), which has since appeared, is, however, an important addition and shows a growing consciousness of the problem involved. One might also add a significant German study, *The Medieval Feeling for Life in the English Renaissance* (1937) by Paul Meissner.[102] There is here no

97 See above, pp. 335 and 340.

98 E. Gilson, "Rabelais franciscain," in his *Les idées et les lettres* (Paris, 1932), pp. 197–241.

99 See above, p. 269 f.

100 R. Tuve, "Critical Survey of Scholarship in the Field of English Literature of the Renaissance," *Studies in Philology*, XL (1943), p. 222.

101 *Ibid.*, pp. 222 ff.

102 P. Meissner, "Mittelalterliches Lebensgefühl in der englischen Renaissance," *Deutsche Vierteljahrsschrift für Literaturwissenschaft und Geistesgeschichte*, XV (1937), 433–72.

indifference to the conceptual issue. On the contrary, Meissner was interested solely in the general principles of interpretation. As a result, his article is possibly the most systematic summary of the medieval preconceptions still remaining in sixteenth century English thought.

American students of the Renaissance have generally shared the disinclination of their English confreres to consider epochal concepts. There are, however, some exceptions. Douglas Bush, for example, has shown an unusual awareness of the historiographical evolution of the Renaissance, and has taken his stand with rare explicitness on the side of those who find the Renaissance filled with medieval traditions. Bush announced his thesis positively, and with much urbane wit, in a monographic study of *Mythology and the Renaissance Tradition in English Poetry* (1932). Though formally restricted to a rather narrow theme, he never hesitated to make broader generalizations nor to point a moral forcefully. And one moral, "to be perhaps relentlessly emphasized, is that the essential quality of Renaissance poetry, at the best as well as at the worst, is its medievalism." [103] Nor was this true only of English poetry. Bush's thesis was more extensive. It was summarized in a paragraph that merits full quotation.

> While the nineteenth century in general saw the Middle Ages and the Renaissance in terms of black and white, modern scholars have in the first place shown the importance of medieval achievement, and, in the second, have made it clear that the Renaissance was no sudden break with the medieval past. In all fields of activity men of the Renaissance were much less emancipated than they thought they were; most of them, even such heralds of modernity as Bacon and Descartes, were rooted in medieval tradition. The medieval mind accepted the irrational if it came in the guise of religion, we accept the irrational if it comes in the guise of science; the difference is called progress. Though, in relation to the general march of mind, the study of myths is a bypath, a main effort in this book will be to show the persistence, for good and ill, of the medieval spirit.[104]

It is an effort manfully sustained throughout the book.

[103] D. Bush, *Mythology and the Renaissance Tradition in English Poetry* (Minneapolis: The University of Minnesota Press, 1932), p. 6; cf. pp. 28 ff; 68 ff; 294 ff.

[104] *Ibid.*, p. 24.

The mainspring of Bush's thought seems to be a deeply rooted feeling for the continuity of intellectual tradition, reinforced by a gently ironical disillusionment with modern progress. He would probably not feel that he was doing his beloved Renaissance writers a service by making them modern. One might note in passing that he also made the Middle Ages less modern than some medievalists would have it.[105] The same turn of thought was evident in Bush's later lectures on *The Renaissance and English Humanism* (1939).[106] Here again he went far beyond the limitations of his title. The first lecture was an excellent general account, certainly the best in our language, of the history of the Renaissance concept. While ruefully identifying himself with the old definition of a scholar — "a siren which calls attention to a fog without doing anything to dispel it" [107] — Bush did in fact offer his own formula for dispelling the mists that surround the problem of the character of the Renaissance and its place in history. It was the same formula as in his earlier work, but more maturely rounded, and extended to include continental as well as English humanism. If anything there was here a more explicit insistence upon the close union between humanism and Christian faith. Bush was, in fact, close to Toffanin in his conception of humanism as a bulwark of Christianity against "irreligious scientific philosophies." [108] It was modern, not medieval, thought that Bush found antithetical to humanism, and there can be no doubt on which side his sympathy lay. Of the general character of continental humanism he concluded:

> The briefest account of it, from the twelfth century to the early sixteenth, reveals a creed and a programme in which the major articles remain constant. Whatever qualifications a larger survey might compel one to make, they would not alter the main conclusion, that the classical humanism of the Renaissance was fundamentally medieval and fundamentally Christian.[109]

The interpretation of humanism in terms of medieval survivals seems to fit English history so much more aptly than the reverse

105 *Ibid.,* p. 18 ff.
106 D. Bush, *The Renaissance and English Humanism* (Toronto: University of Toronto Press, 1939). See especially pp. 32 ff; 93 ff; 100.
107 *Ibid.,* p. 18.   108 *Ibid.,* p. 53; cf. pp. 52 ff; 69; 87 ff.   109 *Ibid.,* p. 68.

tendency to thrust the Renaissance back into the national past, that even those works that emphasize the early origins of English humanism may be discussed here more suitably than in the preceding chapter, to which they would apparently belong. This applies particularly to two recent studies: W. F. Schirmer's *Early English Humanism* (1931) [110] and Roberto Weiss's *Humanism in England during the Fifteenth Century* (1941). Both freely admit the priority of Italy and the debt of English to Italian humanism. What emerges significantly from both is not so much an earlier dating of the beginnings of English humanism as the continuation in it of many medieval, scholastic elements. Weiss, in particular, insisted upon the half-medieval, clerical, and quasi-scholastic character of the early English humanists. "In England humanism was conceived not as a new cultural manifestation or a refinement in taste, but rather as a means of improving some aspects of scholasticism." [111] It was a utilitarian means rather than an end in itself. And the early humanists continued to use many of the methodological weapons of scholasticism. [112] Even in the great humanists of the sixteenth century — Grocyn, Colet, Linacre, and More — the ideals of the new learning represented a compromise with or subordination to medieval culture rather than antagonism to it. [113]

A somewhat similar interpretation of German humanism had previously been presented by Gerhard Ritter, one of the most distinguished students of late medieval scholasticism. It may be taken as typical of recent German efforts to find evidence of continued medieval traditions in the learning of their national Renaissance. Ritter's thesis was most clearly summarized, together with an analysis of the current status of the Renaissance problem as it applies to German history, in a lengthy article entitled "The Historical Significance of German Humanism." (1923). [114] And his conclusion was that its

---

[110] W. F. Schirmer, *Der englische Frühhumanismus; ein Beitrag zur englischen Literaturgeschichte des 15. Jahrhunderts* (Leipzig, 1931).

[111] R. Weiss, *Humanism in England during the Fifteenth Century* (Oxford, 1941), p. 179.

[112] Cf. Schirmer, pp. 74 ff.   [113] Weiss, p. 183.

[114] G. Ritter, "Die geschichtliche Bedeutung des deutschen Humanismus," *Historische Zeitschrift*, CXXVII (1923), 393–453. See also his *Studien zur Spätscholastik*, 2 vols. (Heidelberg, 1921–1922); and *Die Heidelberger Universität, I. Das Mittelalter, 1386–1508*, 3 vols. (Heidelberg, 1936).

historical significance was not very great; certainly it was less revolutionary than its Italian counterpart, or than the Protestant Reformation. Ritter explicitly rejected the nineteenth century liberal tradition which would make the German humanists free and rational champions of enlightenment against the darkness, superstition, and barbarism of the Middle Ages. On the contrary, he argued that what vital force humanism possessed in Germany came from the continuation in it of the strong current of late medieval piety. Moreover, Ritter insisted, there was no quarrel in principle between German humanism and scholasticism. Despite superficial, if sometimes bitter, conflicts on academic grounds, humanists and schoolmen lived amicably enough together in the same universities and learned from one another, so that the humanists were, in fact, half scholastic. Humanism was an essentially literary movement; it made very little contribution to modern scientific or philosophical thought; nor did it create a new view of the world. Where the humanists were active reformers, they owed their ideas and their driving force less to their humanism than to the various reforming impulses inherited from the later Middle Ages. In short, as he commented elsewhere, "humanism, which in Italy helped to bring to light a new idea of the world and life, remained in Germany a mere educational phenomenon which received its *weltanschaulichen* content . . . . from other more original tendencies." [115] It is not irrelevant to note that these more original tendencies had evolved within German national culture, though they might not be exclusively German. They were at any rate not foreign importations as was classical humanism. There is a close relation between Ritter's nationalism and his antagonism to the liberal-rational-classical tradition. So far as possible he treated both German humanism and the Reformation as aspects of the national culture, and he tended to minimize the importance of those elements in them that might be considered alien to the German *Geist*.[116]

115 G. Ritter, "Romantische und revolutionäre Elemente in der deutschen Theologie am Vorabend der Reformation," *Deutsche Vierteljahrsschrift für Literaturwissenschaft und Geistesgeschichte*, V (1927), 376.
116 Cf. G. Ritter, *Luther, Gestalt und Symbol* (Munich, 1925).

DEVALUATION OF RENAISSANCE ART AND LIMITATION OF ITS CHRONOLOGICAL SCOPE: NEW CRITERIA OF JUDGMENT

Recent revisionism in the interpretation of Renaissance art presents a more complex picture than that relating to literature, learning, and verbally expressed *Weltanschauung*. Or at least so it seems to the historian trained in other fields. Revolutionary changes in taste as well as in historical and critical methodology during the past half-century have made the history of art increasingly confusing to the lay scholar. And the confusion has been in no way lessened by the apparently innate tendency of German scholars to manufacture concepts. Even if it were possible in the space available, no one but a specialist would dare attempt a comprehensive analysis of recent historiography and critical theory in the field of Renaissance art. In that as yet unmapped wilderness, the general historian may well be haunted by an uneasy conviction that his compass can no longer be trusted to indicate the magnetic north. Nevertheless, it seems worth while at this point to mention certain trends of interpretation, which, while not always fitting exactly the theme of this chapter, are yet more or less germane to it. They deviate from the Burckhardtian tradition chiefly by the assertion of different value judgments or by the establishment of new criteria of interpretation; yet they may be discussed here, perhaps more fittingly than elsewhere, since their general effect has been to devaluate the art of the Renaissance or to limit its chronological scope, mostly to the advantage of the Middle Ages.

The dominant trend in art history and criticism in the past three or four decades has been the adoption of various "scientific" methodologies, most of which have borrowed heavily from current developments in the science of psychology. They constitute a distinct break with the traditions of the preceding century, when Romantic men of letters wrote loosely about the spirit of art, and cultural historians were content to explain the art of an age as the product of a general social milieu. Since that idyllic age the history of art has become one of the more esoteric branches of the *Geisteswissenschaften*. The new methodologies have concentrated primarily upon the problems of form. To quote one recent critic, "Art history has developed into form history and has interested itself in all other things only in so far as they concern form."[117] In its most objective phases, this exclusive study of form has been essentially unhistorical; it has ignored the basic historical problems of causation and development, and has treated art as an autonomous phenomenon, unrelated to contemporaneous civilization.[118] More commonly, however, the historical method has been maintained by an effort to relate the forms of art to psychological attitudes or intellectual preoccupations perceptible in other fields of expression. This tendency, which owed much of its original impetus to the historical school founded by Wilhelm Dilthey and is perhaps best illustrated by the work of Max Dvořák, has been stronger in Germany than elsewhere. It has served as inspiration, however, for much recent work in other countries, and it has lately been made more familiar to American scholars through the illuminating lectures presented at the Lowell Institute in Boston by Otto Benesch, published under the title, *The Art of the Renaissance in Northern Europe: Its Relation to the Contemporary Spiritual and Intellectual Movements* (1945). But while thus entering the field of intellectual history, the newer history of art has generally remained aloof from the social, economic, and other material considerations of *Kulturgeschichte,* and has, as a result, exerted a more limited influence on the interpretation of the history of civilization in general than did the school of Burckhardt and Taine.

Exclusive preoccupation with form has, however, had a revolutionary effect upon the judgment of medieval and Renaissance art in two important respects. It has freed the history of art from the Romantic habit of judging the art of an age in accordance with the sentimental connotations of its subject matter; and, at the same time, it has emancipated criticism from the preconceptions and the representational or naturalistic standards of classical aesthetic. One result has been the establishing of new bases for distinction between the classical style of

---

[117] J. Jahn, *Die Kunstwissenschaft der Gegenwart in Selbstdarstellungen* (Leipzig, 1924), p. iv.

[118] For discussion of the tendency to separate art theory from history, see H. Lützeler, "Kunsttheorie und Kunstgeschichte Heute," *Neue Jahrbücher für Wissenschaft und Jugendbildung,* VII (1931), 162–174; and J. Strzygowski, *Die Krisis der Geisteswissenschaften* (Vienna, 1923).

the Renaissance and the non-classical Gothic or Baroque; a second has been a new, positive evaluation of both Gothic and post-Renaissance art in their own right, with at times a corresponding devaluation of the Renaissance itself.

These tendencies in historical criticism have also been powerfully reinforced by kindred tendencies in the theory and practice of contemporary art. The revolt against academic representative art, and the various trends of irrationalism, abstraction, expressionism, primitivism, and so forth of the past half-century have combined to remove from the art of the classical Renaissance its halo of perfection. Evidence of this re-evaluation of Renaissance art may be found in abundance. One example, unusually early and unusually explicit, may serve as illustration. In an essay on theoretical aesthetics, simply entitled *Art* (1914), the English post-impressionist critic, Clive Bell, attacked the whole tradition of representative art. In its place, he would set up a new criterion, that of "significant form," which, he maintained, was the sole valid distinction between art and mere illustration. It was the common denominator of all true art. It might exist in conjunction with representative form, but Bell thought it rarely did so. "Formal significance," he asserted, "loses itself in preoccupation with exact representation and ostentatious cunning." [119] It is found at its best in primitive art, but it also appears in eras of intense religious feeling, for "religion, like art, is concerned with the world of emotional reality and with material things only in so far as they are emotionally significant." [120] Applying his aesthetic to the history of art, Bell inverted the traditional curves of periodic rise and decline. From the heights of primitive form, art declined with the Greeks "to peter out in the bogs of Hellenistic and Roman rubbish." [121] But at this point art was saved and significant form restored by Christian emotion, so that a new height was reached in the Byzantine art of the sixth century. This, Bell declared "is the primitive and supreme summit of the Christian slope. The upswing from the levels of Greco-Romanism is immeasurable." [122] The decline thereafter was slight until Giotto, whom Bell regarded as the last great painter

[119] C. Bell., *Art* (London: Chatto and Windus, 1914), p. 23.
[120] *Ibid.*, p. 81.   [121] *Ibid.*, p. 124.   [122] *Ibid.*, p. 129.

before Cézanne. "From the peak that is Giotto the road falls slowly but steadily. Giotto heads a movement toward imitation and scientific picture making. . . . The new movement broke up the great Byzantine tradition, and left the body of art a victim to the onslaught of that strange new disease, the Classical Renaissance." [123]

For the critical study of artistic form as it relates to the Renaissance and adjacent periods, the work of Heinrich Wölfflin and Wilhelm Worringer is of fundamental importance. Though differing in method, both sought a new basis for periodization and synthesis in the scientific study of pure form. Their work resulted in new sets of criteria for the characterization of the Renaissance and for distinguishing its style from that of the Baroque and Gothic respectively. And both exerted a strong influence on the tendency of later art historians to reduce the term "Renaissance" to a style concept, sharply limited in content and time.

Wölfflin's method was to concentrate attention upon what he called "pure visibility," entirely divorced from all consideration of pictorial content, sentimental connotation, or fidelity to nature.[124] He strove to achieve a synthetic organization of periods in the history of art by analyzing the ways in which the artists of the age perceived and presented reality, and by classifying these in schemes of visual imagery. Rejecting the time-honored theory that advance or decline in art was to be determined by the skill with which it imitated nature, Wölfflin regarded Gothic, Renaissance, and Baroque, not as representing an organic development from barbarous limitation to perfection and later decline, but rather as three different types of visual imagery, each equally valid in itself and each the inevitable product of the psychological peculiarity of the age. In practice, Wölfflin applied his theory chiefly to Renaissance and Baroque painting. After two early and relatively conventional histories of these fields,[125] he published his epoch-making methodological treatise, *Principles of Art History: the*

---

[123] *Ibid.*, p. 147 ff.

[124] For discussion of Wölfflin and the theory of pure visibility, see L. Venturi, *History of Art Criticism* (New York, 1936), pp. 271 ff.

[125] H. Wölfflin, *Renaissance und Baroque* (Munich, 1888); *Die klassische Kunst* (Munich, 1898). Eng. trans. (New York, 1903).

Problem of Development of Style in Later Art in 1915.[126] Here he gave schematic form to the contrast between Renaissance and Baroque painting in five antithetical categories: linear vs. painterly; plain vs. recession; closed vs. open form; multiple unity vs. unity; clarity vs. unclearness. Wölfflin made no attempt to explain the reasons for what he believed to be a fundamental psychic change, not, at least, in any way that would be useful to the general historian of civilization. He merely presented evidence, carefully selected, to demonstrate his belief that in each age artists shared a common type of vision and used common schemes of visual imagery. He believed that his categories could be applied to all European art, though he did also note some secondary differences in national character, and he thought that Italian art was at its best in the classical form, German in the Baroque.[127] Unhistorical though it was and largely inapplicable to any form of art other than painting, Wölfflin's work contained a great deal of stimulating suggestion and its influence on later art criticism was very widespread. On the whole, he had made little change in the traditional chronological boundaries of the Renaissance, but his method and criteria, applied to a different selection of examples, could be used to aid the current process of shrinking the area assigned to it.

Meanwhile, from the opposite chronological direction, Wilhelm Worringer had used the psychological study of pure form to establish a new basis for distinction between Renaissance and Gothic. The principles of his methodology were first laid down in a theoretical work, entitled *Abstraction and Empathy* (1908).[128] Later he applied them historically to European art in a companion study of *Form Problems of the Gothic* (1910).[129] The key to Worringer's approach to the problem is to be found in his introductory argument that Gothic art had never been properly understood or appraised in any

[126] H. Wölfflin, *Kunstgeschichtliche Grundbegriffe. Das Problem der Stilentwicklung in der neueren Kunst* (Munich, 1915; I use 6th ed., Munich, 1923). Eng. trans. (London, 1932).

[127] Wölfflin, *Grundbegriffe*, p. 253 f; cf. his *Italien und das deutsche Formgefühl* (Munich, 1931).

[128] W. Worringer, *Abstraktion und Einfühlung* (Munich, 1908).

[129] W. Worringer, *Formprobleme der Gotik* (Munich, 1910; I use ed. Munich, 1927). Engl trans. (New York, Stechert-Hafner, Inc., 1918). For criticism, see G. Weise, "Das Schlagwort vom gotischen Menschen," *Neue Jahrbücher für Wissenschaft und Jugendbildung*, VII (1931), 404–37.

REVOLT OF THE MEDIEVALISTS

but a negative manner, because it had always been judged in the light of classical aesthetic and on the basis of an erroneous notion of the nature of art.

> This error [he continued] expresses itself in the assumption, sanctioned throughout many centuries, that the history of art is equivalent to the history of artistic ability, and that the self-evident aim of this ability is the artistic copying and reproduction of nature's models. The growing truth to life and naturalness of what is represented has in this way, without further question, been esteemed as artistic progress. The question of the artistic will has never been raised, because this will seemed, indeed, definitely established and undebatable. Ability alone has been the problem of valuation, never the will.[130]

In opposition to this preconception, against which Wöllflin was also to rebel, Worringer asserted that the past could do all that it *willed*. "The will, which was formerly undebatable, accordingly becomes the real problem of investigation." But, if the will or intention of the artist is all important, the method of criticism must be primarily psychological. What Worringer did was, in fact, to reverse the method of Taine's "scientific" school, which had proceeded from race, milieu, and moment to the explanation of art. Instead, he proceeded from the direct study of artistic form back to a reconstruction of the psychological character of the race, social milieu, and tradition of the age which had produced it.

Having divided all European art into two great categories — classical and Gothic — characterized by antithetical types of "form will," Worringer posited the existence of two basic psychological types: the classical and Gothic man, respectively. The classical man, as evidenced in the art forms of antiquity and the Renaissance, was completely at home with nature. "The Gothic soul, however, lacks this harmony. With it the inner and the outer world are still unreconciled." [131] As a result of this fundamental dualism, the Gothic form will expressed itself in abstract line, which was the rejection of reality, in a restless activity, which reflected its metaphysical anxiety, and in a kind of

130 Worringer, *Formprobleme der Gotik*, p. 6 f [p. 20 f].
131 *Ibid.*, p. 52 [p. 68].

hysterical play of fantasy, through which the Gothic soul sought salvation from the torment of its inner dichotomy. "This intensified fantastic activity lays hold of the actual, which Gothic man could not yet convert into the natural by means of clear knowledge, and changes it into the phantasmagoria of intensified and distorted actuality." [132] But Worringer's Gothic man did not represent merely a temporary stage in the development of humanity. He was also a racial type, northern if not exclusively Germanic. Worringer was convinced that a disposition to the Gothic could be found only among those peoples in whom there had been a considerable intermixture of Germanic blood. The Germans were "the *conditio sine qua non* of the Gothic." [133] It was they who had "introduced among self-confident peoples the germs of doubt of sense and of distraction of soul, out of which the transcendental pathos of the Gothic then shot up so mightily." [134]

There is something almost Hegelian about the grandeur of Worringer's historical construction, and sober critics regarded the *a priori* quality of his reasoning with some distrust. Nevertheless, his work was widely read, and traces of his characterization of the Gothic mentality can be found well outside the sphere of art history. It clearly underlies Ernst Mehl's analysis of *The World-View of Giovanni Villani* (1927) where, on the ground of his anxious inner dualism and transcendentalism, as contrasted with the serene secularism of the Renaissance, the solid bourgeois author of the *Chronicle* was described as in essence a Gothic man.[135] As this suggests, one effect of Worringer's thesis was to intensify rather than lessen the ancient contrast between Middle Ages and Renaissance. In this respect he was out of harmony with the revisionism of the following decades. Yet, his new criterion for the identification of the Gothic style led more than one watchful eye to note the appearance of Gothic elements in what had commonly been considered early Renaissance. Thus Georg Weise, using criteria that admittedly originated with Worringer, noted a recrudescence of Gothic form, after a period of naturalism, in both

---

[132] *Ibid.*, p. 53 [p. 69].   [133] *Ibid.*, p. 29 [p. 45].
[134] *Ibid.*, p. 127 [p. 146].
[135] E. Mehl, *Die Weltanschauung des Giovanni Villani. Ein Beitrag zur Geistesgeschichte Italiens im Zeitalter Dantes* (Leipzig, 1927), p. 183.

Germany and Italy during the later part of the fifteenth century.[136]
At the same time, Worringer's suggestion that northern Baroque was
a partial revival of the Gothic or northern form will[137] — the constantly recurring Germanic principle — also lent encouragement to
those who would limit the Renaissance more sharply at its other
extremity.

The success of Worringer's thesis may be credited in part to the
fact that he had removed medieval art from under the shadow of
antiquity and the Renaissance and had given it its own place in the
sun, thereby aiding that rehabilitation of the Middle Ages which was
to become such a strong current in the historical scholarship of the
next two or three decades. To a still greater degree, however, the
favorable reception accorded his work by German historians may
have been inspired by the fact that it furnished a new justification for
Germanic art and, at the same time, a new and heartening scientific
foundation for the old Romantic faith in the creative power of the
folk soul and the consequent identification of Gothic and Baroque art
with the German national spirit. Historians, at any rate, who believed
that there was a natural affinity between the Germanic spirit and the
Gothic form might well tend, as did the German Romanticists, to
minimize or deplore the intrusion upon German art of any alien
influence. The effect of this way of thinking is very clear in Georg
Dehio's strongly nationalistic *History of German Art* (1919–1926).[138]
Though admitting foreign influences — French or general European
currents during the High Middle Ages and Italian forms during the
Renaissance — Dehio found throughout the whole history of German
art a constant national character or ground tone, which he preferred
to call Baroque rather than Gothic, but which amounted to much the
same thing. It was, he thought, especially strong in the late Gothic.

A direct line [he wrote] connected the late Gothic with the Baroque;
yes we must decide to think this: perhaps the late Gothic is already

---

[136] G. Weise, "Der doppelte Begriff der Renaissance," *Deutsche Vierteljahrsschrift für Literaturwissenschaft und Geistesgeschichte,* XI (1933), 516 ff; "Das
gotische oder barock Stilprinzip der deutschen und der nordischen Kunst," *ibid.,*
X (1932), 206–43.

[137] Cf. Worringer, *Formprobleme,* pp. 28; 79 f; 127.

[138] G. G. Dehio, *Geschichte der deutschen Kunst* (Leipzig, 1919–26).

the beginning of the Baroque; perhaps we may turn our glance backward and say that the late Gothic merely brought to light what from the beginning lay in the nature of the Gothic, save that it was thrust back by the universal current of the High Middle Ages; perhaps the Baroque is in general the original and basic German tone (die deutsche Ur- und Grundstimmung).[139]

Later, he decided that for the "perhaps" he could substitute an unqualified affirmation.[140] As Worringer had done with the concept of Gothic, Dehio made a distinction between the historical Baroque and the timeless Baroque principle. In this latter and larger sense, he defined Baroque as the antithesis of classical art, as resting upon super-rational foundations rather than upon the identification of beauty with reason. Convinced that Gothic or Baroque, thus defined, represented the unchangeable way of feeling of the Germanic people, Dehio limited the German Renaissance to a brief period of superficial and purely formal adoption of the externals of Italian art. "The late Gothic," he declared, "did not have an actual end; what became known traditionally as the Renaissance was an altered cloak beneath which the late Gothic lived on undisturbed."[141] And again, defining more precisely the periodization of German art: "In the two first decades of the sixteenth century, the late Gothic dominated the mass of production; in the middle, the style material if not the style spirit of the Renaissance set the standard; toward the end a transformation began which cannot be called anything but Baroque."[142]

Dehio thought that the influence of the Renaissance on German art was not only brief and superficial, but, in so far as it was effective, unfortunate if not disastrous. The Reformation and the Renaissance in conjunction, he thought, created a crisis which had catastrophic results for the mid-sixteenth century, and from which, indeed, German art never quite recovered.[143] The Reformation broke the connection between art and religion or, at least, the Church; the Renaissance broke the intimate relation between art and the people. The art of the Renaissance, Dehio insisted, could never be assimilated in spirit by

---

[139] *Ibid.*, II, 149.
[141] *Ibid.*, II, 149.
[140] *Ibid.*, III, 177.
[142] *Ibid.*, III, 176.
[143] *Ibid.*, III, Introduction; cf. G. Dehio, "Die Krisis der deutschen Kunst im sechzehnten Jahrhundert," *Archiv für Kulturgeschichte*, XII (1914), 1–16.

the German people. "It came from another culture." [144] All that could
be taken over was the empty form. Renaissance art in Germany was
therefore aristocratic rather than popular, technically skillful but
spiritually void. "Its roots no longer struck down into the ground
water of national life." [145] This was not an uncommon theme among
German historians in the years during and after the first World War.
A notable example may be found in Richard Benz's bitter article,
The Renaissance, the Fatality of German Civilization (1915).[146]

Not all German nationalists, however, were prepared to credit the
Renaissance with even a regrettable influence on German art. Carl
Neumann, whose thesis that the Italian Renaissance drew its vital
energies from medieval Germanic, rather than antique classical, sources
we have already noted,[147] would, on the other hand, permit no foreign
intrusion to lessen the autonomy or adulterate the national purity of
German culture. In a belligerent review article entitled, *End of the
Middle Ages? Legends of the Dissolution of the Middle Ages by the
Renaissance* (1934),[148] he argued against the conclusions of all those
historians who saw in the Renaissance the beginnings of a new
European civilization. If the Renaissance had any meaning at all, it
was only for Italy. It had none for the North, where the concept is
only an outlived fashionable convention of "the liberal-rationalist"
school of thought.[149] As for sixteenth century German art, "it was in
mind and soul the most unmistakable late Gothic." [150] Neumann insisted that the Renaissance was scarcely an episode in the history of
German culture. The Baroque lived on in the spirit of the Gothic.
And this was true not only of art: the whole civilization of the sixteenth century in Germany was late Middle Ages. It was a living
Gothic, not a posthumous Gothic. The Gothic did not die or decline.
It was the mother of German culture.[151]

144 Dehio, *Geschichte,* III, 175.
145 Dehio, "Krisis der deutschen Kunst," *Archiv für Kulturgeschichte,* XII, 7.
146 R. Benz, "Die Renaissance, das Verhängnis der deutschen Kultur" (1915),
repub. in his *Renaissance und Gotik, Grundlagen deutscher Art und Kunst* (Jena,
1928).   147 See above, pp. 325 ff.
148 C. Neumann, "Ende des Mittelalters? Legende der Ablösung des Mittelalters
durch die Renaissance," *Deutsche Vierteljahrsschrift für Literaturwissenschaft und
Geistesgeschichte,* XII (1934), 124–71
149 *Ibid.,* p. 157.   150 *Ibid.,* p. 162.   151 *Ibid.,* p. 167.

If there was any interchange of artistic traditions, Neumann preferred to see the current of influence run from North to South, a tendency shared by other art historians of similar patriotic bent. Thus, Neumann, Haendecke, and others not only ascribed the original impulse of the Italian Renaissance to the Gothic, but also noted the continuation of northern Gothic elements in the art of the *Quattrocento*.[152] One of the most distinguished exponents of the latter thesis was August Schmarsow, who combined, in a manner reminiscent of Worringer, the scientific study of artistic form with a somewhat less scientific spirit of German nationalism. In his most important work, *The Laws of Composition in the Art of the Middle Ages* (1915–22),[153] Schmarsow established certain "basic concepts" as fundamental for the whole period of medieval art. In two later works, *Gothic in the Renaissance* (1921)[154] and *Italian Art in the Age of Dante* (1928),[155] he then demonstrated the continued existence of these essentially Germanic forms through much of the art of Renaissance Italy. In much the same way, Friedrich Antal also declared that the work of Andrea del Castagno was pure Gothic, while that of the majority of Florentine painters of the mid-fifteenth century was at least strongly marked by Nordic-Gothic traits.[156]

One further tendency of revisionism in the history of art remains to be noted, one which struck directly at the heart of the Burckhardtian interpretation by attacking it on its own grounds, that is, the extension of realism or naturalism in art from the domain of the Renaissance into that of the Middle Ages. Realism was, indeed, an essential part of the Renaissance tradition as formulated by Michelet and Burckhardt. To quote Huizinga, whose own very important revision of that formula will be discussed later:

If one understands by realism the need and the ability to approach in word and picture as closely as possible to the reality of things, and if

[152] Cf. *ibid.*, p. 163; see also above, p. 327 f.

[153] A. Schmarsow, *Kompositionsgesetze in der Kunst des Mittelalters*, 4 vols. (Leipzig, 1915–22).

[154] A. Schmarsow, *Gotik in der Renaissance, eine kunsthistorische Studie* (Stuttgart, 1921).

[155] A. Schmarsow, *Italienische Kunst im Zeitalter Dantes: zur Wesenbestimmung des Trecento,* 2 vols. (Augsburg, 1928).

[156] F. Antal, "Studien zur Gotik im Quattrocento," *Jahrbuch der preussischen Kunstsammlung,* XLVI (1925), 3–32.

the Renaissance signifies the discovery of the world and of man, the
rise of an immediate, individual consideration and perception of
reality, then it seems to follow that realism must in fact be connoted
with the Renaissance.[157]

To make realism instead a characteristic trait of the Middle Ages was
to alter the whole traditional pattern of the contrast between the
medieval and Renaissance *Weltanschauung*. Recent historians of
medieval literature and thought have, it is true, materially altered that
pattern. As was noted in the first section of this chapter, they have
attacked from almost every possible angle the old conception of the
inherent transcendentalism, the exclusive otherworldliness, of the
Middle Ages. In the field of art history, however, the problem was
somewhat more difficult. For there it was necessary to break down
not only old prejudices but also new ones resulting from recent trends
of taste and criticism.

Emile Mâle, whose study of *The Religious Art of the Thirteenth
Century in France* (1913)[158] was very widely read, was one of the
first to protest against the conception of Gothic art as entirely symbolical or idealistic. He found in the detail of Gothic sculpture ample
evidence of a close and loving study of nature.[159] Since then the
realistic quality of much of Gothic art has been more and more commonly recognized.[160] But the accurate copying of natural objects, such
as flowers,[161] in Gothic ornament does not of itself make a realistic
art; and many critics, while recognizing in medieval art an increasing
attention to nature, have interpreted Gothic realism either as a partial
phenomenon in an art dominated by idealism and symbolism or as a
late and decadent development. Huizinga portrayed realism as a
symptom of decline, thereby fitting it into his picture of the waning

---

[157] J. Huizinga, "Renaissance und Realismus," in his *Wege der Kulturgeschichte*
(Munich, 1930), p. 140; and see below, p. 375 f.

[158] E. Mâle, *L'art religieux du XIIIe siècle en France: étude sur l'iconographie
du Moyen Age et sur ses sources d'inspiration* (Paris, 1913; I use 6th ed. Paris,
1925). Eng. trans. (New York, 1913).

[159] *Ibid.*, pp. 48 ff.

[160] See survey of recent opinion in L. White, "Natural Science and Naturalistic
Art in the Middle Ages," *American Historical Review*, LII (1947), 421–35.

[161] Cf. D. Jalabert, "La flore gothique: ses origines, son évolution du XIIe au
XVe siècle," *Bulletin monumental*, XCI (1932), 181–246.

Middle Ages. Hubert Schrade, too, included realism in the Gothic only as a late, secular development which broke the relation between myth and art.[162] Walter Goetz came closer to making realism a characteristic indigenous to the Middle Ages in his study of *The Development of a Sense of Reality from the Twelfth to the Fourteenth Century* (1937),[163] but he thought that it did not find expression in art until about the end of the thirteenth century with the painting of Giotto and his contemporaries. The task of fitting realism or naturalism and idealism together into a synthetic interpretation of the nature of Gothic art was, however, accomplished with brilliant effect by Max Dvořák in a long article entitled "Idealism and Naturalism in Gothic Sculpture and Painting" (1918).[164]

One of the most brilliant practitioners of art history as *Geistesgeschichte*, Max Dvořák was convinced that medieval art could be understood only by understanding its intellectual foundations. He considered Worringer's interpretation brilliant but arbitrary and fantastic, applicable, in any case, to one aspect only of Gothic art.[165] Rejecting both Worringer's *"a priori* form will," on the one hand, and the older methods of materialistic *Kulturgeschichte,* on the other, Dvořák strove to interpret medieval art by relating it to kindred intellectual tendencies in literature and philosophy. The closest parallel to the harmonious combination of the ideal and the natural in Gothic art he found in Thomist philosophy. Like the scholastic system, Gothic art set up a hierarchy of values; it treated the supernatural world ideally, the natural world naturally. Moreover, medieval philosophy, with its ever-present comparison of the sensible world with the supersensuous and eternal, gave the artist a new conception of the significance of nature. And at the same time a new conception of spiritual personality lent life and individuality to artistic portrayal of the human form.[166] The discovery of personality and nature, then, did not come as an emancipation from medieval ecclesiastical ideals, nor as an inde-

---

[162] H. Schrade, "Über Symbolismus und Realismus in der Spätgotik," *Deutsche Vierteljahrsschrift für Literaturwissenschaft und Geistesgeschichte,* V (1927), 78–105.

[163] See above, p. 306.

[164] M. Dvořák, "Idealismus und Naturalismus in der gotischen Skulptur und Malerei," *Historische Zeitschrift,* CXIX (1918), 1–62; 185–246.

[165] *Ibid.,* CXIX, 6.   [166] Cf. ibid., CXIX, 185 ff.

pendent secular Renaissance. It was rooted in the Christian spiritualism of the medieval world.[167] But medieval realism, rising as it did from a foundation of spiritualism, was inherently subjective.[168] It was, therefore, a new and independent observation of nature, not a revival of antique naturalism. Its outstanding trait was "the once seen and individually characteristic." [169]

THE RENAISSANCE INTERPRETED AS CONTINUATION OR DECLINE OF THE MIDDLE AGES

The final logical step in the process described in this chapter was to deny the existence of the Renaissance as a new age in the history of civilization and to annex it to the Middle Ages. The historians discussed in the foregoing pages were for the most part content to demonstrate the existence of Renaissance characteristics in the Middle Ages or of medieval traits in the Renaissance. We have now to deal with those writers who were convinced of the preponderant similarity of the two ages, a similarity outweighing incidental differences. Without exception they viewed the Renaissance from the direction of the Middle Ages. Denying to it all significant originality, they regarded it as the end of the Middle Ages rather than as the beginning of modern times. Viewed thus, it was almost inevitable that the age should seem one of decline, even decadence, rather than of fresh and youthful vigor. And this impression was intensified by the underlying antagonism toward the Renaissance which is explicit or implicit in all the works to be noted. Leaders of the most extreme reaction against the Burckhardtian tradition, their authors were conscious revisionists and frequently displayed an irritated animosity toward the concept of the Renaissance and, by a kind of carry over of emotional intensity, toward the age itself. Or perhaps the emotional progression worked in the other direction. In any case, their work represents the ultimate phase in the revolt of the medievalists.

---

[167] *Ibid.*, CXIX, 195.
[168] For discussion of Dvořák's differentiation between subjective realism of the Middle Ages and the objective *Gesetzmässigkeit* of Renaissance art, see above, p. 251 f.
[169] Dvořák, "Idealismus und Naturalismus," *Historische Zeitschrift*, CXIX, 198.

There are books which exert as much influence through a striking title as through the more carefully qualified argument contained within their covers. Such a book was Haskins' *Renaissance of the Twelfth Century,* and such also Jacob Huizinga's *The Waning of the Middle Ages* (1919),[170] which was in a way its geometrical complement. It is that fact that justifies its inclusion here, even though Huizinga's thesis, like that of Haskins, was less revolutionary than it has sometimes been taken to be. Huizinga limited his study to France and the Netherlands in the fourteenth and fifteenth centuries, a period which French tradition, at least, had seldom claimed for the Renaissance. And he did admit the existence of a Renaissance,[171] though he had grave doubts about it. He considered the historical concept implied in the term distressingly protean, a dangerous and unreliable, yet somehow indispensable, tool for the use of historians, and he would limit it to an irreducible minimum in time, scope, and content. Noting the regrettable tendency of some historians to thrust the Renaissance back into the Middle Ages, he added:

On the other hand, the Renaissance, when studied without preconceived ideas, is found to be full of elements which were characteristic of the medieval spirit in its full bloom. Thus it has become nearly impossible to keep up the antithesis, and yet we cannot do without it, because Middle Ages and Renaissance by the usage of half a century have become terms which call up before us, by means of a single word, the difference between two epochs, a difference which we feel to be essential, though hard to define, just as it is impossible to express the difference of taste between a strawberry and an apple.

To avoid the inconvenience inherent in the unsettled nature of the two terms Middle Ages and Renaissance, the safest way is to reduce them, as much as possible, to the meaning they originally had — for instance, not to speak of Renaissance in reference to Saint Francis of Assisi or the ogival style.[172]

[170] J. Huizinga, *Hersttij der Middelleeuwen; Studie over Levens-en Gedachtenvormen der veertiende en vijtiende eeuw in Frankrijk en de Nederlanden* (Haarlem, 1919). I cite from the English translation, revised under the author's supervision, *The Waning of the Middle Ages* (Longmans, Green and Co., London, 1924).
[171] Cf. *ibid.,* pp. 22; 30 f; 296 ff. In one place he equated Renaissance with "new modes of expression" (p. 46).
[172] *Ibid.,* p. 252.

But if Huizinga's interpretation was not as revolutionary as it might have been, it was still revolutionary enough to give aid and comfort to the annexationist wing of medieval scholarship. The impact of his work came less from the explicit statement of his thesis than from the total impression left by a book filled with evocative imagery. In a sense, Huizinga was a true disciple of Jacob Burckhardt. His work was psychological *Kulturgeschichte* in the Burckhardtian manner. But he looked at the age from the opposite direction, and his late medieval man was Burckhardt's Renaissance man, seen, as it were, from the rear. Huizinga was himself conscious of the one-sidedness of his view. In the preface to the English edition he wrote:

> History has always been far more engrossed by problems of origins than by those of decline and fall. When studying any period, we are always looking for the promise of what the next is to bring. . . . But in history, as in nature, birth and death are equally balanced. The decay of overripe forms of civilization is as suggestive a spectacle as the growth of new ones. And it occasionally happens that a period in which one had, hitherto, been mainly looking for the coming to birth of new things, suddenly reveals itself as an epoch of fading and decay. The present work deals with the history of the fourteenth and fifteenth centuries regarded as a period of termination, as the close of the Middle Ages.

Despite the inclusion of France in the scope of his study, Huizinga concentrated attention primarily upon the Burgundian Netherlands, a fact which made his thesis more significant than it might otherwise have been. For the Renaissance was generally considered to have begun earlier in the Netherlands than in any other land north of the Alps. They were second only to Italy in the early growth of urban culture, and their artists were the principal rivals of the great Italians of the *Quattrocento*. There, as nowhere else outside of Italy, could be found a similar wealth and luxury, the extravagant magnificence of court life, the glaring contrasts of wealth and poverty created by an incipient capitalism. Huizinga found in the Burgundian court a conscious desire to make social life a work of art, and in the fashions of the day evidence of "an overflowing aesthetic craving," [173] all of which

[173] *Ibid.*, p. 46 f.

was very reminiscent of Burckhardt's Italian Renaissance. Consciously reminiscent, too, was Huizinga's emphasis on honor and the desire for fame, which he found to be characteristic of that decadently chivalrous society.[174] In both morality and religion it was a period of disequilibrium, marked by excessive violence of passion and by a tendency to reduce religious concepts to forms of sensuous imagery.[175] But in all this Huizinga saw not the stirrings of a new age coming to birth, but rather the decadent overripeness of a civilization that had passed its prime and had lost vitality. He was most convincing when dealing with the pseudo-chivalrous court of the Burgundian dukes; for there an uprooted feudal society, enjoying the luxury produced by urban industry and commerce, still kept up feudal social forms and ideas which had lost all contact with reality. This is an impression further borne out by Otto Cartellieri's more detailed study of *The Court of the Dukes of Burgundy* (1926).[176]

When he turned to art, always one of his principal interests, Huizinga was on more controversial ground. But realization of that fact did not make him alter his thesis. On the contrary, it was, he wrote, the study of the art of the Van Eycks and their contemporaries that first led him to his interpretation of their age.[177] On this point he was emphatic.

> Nor should the art of Claus Sluter and the brothers Van Eyck be called Renaissance. Both in form and in idea it is a product of the waning Middle Ages. If certain historians of art have discovered Renaissance elements in it, it is because they have confounded, very wrongly, realism and Renaissance. Now this scrupulous realism, this aspiration to render exactly natural details, is the characteristic feature of the spirit of the expiring Middle Ages. It is the same tendency which we encountered in all the fields of thought of the epoch, a sign of decline and not of rejuvenation. The triumph of the Renaissance was to consist in replacing this meticulous realism by breadth and simplicity.[178]

[174] *Ibid.*, p. 58 f.
[175] Cf. *ibid.*, p. 136 ff.
[176] O. Cartellieri, *Am Hofe der Herzöge von Burgund; kulturhistorische Bilder* (Basel, 1926). Eng. trans. (London, 1929).
[177] Huizinga, p. v.
[178] *Ibid.*, p. 252 f.

Later, in a special study of the concepts "Renaissance and Realism" (1930),[179] he declared that, on the basis of its realism, the Italian *Quattrocento* should also be considered fundamentally medieval. The mature Dürer, on the other hand, after he had abandoned indiscriminate attention to detail for a unified ideal beauty, became one of the exponents of the Renaissance. Here again we find Huizinga recognizing the existence of a Renaissance, but limited in time and content to the period of classic form.

Despite his half-hearted concessions to the time-honored concept, Huizinga must be numbered among the destructive critics of the Renaissance tradition. So much is made doubly clear in the article on "The Problem of the Renaissance" (1920),[180] in which he examined the historical evolution as well as the validity of the Renaissance concept. He was prepared to admit the usefulness of the periodic concept, even its indispensability; but by the time he had finished his analysis of its inconsistencies and bewildering metamorphoses, and had demonstrated the medieval content of the age and deprived it of most of the distinguishing peculiarities ascribed to it by tradition, there seemed little left worth fighting for.

What *The Waning of the Middle Ages* had done for France and the Netherlands, Rudolf Stadelmann's essay, *The Spirit of the Outgoing Middle Ages* (1929),[181] did for Germany in the period before the Reformation. Stadelmann had originally intended to write a general history of late medieval culture, but gave up the plan when Huizinga's book appeared.[182] Accepting this anticipation of his own intention with admirable good grace, he determined to limit the scope of his study to the intellectual history of Germany, as illustrated by the *Weltanschauung* of a series of writers from Nicholas of Cusa to Sebastian Franck. The impact of his work, however, went far beyond the formal limits of his subject. Stadelmann was a conscious revisionist

---

[179] J. Huizinga, "Renaissance und Realismus," in his *Wege der Kulturgeschichte* (Munich, 1930), pp. 140–64; see especially, p. 157.

[180] J. Huizinga, "Renaissance Studien: I. Het Problem," *De Gids*, IV (1920); German translation in his *Wege der Kulturgeschichte*, pp. 89–139.

[181] R. Stadelmann, *Vom Geist des ausgehenden Mittelalters, Studien zur Geschichte der Weltanschauung von Nicolaus Cusanus bis Sebastian Franck* (Halle, 1929).

[182] Cf. *ibid.*, Preface.

who wrestled manfully with the "Problem of the Renaissance"; [183] and he took his stand firmly with those who would look at the Renaissance from the direction of the High Middle Ages. It was, he admitted, a one-sided view, but he argued that a phenomenon can be seen significantly only from a fixed point, i.e., from one side.[184] In all this he was at one with Huizinga, but in other respects he was much closer to Dilthey, whose famous essay *Intuition and Analysis of Men in the Fifteenth and Sixteenth Centuries* he took as his model. He accepted Dilthey's methodology and his criteria, but what he did to Dilthey's conception of the *Weltanschauung* of the age was very much what Huizinga had done to Burckhardt's. Where Dilthey had seen the dawn of modern philosophy and the modern spirit, Stadelmann saw only the end of an era, characterized by the tired, resigned tone of a *fin de siècle*.[185] The chapter headings indicate the tone as well as the content of his analysis of what had generally been considered the German Renaissance: "Skepticism," "Resignation," "Emancipation," "Pessimism." The peculiar traits of the age, Stadelmann thought, were "an undeveloped mysticism, a pietistic resignation, a spiritual individualism, a rational philosophy of religion," [186] all of which added up to a generally "defeatist" attitude. The intellectual atmosphere was one prone to compromise, a fit climate to nourish the Erasmian *Bildungsreligion*. Luther, on the other hand, with his faith in objective revelation and his personal acquaintance with the Devil, lived in an entirely different atmosphere.[187] Stadelmann thought it a much healthier one. Compared with Luther, the men of the preceding generation were feckless creatures, "complicated individualists" without ideal drive, "problematical natures" who sought in vain to find secure footing in a world that was disintegrating under them. They all "carried the mark of a hidden sorrow, as though they secretly longed for a cool hand to be placed on their brows. . . . They are the noteworthy boundary posts of an age approaching its end." [188] It may be

---

[183] See R. Stadelmann, "Zum Problem der Renaissance," *Neue Jahrbücher für Wissenschaft und Jugendbildung*, X, (1934), 49–63.

[184] Stadelmann, *Vom Geist*, p. 3.

[185] Cf. Stadelmann, "Zum Problem," *Neue Jahrbücher*, X, 50; *Vom Geist*, pp. 6 ff.

[186] *Ibid.*, p. 278.   [187] *Ibid.*, pp. 279 ff.   [188] *Ibid.*, p. 285.

that Stadelmann found them all too closely akin to his own somewhat lost generation.

It was the phenomenon of cultural decadence that seems to have especially preoccupied both Huizinga and Stadelmann. With most of the other historians who regarded the Renaissance as the end or decline of the Middle Ages, that was a matter of secondary importance. Their interest was concentrated primarily on defence of the great but long undervalued culture of the High Middle Ages, and their relative depreciation of the achievements of the Renaissance was, as it were, incidental. We have, in short, to deal here with those historians who carried the rehabilitation of the Middle Ages to the point of invidious comparison.

French chauvinism, which could at times rival in intensity its trans-Rhenish counterpart, furnished one of the motives that might lead to such a tendency. Unlike the Germanic nationalists, however, the French seldom showed animosity toward the influence of classical antiquity. They merely claimed that it had first been revived by medieval France rather than by Renaissance Italy. The French, too, could claim with good reason that France was the home of medieval scholastic learning and Gothic art, and the source of a very large part of both medieval and Renaissance vernacular literary tradition. Such emphasis on the priority of medieval France was not incompatible with a moderately revised conception of the Renaissance. Carried to extremes, however, it might lead to complete rejection of the originality of the later Italian movement. What then resulted was not simply the discovery of a medieval Renaissance, but the dogmatic assertion that the High Middle Ages were *the* Renaissance and the period traditionally so named merely a rather watered down continuation thereof. Oddly enough it was a Swedish scholar, Johan Nordström, who propounded this interpretation, thus succeeding in becoming more Gallic than the Gauls.

Throughout the whole of his belligerent essay, *Middle Ages and Renaissance* (1933),[189] Nordström dwelt consistently on the theme

---

[189] J. Nordström, *Moyen Age et Renaissance, essai historique* (Paris, 1933). The Swedish original appeared in *Norstedts Världshistoria*, ed. S. Tunberg and S. E. Bring, VI (Stockholm, 1929).

of the priority, originality, and general superiority of medieval French culture as compared with that of Renaissance Italy. The key to his emotion seems to be, it is true, less a specifically French national feeling than a more generally northern resentment of Italian claims to cultural leadership. Medieval French culture he regarded as the source of a general European Renaissance, to which the later Italian culture added nothing significant.

> In proportion as medieval studies advance [he wrote], it becomes evident that one must give to the notion "Middle Ages" a meaning at once larger and more carefully defined: likewise, it becomes necessary to revise completely the traditional conception which has made us see in the Italian Renaissance the matrix of our civilization. What we have learned to think of as the great contributions of that Renaissance to western culture appear more and more, in their principal lines, a simple continuation or a transformation under the influence of the ethnical Italian character of the traditions of the Middle Ages. But these were formed mostly to the north of the Alps during the first two centuries of the second millenium, in the midst of that civilization which embraced almost all the West and of which France had been the most glorious creator. Before Italy appeared, relatively late, as a nation directing culture, we may well speak of a "European Renaissance," which had laid the mighty foundations on which the multiple forms of higher civilization in our part of the world would be built.[190]

After a sketch of the historical development of the Renaissance concept, in which a lengthy and bitter criticism of Burckhardt holds the central position, Nordström proceeded to demonstrate this thesis point by point. Taking the modern and secular traits traditionally ascribed to the Renaissance one by one — national consciousness, urban culture, individualism, classical humanism, liberation of reason, Platonic philosophy, empirical study of the natural sciences, intense interest in man and nature, the growth of a worldly and consciously refined society, realism and classical influences in art — Nordström repeated in regard to each his constant formula: these things were not originated by Renaissance Italy; they were already fully matured in medieval France. Turning finally to the history of Italy, he declared that "in all that concerned higher culture as a whole, it long remained a French

[190] *Ibid.*, p. 12 f; cf. p. 8.

province." [191] Its civilization began to assume a national character only during the fourteenth century. Even then, medieval northern traditions continued to exert a powerful influence. The argument of this final chapter might be summarized, without departing far from objective justice, in two axiomatic statements: first, what was admirable in the culture of Renaissance Italy was neither unique nor original; and, second, what was original and peculiar was generally deplorable.

Nordström's thesis was too obviously over-stated to win general acceptance. It was, however, widely noted. Italian scholars rejected it with considerable indignation.[192] Non-Italian medievalists tended to regard it as an unfortunately extreme statement of an interpretation which contained a kernel of truth and which might well have a salutary effect.[193] And some French nationalists accepted it in toto. Among the latter, Jacques Boulenger carried Nordström's argument to its logical conclusion in an article significantly entitled, "The True Century of the Renaissance" (1934).[194] Here Boulenger asserted with a notable absence of qualification that the Renaissance "did not in any way begin in the fifteenth century, and its properly Italian aspect was only one of its late aspects: it began in the twelfth century or thereabouts." [195] Boulenger repeated all of Nordström's arguments, summarized and heightened, if possible, in tone. It was twelfth century France, not fifteenth century Italy, which saw "the rebirth of national sentiment," a rather puzzling phrase, and also the rebirth of intellectual curiosity, ancient science, classical latinity, and, in short, the beginnings of all modern European culture.

Still another motive for depreciation of the Renaissance in relation to the Middle Ages is to be found in Catholic feeling for the great age of the Church and of scholastic philosophy. That this might lead to partial denial of the originality of the Renaissance and to emphasis

191 Ibid., p. 153.
192 See, for example, I. Siciliano, Medio Evo e Rinascimento (Milan, 1936), pp. 36–50; and E. Anagnine, "Il problema del Rinascimento," Nuova rivista storica, XVIII (1934), 573–94. Anagnine's conclusion is to the point: "Volendo troppo provare, il Nordström non ha in sostanza provata nulla."
193 Cf. D. Bush, The Renaissance and English Humanism (Toronto, 1939), p. 25 f.
194 J. Boulenger, "Le vrai siècle de la Renaissance," Humanisme et Renaissance. I (1934), 9–30.
195 Ibid., p. 9.

upon the survival in it of scholastic and essentially Catholic ways of thought has been abundantly illustrated above. It might also lead to complete annexation of the Renaissance to the Middle Ages. Such was the interpretation offered, for example, by François Picavet, one of the most influential teachers of medieval philosophy at Paris in the early years of this century. Defining the Middle Ages as "essentially a theological period, which gave preponderant place to questions relating to God and immortality, or more exactly, to God and the means by which men may be united with Him," he concluded that the medieval period gave way gradually to modern civilization only during the seventeenth century.[196] The most serious depreciation of the Renaissance, however, is found more commonly in another tendency of recent Catholic thought, which, while springing from the same source, has resulted in a quite different attitude. Though it is not entirely germane to the present discussion, it may be worth noting here that a number of recent Catholic writers have reacted against the Burckhardtian Renaissance chiefly in the way of a complete reversal of value judgments. That is, they have accepted the traditional interpretation as substantially accurate, but have condemned the Renaissance, so pictured, as the source of modern error. Thus Jacques Maritain, in diagnosing the ills of the modern world, defined it as "a certain type of civilization, spiritually dominated from the beginning by the humanism of the Renaissance, the Protestant Reformation, and the Cartesian reform," a civilization in which culture "has become separated . . . . from the sacred and has been turned back on man himself." [197] In much the same spirit Christopher Dawson restated the traditional contrast between Middle Ages and Renaissance:

> The Renaissance has its beginning in the self-discovery, the self-realization, and the self-exaltation of man. Medieval man had attempted to base his life on the supernatural. His ideal of knowledge

---

[196] F. Picavet, *Esquisse d'une histoire générale et comparée des philosophies médiévales* (Paris, 1905), pp. 41–45.

[197] J. Maritain, "Religion and Culture," in J. Maritain, P. Wust, and C. Dawson, *Essays in Order* (New York: Sheed and Ward, 1931), p. 14. Cf. J. Maritain, *True Humanism* (New York, 1938); and I. C. Isola, *Critica del Rinascimento*, 2 vols. (Livorno, 1907); and Baudrillart, cited above, p. 264.

was not the adventurous quest of the human mind exploring its own kingdom; it was an intuition of the eternal verities, which is itself an emanation from the Divine Intellect. . . . The men of the Renaissance, on the other hand, turned away from the eternal and the absolute to the world of nature and human experience. They rejected their dependence on the supernatural, and vindicated their independence and supremacy in the temporal order. But thereby they were gradually led by an internal process of logic to criticize the principles of their own knowledge and to lose confidence in their own freedom. The self-affirmation of man gradually led to the denial of the spiritual foundations of his freedom and knowledge.[198]

This interpretation concedes to the Renaissance a certain reprehensible originality. It admits that the Renaissance added something new. Etienne Gilson refused to grant the Renaissance even that faint praise. His thesis, already referred to in its several aspects,[199] was always consistent: the Renaissance had created nothing new that was of value, since all the most important elements of its culture already existed in the Middle Ages. But, while adding nothing, it had lost much. Argument in support of this interpretation runs through the greater part of Gilson's work, but the whole thesis was summed up in his essay on "Medieval Humanism and the Renaissance" in one classically balanced epigram: "The difference between the Renaissance and the Middle Ages was not a difference by addition but by subtraction. The Renaissance, as it has been described to us, was not the Middle Ages plus man, but the Middle Ages minus God, and the tragedy is that in losing God the Renaissance was losing man himself." [200]

Finally, and from a very different point of view, those scholarly medievalists whose research has been devoted to the defense and illustration of medieval science, and who have found the Renaissance writers lacking in that field, have tended to minimize the original contributions of the Renaissance and to regard it as simple decline of medieval civilization. For that matter, scholarly medievalists in general, viewing the Renaissance from the direction of their own field of

[198] C. Dawson, "Christianity and the New Age," in *Essays in Order*, p. 160 f.
[199] See above, pp. 335; 340; 354.
[200] E. Gilson, "Humanisme médiéval et Renaissance," in his *Les idées et les lettres* (Paris, 1932), p. 192.

study, have not unnaturally been more impressed by what was to them familiar than by what was new in that transitional age. But the historians of science seem to have a more positive conviction that the Renaissance marked a falling away from the vigorous thought of the scholastic age. As George Sarton put it, "from the scientific point of view, the Renaissance was *not* a renaissance." It was, he added, "less a genuine revival than a halfway rest between two revivals."[201] This is a significant attack upon the Burckhardtian conception of the Renaissance as the birth hour of the modern world and one that must be taken seriously; for their can be no doubt that natural science is one of the outstanding attributes of modern civilization.[202] And even though, as Sarton admitted and as Leonardo Olschki has demonstrated at length,[203] the unlearned but practical technicians of the age, craftsmen, artists, engineers, and the like, did make important contributions to the progress of science, there can also be little doubt that the humanists were not scientists nor much concerned with scientific theory. They may even have been, as Sarton insisted, "anti-scientific." They were men of letters, with other interests, perhaps equally scholarly and rather more humane. One may, however, recognize their scientific limitations without therefore considering them "supercilious dilettanti," or going so far as Sarton does in depreciation of their work, as, for example, in the following quotations:

> In the eternal conflict between matter and form, the pendulum had swung back to the latter, and for a century or two, style overruled knowledge, truth, even morality.[204]

And again:

> From the philosophical as well as from the scientific standpoint this was undoubtedly a regression. As compared with medieval scholasti-

[201] G. Sarton, "Science in the Renaissance," in J. W. Thompson, G. Rowley, F. Schevill, and G. Sarton, *The Civilization of the Renaissance* (Chicago: The University of Chicago Press, 1929), p. 76; cf. G. Sarton, *Introduction to the History of Science,* 2 vols. (Washington, 1927–31).

[202] For discussion of this aspect of the Renaissance problem, see D. B. Durand, "Tradition and Innovation in Fifteenth Century Italy," *Journal of the History of Ideas,* IV (1943), 1–20.

[203] L. Olschki, *Geschichte der neusprachlichen wissenschaftlichen Literatur,* 3 vols. (Heidelberg, Leipzig and Halle, 1919–27); see above, pp. 220 ff.

[204] Thompson et al., *Civilization of the Renaissance,* p. 77.

cism, dull but honest, the characteristic philosophy of that age, the Florentine Neo-Platonism, was a superficial mixture of ideas too vague to be of real value. . . . Much of the critical work which had been done by their [the humanists'] medieval forerunners, whom they could not understand and despised accordingly, was carelessly undone by them.[205]

Finally:

It is not true to say (as is so often done) that the humanists introduced freedom of thought. They destroyed some medieval prejudices which blocked the way; they broke some old shackles, but introduced new ones; they questioned the authority of dogmas, but accepted the authority of the ancients; they tore down cumbersome restraints, but replaced them by something infinitely worse, spiritual anarchy; they smothered scholasticism, but put in its stead literary ideals too vague to be effective. They looked backward, not forward. They created beauty, plenty of it, but not truth, and without truth, everything becomes arbitrary and insecure, and whatever freedom there is, is a sham.[206]

One might ask, on good precedent, "What is truth?" The succeeding sentence gave Sarton's answer: "The only remedy which could have cured them was a direct appeal to nature — experimental science — but this they hardly understood." This should be a comforting thought to our generation, which at least understands experimental science, even though it is not entirely convinced that it has thereby found the truth that will prevent all things from becoming arbitrary and insecure.

Proceeding from much the same premises, Lynn Thorndike has gone even further than Sarton in rejecting the conception of the Renaissance. For Thorndike, the Renaissance is always "the so-called Renaissance." The theme of the unbroken continuity of medieval tradition and a tendency to underrate the original achievements of the men of the fifteenth and sixteenth centuries runs throughout the later part of his great *History of Magic and Experimental Science*.[207] And in his general discussions of the historiographical problem, there is evidence

---

[205] *Ibid.*, p. 79.   [206] *Ibid.*, p. 94.

[207] L. Thorndike, *A History of Magic and Experimental Science*, 6 vols. (New York, 1923–41). For discussion, see D. B. Durand, "Magic and Experimental Science: The Achievement of Lynn Thorndike," *Isis*, XXXIII (1942), 691–712.

of an almost personal antipathy toward not only the concept of the Renaissance, but also the age to which it has been applied. In the introductory chapter to the series of studies entitled *Science and Thought in the Fifteenth Century* (1929), for example, he raised the question "whether there was not a falling off in civilization in general and in scientific productiveness in particular after the remarkable activity of the twelfth and thirteenth centuries — in short, whether instead of a renaissance something of a backsliding did not set in with Petrarch." [208] Like Sarton, Thorndike apparently found it difficult to forgive the humanists for their devotion to literary form, which he thought a poor substitute for the close logical reasoning of the schoolmen.

> Was not humanism [he asked] in part an easier way for princes and their sons who found the existing university requirements too harsh, and for those in general who preferred to write poems, letters, and orations, instead of following intricate arguments and arranging their own thought in a systematic orderly manner? To escape this stern necessity, the humanists glorified what had been a grammar-school subject, Latin, into the sum and substance of culture. . . . Indeed, leisure and cultured ease were the ideal of many humanists, as against either great literary productivitiy or sustained reasoning.[209]

It might be suggested that Renaissance men could have found some still easier way of avoiding the stern necessity of systematic thought than by the study of ancient literature. They might, indeed, have simply remained illiterate, as many medieval princes and their sons were content to do. But such an objection is frivolous. The problem raised by Thorndike's argument, as by so many other interpretations, is one of criteria. If a civilization is to be judged by its proficiency in one form of logical ratiocination, and if the Middle Ages are to be equated with scholastic speculation in the natural sciences while the Renaissance is equated with humanist dilettantism, Thorndike's thesis may well be justified. Such criteria, however, are too narrow to serve as basis for an adequate interpretation of any civilization.

[208] L. Thorndike, *Science and Thought in the Fifteenth Century* (New York, *Columbia University Press,* 1929), p. 10; see also his "Renaissance or Prenaissance?," *Journal of the History of Ideas,* IV (1943), 65–74.
[209] Thorndike, *Science and Thought,* p. 13.

CHAPTER TWELVE

Conclusion

THE PURPOSE OF THIS BOOK has been to study the mirrored reflections of the Renaissance, not the historical actuality. These reflections are also historical facts, but they belong less to the history of the Renaissance than to that of modern historiography, or in a more general way to the history of modern thought. Yet, what is mirrored in the writings we have studied, though often seen darkly as in a glass, is always the same concrete phenomenon, the actuality of an epoch of crucial importance for the evolution of Western civilization. And it has been my hope that by viewing this phenomenon through the eyes of successive generations we might be able to see it for ourselves a little more clearly and completely, with a greater awareness of the subjective biases that tend to make us see it in this or that light. The conclusions to be drawn from our study, then, are of various kinds, depending on whether we regard it as a contribution to the history of historiography or to modern intellectual history or as a possible aid to achieving a more satisfactory interpretation of the Renaissance itself.

Viewed simply as an essay in the history of historiography, it may be considered, first of all, as an object lesson in historical relativism. As we follow the interpretations of the Renaissance presented by generation after generation, and within each generation by one historian after another, we must be impressed by the degree to which the historian's reconstruction of the past is conditioned by the intellectual environment of his time and place and also by his own character, interests, and experience. At the same time our study might serve as a case history to demonstrate the effect of tradition upon historical thought, for the historian's view of the past is also conditioned constantly by the works of his predecessors. Even if it were possible for him to draw all his material directly from the sources, the scope and point of view of his inquiry, his choice of sources and the questions he would ask of them, would all be influenced by the way in which these problems had been solved in the past. One conclusion, then, that may be fairly drawn from our study is that historical interpretations are not isolated acts. They are part of an evolving, constantly changing, but continuous tradition. In the growth of this tradition branches may strike out in diverse directions, but they spring from the trunk of the parent tree. It follows, therefore, that no interpretation of the Renaissance or, we may assume, that of any other historical phenomenon can be fully understood except in relation to the tradition from which it springs. Finally, as we review the past histories of the Renaissance, we cannot but be impressed by the immense growth of historical consciousness since the days when the humanists laid the foundations of modern historiography. Our knowledge of history has broadened and deepened, has become immeasurably richer. Yet that very richness presents a problem that is becoming increasingly serious. It is an embarrassment of wealth. Man can perceive reality, including historical reality, only after the manner of being that he has, and that being is finite. There is a limit to the amount of knowledge his mind can encompass. Hence the broadening of historical knowledge has been accompanied by a narrowing of the historian's view, in too many instances, to a small segment of history. The interpretation of an historical period such as the Renaissance may thus be conditioned by the historian's specialized concern with one aspect of its culture as well as by current modes of thought or inherited traditions, a fact amply demonstrated in the foregoing pages.

Though primarily an essay in the history of historiography, our study has also certain implications for the broader field of intellectual history. The two fields are, indeed, related by a constant chain of interaction. Not only is the historian's view of the past conditioned by the intellectual environment in which he lives; it becomes in turn an active force in shaping that environment. This latter aspect of the interaction between historical thought and the general climate of opinion has remained rather implicit than explicit throughout our study. But it is obvious enough that interpretations of the Renaissance have at times exerted a very considerable influence upon thought in a variety of fields, ranging all the way from aesthetics to the philosophy of history. They have also served the propagandist purposes of such widely differentiated movements as the Protestant Reformation, the French Revolution, and chauvinistic nationalism. The habit of thinking historically has become so nearly universal in the past two centuries that there is scarcely a problem in contemporary life the solution of which is not influenced, for good or ill, by the interpretation of history. For that reason, if for no other, it is of vital importance that our conception of the past should be as close as possible to objective truth, that it should at least be as free as possible from distortion by conscious or unconscious bias.

Let us return, then, to the idea that was the original inspiration for this book: the hope that a study of the interpretations of the Renaissance during the past five hundred years might aid us in achieving a truer conception of the Renaissance itself, the Renaissance as historical actuality. It may be that the first impression left by our study, with all its implied historical relativism, will be the disillusioned conviction that there have been too many interpretations already, and that any new interpretation, being the product of our own time and ephemeral as are all things temporal, will scarcely be worth the effort. But the historian cannot, in fact, abandon the task of attempting to understand the past and of trying to interpret it in some way that will have meaning, if only for his own generation. And the multiplicity of interpretations, properly considered, may aid him in accomplishing that task. A study of the origins and growth of these interpretations should enable him to assess more exactly the point of view of other historians and hence the degree of validity to be ascribed to their work. At the same time, it should make him more consciously aware of his own point of view. If the historian is to interpret the past at all, he must have a point of view, but he may come closer to objectivity if that point of view is consciously recognized and hence not regarded as absolute. Further, the multiplicity of interpretations has contributed to our knowledge as well as to our confusion. Each interpretation has added something to our ability to view the Renaissance in its entirety.

It has been said that, though the historian may make history, he does not make it out of whole cloth. Except for the few examples of that lunacy that emanates from mystical racism, none of the interpretations we have considered are entirely divorced from reality. The mirror of historical writing may reflect only one facet of actuality, and the reflection may be warped or clouded, but each successive reflection makes it more nearly possible to see the objective phenomenon from all sides as a complete entity. What the foregoing study indicates, then, if we read its lesson aright, is that the time is ripe for a new and more comprehensive synthesis.

The very confusion of concepts regarding the Renaissance demonstrates the need for interpretation. More than ever in our time this is the primary desideratum. Research is needed, too, especially in those fields of intellectual, economic, and social history that have attracted the attention of historians only in fairly recent times. Even there, however, the volume of available data is already very great. The historian who would try to understand in a general way what happened during the period we know as the Renaissance and to fit it into its proper place in the evolution of Western civilization must select, arrange, and interpret a vast amount of material. Most historians will no doubt continue to work within special fields. That is the inevitable result of that embarrassment of riches which has made comprehensive knowledge, not to mention the discovery of new data, possible only within a limited field. And it is by no means undesirable. But even the specialist must have some larger conception of the nature of the age if he is to avoid the danger of viewing his chosen segment in false perspective. Much of the confusion within special fields has been fostered by the lack of an adequately founded and comprehensive synthesis of the age as a whole.

Conversely, the instability of many interpretations of the Renaissance has resulted from their being set upon too narrow a foundation. Too often the procedure has been to assume a general interpretation of the period from data pertaining exclusively to a special field, rather than to interpret the history of the special field in accordance with a general synthesis constructed from a study of the total complex of Renaissance civilization. Until about the middle of the nineteenth century, this procedure could scarcely be avoided. The history of civilization as an historical genre had scarcely been born, and the concept of the Renaissance was limited almost entirely to the history of learning, literature, art, or religion. The "rebirths" in these various fields thus remained isolated phenomena. They set the tone for historians' attitudes toward the age that had produced them, but they were not themselves interpreted in their proper character as aspects of a total configuration of culture. Both Voltaire and Michelet made tentative efforts to remedy this situation, but it was Burckhardt who first established the Renaissance firmly as an epoch in the history of civilization. His synthesis included much of the political and social and some of the economic life of the period, as well as the more commonly considered aspects of intellectual culture, all interpreted in relation to a spirit or mentality which he regarded as characteristic of the age. It was a broad yet closely integrated interpretation. Unfortunately, the foundation upon which it, too, rested was in many respects inadequate. Burckhardt's knowledge of the Middle Ages was insufficient, and his conception of medieval civilization was distorted by traditional prejudices. As a result, his Renaissance was cut off from its natural roots. It was, to some extent, a static phenomenon, standing isolated in time, without, as it were, visible means of support. Further, while interpreting the Renaissance as the dawn of modern civilization, and hence a general European phenomenon, Burckhardt identified its spirit with the peculiar genius of the Italian people and traced its historical origins to conditions that were peculiar to Italy. Finally, his whole synthesis rested upon data carefully selected to illustrate a limited number of typical characteristics.

Since the publication of *The Civilization of the Renaissance in Italy*, a host of historians have labored to fill in Burckhardt's pattern, and have extended it, by the theory of diffusion, to the lands beyond the Alps. More recently, other hosts of historians have labored with equal zeal to disintegrate his pattern. But neither the work of the traditionalists nor that of the revisionists, if they may be so designated, has resulted in a synthesis broader or more inclusive than Burckhardt's own. Almost without exception their data have been drawn principally from some specialized field of research. And in most instances new interpretations have been oriented upon national claims to priority, or upon some one set of ideas, a single branch of intellectual or aesthetic culture, or even a single psychological attitude. The overwhelming tendency has been to interpret the Renaissance exclusively in terms of immaterial factors — aesthetic forms, ideologies, religion, *Weltanschauung,* psychological characteristics, and so forth. The more material factors — the economic, social, and political conditions, which form so large a part of the civilization of any age — have generally been slighted as elements in an interpretation of Renaissance culture. On the other hand, historians for whom economic, social, or political history is a primary concern have too seldom bothered to offer a general interpretation of the culture of the age. They have thus contributed less than they might have done to restore the balance and to make possible a rounded and comprehensive synthesis.

Through all the recent interpretations of the origins, motive forces, and basic character of Renaissance civilization, the major trend of revisionism has been to break down the contrast between the Renaissance and the preceding era. This has been on the whole a healthy tendency, sanctioned by our modern conviction of the evolutionary nature of historical development. In extreme cases, however, it has led to the thesis that the Renaissance was merely a continuation of the Middle Ages, an interpretation surely as one-sided as Burckhardt's belief that it was the dawn of the modern age, and based on as restricted a selection of data. There is undoubtedly more truth in the compromise solution, frequently implied or stated in passing comment, that the Renaissance was an age of transition. But this thesis has yet to be worked out in a full synthesis. It is in any case meaningless unless accompanied by a systematic analysis both of the essential differences between medieval and modern civilization and of what was peculiar to the transitional age itself.

I do not mean to imply that historians should seek to discover anew the "spirit of the Renaissance" in the sense of a *Zeitgeist* that will serve as the key to open all doors. My insistence upon the value of synthesis rests simply upon a conviction, which may be in essence an act of faith, that the events of the past are not isolated phenomena, that history is not a meaningless chaos of unrelated facts. To support this conviction with adequate proof, even could I do so, would require an essay in the philosophy of history too lengthy for inclusion here. Here I can do no more than state a *credo,* and one shared by an increasingly large number of historians. It is the belief that all elements of a civilization are related to one another as parts of a total configuration, just as, by the dynamic nature of history, they are related in causal sequence to the past and the future.

The need for synthesis in broad outlines will naturally seem less apparent to the historian engaged in detailed analysis of specialized fields. But as I have observed, the lack of a larger synthesis often leads to distortion of perspective in the treatment of detail. It may also lead to an unhappy reversal of logical procedure in the way of over-hasty generalization from data of a special sort. What is more to the point, however, the historian actually cannot avoid forming some notion of the nature of the age in which his special field lies. Whether he will or no, consciously or unconsciously, he will form some conception of it, and that conception will give shape and color to his treatment of any aspect of its civilization. There is less danger of distortion if that conception, however misguided, is a conscious one and therefore the object of thought, than if it is merely an unconscious preconception, by which the historian is unwittingly guided in the selection, arrangement, and evaluation of his material. Carl Becker used to observe that there was an erroneous assumption involved in the belief that by not giving thought the historian could add a cubit to his stature. It would be well, too, if the historian were not only to possess a well thought out interpretation of the age, but also to state it explicitly, if only as a *caveat emptor.* If he errs — and what historian can avoid the fate of all humanity? — his error will then be the less insidious. In the not so distant past the historian could absolve his conscience with the pleasing fallacy that the facts might speak for themselves. We are now much too aware of the subjective nature of historical thought to accept that easy solution of the historian's problem. The facts of history, as they appear in history books, speak with the tongues of men and in a great variety of idiom.

To argue the desirability of a synthetic interpretation of an age presupposes, of course, that one admits the value of historical periodization.[1] This is an admission that not all historians, particularly in this country, are prepared to make. There are, in fact, valid, logical objections to any form of periodization. It is an arbitrary construction imposed upon the unbroken flow of historical actuality. Yet without it the historian cannot think, much less talk or write about the past. He may, indeed, narrate the sequence of events in mere chronological order, but he cannot possibly discuss the material or intellectual conditions of the past without the aid of some periodic device. It is simply impossible to comprehend, much less interpret for others, the complex pattern of changing conditions as it occurred minute by minute. The historian may vary the length of his periods in accordance with the intensity of his study, but whether they be years, decades, generations, centuries, or epochs, they are the indispensable tools of his trade. If his concern is with the history of civilization, his periods must be large enough to be convenient, yet not so large as to be meaningless. He will not achieve an adequate interpretation of the period we know as the Renaissance by treating it a decade at a time, nor by annexing it to the already over-large medieval or modern eras. The problem of the Renaissance, then, cannot be solved simply by abandoning the periodic concept, by, as it were, ignoring it in the hope that it will go away. In our present state of confusion regarding it, we may be tempted to do just that. But to do so is to follow a counsel of despair and implies an abdication of the historian's office as interpreter of the past. Something of crucial importance took place during the three centuries or so commonly included in the Renaissance period. And the historian needs some periodic concept to apply to it as an indispensable instrument of thought, discussion, and interpretation.

One may be willing to grant the necessity of a periodic concept, however, and still object to the term "Renaissance" which tradition has attached to it. The term is undoubtedly misleading, and reflects an inadequate, if not positively erroneous conception of the significance of the age. It is, however, no more misleading nor biased in its connotation than the term Middle Ages, which many of the most bitter

---

[1] R. G. Collingwood has recently remarked that "the attempt to distinguish periods in history is a mark of advanced and mature historical thought, not afraid to interpret facts instead of merely ascertaining them." R. G. Collingwood, *The Idea of History* (Oxford, 1946), p. 53.

critics of the Renaissance still use without apparent qualms. Both terms had their origin in the same notion of the historical development of Western civilization, and there is not much justification for either except that it is sanctioned by tradition and that there is no commonly accepted substitute. There seems little point in accepting one term while rejecting the other, as Henry Osborn Taylor did with results more confusing than otherwise.[2] Until historians can agree upon a complete new scheme of periodization, the term "Renaissance," despite all confusion as to its meaning, carries a more generally recognized connotation than any other term we could employ. As Henri Hauser once remarked in this connection, "It seems to me that, save in the case of absolute necessity, it is a grave matter to renew in the scientific domain the miracle of the confusion of tongues."[3] And we might add the sage comment of that dean of medievalists, Charles Homer Haskins. After noting the misleading character of the term *renaissance,* wherever applied, he concluded:

> Nevertheless, it may be doubted whether such a term is more open to misinterpretation than others, like the *Quattrocento* or the sixteenth century, and it is so convenient and so well established that, like Austria, if it had not existed we should have to invent it. There was an Italian Renaissance, whatever we choose to call it, and nothing is gained by the process which ascribes the Homeric poems to another poet of the same name.[4]

If, then, we admit the desirability of synthesis and the need for a scheme of periodization which will recognize the existence of the Renaissance as an epoch in the history of Western civilization, we come to the heart of the methodological problem: how are we to establish an adequate basis for the interpretation of the age? In any work of synthesis, the first task is to decide what are the characteristic traits

[2] H. O. Taylor entitled his fine study of the intellectual history of Europe from the Church Fathers to Dante, *The Medieval Mind,* 2 vols. (New York, 1911), but refused to use the term Renaissance in the sequel devoted to the three following centuries, which thus appeared under the chronologically inadequate and misleading title, *Thought and Expression in the Sixteenth Century,* 2 vols. (New York, 1920).

[3] H. Hauser, "De l'humanisme et de la Réforme en France," *Revue historique,* LXIV (1897), 259 f.

[4] C. H. Haskins, *The Renaissance of the Twelfth Century* (Cambridge, Mass.: Harvard University Press, 1927), p. 5.

of the civilization of an age and to arrange them in a hierarchical order of importance. This is in fact the procedure followed, though not followed far enough, by historians who build their synthesis around such concepts as the Age of Faith, the Age of the Reformation, the Age of Mercantilism, the Enlightenment, the Industrial Revolution, the Romantic Era, or the Age of Nationalism. But these are prejudiced terms, not so much because they suggest an original bias, as because they concentrate attention too exclusively upon one aspect of the life of the age to serve as the basis for a general synthesis. Such was also the error of the humanists who portrayed the Renaissance as the age of the rebirth of classical culture and named it accordingly. Abuse of a method, however, does not prove the method to be unsound. Let me repeat: one cannot interpret history without a point of view. One cannot, therefore, avoid the necessity of arranging the various categories of historical activity in some order of relative importance. With the attempt to solve this problem, which involves the direction of approach to synthesis and also the weighing of evidence drawn from one field against that taken from another, we enter upon the most controversial ground. For here we have to deal with value judgments, and these are always peculiarly susceptible to subjective bias. The historian can scarcely avoid the temptation to regard as most important in the past what seems most important to him, what he values or what interests him most. All that can be asked of him is that he give earnest thought to the problem before deciding what factors in the civilization of the age he regards as most important for a general synthesis, and also that he should not, in constructing his synthesis, neglect those which he regards as less important or which he finds to be in contradiction to his major thesis.

Many interpretations, indeed, have failed not only because the foundation was too narrow, but also because the structure itself was not sufficiently flexible to tolerate the inconvenient fact and the contrary instance. A critical examination of the interpretations of the Renaissance from this point of view may suggest certain further methodological conclusions.

In the first place, those traits that may serve as focal points for synthesis need not be — almost certainly will not be — universally characteristic of the civilization of the age. The assumption that any feature proven to be typical is in fact universal has led to many an over-stated thesis and to much unnecessary revisionism. Transcendentalism may well be regarded as a major characteristic of medieval thought without it being necessary to prove that it was characteristic of all medieval thought, and scattered evidence of contrary currents, while important for filling in the picture of the age, does not materially alter its main outlines. It would be almost impossible, in fact, to discover any single trait of either medieval or modern civilization to which exceptions could not be found. This should be taken for granted. He who proves too much proves nothing. The historian must be satisfied to found his synthesis on characteristic features of relative validity, upon a judicious weighing of more and less, rather than upon the hopeless search for absolute uniformity. This weighing of more and less is especially important in relation to the Renaissance, for, in accordance with its transitional character, standing as it did between two fairly well integrated types of civilization, its own civilization was in a peculiarly fluid state, filled with contrasting elements.

In the second place, it is in the nature of historical evolution that each age will carry over a vast number of ideas, institutions, and forms of behavior from the preceding age. We must not expect, then, to find absolute contrast between successive ages at any point. Failure to recognize this has, however, been a further cause of much over-statement and unnecessary revision. The fact that scholastic methodology was still an active ingredient in the philosophy of the fifteenth and sixteenth centuries should surprise no one, nor does its discovery prove that Renaissance philosophy, much less the Renaissance as a whole, was essentially medieval. For that matter, Etienne Gilson is a better Thomist than any who lived during the Renaissance, yet he lives more or less in the twentieth century. What may be a major characteristic of one age may continue as a minority phenomenon in the succeeding one. Further, there are peculiar dangers involved in the effort to trace the continuity of tradition through a changing age. It often happens that institutional and ideal forms outlast their original content and are utilized by successive generations to organize or express something so altered as to be essentially new.

A third problem involved in any periodic synthesis, and one of the most difficult, is that posed by the continuous historical development within each age as well as from one age to another. Any general description of conditions must be subject to constant chronological qualification. Otherwise, the resultant synthesis presents no more than a static cross section of history and is therefore essentially unhistorical. For the same reason, the line of demarcation between historical periods can never be anything but arbitrary. No broad changes in the character of a civilization occur overnight. Here the historian must simply use his best judgment in deciding at what point the balance of more or less reaches a position of equilibrium. The whole problem is further complicated by the fact that the rate of change varies widely from one field to another, and also from one place to another. The historian may find that German civilization as a whole is still characteristically medieval at a time when that of Italy has ceased to be so. Or he may find that one aspect of Italian culture is still decidedly medieval, while another has changed almost beyond recognition. The point at which he will then place his line of chronological demarcation will depend, as does so much else, upon the relative importance he assigns to the various categories of historical activity.

This brings us back once more to the heart of the problem, to the essential question of the nature of Renaissance civilization, viewed in its entirety as a European phenomenon. But to attempt to answer that question would not be appropriate here. To do so would entail the writing of another book. If this study of past interpretations should help to make historians more conscious of all that is involved in the problem, it will have served its purpose.

THE FOLLOWING BIBLIOGRAPHY is not intended to include either works dealing directly with the history of the Renaissance or general works of historiography. These can be found listed in many places and, so far as they are related to the foregoing discussion, they are amply cited in the footnotes or index. Studies of particular historians or aspects of historiography can also be found easily in the footnotes. I have limited my bibliography, therefore, to studies of the origins and development of the concepts Middle Ages and Renaissance, discussions of varying trends of interpretation, and reviews of the recent literature on the Renaissance. These seem worth listing, not only because they pertain directly to the purpose of the book, but also because no adequate bibliography of the kind exists. Moreover, most of these studies are in the form of articles and hence are more difficult to find than books which would be listed under subject headings in any good library. A number of surveys of recent scholarship in the period of the Renaissance published in this country were prepared under the auspices of the Committee on Renaissance Studies of the American Council of Learned Societies. These are noted in the bibliography as "Renaissance Studies."

Allen, D. C., "Latin Literature," *Modern Language Quarterly,* II (1941), 403–20. (Renaissance Studies.)

Anagnine, E., "Il problema del Rinascimento," *Nuova rivista storica,* XVIII (1934), 555–94. (Review of recent studies and criticism especially of Walser and Nordström.)

Arezio, L., "Rinascimento, umanesimo e spirito moderno," *Nuova antologia,* CCLXXII (1930), 15–38. (Criticism of Toffanin's thesis.)

Bainton, R. H., "Changing Ideas and Ideals in the Sixteenth Century," *Journal of Modern History,* VIII (1936), 417–43. (Review of recent trends and discussion of intellectual change in the sixteenth century.)

Barnick, H., *Die Stellung der englischen Romantik zur italienischen Renaissance* (Freiburg im Breisgau, 1927). (Dissertation.)

Baron, H., "Zur Frage des Ursprungs des deutschen Humanismus und seiner religiösen Reformbestrebungen. Ein kritischer Bericht über die neuere Literatur," *Historische Zeitschrift*, CXXXII (1925), 413–46. (Review of studies since Hermelink.)

―――― "Literarische Wegweiser durch die italienische Geschichtsforschung der Gegenwart," *Historische Zeitschrift*, CXXXIII (1926), 325–34.

―――― "Renaissance in Italien. Literaturbericht," *Archiv für Kulturgeschichte*, XVII (1927), 226–56; XXI (1931), 95–128; 215–39; 340–56. (Review of studies since 1914. Valuable.)

Baumgarten, F. F., *Das Werk C. F. Meyers. Renaissance Empfindungen und Stilkunst* (2nd ed. Munich, 1920). (Contains good study of development of *Renaissancismus* in the nineteenth century.)

Bernhart, J., "Vom Geistesleben des Mittelalters. Ein Literaturbericht," *Deutsche Vierteljahrsschrift für Literaturwissenschaft und Geistesgeschichte*, V (1927), 172–211.

Borinski, K., "Die Weltwiedergeburtsidee in den neueren Zeiten," *Sitzungsberichte der Bayerischen Akademie der Wissenschaften*, Jahrgang 1919, 1 Abh. (Important study of the origins and evolution of the Renaissance concept.)

Bräm, E. M., *Die italienische Renaissance in dem englischen Geistesleben des 19. Jahrhunderts im besondern bei John Ruskin, John Addington Symonds und Vernon Lee* (Brugg, 1932).

Brandi, K., *Das Werden der Renaissance* (Göttingen, 1908). (Brief but excellent study of the growth of the idea of the Renaissance.)

―――― "Renaissance und Reformation, Wertung und Umwertung," *Preussische Jahrbücher*, CC (1925), 120–35. (Criticism of Burdach's thesis.)

Brecht, W., "Neue Literatur zum italienischen Humanismus," *Deutsche Vierteljahrsschrift für Literaturwissenschaft und Geistesgeschichte*, VI (1928), 767–80. (Good review of most important works, 1922–28.)

Buck, A., "Das Problem der italienischen Renaissance in der neuesten Forschung," in *Italienische Kulturberichte* (*Leipziger Romanistische Studien*, III, 1937), II, 179–213. (Excellent review.)

Burdach, K., "Sinn und Ursprung der Worte Renaissance und Reformation," *Sitzungsberichte der preussischen Akademie der Wissenschaften,* Jahrgang 1910, pp. 594–646. (Fundamental for Burdach's thesis and for origins of Renaissance concept.)

—— "Die seelischen und geistigen Quellen der Renaissancebewegung," *Historische Zeitschrift,* CXLIX (1933–34), 477–521. (Contains review of reception of his interpretation.)

Burr, G. L., "How the Middle Ages got their Name," *American Historical Review,* XX (1914–15), 813–15.

Bush, D., *The Renaissance and English Humanism* (Toronto, 1939). (Chapter I is an excellent study of modern theories of the Renaissance.)

Cantimori, D., "Sulla storia del concetto di Rinascimento," *Annali della R. Scuola normale superiore di Pisa,* Serie II, I (1932), 229–68. (Most important Italian study of history of Renaissance concept.)

Chamard, H., *Les origines de la poésie française de la Renaissance* (Paris, 1932). (Contains good historiographical introduction, pp. 17–38.)

Dove, A., "Der Streit um das Mittelalter," *Historische Zeitschrift,* CXVI (1916), 209–30. (Argues that concept of Middle Ages is a meaningless legacy from the humanist tradition.)

Durand, D. B. and Baron, H., "Tradition and Innovation in the Fifteenth Century Renaissance," *Journal of the History of Ideas,* IV (1943), 1–49. (Discussion of the problem and review of recent trends, chiefly in the history of science and political theory.)

Eppelsheimer, H. W., "Das Renaissance-Problem," *Deutsche Vierteljahrsschrift für Literaturwissenschaft und Geistesgeschichte,* XI (1933), 477–500. (Part I is a sketch of the history of the concept; Part II a methodological essay on the Renaissance as a problem in *Geistesgeschichte.*)

Ernst, F., "La tradition médiatrice de la Suisse aux XVIIIᵉ et XIXᵉ siècles," *Revue de littérature comparée,* VI (1926), 549–607. (On rôle of Burckhardt and other Swiss historians in shaping the idea of the Renaissance.)

Escher, K., *Die Kunst der Renaissance* (Potsdam, 1924). (Introduction discusses the development of the Renaissance concept.)

Falco, G., *La polemica sul medio evo* (Turin, 1933). (History of the conception of the Middle Ages from humanism to Romanticism.)

Fife, R. H., "The Renaissance in the Changing World," *The Germanic Review,* IX (1934), 73–95. (Review of recent trends.)

Frey, D., *Gotik und Renaissance als Grundlagen der modernen Weltanschauung* (Augsburg, 1929). (Introduction discusses recent trends of interpretation.)

Gebhart, É., "La renaissance italienne et la philosophie de l'histoire," *Revue des deux mondes,* LXXII (1885), 342–79. (Discussion of Burckhardt's interpretation.)

Gentile, G., "Umanesimo e Rinascimento," *Rivista di cultura,* I (1920), 145–57. (Discussion of the Renaissance problem.)

Gilbert, F., "Political Thought of the Renaissance and Reformation," *The Huntington Library Quarterly,* IV (1941), 443–68. (Renaissance Studies.)

Goetz, W., "Mittelalter und Renaissance," *Historische Zeitschrift,* XCVIII (1907), 30–54. (A pioneer essay on the history of the Renaissance concept. Excellent.)

Gordon, G. S., *Medium Aevum and the Middle Ages,* S. P. E. Tract, No. XIX (1925). (Philological study of origins of the term.)

Green, O. H., "A Critical Survey of Scholarship in the Field of Spanish Renaissance Literature, 1914–44," *Studies in Philology,* XLIV (1947), 228–64. (Renaissance Studies.)

Hefele, H., "Zum Begriff der Renaissance," *Historisches Jahrbuch der Görresgesellschaft,* XLIV (1929), 444–59. (Review of recent trends and argument in favor of a political interpretation.)

Heussi, K., *Altertum, Mittelalter und Neuzeit; ein Beitrag zum Problem der historischen Periodisierung* (Tübingen, 1921). (Fundamental study of periodization.)

Heisenberg, A., "Das Problem der Renaissance in Byzanz," *Historische Zeitschrift,* CXXXIII (1926), 393–412. (Reply to Neumann's thesis.)

Heyfelder, E., "Die Ausdrücke 'Renaissance' und 'Humanismus'," *Deutsche Literaturzeitung,* XXXIV (1913), 2245–50. (Examples of the use of the terms in Germany before Burckhardt and Voigt.)

Hildebrand, R., "Zur sogenannten Renaissance," *Zeitschrift für den deutschen Unterricht,* VI (1892), 377–82. (Early reaction against the Burckhardtian conception.)

Huber, R. M., "Recent Important Literature Regarding the Catholic Church During the Late Renaissance Period (1500–1648)," *Church History,* X (1941), 3–37. (Renaissance Studies.)

Huizinga, J., "Das Problem der Renaissance," in his *Wege der Kulturgeschichte* (Munich, 1930), pp. 89–139. (History of the growth of the conception and discussion of the problem. Very good.)

Jacob, E. F., "The Fifteenth Century: Some Recent Interpretations," *Bulletin of the John Rylands Library,* XIV (1930), 386–409.

——— "Changing Views of the Renaissance," *History,* N. S. XVI (1931–32), 214–29. (Both articles discuss recent trends with emphasis on the tendency to break down the distinction between Middle Ages and Renaissance.)

Janner, A., "Individualismus und Religiosität in der Renaissance," *Deutsche Vierteljahrsschrift für Literaturwissenschaft und Geistesgeschichte,* XIII (1935), 357–77. (Review of recent trends; favorable to the Burckhardtian tradition.)

Joachimsen, P., "Vom Mittelalter zur Reformation," *Historische Vierteljahrsschrift,* XX (1920–21), 426–70. (Chiefly criticism of Burdach's thesis, with some constructive suggestions.)

Johnson, F. R. and Larkey, S. V., "Science," *Modern Language Quarterly,* II (1941), 363–401. (Renaissance Studies.)

Kaufmann, R., *Der Renaissancebegriff in der deutschen Kunstgeschichtschreibung* (Basel, 1932). (Dissertation.)

Kluge, O., "Das Renaissanceproblem und sein jüngster Lösungsversuch," *Neuphilologische Monatsschrift,* VI (1935), 134–40. (Review of Walser and others. Slight.)

Koebner, R., "Zur Begriffsbildung der Kulturgeschichte," *Historische Zeitschrift,* CXLIX (1933), 10–34; 253–93. (Discussion of the concepts of culture and individualism, chiefly in the works of Burckhardt and Huizinga.)

Kristeller, P. O. and Randall, J. H., "The Study of the Philosophies of the Renaissance," *Journal of the History of Ideas,* II (1941), 449–96. (Renaissance Studies.)

Kunstmann, J. G., "German Literature," *Modern Language Quarterly,* II (1941), 421–38. (Renaissance Studies.)

Lehmann, P., *Vom Mittelalter und von der lateinischen Philologie des Mittelalters* (Munich, 1914). (Fundamental study of the origins of the concept and term Middle Ages.)

Lockwood, D. P. and Bainton, R. H., "Classical and Biblical Scholarship in the Age of the Renaissance and Reformation," *Church History*, X (1941), 3–21. (Renaissance Studies.)

Luzzatto, G., "The Study of Medieval Economic History in Italy: Recent Literature and Tendencies," *Journal of Economic and Business History*, IV (1931–32), 708–27. (Valuable review.)

Martin, A. von, "Das Problem der mittelalterlichen Weltanschauung," *Deutsche Vierteljahrsschrift für Literaturwissenschaft und Geistesgeschichte*, III (1925), 485–500. (Review of recent interpretations and discussion of the problem.)

—— *Coluccio Salutati und das humanistische Lebensideal* (Leipzig, 1916). (Introduction has good discussion of Renaissance as a problem in historiography.)

Mommsen, T., "Petrarch's Conception of the 'Dark Ages'," *Speculum*, XVII (1942). 226–42.

Nelson, E. W., "Recent Literature Concerning Erasmus," *Journal of Modern History*, I (1929), 88–102. (Valuable study in a restricted field.)

Nelson, N., "Individualism as a Criterion of the Renaissance," *The Journal of English and Germanic Philology*, XXXII (1933), 316–34. (Review of recent discussion of a crucial problem.)

Nerrlich, P., *Das Dogma vom klassischen Altertum in seiner geschichtlichen Entwicklung* (Leipzig, 1894).

Neumann, C., "Ende des Mittelalters? Legende der Ablösung des Mittelalters durch die Renaissance," *Deutsche Vierteljahrsschrift für Literaturwissenschaft und Geistesgeschichte*, XII (1934), 124–71. (Review of recent trends and argument against the traditional conception. Valuable but tendentious.)

—— "Byzantinische Kultur und Renaissancekultur," *Historische Zeitschrift*, XCI (1903), 215–32. (Argument against the classical origins of the Renaissance.)

—— "Neue Kunstliteratur, besonders zur spätgotischen Zeit," *Deutsche Vierteljahrsschrift für Literaturwissenschaft und Geistesgeschichte*, IV (1926), 270–314.

Nordström, J., *Moyen-âge et Renaissance* (Paris, 1933). (Contains historical sketch of the interpretations of the Renaissance and vigorous attack on the traditional conception from a French nationalist point of view.)

Nussbaum, F. L., "The Economic History of Renaissance Europe; Problems and Solutions during the Past Generation," *Journal of Modern History*, XIII (1941), 527–45. (Renaissance Studies.)

Occhini, B., "Medioevo e Rinascimento," *La Rinascita*, V (1942), 3–46.

Panofsky, E., "Renaissance and Renascences," *Kenyon Review*, VI (1944), 201–36. (Defends the Renaissance as a style concept.)

Pauck, W., "The Historiography of the German Reformation During the Past Twenty Years," *Church History*, IX (1940), 3–38. (Renaissance Studies.)

Philippi, A., *Der Begriff Renaissance; Daten zu seiner Geschichte* (Leipzig, 1912). (Contribution to the history of the Renaissance as a concept in the history of art.)

Plattard, J., " 'Restitution des bonnes lettres' et 'renaissance'," in *Mélanges offerts par ses amis et ses élèves à M. Gustave Lanson* (Paris, 1922), pp. 128–31. (Brief but heavily documented article on use of these terms in the sixteenth century.)

Rehm, W., *Das Werden des Renaissance Bildes in der deutschen Dichtung vom Rationalismus bis zum Realismus* (Munich, 1924).

—— *Der Renaissancekult um 1900 und seine Ueberwindung* (Stuttgart, 1929).

Ritter, G., "Die geschichtliche Bedeutung des deutschen Humanismus," *Historische Zeitschrift*, CXXVII (1923), 393–453. (Contains astute comments on recent trends.)

Rupprich, H., "Deutsche Literatur im Zeitalter des Humanismus und der Reformation: ein Bericht," *Deutsche Vierteljahrsschrift für Literaturwissenschaft und Geistesgeschichte*, XVII (1939), Referatenheft, pp. 83–133. (Comprehensive review but with little discussion of important works.)

Schaeffer, E., "Das moderne Renaissance-Empfinden," *Die neue Rundschau*, XVI (1905), 769–84. (Valuable review of the concept in *belles lettres* since Schiller.)

Schmalenbach, H., *Das Mittelalter, sein Begriff und Wesen* (Leipzig, 1926).

Seton, K. E., "Some Recent Views of the Italian Renaissance," *Report of the Annual Meeting of the Canadian Historical Association, 1947*, pp. 5–34. (One of the best reviews of recent literature on the Renaissance.)

Simone, F., "La coscienza della Rinascita negli humanisti," *La Rinascita*, II (1939), 838–71; III (1940), 163–86. (Fundamental study of the first stage in the growth of the Renaissance concept.)

Smith, C. S. and Duneen, W., "Recent Works on Music in the Renaissance," *Modern Philology*, XLII (1944), 41–58. (Renaissance Studies.)

Società Filologica Romana, *Un cinquantennio di studi sulla letteratura italiana (1886–1936)*, 2 vols. (Florence, 1937). (Has several articles on studies of the Renaissance period.)

Soffici, A., "L'essenza del Rinascimento," *La Rinascita*, IV (1941), 113–19. (Discussion of the Renaissance problem.)

Spangenberg, H., "Die Perioden der Weltgeschichte," *Historische Zeitschrift*, CXXVII (1922–23), 1–49. (Discusses growth of the concept of the Middle Ages and argues against division between medieval and modern periods at 1500.)

Stadelmann, R., "Grundformen der Mittelalterauffassung von Herder bis Ranke," *Deutsche Vierteljahrsschrift für Literaturwissenschaft und Geistesgeschichte*, IX (1931), 45–88.

―――― "Zum Problem der Renaissance," *Neue Jahrbücher für Wissenschaft und Jugendbildung*, X (1934), 49–63. (Analysis of recent trends.)

Streiter, R., "Gotik oder Renaissance," in his *Ausgewählte Schriften* (Munich, 1913). (Criticism of Schmarsow's thesis.)

Thorndike, L., "Renaissance or Prenaissance?," *Journal of the History of Ideas*, IV (1943), 65–74. (Review of recent trends and argument against the concept of the Renaissance.)

Toffanin, G., "Orientamenti bibliografici sull' umanesimo," *La Rinascita*, I, 4 (1938), 54–62. (Good review.)

―――― "De Sanctis e il Rinascimento," La Rinascita, IV (1941), 169–205.

Troeltsch, E., "Entwicklung des modernen Renaissancebegriffs," in his *Gesammelte Schriften* (Tübingen, 1925), IV, 830–32. (Unfinished, but useful for references.)

Turbeville, A. S., "Changing Views of the Renaissance," *History,* N. S. XVI (1931–32), 289–97. (From traditional point of view. Rather slight.)

Tuve, R., "A Critical Survey of Scholarship in the Field of English Literature of the Renaissance," *Studies in Philology,* XL (1943), 204–55. (Renaissance Studies.)

Varga, L., *Das Schlagwort vom "finsteren Mittelalter,"* (Vienna, 1932). (Study of the origins and development to the end of the eighteenth century of the concept of the dark Middle Ages.)

Volpe, G., "La Rinascenza in Italia e le sue origini," in his *Momenti di storia italiana* (Florence, 1925), pp. 95–127. (Criticism of Neumann's thesis.)

Wackernagel, M., "Neue Umwertungen in der Kunstgeschichte," *Neue Züricher Zeitung* (1923), No. 1770. (Discusses recent decline in interest in Renaissance art.)

——— "Die italienische Renaissance in der kunstgeschichtlichen Literatur der letzten sechs Jahre," *Deutsche Vierteljahrsschrift für Literaturwissenschaft und Geistesgeschichte,* VI (1928), 742–66.

Weisbach, W., "Renaissance als Stilbegriff," *Historische Zeitschrift,* CXX (1919), 250–80. (Discussion of the concept and its development in the history of art.)

Weise, G., "Das Schlagwort vom gotischen Menschen," *Neue Jahrbücher für Wissenschaft und Jugendbildung,* VII (1931), 404–37.

——— "Vom Menschenideal und von den Modewörtern der Gotik und der Renaissance," *Deutsche Vierteljahrsschrift für Literaturwissenschaft und Geistesgeschichte,* XIV (1936), 171–222.

——— "Der doppelte Begriff der Renaissance," *Deutsche Vierteljahrsschrift für Literaturwissenschaft und Geistesgeschichte,* XI (1933), 501–29. (Studies the history of the concept and argues for a distinction between realism and classicism in the conception of Renaissance art.)

Weisinger, H., "Renaissance Theories of the Revival of the Fine Arts," *Italica,* XX (1943), 163–70.

——— "The Self-Awareness of the Renaissance as a Criterion of the Renaissance," *Papers of the Michigan Academy of Science, Arts, and Literature,* XXIX (1944), 561–67.

———— "Who Began the Revival of Learning? The Renaissance Point of View," *ibid.* XXX (1944), 625–38.

———— "The Renaissance Theory of the Reaction against the Middle Ages as a Cause of the Renaissance," *Speculum*, XX (1945), 461–67. (The four articles by Weisinger are studies of the origins of the Renaissance concept in humanist writings.)

Wiley, W. L., "The French Renaissance Gallicized," *Studies in Philology*, XXXIV (1937), 248–59. (Review of recent French nationalist interpretations.)

Wilkinson, W. W. J., "The Meaning of the Renaissance," *Thought*, XVI (1941), 444–56. (Discussion of recent trends with special attention to Olgiati. Catholic point of view.)

Will, S. F., "French Literature," *Modern Language Quarterly*, II (1941), 439–64. (Renaissance Studies.)

412